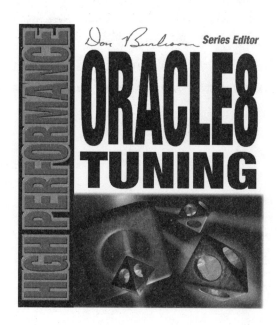

Don Burleson **Series Editor**

HIGH PERFORMANCE

ORACLE8 TUNING

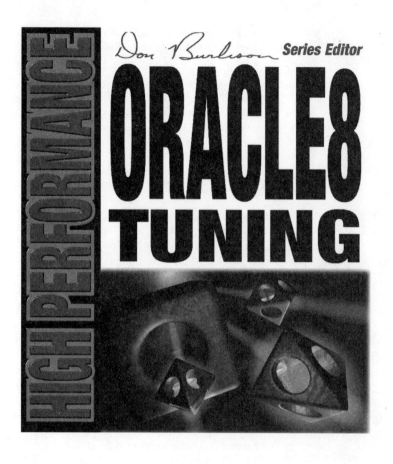

HIGH PERFORMANCE

Don Burleson **Series Editor**

ORACLE8 TUNING

Don Burleson

CORIOLIS GROUP BOOKS

an International Thomson Publishing company I⊤P®

Albany, NY • Belmont, CA • Bonn • Boston • Cincinnati • Detroit • Johannesburg • London
Madrid • Melbourne • Mexico City • New York • Paris • Singapore • Tokyo • Toronto • Washington

High Performance Oracle8 Tuning
Copyright © 1998 by The Coriolis Group, Inc.

Limits of Liability and Disclaimer of Warranty
The author and publisher of this book have used their best efforts in preparing the book and the programs contained in it. These efforts include the development, research, and testing of the theories and programs to determine their effectiveness. The author and publisher make no warranty of any kind, expressed or implied, with regard to these programs or the documentation contained in this book.

The author and publisher shall not be liable in the event of incidental or consequential damages in connection with, or arising out of, the furnishing, performance, or use of the programs, associated instructions, and/or claims of productivity gains.

Trademarks
Trademarked names appear throughout this book. Rather than list the names and entities that own the trademarks or insert a trademark symbol with each mention of the trademarked name, the publisher states that it is using the names for editorial purposes only and to the benefit of the trademark owner, with no intention of infringing upon that trademark.

The Coriolis Group, Inc.
An International Thomson Publishing Company
14455 N. Hayden Road, Suite 220
Scottsdale, Arizona 85260

602/483-0192
FAX 602/483-0193
http://www.coriolis.com

Printed in the United States of America

ISBN 1-57610-217-3

10 9 8 7 6 5 4 3 2

Publisher
Keith Weiskamp

Project Editor
Toni Zuccarini

Production Coordinator
Denise Constantine

Cover Design
Anthony Stock

Layout Design
Nicole Colón

CD-ROM Development
Robert Clarfield

*This book is dedicated to the memory of
Louis F. Burleson, who taught me that there
is always room at the top.*

*When distant and unfamiliar and complex
things are communicated to the masses of people,
the truth suffers a considerable and often a
radical distortion. The complex is made over into
the simple, the hypothetical into the dogmatic,
and the relative into an absolute.*

—*Walter Lippmann*

Acknowledgments

It is never possible to create a high-quality technical book in a vacuum; rather, such a book is the accumulation of tips and techniques from hundreds of technical experts. Special thanks are in order to Jenny and Andy Burleson, who lovingly tolerated my long hours of research; to Toni Zuccarini, whose editing repaired my atrocious grammar; to Rob Clarfield, who managed the CD; to Mike Ault, for his expert reviews; and to Keith Weiskamp, whose vision and foresight made this book a reality.

A Note From Donald Burleson

Today's Oracle professionals are standing at the turning point. As Oracle technology moves into the twenty-first century we are seeing the complexity of database systems becoming almost unfathomable. Today's Oracle professional must be an expert in database performance and tuning, database administration, data warehousing, using Oracle with the Web, using OLAP and spatial data, and many other areas. These robust new features of Oracle present unique challenges to anyone who must use Oracle technology to deliver solutions to complex data-oriented challenges.

Oracle, the world's leading database management system, provides a mind-boggling wealth of features and options—far more than one Oracle professional can easily digest. The Oracle market is filled with new possibilities as Oracle introduces the management of objects, data warehouses, and Web-enabled applications; Oracle professionals everywhere are struggling to understand how to exploit these new features.

It is no longer acceptable for Oracle professionals to be generalists—they must become intimately familiar with all facets of Oracle technology and understand how these technologies interoperate. Rather than simply breadth of knowledge, the Oracle professional must have enough depth to effectively apply the technology. To get this knowledge we must rely on experts to guide us through the labyrinth of complicated tools and techniques, and we do not have the luxury of wading through mundane technical manuals.

What we need is clear, concise advice from seasoned Oracle professionals. That is the purpose of The Coriolis Group's High Performance Oracle series. As you are challenged to keep pace with this exciting new technology, we are challenged to provide on-point books to help guide you through the myriad of Oracle features and ensure your success.

Don Burleson

Raleigh, North Carolina

Contents

Chapter 2   Logical Performance Design   65

Chapter 3   Physical Performance Design   117

Introduction

This book was written because there is a real need for a comprehensive book for the application developer and DBA who must implement fast, efficient, and reliable client/server applications. Unlike other theoretical books on this subject, *High Performance Oracle8 Tuning* provides tangible examples and easy-to-understand techniques for getting the most out of your database and client/server applications. Until now, there have been no books in the marketplace that address client/server as a whole and provide an overall strategy for tuning. *High Performance Oracle8 Tuning* fills this void in the Oracle universe, and is designed to give you easy-to-understand, real-world advice to get your Oracle system working the way you want.

Oracle developers are struggling to understand how the new object extensions are going to change the way that their applications are designed and implemented. Oracle's commitment to objects is not just acknowledgment of a fad; the benefits of being able to support objects is very real, and the exciting new extensions of Oracle8 are going to create a new foundation for the database systems of the twenty-first century. This book recognizes the profound changes that are being introduced for object support in Oracle8, and gives clear definitions and working code examples for the new Oracle8 object constructs. Throughout the book, I show how the Oracle8 object features can be used in the design of high performance applications. Best of all, this book shows the reader when it makes sense to utilize the object features and also addresses the performance implications of using Oracle8 objects.

A major shortcoming of many other Oracle performance books is their failure to explain Oracle tuning in simple English. Clogged with jargon and technical terminology, these books are difficult for even the most seasoned Oracle professionals to comprehend. *High Performance Oracle8 Tuning* was written with the Oracle professional in mind. I have attempted to explain complex database interactions in plain English so developers can immediately begin tuning their Oracle applications. And rather than describing each feature of Oracle, this text zeros in on those proven techniques that have the most immediate performance gains. Throughout the book, I use actual code examples from Oracle databases and guide the developer through all of the implementation steps, from initial planning to final rollout, drawing on my many years of real-world experience in tuning large applications and focusing on the effective use of Oracle and client/server technology. The CD-ROM that is included with the text will allow you to immediately begin monitoring and tuning your Oracle databases.

The focus of this book is on the application of Oracle performance and tuning techniques to real-world systems. The reader is guided step by step through all of the complex performance analysis techniques and is provided with numerous code listings, ready-to-run scripts, and other tools that can be immediately used to assist in the diagnosis and treatment of performance problems. The text also concentrates on specific components of Oracle performance, describing each in detail.

High Performance Oracle8 Tuning also introduces the evolution and internals of database management and client/server technology and shows how proven techniques can be used to fully exploit Oracle—through the use of existing hardware and software resources. Furthermore, it will show the professional applications developer how he or she can intelligently use the client/server paradigm to implement fast and efficient systems.

Many of the existing publications that address Oracle tuning fail in several important areas. They feel compelled to describe each and every parameter within Oracle without any regard for the major techniques that ensure fast performance. Oracle professionals must wade through dozens of irrelevant pages to find the tools that they need to tune their database. In addition, all of the existing Oracle performance and tuning books solely address performance and tuning for an existing database and completely fail to discuss how effective design prior to the construction of a new database can dramatically improve Oracle performance. *High Performance Oracle8 Tuning* takes a holistic approach to Oracle tuning, recognizing that Oracle performance is impacted during all of the phases of systems development. Hence, we look at how Oracle analysis and design can be leveraged to create Oracle databases that make the most of the available resources. No amount of tuning can help a poorly designed database, and this book takes the reader through the Oracle analysis and design phase, illustrating performance techniques with clear, easy-to-understand examples.

Written by a practicing Oracle DBA with 15 years experience, this book is indispensable for all Oracle professionals who must analyze, design, code, and tune their Oracle databases for maximum performance. Just the exhaustive collection of tuning scripts that I've included on the CD-ROM will be worth the cost of the book. These scripts allow you to quickly gain insight into your database and apply corrective tuning before your system becomes crippled.

While the process of determining Oracle performance problems is phenomenally complex, the concepts behind Oracle tuning are quite simple and very straightforward. *High Performance Oracle8 Tuning* explains Oracle tuning in a simple, easy-to-understand fashion, with dozens of clear illustrative examples. I've done all of the laborious script writing, so you can quickly apply the scripts to identify your performance problems.

—Don Burleson

burleson@frontiernet.net

What's New In Oracle8

CHAPTER

1

What's New In Oracle8

Oracle8 reflects the next progression of database architectures—object-oriented databases. Early file managers stored data, network databases stored data and relationships, now object-oriented databases store data, data relationships, and the behaviors of the data, all inside the database engine.

In general, the Oracle8 engine is remarkably similar to the relational engine found in Oracle7.3 but with major extensions to the relational architecture and the addition of table and index partitioning. It is interesting to note that Oracle has not discarded the idea of creating a "universal" database engine. In fact, Oracle is calling Oracle8 the *Oracle Universal Server*, adding text, multidimensional, and object capabilities to the relational engine. Some of the most exciting enhancements involve the introduction of Oracle ConText, and the incorporation of the Oracle Express multidimensional database. But most important, Oracle8 has coupled an object layer with the relational engine. This last enhancement is so important that we'll discuss the object layer in detail after taking a quick look at Oracle ConText and Oracle Express.

Oracle ConText

A text searching option called *Oracle ConText* has also been added to the relational engine of Oracle8. Oracle ConText allows thematic word searching capabilities against Oracle's relational database. Although the ConText option indexes on each word within the text, the real power of the text retrieval system is located in the front-end software. While this represents a major improvement over Oracle Book (which is now obsolete), it remains to be seen how ConText will compete in the marketplace as a text search engine. There are two fundamental ways to measure the accuracy of text retrieval:

- *Precision*—The ability to retrieve only relevant documents (no false or "noisy" hits).

- *Recall*—The ability to retrieve all relevant documents in a given data collection.

Together, precision and recall represent the overall accuracy of a text retrieval system. Another phrase frequently heard in conjunction with concept-based searching is *natural language.* Morphology is commonly used by text databases to simulate natural language queries. Morphology recognizes basic units of meaning and parts of speech. To understand morphology, consider the phrase *Please write to Mr. Wright right now.* From the initial review, it is still unclear how well Oracle ConText will be able to compete with the other, more established text engines, such as ConQuest, Fulcrum, and Folio.

Oracle Express

Oracle Express is a robust multidimensional database that supports both MOLAP (Multidimensional Online Analytical Processing) and ROLAP (Relational Online Analytical Processing). Unlike in Oracle7.3, where the Express multidimensional database is installed independently of Oracle, Oracle8 incorporates the Express product into the Oracle8 kernel. This implies yet another change for Oracle DBAs, who must now manage both the relational and multidimensional components of Oracle. Oracle Express is now offered on NT and Unix platforms. The basic reporting functions of Express have been enhanced to provide forecasting and model building.

Originally a multidimensional database called IRI Express (IRI was the company that originally developed Express), Oracle Express was originally a MOLAP tool for data warehouse analysis. As Oracle Express, the tool has been enhanced so that it does not require data to be preloaded into its internal multidimensional data structures. This enhancement allows Express to read relational data directly from relational Oracle, dynamically transforming and aggregating the data for multidimensional presentation. This approach is called ROLAP, and the dual MOLAP and ROLAP functionality means that Express can now compete against other relational back-end products, such as Holos and MetaCube.

Now that we've taken a summary look at Oracle ConText and Oracle Express, let's turn our attention toward Oracle8's database object layer.

The Basics Of Database Objects

Rather than rebuild the Oracle engine as an object-oriented architecture, Oracle decided to keep the base relational engine and add object functionality on top of the standard relational architecture. While claiming to be an active member in the Object Management Group (OMG), Oracle has departed from OMG's standard for "pure" object databases as defined by the Object Data Management Group (ODMG). Instead, as I mentioned, Oracle provides a generic relational database while extending the architecture to allow objects. The object layer of Oracle8 has implemented a number of new features. In this section, we'll address the following object-related issues:

- Abstract data types—Oracle's user-defined types
- Aggregate object definitions
- Coupling of data and behavior
- Polymorphism
- Encapsulation
- Extensibility

Abstract Data Typing

Rather than being constrained to the basic relational data types of **int**, **varchar**, and **float**, Oracle8 allows the definition of data types to be composed of many subtypes. Oracle calls abstract data typing *user-defined types*, or UDTs. For example, the following data definition could be implemented in Oracle8 as a **full_address_type** data type:

```
CREATE TYPE full_address_type  (
street_address    varchar(30),
city_address      varchar(30),
state_abbr        char(2),
zip_code          char(5));
```

In this manner, aggregate data types can be defined and addressed in a table definition just like any other relational data type. In the following example, you can see the **phone_nbr** and **full_address_type** data types being used in a table definition:

```
CREATE TYPE customer_t AS OBJECT (
    cust_name            full_name,
    cust_phone           phone_nbr,
    cust_address         full_address_type);

CREATE TABLE CUSTOMER OF customer_t;
```

Here, you can see that a single data "field" in a table can be a range of values or an entire table. This concept is called *complex*, or *unstructured*, data typing. The domain of values for a specific field in a relational database can be defined with this approach. This ability to nest, or embed, data tables allows relationship data to be incorporated directly into the table structure. For example, the **Occupation** field in the table in Figure 1.1 establishes a one-to-many relationship between an employee and a valid occupation. Also, note the ability to nest the entire **SKILLS** table within a single field. In this example, only valid skills can reside in the **Skills** field, and this implements the relational concept of *domain integrity*.

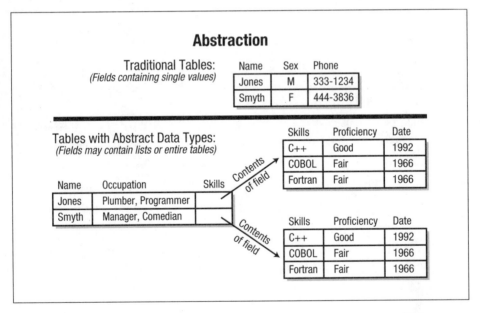

Figure 1.1

An example of abstract data types (ADTs).

Defining Aggregate Objects

In Oracle8, aggregate objects can be defined and preassembled for fast retrieval. For example, a **REPORT_CARD** object might be defined for a university database. The **REPORT_CARD** object could be defined such that it is assembled at runtime from its atomic components (similar to an Oracle view), or the **REPORT_CARD** could be preassembled and stored in the database. These aggregate objects can have methods (such as stored procedures) attached to them, such that an Oracle object couples data and behavior together. Details about the implementation of Oracle aggregate objects are found in Chapter 2.

The introduction of aggregate objects presents a huge improvement over the traditional requirement that all data is modeled at its smallest, most atomic level (i.e., third normal form). Oracle8 now allows the database designer to model the real world as it exists, defining both the small, atomic data items, as well as the aggregate objects that are composed from the atomic items.

From a performance perspective, this presents the Oracle8 designer with a tremendous opportunity to "pre-build" and "pre-sort" data items within the database. Rather than having to re-create aggregate objects with Oracle views every time an aggregate object is requested, Oracle8 allows the aggregate to be pre-created and referenced as an independent object. The proper use of aggregate objects within Oracle8 will greatly improve database performance because all of the overhead involved with table joining and sorting are removed, and the pre-built object can be quickly assembled from the object IDs that comprise the aggregate object.

Coupling Of Data And Behavior

The Oracle8 engine allows for the direct coupling of a database entity (a table or object) with a set of predefined behaviors called *methods*. Methods can be either procedures or functions and are created in the type body specification. In this fashion, calls to Oracle are made by specifying an object name and the method associated with the object. For example:

```
CUSTOMER.check_credit(123);
```

This call tells Oracle to invoke the **check_credit** method (in this case a procedure since it updates the database) that is attached to the **CUSTOMER** object, using the supplied parameter, in this case the customer number. As you might expect, this new way of invoking database calls has important ramifications for developers and DBA staff. Oracle8 automatically creates methods for the creation of a new row (called a constructor) and a method for dropping the row (called a destructor).

For developers, object applications within Oracle8 can be SQL-less and will consist entirely of calls to Oracle8 methods (called member functions). Of course, this has the important benefit of making applications portable across platforms, while also making it very easy to find and reuse code. In addition, because each method is encapsulated and tested independently, the pretested methods can be assembled with other methods without worry of unintended side effects.

For DBAs, the coupling of data with behaviors dramatically changes the way database administration tasks are performed. Instead of only managing data and tables, the Oracle8 DBA will also be responsible for managing objects and the methods associated with each object. These new "object administrator" functions will need to be defined so developers know the functions of methods and the parameters for each method.

Polymorphism

Polymorphism is the ability of different objects to receive the same message and behave in different ways. Oracle has supported pseudopolymorphism since the Oracle7 days by allowing identically named stored procedures to be differentiated by their input parameters, but Oracle8 expands the concept.

Polymorphism has many parallels in the real world. For example, an event, such as a volcanic eruption, has many different effects on living organisms in the area: The poisonous gases might kill all air-breathing animals, while at the same time nourish the small marine organisms nearby. The single behavior of **ERUPTION** has different effects on objects within the **ANIMAL** class. Another analogy can be found in the business world. For example, the event of **PROMOTION** has different behaviors depending on the class of **EMPLOYEE** that receives the **PROMOTION. MANAGEMENT** objects might receive stock options and country club memberships not offered to **STAFF** objects.

In real-world experience, the steering mechanism on an automobile can be considered polymorphic. The steering has a common user interface (the steering wheel), and the complex internals of the steering mechanism are hidden from the user. While the steering mechanism may be very different (rack-and-pinion or power steering), the interface remains the same.

While his name might not sound familiar to you at first, Ron Popeil was a master of polymorphism. Many folks might remember the heyday of Ronco and Popeil, where polymorphic products were advertised at the national level. Consider the statement, "It's a hair cream AND a floor wax!" If this is indeed true, the method **spread_it_on** would invoke very different processes depending upon whether you are applying the cream to a floor or a person's head.

The concept of polymorphism originally came from the programming concept of overloading. *Overloading* refers to the ability of a programming function to perform more than one type of operation depending on the context in which the function is used. For example, consider the following Basic program:

```
REM    Sample Basic program to show polymorphism

REM    Increment the counter

COUNTER = COUNTER + 1

REM Concatenate the String

N$ = "Mr. Burleson"
S$ = "Hello there, " + N$

END
```

In this example, the operator + is used to indicate addition in one context and concatenation in another context. But what determines the way the operator will function? Clearly, the Basic compiler knows that the + operator means addition when it is used in the context where a number is passed as an argument, and the compiler knows concatenation is required when character strings are passed as an argument to the operator.

The overriding implication of polymorphism is that a standard interface can be created for a related group of objects. The specific action performed by an object depends on the message passed to the interface. Because the programmer is no longer concerned with the internal constructs of the object, extremely complex programs can be created. The programmer only needs to understand the interface to use the object.

In the real world, polymorphism can be described by looking at standard interfaces. For example, in most PC-based software, the F1 key has a special meaning. Often, pressing F1 invokes a context-sensitive help function. These help functions have vastly different methods and different data storage techniques, but the standard interface (F1) is polymorphic.

All communication between objects and their behaviors is accomplished with messages passed as behaviors. For example, consider the two objects **rush_order** and **cod_order**. Both objects belong to the **ORDER** class. When a message such as **prepare_invoice** is called, it can contain sub-behaviors such as **prepare_invoice** and **compute_charges** (see Figure 1.2). The message **prepare_invoice** directs the system to compute the shipping charges. Different procedures will then be invoked depending on whether the receiving object is a **rush_order** object or a **cod_order** object—even though they are both objects within the **ORDER** class. A rush order includes overnight mail calculations, while a COD order contains additional computations for the total amount due. This is equivalent to the following procedural language code:

```
IF (rush_order)
    COMPUTE SHIPPING = TOT_AMNT * .25
ELSE
    COMPUTE SHIPPING = TOT_AMNT * .10

IF (cod_order)
    COMPUTE TOT_DUE = TOT_AMNT + SHIPPING
ELSE
    COMPUTE TOT_DUE = 0
```

Polymorphism is achieved in Oracle8 by creating stored procedures or functions with the same names but with different data types for the input function. To Oracle8, two procedures with the same name and different input parameters are considered different procedures, and different code will be invoked, depending on the data type that is passed as an argument to the procedure. For example, you could define two Oracle functions called **add_them**. One **add_them** function could accept two integers, while the other function could accept two character strings. If you call **add_them** with numbers, the function will add the numbers. On the other hand, if you call

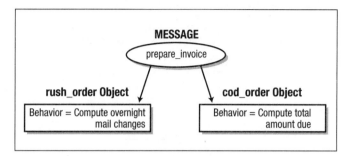

Figure 1.2
An example of polymorphism.

add_them with character strings as input, the other **add_them** function will be invoked and Oracle will concatenate the strings together.

In future releases of Oracle8, Oracle has promised that class hierarchies will be supported. With class hierarchies, polymorphism will also be used by associating methods within two distinct object tables in a class hierarchy. For example, you might have two object tables, **CONTRACTOR** and **EMPLOYEE**, each of which have a method called **compute_pay**. When the **compute_pay** method is invoked, Oracle will interrogate the type of the object and invoke the appropriate method. Again, here we see polymorphism because Oracle8 will be able to invoke the appropriate **compute_pay** method.

Encapsulation

Encapsulation means that each object within a system has a well-defined interface with distinct borders. In plain English, encapsulation refers to the localized variables that can be used within an object behavior and cannot be referenced outside of that behavior. This closely parallels the concept of information hiding. Encapsulation also ensures that all updates to a database are performed by using (or by way of) the behaviors associated with the database objects.

Code and data can be enclosed together into a *black box*. These boxes can then function totally independent of all other objects within the system. (See Figure 1.3.) From a programming perspective, an object is an encapsulated routine of data and behaviors. Objects can contain **public** variables (variables used to handle the interfaces to an object) and **private** variables (variables known only to an object). Once created, an object is treated as a variable of its own type.

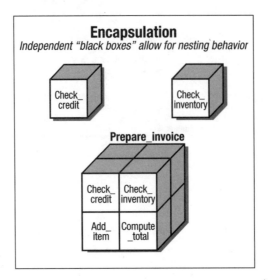

Figure 1.3
An example of encapsulation.

Encapsulation is used in non-database object-oriented applications to ensure that all operations are performed through the programmer-defined interface and data cannot be modified outside of the application shell. But what about ad hoc queries and updates? It appears that any declarative database language, such as SQL, that allows external retrievals and updates does not follow the dictates of encapsulation; therefore Oracle SQL is inconsistent with object-oriented database management.

For example, a relational database could be defined to have a behavior called **add_line_item**, which serves to check inventory levels for an item and add an item to an order only if sufficient stock is available. This behavior ensures that orders are not entered for out-of-stock items. However, with a language such as SQL, the object-oriented behavior could be bypassed, and **line_item** records could be added without any regard for inventory levels.

Remember, encapsulation is predicated on the requirement that an object can only be accessed via its methods. Because encapsulation and SQL are clearly incompatible, the only conclusion that can be reached is that encapsulation can be violated in Oracle8 by using ad hoc tools such as SQL*Plus, which allow the Oracle8 methods to be bypassed.

In a sense, Oracle8 enforces a primitive form of encapsulation by creating default constructors and destructors for each object definition; but Oracle8 SQL allows Oracle8 objects to be accessed independently from their methods. Surely, some of the object-oriented purists will criticize this shortcoming, but careful planning can overcome this feature of Oracle8.

Extensibility

Extensibility is the ability of a database engine to add new behaviors to an existing application without affecting the existing application shell. This is an especially powerful concept because it allows the database to extend existing class hierarchies, guaranteeing that no unintended side effects from the introduction of a new object class will occur. As for Oracle8, we will not be seeing class hierarchies (and the inheritance and extensibility that are associated with class hierarchies) until the introduction of Oracle8.2.

When a future release Oracle8 is enhanced to provide for extensibility, there will be a huge improvement in the ability of the database engine to extend upon existing methods, dramatically reducing the time required to make modifications to databases. To understand the concept of extensibility, consider a company that provides payroll services for businesses in many states. Some payroll computations are global (for example, **Gross_pay** = **hours_worked** * **payrate**), while other computations are specific to a municipality or state. Using Oracle8, an existing object class definition can be extended, such that the new object behaves exactly like its superclass definition (with whatever exceptions are specified). For example, if New York City instituted a new payroll rule for New York City residents, then the general definition for New York payroll customers could be extended with a new class definition for New York City payroll customers. The only method that would be attached to this class definition would be the code specific to New York City—all other methods would be inherited from existing superclasses. Remember though, Oracle does not currently support class hierarchies and inheritance, but it is planned for a later release of Oracle8.

Now that you're a little more familiar with some of the changes implemented in Oracle8, including Oracle8's object layer, let's take a look at the issues facing the Oracle professional as they include object design into their Oracle structures.

Object-Oriented Design Issues

Oracle's object-oriented approach borrows heavily from the C++ and Smalltalk languages. Both of these languages allow for the storing of behaviors with data, such that data and business rules also share a common repository.

With the properties of encapsulation, abstraction, and polymorphism, object technology systems are moving toward a unified data model that models the real world far more effectively than previous modeling techniques. Furthermore, a properly designed object-oriented model promises to be maintenance-free, because all changes to data attributes and behaviors become a database task—not a programming task.

Let's take a look at a human analogy to the object-oriented approach. It is very natural for humans to recognize objects and to associate objects with classes. It is also a very natural concept to associate an object with its expected behaviors. Even as very young children, people learn to associate behaviors with certain characteristics of objects. For example, it is not uncommon to visit the zoo and hear a three-year-old call all four-legged animals "doggies." The child has learned to associate the object class (dog) with a data attribute (four legs). Later, a child will refine the object-oriented paradigm, associating other data attributes with animal objects. A child also learns to associate behaviors (such as playing, having fun, feeling pain, and so forth) with different visual and auditory stimuli. Many young children learn to associate unpleasant sensations (pain) with a visit to the adult who wears a white lab coat (the doctor). McDonald's corporation has spent millions of dollars exploiting this principle (much to the consternation of many parents), associating pleasant behavior with objects such as golden arches, Happy Meals, and Ronald McDonald.

Behaviors must be dynamic, and human experience shows that human associations of behaviors with data attributes also change with time. In the 1930s, people with tattoos were usually categorized as belonging to the **sailor** class. In the 1970s, tattoos were generally categorized as belonging to the **criminal** class. Today, tattoos are indicative of the **college_student** class of humans. The ODMG object model partially addressed this issue, whereby objects are assigned lifetimes by the object-oriented database system. Unfortunately, the concept of object lifetimes has not been included in Oracle8.

Humans are also familiar with the concept of abstraction. For example, intangible objects such as *time* are easily understood, and the conceptual, nonconcrete existence of time has meaning to most individuals.

The distinguishing characteristic of the object-oriented database is its ability to store data behavior. But how is the behavior of data incorporated into a database? At first glance, this might seem to be a method for moving application code from a program into a database. While it is true that an object-oriented database stores behaviors, these databases must also have the ability to manage many different objects—each with different data items.

But there is more to object-oriented design than the simple coupling of data and behavior. We must also be able to plan for polymorphism and inheritance, which are achieved by adding class hierarchies into the database design. These class hierarchies are commonly called IS-A relationships.

Designing IS-A Relationships

One of the basic concepts behind object-orientation is to provide a mechanism whereby different variants of the same entity can be modeled. In object-oriented databases, these variants may have different data attributes and methods, and the process of creating these structures is call *building a class hierarchy*. While Oracle 8.0 does not yet support the definition of class hierarchies, it has been promised for later releases of Oracle. The IS-A relationship (pronounced "is a") is a data relationship that indicates a type/subtype data relationship. While traditional Entity/Relation modeling deals only with single entities, the IS-A approach recognizes that many types or classes of an individual entity can exist. In fact, the IS-A relationship is the foundation of object-oriented programming, which allows the designer to create hierarchies of related classes and then use inheritance and polymorphism to control which data items will participate in the low-level objects.

After establishing a class hierarchy with the E/R model, the object-oriented principle of *generalization* is used to identify the class hierarchy and the level of abstraction associated with each class. Generalization implies a successive refinement of a class, allowing the superclasses of objects to inherit data attributes and behaviors that apply to the lower levels of a class. Generalization establishes *taxonomy hierarchies*. Taxonomy hierarchies organize classes according to their characteristics in increasing levels of detail. These hierarchies begin at a very general level and then proceed to a specific level, with each sublevel having its own unique data attributes and behaviors.

In Figure 1.4, the IS-A relationship is used to create a hierarchy within the **CUS-TOMER** and **ORDER** entities. All of the lower-level classes inherit the data definitions and behaviors from the base classes. Data structures are inherited when an object is created (using the constructor method), and the database builds the data structure for the object. Methods are inherited at runtime when a method is called and the database searches the class hierarchy for the appropriate method. The IS-A relationship is used to model the hierarchy, which is created as the class entity is decomposed into its logical subcomponents. Customers can be **preferred_customers** or **new_customers**, and orders can be **cod_orders** or **prepaid_orders**, each with their own data items and behaviors. Data items generic to customers and orders reside in the **CUSTOMER** and **ORDER** entities, while data items unique to **preferred_customers** (such as **percent_discount**) reside in the lower-level entities.

Let's look at another example. Consider the application of the IS-A relationship for a vehicle dealership, as shown in Figure 1.5. As you can see, the highest level in the hierarchy is **VEHICLE**. Beneath the **VEHICLE** class, you might find **CAR** and **BOAT** subclasses. Within the **CAR** class, the classes could be further partitioned into classes for **TRUCK**, **VAN**, and **SEDAN**. The **VEHICLE** class would contain the data items unique to vehicles, including the vehicle ID and the year of manufacture. The **CAR** class, because it IS-A **VEHICLE**, would inherit the data items of the **VEHICLE** class. The **CAR** class might contain data items such as the number of

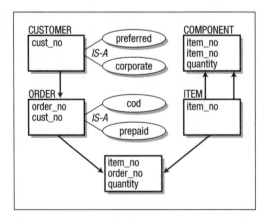

Figure 1.4
An Entity/Relation model with added IS-A relationships.

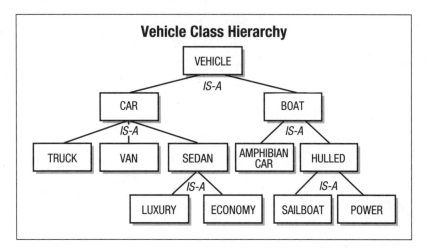

Figure 1.5
A sample class hierarchy.

axles and the gross weight of the vehicle. Because the **VAN** class IS-A **CAR**, which in turn IS-A **VEHICLE**, objects of the **VAN** class inherit all data items and behaviors relating to the **CAR** and **VEHICLE** classes.

These types of IS-A relationships, while valid from a data modeling viewpoint, do not have a simple implementation in Oracle8. Because current Oracle8 releases do not support hierarchical relationships, it is currently impossible to directly represent the fact that a database entity has subentities. However, this type of relationship can be modeled in Oracle8 in two ways.

The first technique is to create subtables for car, boat, sedan, and so on. This encapsulates the data items within their respective tables, but it also creates the complication of doing unnecessary joins when retrieving a high-level item in the hierarchy. For example, the following SQL would be required to retrieve all the data items for a luxury sedan:

```
SELECT
        VEHICLE.vehicle_number,
        CAR.registration_number,
        SEDAN.number_of_doors,
        LUXURY.type_of_leather_upholstery
```

```
FROM
        VEHICLE,
        CAR,
        SEDAN,
        LUXURY
WHERE
VEHICLE.key = CAR.key
AND
CAR.key = SEDAN.key
AND
SEDAN.key = LUXURY.key;
```

The second approach is to create a megatable, with each data item represented as a column (regardless of whether it is needed by the individual row). A **TYPE** column could identify whether a row represents a car, van, or sailboat. In addition, the application must have intelligence to access only those columns applicable to a row. For example, the sail-size column would have meaning for a sailboat row, but would be irrelevant to a sedan row.

The IS-A relationship is best suited to the object-oriented data model, where each level in the hierarchy has associated data items and methods, and inheritance and polymorphism can be used to complete the picture. It is important to note that not all classes within a generalization hierarchy will be associated with objects. These *noninstantiated* classes only serve the purpose of passing data definitions to the lower-level classes. The object-oriented paradigm allows for abstraction, which means that a class can exist only for the purpose of passing inherited data and behaviors to the lower-level entities. The classes **VEHICLE** and **CAR** probably would not have any concrete objects, while objects within the **VAN** class would inherit from the abstract **VEHICLE** and **CAR** classes.

Multiple inheritance can be illustrated by the **AMPHIBIAN_CAR** class. Instances of this class probably would inherit data and behaviors from both the **CAR** and the **BOAT** classes.

It is important to note one very big difference between one-to-many relationships and IS-A relationships. The IS-A construct does not imply any type of recurring association, while the one-to-many and many-to-many relationships imply multiple occurrences of the subclasses. In the previous example, the entire class hierarchy describes vehicles associated with the **ITEM** entity in the overall database. The fact that a class hierarchy exists *does not* imply any data relationships between the classes.

While one **CUSTOMER** can place many **ORDER**s, it is not true that one **CAR** can have many **SEDAN**s.

Now that you have a general understanding of object-oriented design principles, let's see how the principles are designed and implemented within the Oracle8 object model.

Designing With Objects

There is a tremendous amount of confusion surrounding the way Oracle8 implements the database object model. The following sections explore how Oracle8 object features can be used to design robust object systems. In addition, Oracle designers are shown how to plan for the use of these features.

Defining Abstract Data Types

Unlike Oracle7, which only provides a handful of built-in data types, Oracle8 allows for the creation of abstract data types (as mentioned earlier in this chapter). The data types offered in Oracle7 were sufficient for most relational database applications, but developers are now beginning to realize that the ability to create abstract data types can greatly simplify database design and improve system performance. While these abstract data types are popular within languages such as C++, they have only recently been introduced into the mainstream world of database objects.

Oracle8 has implemented abstract data types by including a **CREATE TYPE** definition. This definition is used to define the domains of the subtypes that exist within a new data type. At the most basic level, an abstract data type is nothing more than a collection of smaller, basic data types that can be treated as a single entity. While this is a simple concept, the changes in Oracle database design will be dramatic.

It is interesting to note that the ability to represent abstract data types was commonly used within pre-relational databases and was lost when the relational model was introduced. In pre-relational databases, there were only a few allowable data types (numeric and character), but these databases allowed for the atomic values to be grouped into larger units. These larger units could then be easily moved around within the database. For example, a **full_address** construct could be defined and copied into numerous record definitions, where it could be manipulated as if it were a single unit.

While pre-relational databases such as IMS and IDMS supported ADTs, the *strong typing* features were only introduced around 1990, with the first commercial object-oriented databases. Also, many of Oracle8's "new" features have been available for years in other database management systems. For instance, UniSQL, the relational/object-oriented database developed by Dr. Wong Kim, supports the concept of nested tables whereby a data field in a table can be a range of values or an entire table. With this approach, the domain of values for a specific field in a relational database can be defined. The ability to nest data tables allows for relationship data to be incorporated directly into a table structure.

By the way, Oracle8 provides for strong typing when an object ID column is defined within a table. For example, we could define a column inside an **ORDER** table that would contain the OID of the customer that placed the order. In the table definition, Oracle8 allows only OIDs belonging to **customer** rows to be placed into this column. In the following example, we have created an **ORDER** table with a column called **customer_placing_order** that will only accept OIDs that are from a **customer** row. As you can see, this is done with the **SCOPE IS** parameter:

```
CREATE TYPE customer_type AS OBJECT (
    customer_name       full_name,
    customer_address    full_address
    );

CREATE TABLE CUSTOMER OF customer_type;

CREATE TYPE order_type AS OBJECT (
  order_date                  date,
  shipping_details            varchar(200),
  customer_placing_order   REF customer_type SCOPE IS CUSTOMER);
```

We can see from the above code that Oracle's **REF** parameter is used to define a column that is designed to contain the OID of an Oracle row. Oracle's **DEREF** parameter is used to dereference this OID to return the data at the location pointed to by the OID.

Now that you understand the basic idea behind abstract data types, let's explore some of the compelling benefits to this approach. There are several reasons why ADTs are useful within an Oracle8 design:

- *Encapsulation*—Because each abstract data type exists as a complete entity, including the data definitions, default values, and value constraints, this entity ensures uniformity and consistency. Once defined, an abstract data type can participate in many other abstract data types, such that the same logical data type always has the same definition, default values, and value constraints, regardless of where it appears in a database.

- *Reusability*—As a hierarchy of common data structures is assembled, it can be reused within many definitions, saving coding time and ensuring uniformity.

- *Flexibility*—The ability to create real-world data representations of data allows the database object designer to model the real world as it exists.

As you can see, there are many compelling reasons to have abstract data typing, provided that the data types are properly analyzed and incorporated into the database object model. Let's take a look at some of the implementation issues that relate to Oracle8 and abstract data typing.

Designing With Oracle Abstract Data Types

One of the shortcomings of Oracle7 was the requirement to model all entities at their smallest level. For example, if you wanted to select the address information for a customer, you were required to manipulate **street_address**, **city_address**, and **zip_code** as three separate statements. Now, with Oracle8's abstract data typing, you can create a new data type called **full_address** and manipulate it as if it were an atomic data type. As mentioned earlier, while this is a huge improvement for Oracle, it is interesting to note that pre-relational databases supported this construct, and COBOL has always offered ways to create data types composed of subtypes. For example, in COBOL, you can define a full address as follows:

```
05  CUSTOMER-ADDRESS.
    07 STREET-ADDRESS       PIC X(80).
    07 CITY-ADDRESS         PIC X(80).
    07 ZIP-CODE             PIC X(5).
```

You can then move the **CUSTOMER-ADDRESS** as if it were an individual entity, like this:

```
MOVE CUSTOMER-ADDRESS TO PRINT-REC.
MOVE SPACES TO CUSTOMER-ADDRESS.
```

By the same token, an object database allows the definition of a **full_address_type** data type, as follows:

```
CREATE TYPE full_address_type (
    street_address      char(20),
    city_address        char(20),
    state_name          char(2)
    zip_code            number(9));
```

You could then treat **full_address_type** as a valid data type, using it to create tables and select data, as follows:

```
CREATE TABLE CUSTOMER AS OBJECT(
    cust_name           full_name_type,
    cust_address        full_address_type,
    . . .
    );
```

Now that an Oracle table is defined, you could reference **full_address_type** in your SQL, just as if it were a primitive data type:

```
SELECT DISTINCT full_address_type FROM CUSTOMER;

INSERT INTO CUSTOMER VALUES (
    full_name_type ('ANDREW','S.','BURLESON'),
    full_address_type ('123 1st st.','Minot, ND','74635');
```

Note that the Oracle SQL **SELECT** statements change when accessing rows that contain abstract data types. Following is the Oracle SQL syntax required to select a component within the **full_address_type** type:

```
SELECT full_address.zip_code
FROM CUSTOMER
WHERE
full_address.zip_code LIKE '144%';
```

Now, let's take this concept of abstract data types one step further and consider how abstract data types can be nested within other data types.

Nesting Abstract Data Types

The primary reason for the introduction of abstract data types is to gain the ability to reuse components in a consistent fashion across the entire database domain. Because data types are created to encapsulate other data types, DBAs need to be able to nest abstract data types within other abstract data types. For example, you could create a data type that encapsulates the data in a table, and then use the data type in a table definition, as follows:

```
CREATE TYPE  customer_stuff_type AS OBJECT  (
   customer_name      full_name_type,
   customer_address   full_address_type);
```

With the **customer_stuff_type** type defined, the table definition becomes simple:

```
CREATE TABLE CUSTOMER (customer_data   customer_stuff_type);
```

or

```
CREATE TABLE CUSTOMER OF customer_stuff_type;
```

By using this kind of abstract data typing, you are essentially duplicating the object-oriented concept of encapsulation. That is, you are placing groups of related data types into a container that is completely self-contained and has the full authority of the innate relational data types, such as **int** and **char**.

Displaying nested abstract data types is performed in the same fashion as the sample queries presented earlier, with the exception that the target data types would require several *dots* to delimit the levels of nesting within the data structure. For example, the following query will display the **street_address** for a customer:

```
SELECT customer_stuff.customer_name.zip_code
FROM CUSTOMER
WHERE customer_stuff.customer_name.zip_code LIKE '144%';
```

Here, you can see that a reference to **zip_code** must be prefaced with **customer_name** because it participates in this data type. Furthermore, the **customer_name** data type is nested within the **customer_stuff** data type. Hence, the proper SQL reference to **zip_code** is expressed as follows:

```
customer_stuff.customer_name.zip_code
```

Now that you have a general understanding of the function and operation of abstract data types within Oracle8, let's take a look at how "pointers" are being used in Oracle to establish relationships between table rows.

Using Object IDs

Before we begin our discussion of navigating Oracle databases with pointers, it is important to understand exactly what object IDs represent and how they are implemented within Oracle8. In pre-relational databases, each record in a database had a distinct database address. The addresses were similar to Oracle **ROWID**s in that the addresses corresponded to a physical database block. Also included in the address was the offset or displacement of the target record into the block. For example, an address of 665:2 referred to the second record in database block number 665. Once defined, these addresses could be stored inside other records, essentially allowing one record to point to another record. These pointers became the foundation of establishing relationships between entities in pre-relational times.

In today's object databases, objects stored in an object table have an object ID, which is commonly called an *OID*. An OID is guaranteed to be globally unique. Each OID consists of a 128-byte hexadecimal value. By itself, an OID cannot be used to locate an object instance, only a **REF** (or *reference*, discussed later in this chapter), which contains location data, can be used to locate an object instance.

Oracle8 uses the concept of the **ROWID** (introduced in Oracle7) to uniquely identify each row in each table in a database. The **ROWID** in Oracle7 is a **varchar2** representation of a binary value shown in hexadecimal format. It is displayed as

```
bbbbbbbbssssffff
```

where:

- **bbbbbbbb** is the block ID
- **ssss** is the sequence in the block
- **ffff** is the file ID

In cases where a primary key for a table allows duplicate values, the **ROWID** can be used to detect and eliminate the duplicate rows. In the following SQL, the **ROWID**s for duplicate customers are displayed:

```
SELECT

   ROWID,
   cust_no
FROM
     CUSTOMER A
WHERE
A.cust_nbr >
   (SELECT
       min (B.ROWID)
       FROM
       CUSTOMER B
       WHERE
       A.cust_nbr = B.cust_nbr
   );
```

New with Oracle8 is the concept of objects and OIDs. Oracle8 objects have identifiers added to **ROWID**s, giving an **EXTENDED ROWID** format, which is 10 bytes long as opposed to the 6-byte format that was used in Oracle7. The Oracle8 **ROWID** is a **varchar2** representation of a base-64 number. The Oracle8 **ROWID** is displayed as

```
oooooofffbbbbbbsss
```

where:

- **oooooo** is the data object number

- **fff** is the relative file number

- **bbbbbb** is the block number

- **sss** is the slot number

In Oracle8, DBAs have the ability to create a distinct OID to uniquely identify each row within a table. As mentioned, these OIDs are 128 bytes in length. Oracle guarantees that OIDs will remain unique to the database software even after they have been deleted. Like a traditional pointer found in legacy databases, OIDs can be embedded into columns, providing the ability to point to other rows in the database.

As mentioned earlier, many pre-relational databases employed pointers and used linked-list data structures. These data structures created embedded pointers in the prefix of each occurrence of a database entity. The pointers were used to establish one-to-many and many-to-many relationships among entities. Although the design of pointer-based databases was very elegant in the sense that foreign keys were not needed to establish data relationships, there were serious problems with implementation. Network databases, such as CA-IDMS, and hierarchical databases, such as IMS, were very difficult to navigate because the programmer had to remain aware of the location, name, and type of each pointer in the database. Developers did not have the luxury of a declarative language such as SQL.

The introduction of OIDs dramatically changes Oracle database design. Because developers will now be able to dereference an OID to get the values that an object contains, SQL joins are no longer required. However, there is a downside. Because the data relationships are hard linked with embedded pointers, the addition of a new OID will require special utility programs to "sweep" each and every affected object in the database. Also, when an Oracle8 object is deleted, the programmers must know what objects have OIDs that contain the address of the deleted object. Hence, it is possible in Oracle8 to have orphan OIDs that point to deleted objects. Oracle8 addresses this issue with the SQL extension **IF oid_column IS DANGLING**, which will return **TRUE** if the OID reference points to a deleted object.

As promised, now that we've clarified the concept of OIDs, we are ready to address how to navigate Oracle databases using pointers as an alternative to **JOIN** operations.

Navigating With Pointers (OIDs)

One major feature of the relational database model is the requirement that rows be addressed by the contents of their data values (with the exception of the **ROWID** construct). Now, within Oracle8, database designers have an alternative access method for rows, such that rows can be identified by either their data values or by their OIDs. For example, you can issue the following Oracle query:

```
SELECT
      customer_stuff
```

```
FROM
     CUSTOMER
WHERE
     customer_ID = 38373;
```

In Oracle8, you can also use SQL to address rows by their OIDs, thereby allowing the following pointer-based database navigation:

```
SELECT
       customer_stuff
FROM
     CUSTOMER
WHERE
   OID = :host_variable;
```

The concept of retrieval by OIDs implies that you can now navigate your Oracle database one row at a time with PL/SQL, capturing an OID as you retrieve a row, using that OID to access another row, and so on. In traditional Oracle SQL however, the access path is not evident and is hidden because the access is determined by the SQL optimizer.

Now that we have a high-level understanding of OID-based database navigation, let's take a look at how an Oracle database can be designed to contain repeating groups within a row definition. This feature is called *non-first normal form design*, since the introduction of repeating groups violates Codd's first normal form rule.

Using Non-First Normal Form Design

For many years, the idea of repeating data items within an object has been repugnant to Oracle designers. The tenets of data normalization dictated that the removal of repeating data items was the very first step toward a clean data model. However, many of the earlier databases such as IDMS allowed for repeating groups to be defined. The introduction of lists of values into relational databases was first implemented by the UniSQL database. At the time, this non-first normal form modeling ability was treated with suspicion and raised the ire of the titans of relational modeling. However, repeating groups soon became more respectable, and C. J. Date introduced a concept into the relational model called a *set* to allow repeating groups to fit into the relational paradigm. Today, database designers recognize that there are specific instances where the introduction of a repeating group enhances an Oracle8 database design.

Repeating Groups To Enhance Database Design

Assuming it is now acceptable to violate first normal form and introduce repeating groups into a table, a set of rules needs to be developed dictating when repeating groups are acceptable. The following guidelines apply:

- Repeating data items should be small in size.

- Repeating data items should be static and rarely changed.

- Repeating data should never need to be queried as a set. That is, you should never need to select all of the repeating values within a single SQL query.

To illustrate this principle, consider this scenario: Suppose you are designing a university database and you notice a student can take the ACT exam up to three times, and your database must capture this information. Without repeating groups, you have two choices:

- You can create unique columns within your student table, naming each repeating group with a subscript, as follows:

```
CREATE TABLE STUDENT (
    student_ID      number(5),
    . . .
    act_score_one   number(3),
    act_score_two   number(3),
    act_score_three number(3))
```

- You can normalize out the repeating groups and move them into another table, like this:

```
CREATE TABLE ACT_SCORE (
    student_ID   number(5),
    act_score    number(3));
```

Now, let's take a look at how the repeating group might be implemented inside an Oracle8 student table:

```
CREATE TYPE act_type as varrary(3) OF act_score;

CREATE TABLE STUDENT (student_id number(5), act_scores act_type);
```

Here, you can see that a data structure has been defined that can use an implied subscript to reference the data. For example, to insert the test scores for Don Burleson, you could enter:

```
INSERT INTO
            STUDENT
VALUES
     act_type(
                act_score(300),
                act_score(566),
                act_score(624))
WHERE
student_name.last_name = 'Burleson'
AND
student_name.first_name = 'Don';
```

To select the test score for Don Burleson, you could query the **act_score**s by referring to the subscript of the data item in your Oracle SQL, as follows:

```
SELECT
        act_score(1),
        act_score(2),
        act_score(3)
FROM
        STUDENT
WHERE
student_name.last_name = 'Burleson'
AND
student_name.first_name = 'Don';
```

You should now have a basic understanding of the concept of using repeating values within a database object or relational table. Let's move on and take a look at the advantages and disadvantages of this approach. After that, we'll look at how to determine when to use repeating groups.

Advantages Of Repeating Groups

The primary advantage of designing repeating groups is performance. Repeating groups are available when a table row is fetched without having to join another table (as required when using Oracle7). Also, as you can see in the previous example, less disk space is consumed because you do not have to create another table to hold the

ACT scores and duplicate a foreign key into the new table. Remember, if you create another table, you will need to redundantly duplicate the **student_ID** for each and every row of the **ACT_SCORE** table.

Disadvantages Of Repeating Groups

The main disadvantage of repeating groups is that they cannot easily be queried as a distinct set of values within Oracle SQL. In other words, you are not able to query to see all students who have received an ACT score greater than 500 without writing a PL/SQL snippet such as the following:

```
DECLARE
CURSOR c1 IS
     SELECT * FROM STUDENT;
BEGIN
    OPEN c1;
    FETCH c1 INTO score;
   FOR score IN c1
   LOOP

     FETCH c1 INTO score;

     FOR i  IN act_score.first...act_score.last LOOP

       IF act_score(i) > 500
       THEN
          dbms_output.put_line(student_name);
       END IF
    END LOOP
  END LOOP
```

Another, somewhat clumsy, alternative in Oracle8 SQL would be to use the SQL **UNION** operator. As you can see in the following code snippet, this involves creating a view to hold the values in a single column:

```
CREATE VIEW  ALL_ACT AS
(
SELECT act_score(1) FROM STUDENT
UNION
SELECT act_score(2) FROM STUDENT
UNION
```

```
SELECT act_score(3) FROM STUDENT
);
SELECT act_score FROM ALL_ACT WHERE act_score > 500;
```

Determining When To Use Repeating Groups

The central question is simple: Is it worth the extra performance and disk savings to use the repeating groups? To answer this question, let's see what would happen if you were to remove the repeating group of **act_score** and place the scores in a table called **ACT_SCORE**. You could then query the table to easily get the list of students, like this:

```
SELECT student_name
FROM STUDENT, ACT_SCORE
WHERE
   ACT_SCORE.student_ID = STUDENT.student_ID
   AND
   act_score > 500;
```

When you use repeating groups or nested tables, you do not know in advance how many cells of a **varray** contain data or how many rows exist inside a store table. Therefore, you need to test to see how many values are present. Oracle8 provides several PL/SQL functions to determine the **first** and **last**, as well as **prior** and **next** values within a collection. The following code sets the value of **j** to the number of ACT scores, so our PL/SQL loop will iterate the appropriate number of times:

```
j:=act_score.last

FOR i - 1 TO j
LOOP
   . . .
END LOOP
```

In short, repeating groups can be very useful within an Oracle8 design when the repeating groups are small and have a common number of repeating values. In these instances, repeating groups will greatly improve performance in circumstances where you need to avoid the additional Oracle overhead involved in joining several tables.

Now, let's take a look at how repeating values appear in the Oracle object/relational model and discuss how they can be used with abstract data types.

Repeating Groups And Abstract Data Types

The Oracle8 engine uses the varying-array language construct of PL/SQL (the **varray**) to indicate repeating groups. This means that you can use the **varray** mechanism to declare repeating groups within table columns.

There are two ways to implement repeating groups in Oracle8. You can define re-peating groups of data items, or you can define repeating groups of OIDs to rows in another table. Let's look at OIDs first, and then examine the equivalent structure with repeating groups of data values.

Repeating Groups Of OIDs

The easiest way to address repeating groups of OIDs is to examine an example. The following SQL adds a repeating group called **job_history** to a customer table. First, a **TYPE** needs to be created called **job_history** with a maximum of three values:

```
CREATE TYPE full_address_type (
     street_address     char(20),
     city_address       char(20),
     state_name         char(2),
     zip_code           char(5));

CREATE TYPE job_details AS OBJECT (
     job_dates               char(80),
     job_employer_name       char(80),
     job_title               char(80),
     job_address             full_address_type);

CREATE TYPE job_history_type  IS
     varray(3) OF REF job_details;
```

Now that the data types are defined, here is how you can create the Oracle8 object using the data types:

```
CREATE TABLE CUSTOMER (
     customer_name     full_name_type,
     cust_address      full_address_type,
     prior_jobs        job_history_type);
CREATE TABLE JOB_HIST OF job_details;
```

A repeating list of references has been created, so you can store **job_hist** objects, capture the OIDs for these objects, and store them as reference columns in the

prior_jobs column. Then, you can extract the data from the remote object using the following **DEREF** statement:

```
SELECT DEREF(CUSTOMER.prior_jobs.job_title(3))
FROM CUSTOMER
WHERE
CUSTOMER.customer_name.last_name LIKE 'JONES%';
```

As you might guess, accessing remote rows by OID is far faster than accessing **job_history** rows with an SQL join. However, there is another Oracle8 method that is even faster than dereferencing an OID. Oracle8 allows for a repeating group to be stored directly inside a table with repeating groups of data values. Let's take a look at how these repeating groups of data values can appear in Oracle8.

Repeating Groups Of Data Values

As you saw before, you can use the **varray** construct to indicate repeating groups, so it is a safe assumption that a **varray** mechanism can be used to declare the **job_history** item. For example:

```
CREATE TYPE full_address_type (
    street_address      char(20),
    city_address        char(20),
    zip_code            char(5));

CREATE TYPE job_details (
    job_dates               char(80),
    job_employer_name       char(80),
    job_title               char(80)
    job_address             full_address_type);

CREATE TYPE job_history_type (
    varray(3) OF job_details);
```

Now you can create the **CUSTOMER** table using the data types that have been defined:

```
CREATE TABLE CUSTOMER AS OBJECT (
    customer_name       full_name_type,
    cust_address        full_address_type,
    prior_jobs          job_history_type);
```

A table has been created with three occurrences of job history details. As you have already seen, you need to subscript **prior_jobs** to tell the database which one of the three items you want. The following code shows how to do this:

```
SELECT CUSTOMER.prior_jobs.job_title(3)
FROM CUSTOMER
WHERE
CUSTOMER.customer_name.last_name LIKE 'JONES%';
```

Here we see that we have created a repeating list within our table definition. (See Figure 1.6.) The following code selects the first previous employer's street address:

```
SELECT CUSTOMER.prior_jobs.job_address.street_address(1)
FROM CUSTOMER
WHERE
CUSTOMER.customer_name.last_name LIKE 'JONES%';
```

Note that it is possible in Oracle8 to make the repeating groups contain either data or pointers to rows within other tables. But what happens when you nest data types that have repeating groups? In pre-relational databases, it was easy to create a record

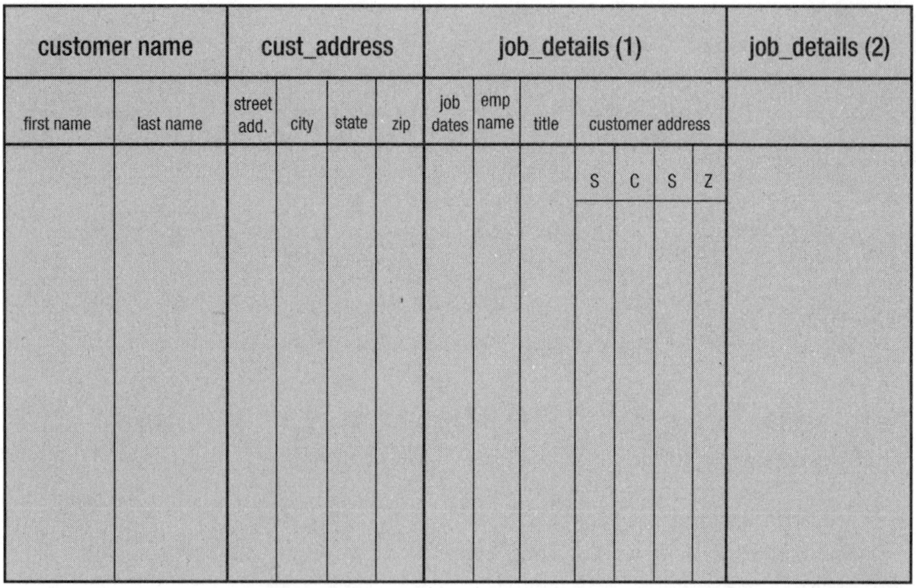

customer name		cust_address				job_details (1)							job_details (2)
first name	last name	street add.	city	state	zip	job dates	emp name	title	customer address				
									S	C	S	Z	

Figure 1.6
A repeating list within an Oracle table column.

that contained a finite repeating group. For example, in COBOL a record definition could be defined to contain three repeating groups of job history information:

```
03 EMPLOYEE.
   05 EMPLOYEE-NAME        PIC X(80).
   . . .
   05 JOB-HISTORY OCCURS 3 TIMES.
      07 JOB-DATE          PIC X(80).
      07 JOB-EMPLOYER-NAME PIC X(80).
      07 JOB-TITLE         PIC X(80).
      07 EMPLOYER-ADDRESS
         09 STREET-ADDRESS PIC X(80).
         09 CITY-ADDRESS   PIC X(80).
         09 ZIP-CODE       PIC X(80);
```

So in COBOL, the **JOB-HISTORY** component is referenced by a subscript, as we see in the following examples.

```
MOVE JOB-HISTORY(2) TO OUT-REC.
MOVE 'DATABASE ADMINISTRATOR' TO JOB-TITLE(3).
```

Database designers will note that the use of Oracle8 **varray**s is a direct violation of first normal form.

If it is possible to allow for repeating values within a table cell, why not allow a reference to an entirely new table? This is a valid option within Oracle8 and is called a *nested table*. In the next section, we'll look at pointing to tables.

Pointing To Tables

Imagine a database that allows nesting of tables within tables such that a single cell of one table can point to another table. While this concept might seem very foreign on the surface, it is not too hard to understand if you consider that many real-world objects are made up of subparts.

Recall our discussion of OIDs. In order to establish data relationships between database entities, a pointer must be persistent, unique, and nonexpiring. In relational databases, a relational **ROWID** is used to identify a row. Unfortunately, a **ROWID** is the number of a physical database block and row displacement within the data block. The problem is that such a relational row could be moved unintentionally to another block or, worse, deleted accidentally. To address this problem, Oracle created OIDs for each row. That way, every row is always uniquely identified, regardless of the row's status or physical placement on database blocks. Furthermore, a database row can be deleted, and the OID associated with the row will never be reused by Oracle.

To create a table with OIDs, a data type must be created that contains all the necessary row information. In the following example, assume that the data type **customer_stuff** contains the required data structures for a **CUSTOMER** table. In a traditional relational database, you could create the table like this:

```
CREATE TABLE CUSTOMER (customer_data          customer_stuff);
```

With the introduction of OIDs, the table creation syntax is changed slightly. The following example will create the exact same table as the preceding example, with the exception that the table will contain an OID for each row created within the **CUS-TOMER** table:

```
CREATE TYPE customer_stuff AS OBJECT (
customer_name      full_name,
cust_address       customer_address,
prior_jobs         job_history);

CREATE TABLE CUSTOMER OF customer_stuff;
```

It has always been a shortcoming of the relational model that only atomic items could be directly represented, and relational views were required to assemble aggregate objects. The object technology professors used to make fun of the relational model's inability to represent aggregate objects, stating that it is like disassembling your car every evening when you arrive home from work, only to have to reassemble the car the next time you want to go for a drive. At last, nested abstract data types allow Oracle users to represent real-world objects without resorting to views. (See Figure 1.7.)

Let's take a look at how this type of recursive data relationship can be represented within Oracle. The following SQL creates a **TYPE** definition for a list of orders. This list of pointers to orders might become a column within an Oracle table, as follows:

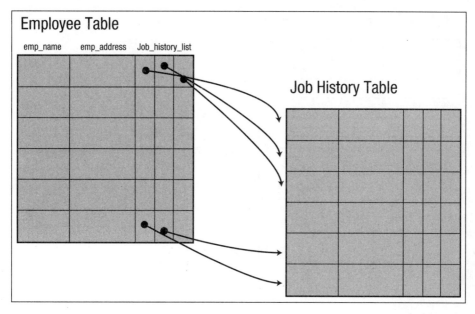

Figure 1.7
Pointers to other database rows.

```
CREATE TYPE order_set  AS TABLE OF order;

CREATE TYPE customer_stuff_type  AS OBJECT(
    customer_id           integer,
    customer_full_name    full_name,
    order_list            order_set);

CREATE TABLE CUSTOMER OF customer_stuff_type
   NESTED TABLE order_list;
```

Here, you can see the new style of table creation syntax. While Figure 1.7 shows the pointer structure as it would look conceptually, the object/relational databases must utilize internal arrays to implement these repeating groups of pointers. In Oracle8, variable-length arrays are used to represent this structure, as shown in Figure 1.8.

In Figure 1.8, a list of pointers is nested within each column, and each cell within a column contains a list of pointers to rows in the **ORDER** table. Using object-oriented SQL extensions, you can now pre-join with the **ORDER** table to add the three orders for this customer, as follows:

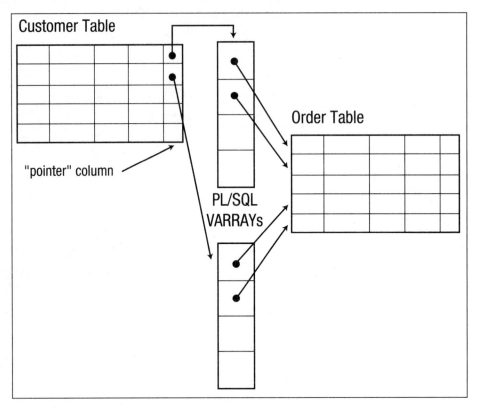

Figure 1.8
The Oracle8 representation of repeating lists of pointers to rows.

```
UPDATE CUSTOMER
   SET order_list (
       SELECT REF(order)      /* this returns the OIDs from all order rows
                              */
       FROM ORDER
       WHERE
       order_date = SYSDATE
       AND
       ORDER.customer_ID = (123)
   )
```

Here, you can see the use of the **REF** operator, which returns the reference, or OID, of the requested rows. This is similar to the retrieval of **ROWID**s in a relational database, except that you are now storing the row information inside a relational table.

Now, let's take a look at how you can navigate between tables without having to join tables together. Remember from our earlier discussion, that the object/relational model provides for two ways to retrieve data from your database. You can use SQL to specify the desired data and let the SQL optimizer choose the access path, or you can navigate your database, one row at a time, to gather the required information. Following is the code to return the contents of the three rows that are contained in the **order_list varray**:

```
SELECT DEREF(order_list)
FROM CUSTOMER
WHERE
customer_id = 123;   /* This will return 3 rows in the order table */
```

The important point in the preceding example is that you can navigate between tables without ever performing an SQL join. Consider the possibilities. You would *never* need to embed a foreign key for the **CUSTOMER** table in the order record because you could store the pointers in each customer row. Of course, you would never be able to perform a relational join between the **CUSTOMER** and **ORDER** tables, but this would not really make any difference as long as you have maintained the ability to navigate between customers and orders with pointers.

Of course, these are one-way pointers from customers to orders, and you would not have a method to get from the **ORDER** table to the **CUSTOMER** table unless you embed a pointer to point to the row that contains the customer for each order. You can do this by creating an owner reference inside each order row that contains the OID of the customer who placed the order.

Let's look at how this type of recursive data relationship might be represented in an object/relational database such as Oracle8:

```
CREATE TYPE order_type AS OBJECT (
    order_date     date,
    total_amount   number)

CREATE TABLE ORDER_LIST AS TABLE OF order_type;

CREATE TYPE customer_type AS OBJECT (
    customer_id                integer,
    customer_full_name         full_name,
    customer_full_address      full_address_type,
```

```
      . . .
      cust_order_list              order_list);

CREATE TABLE CUSTOMER OF customer_type
   NESTED TABLE cust_order_list;
```

Here, you can see the **ORDER** table is conceptually nested within the **CUSTOMER** table (more about nesting in the next section). So, where do you go from here? How do you populate this new structure? Let's take a look at how this table might be populated:

```
INSERT INTO CUSTOMER VALUES (
    full_name ('ANDREW','S.','BURLESON'),
    customer_address('246 1st St.','Minot, ND','74635');
```

Here comes the part where you can see the performance gain. You can now pre-join the **CUSTOMER** table with the **ORDER** table to add the three orders for this customer:

```
UPDATE CUSTOMER
   SET order_list (
       SELECT REF(order)     /* OID reference */
       FROM ORDER
       WHERE
       order_date = SYSDATE
       AND
       ORDER.customer_ID = (123)
   )
```

So, what do you have here? It appears that the **order_list** entry in the **CUSTOMER** table will contain pointers to the three orders that have been placed by this customer. As such, you are able to reference these pointers without having to perform a relational join:

```
SELECT DEREF(order_list)
FROM CUSTOMER
WHERE
customer_id = 123;  /* This will return 3 rows in the order table */
```

This query will return a pointer to the three rows in the **ORDER** table. It should then be a simple matter to dereference these pointers to retrieve the contents of the

ORDER table. Depending on the vendor implementation of SQL, it might look something like this:

```
SELECT DEREF(order_list)
FROM CUSTOMER
WHERE customer_ID = 123;
```

Now, let's take a more in-depth look at the ability of Oracle8 to nest tables.

Using Nested Tables

As we've discussed at various points in this chapter, the new object/relational database contains a very interesting pointer structure that allows a single cell in an entity to contain a whole other entity. In this fashion, it is possible to create a structure where objects (or tables) can be nested within other objects (or tables). For an object/relational database, this means that the values in a single column within a table can contain an entire table. These subtable tables, in turn, can have single column values that point to other tables, and so on, ad infinitum. Figure 1.9 illustrates this concept.

While the application of this new data structure is not apparent, it does present exciting possibilities for modeling complex aggregate objects. In C++ object-oriented databases, such as ONTOS and Objectivity, database designers can create a structure where an object contains a list of pointers. Each of these pointers points to a separate list of pointers. In turn, these pointers point to other objects in the database. In C language parlance, this structure is known as ****char**, which is called a pointer to a pointer to a character.

In Oracle8, this structure is implemented by using what is called a *store table*. The top-level table contains a cell that is defined as a pointer to a table. The column defined as a pointer to a whole table has one big restriction in that each and every pointer must point to a table with the exact same definition. In other words, each column value must contain a pointer to a table that is defined with the exact same definition.

While it appears that each cell points to a whole table, the object/relational databases implement this structure by defining a store table. A *store table* is an internal table that is tightly coupled with the owner table. In essence, a store table is nothing more than an internal table defined as subordinate to the owner table with a fixed set of columns.

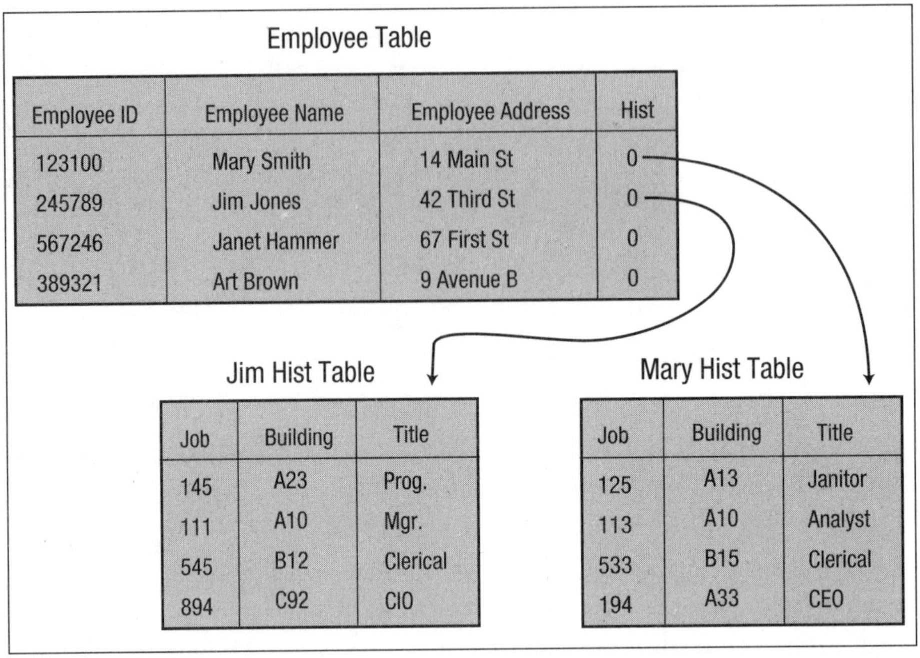

Employee Table

Employee ID	Employee Name	Employee Address	Hist
123100	Mary Smith	14 Main St	0
245789	Jim Jones	42 Third St	0
567246	Janet Hammer	67 First St	0
389321	Art Brown	9 Avenue B	0

Jim Hist Table

Job	Building	Title
145	A23	Prog.
111	A10	Mgr.
545	B12	Clerical
894	C92	CIO

Mary Hist Table

Job	Building	Title
125	A13	Janitor
113	A10	Analyst
533	B15	Clerical
194	A33	CEO

Figure 1.9
Nesting tables within tables.

Let's illustrate the use of this data structure with a simple example. Let's return to the university database. The university database has a many-to-many relationship between courses and student entities. A student can take many courses, and a course has many students. In a traditional relational system, this relationship between students and courses would be implemented by creating a junction table between the student and course entities, and copying the primary keys from the student and course tables into this entity. In our example, this entity is called **grade**, and the grade entity contains the **student_ID** and **course_ID** columns as foreign keys. (See Figure 1.10.)

Now, let's take a look at how this could be implemented using pointers to whole tables. To produce a class schedule for a student in a traditional relational implementation, you would need to select the **student** row, join with the **GRADE** table, and finally join with the **CLASS** table, as follows:

```
SELECT
        student_full_name,
        course_name,
        course_date,
```

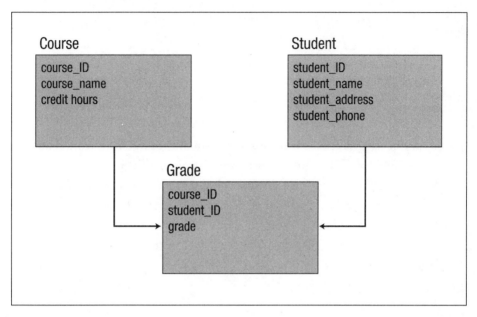

Figure 1.10
The physical implementation of a store table.

```
      grade
FROM
      STUDENT, GRADE, COURSE
WHERE
      student_last_name = 'Burleson'
      AND
      STUDENT.student_ID = GRADE.student_ID
      AND
      GRADE.course_ID = COURSE.course_ID;
```

To avoid the three-way SQL join of the tables, you could choose to create a store table that is subordinate to the **STUDENT** table. This table would contain the **course_name**, **course_date**, and **grade** for each student:

```
CREATE TYPE student_list_type (
      student_full_name      full_name,
      student_full_address   full_address,
      grade                  char(1));

CREATE TYPE student_list AS TABLE OF student_list_type;

CREATE TYPE course_type AS OBJECT (
```

```
course_name          varchar(20),
dept_ID              number(4),
credit_hrs           number(2),
student_roster       student_list);

CREATE TABLE COURSE OF course_type
  NESTED TABLE student_roster;
```

Here, you can see that the **student_roster** column of the **COURSE** table contains a pointer to a table of **TYPE student_list_type**. Herein lies the illusion. While it appears to the application that each distinct column value points to a whole table, in reality, the column points to a set of rows within the store table. The store table is common to all of the columns that contain this pointer structure, and the store table contains a special column that points to the owner of the row in the parent table. (See Figure 1.11.) This column is called **SETID$** and it exists for each row in the store table.

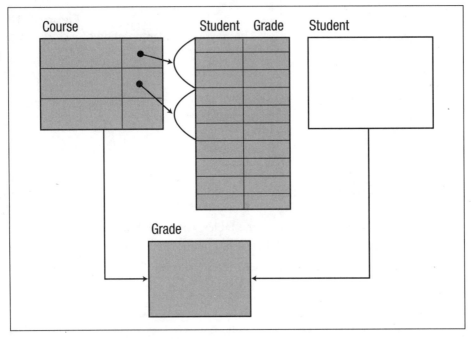

Figure 1.11

A sample many-to-many data relationship for a university.

While the idea of nesting tables within tables is an excellent method for modeling hierarchical structures, there is still some question about the application of this data structure to real-world data models. The nice feature of nested tables is that a single **SELECT** statement can return the applicable rows of a store table, thereby simplifying a query. Because the nested table is really just another table with the same column structure for each row, there is still some question about whether it is better to use this structure or to simply create another table.

Now that we understand the basics of OIDs and pointers, we are ready to take a look at one of the most sophisticated construct in Oracle8, the multidimensional array of object IDs.

Reviewing The Implications Of OIDs For Oracle Design

By this point in the chapter, you should be able to see that the ability to support abstract data types provides database designers with very a powerful tool, giving designers the ability to:

- Store repeating groups within a cell of a table.

- Nest tables within tables.

- Provide pointer-based navigation for relational data.

- Represent aggregate objects.

Consider the ramifications for item pointer-based navigation to relational data. If you are allowed to bypass SQL, imagine the possibilities! With Oracle8, you can navigate a data model without having the overhead of joining tables together. More important, you now have the ability to represent complex objects. This means that you can pre-create objects that are composed of sub-objects without having to build them each time you want to see them. Because aggregate objects have an independent existence, you can attach methods to these objects. In addition, you can also save database overhead by pre-creating complex database objects and having them instantly available to the database.

One of the most exciting new features of Oracle8 is the ability to create real-world objects that exist in the database. One of the shortcomings of relational databases was the requirement that all data is stored at its smallest (i.e., third normal form) size, and that aggregate objects must be built by joining tables together. Oracle8 has now removed this restriction, and aggregate object can be pre-built from their components and stored within the database. Let's take a look at how this works.

Designing Aggregate Objects

In order to create an aggregate object, we need to understand the nature of aggregation within Oracle8. Using the Oracle8 features of abstract data types, you can define a new object called **ORDER_FORM** that contains pointers to the various components that comprise an order form. Note that it is never necessary to rebuild an **ORDER_FORM** object unless items are deleted or added to the **ORDER_FORM**. For example, when the **quantity_ordered** column in the **ORDER_LINE** table is changed, the **ORDER_FORM** object automatically picks up this new value when the **order_line** row is dereferenced.

Here's how it works. First, you need to define a pointer to return the row that corresponds to the customer who placed an order. Let's assume that you have already created a UDT for the entire **customer** row and defined the **CUSTOMER** table as follows:

```
CREATE TABLE CUSTOMER (customer_data    customer_adt);
```

You can now create a **customer_ref TYPE** to hold the pointer to the customer:

```
CREATE TYPE customer_ref AS TABLE OF customer_adt;
```

Because you will be retrieving one **order** row, you can do the same thing for the **ORDER** table row.

```
CREATE TYPE order_ref AS TABLE OF order_adt;
```

Therefore, the first component of the **ORDER_FORM** object will be the reference to the **customer** and **order** rows:

```
CREATE TABLE ORDER_FORM (
   customer      customer_ref,
   order         order_ref);
```

Okay, now that you have the customer and order data, you need to establish pointers to represent the many-to-many relationship between the **ORDER** and **ITEM** tables.

To accomplish this, you start by defining a repeating group of every **order_line** for each order:

```
CREATE TYPE item_list
   AS TABLE OF order_line;
```

This code defines **item_list**. Now, you have to define **ORDER_FORM**:

```
CREATE TABLE ORDER_FORM (
    customer      customer_ref,
    order         order_ref,
    lines         item_list);
```

Next, you need to establish pointers to every item referenced in the **ORDER_LINE** table. But, how do you do this? You do not know the **item_ID** numbers that participate in the order until you retrieve the **order_line** rows. Therefore, you need to establish owner pointers inside each **order_line** row so that you can dereference the item table. Let's assume that the **LINE_ITEM** table has been defined to include a reference pointer to the **ITEM** table, as follows:

```
/* example of an owner pointer */
CREATE TYPE item_ref  AS TABLE OF item_type;

CREATE TABLE line_item_type AS OBJECT (
    order_ID          integer,
    item_ID           integer,
    item_pointer      REF item_type,
    quantity_ordered integer);

CREATE TYPE line_items AS varray(30) OF line_item_type;
```

So, let's see how you can display all of the data for the **ORDER_FORM** object:

```
CREATE TABLE ORDER_FORM AS OBJECT(
    customer          REF customer_type,
    order             REF order_type,
    lines             line_items);

SELECT
   DEREF(customer),
   DEREF(order),
   . . .
;
```

Defining Oracle Objects

As discussed earlier in the chapter, a row can only be referenced if it has been defined with an OID. To do this the table must be defined as:

```
CREATE TABLE CUSTOMER OF customer_stuff_type;
```

as opposed to:

```
CREATE TABLE CUSTOMER (customer_data  customer_stuff_type);
```

*These table definitions are the same. The only difference is that the first has a column called **OID$** that contains a unique OID for each row. Also, the **customer_stuff_type** must be defined with the **AS OBJECT** clause.*

Now that we understand how to create Oracle8 objects, we are ready to look at the coupling of these objects with Oracle8 methods. The process of coupling data and methods requires careful design, and this process usually begins with the specification of "prototypes" for each of the Oracle8 methods.

Designing Method Prototypes

The starting point for the successful coupling of Oracle8 data and methods is the creation of the method prototypes. For the purposes of this example, the data type definitions are taken from the data dictionary and the pseudocode is taken from the mini-spec to aid in our discussion of the hierarchical mapping of methods. In this analysis, a set of data flow diagrams (DFDs) is referenced, beginning at level one (describing the **fill_order** process) and including all of the lower-level data flow diagrams.

Let's begin this discussion by listing each process and showing the sub-methods within each process, as follows:

```
1 - fill_order
   1.1 - check_customer_credit
   1.2 - check_inventory
      1.2.1 - check_stock_level
      1.2.2 - generate_backorder_notice
      1.2.3 - decrement_inventory
```

```
  1.2.4 - prepare_packing_slip
1.3 - prepare_invoice
  1.3.1 - compute_order_cost
  1.3.2 - compute_shipping_charges
  1.3.3 - add_handling_charge
  1.3.4 - assemble_invoice
```

This hierarchy should help you to see how methods are nested within other methods. Once this natural hierarchy has been developed, you are ready to define the mapping of these processes to your database classes.

As you probably know, the lowest level data flow diagrams represent *functional primitives*, or processes that cannot be decomposed into smaller processes. Of course, functional primitive processes become methods, but does this mean that they will never have subcomponents? If an analyst has performed the job properly, there will be no sub-methods in these processes with the exception of standalone methods, such as a **compute_shipping_charges** method.

Beginning with the primitive processes, you can design a method that accepts the same values as noted on the DFD and returns the same values to the program that invokes the method. For example, you might have a process called **compute_shipping_charges** that accepts a **valid_in_stock_order** as input. Inside this process, it gathers the weight and cost of the items, computes the charges, and returns the shipping charge and total weight.

Essentially, a prototype is a formal definition of a method that describes all of the input and output data flows. The accepted form for a prototype is:

```
return_data_type Method_name
    (input_data_name_1 input_data_type_1,
     input_data_name_2 input_data_type_2,
     . . .);
```

Before going into more detail, let's review the possible data types that can be used by methods. These data types can be used to return a data value or they can be accepted by the method as an input parameter:

- **int**—Integer value

- **varchar**—Variable length character string

- **TYPE**—Pointer to a data structure (identical to an Oracle8 OID)

TYPE is the most confusing data type for most object novices because it refers to pointers. A pointer in an object database is an OID that points to the object that will supply the values to the method. Because Oracle8 supports *strong data typing* through the use of the **SCOPE** clause of the **CREATE TABLE** statement, you must differentiate between the different types of OIDs. For example, a pointer to an order (***order**) is quite different from a pointer to a customer (***customer**) object. As a practical matter, it is more efficient to pass a pointer to the data than it is to pass the data itself because the pointer (OID) is more compact.

*The idea of strong typing is alive and well within Oracle8. Oracle8 provides for the use of the **SCOPE** verb in the **CREATE TABLE** statement to limit the type of a reference column to a particular OID table. For example, if you define a customer table with a **varray** of OIDs to orders for a customer, you can use the **SCOPE** clause to ensure that only OIDs from the **ORDER** table are stored within these columns. For more information on **SCOPE**, see Chapter 5, Tuning Oracle SQL.*

In object database parlance, you design a prototype for each process on your DFDs. Let's illustrate this by examining how to design the prototype for the **compute_shipping_charges** method, which accepts a **valid_in_stock_order** and outputs the **shipping_charge** for the order. Therefore, you could create a prototype that shows **compute_shipping_charges** as returning an integer (the shipping charge) and accepting a pointer to an order object:

```
int compute_shipping_charge(valid_in_stock_order *order);
```

For the purpose of this example, assume that the **valid_in_stock_order** contains the following four values, which are required for the process to compute the shipping charges:

- Weight in pounds
- Desired class of shipping
- Origination ZIP code
- Destination ZIP code

So, how do you get these data items when you are only given an OID for the order? The method will dereference the OID, go to the order object, and gather the required information. This means the method will grab the OID and issue the appropriate SQL to accept data items from the object. Here is what the SQL within the **compute_shipping_charges** method might look like:

```
SELECT
    item_weight,
    shipping_class,
    origination_zip_code,
    destination_zip_code
FROM
    ORDER O
WHERE
    REF(O) = :valid_in_stock_order;
```

This function returns the shipping charge, expressed as an integer number. If you did not pass the pointer to the order object to this method, the prototype for **compute_shipping_charges** becomes far more complicated, as you can see here:

```
int compute_shipping_charge
    (weight int, class char(1),
     origination_zip_code number(9),
     destination_zip_code number(9));
```

Note that the first token **int** refers to the data type of the value returned by the method. For methods that do not return a value, the first token in the prototype is **void**. For example, a method called **give_raise** would not return a value and could be prototyped as:

```
void give_raise(emp_ID number(9), percentage int);
```

Now that you understand the basics of prototyping, let's prototype some methods. To prototype the methods, we need to know the names and data types of all input data, and the name and data types of the returned value. These are generally derived from the data flow diagrams in the initial systems analysis:

```
*order      fill_order(cust_info *customer);

int         check_customer_credit(cust_info *customer);
```

```
int           check_inventory(item_number int);

*invoice      prepare_invoice(valid_in_stock_order *order_form);

int           check_stock_level(item_number int);

*backorder    generate_backorder_request(item_number  int);

void          decrement_inventory(item_number int);

*packing_slip prepare_packing_slip(valid_in_stock_order *order_form);

int           compute_order_cost(valid_in_stock_order *order_form);

int           compute_shipping_charges(valid_in_stock_order *order_form);

int           add_handling_charge(total_weight int);

*invoice      assemble_invoice(item_total_cost int,
                               shipping_charge int,
                               handling_charge int);
```

Let's describe these prototypes, so you are comfortable with the definitions. In these prototypes, you can see that some methods return an integer number, some return values, and others return pointers to objects. In object-oriented databases, it is not uncommon to combine assignment statements with method calls. For example, the following process code will compute the shipping charges for the order and assign the result to a variable called **my_shipping_charges**:

```
my_shipping_charges = compute_shipping_charges(:my_order_form_OID);
```

By the same token (excuse the pun), you can also return an OID in a method call, so you can embed an OID into another object. In the following code, assume you have defined the data type for **order_OID** as a pointer to an order. You can now do two things in a single statement. You can invoke the **fill_order** method and, at the same time, return the OID of the new order object into the **order_OID** variable, as follows:

```
order_OID = fill_order(:cust_info);
```

As you can see, a complete specification for each method has been created, stating the name and data type of every input and output variable. It is a requirement that each of these methods is independently tested, and the internal variable might not be known to the calling method. This is known as *information hiding*, and it is used when **private** variables are declared and used within a method. Remember, one of the goals of object-oriented database methods is to make each method into a reusable black box that can always be counted on to function properly. This is the foundation of object method reusability.

Let's now introduce the Oracle8 model into this system. As you probably know by now, there are several components used to describe an object/relational database design. First, you have to address the object/relational model for the base objects. Figure 1.12 displays the base classes in the order processing system and describes the indexes, tablespaces, and subclasses for each class definition.

Next, take a look at the aggregate class diagram shown in Figure 1.13. Here, you can see two aggregate class definitions, their internal pointer structures, and the index and tablespace information for all classes entirely composed of pointers to other objects.

Note that in the models, both base classes are shown, as well as the aggregate classes. The question becomes, how do you map your method prototypes to these classes? Because the object-relational model represents all objects as tables, the availability of aggregate objects will now allow the coupling of aggregate methods with the owner table. In this fashion, an aggregate object will know how to behave based on these methods.

Automatic Method Generation

In most object-oriented and object/relational databases, the basic methods for all objects are created automatically at the time an object class is defined. These basic methods are used when objects are created, deleted, updated, and displayed, and correspond to the **INSERT**, **DELETE**, and **UPDATE** SQL verbs. It is important to recognize that methods exist in the following forms within a database engine:

- *Standalone*—These methods are not associated with a database class.

- *Base class*—These methods affect the lowest-level objects within a database.

- *Aggregate class*—These methods operate on the aggregate objects and can reference data within component objects.

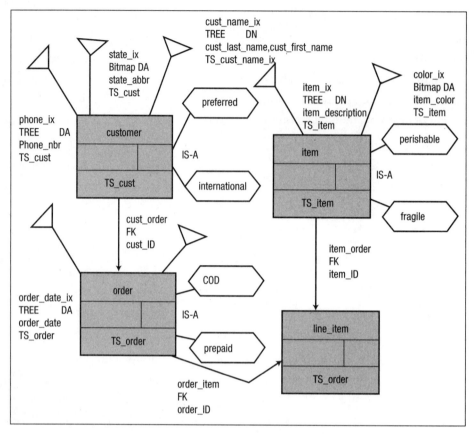

Figure 1.12
An object/relation diagram for the order processing system.

However, more complex methods can be coupled to their target objects. For example, an **order_form** object might contain a method called **check_payment_history**, which performs detailed checks into the prior payment history for a customer who is placing an order.

Now, let's take a look at an analysis of the methods that might be associated with these objects. Whenever a method of the same name appears in more than one class definition, the database will look first at the object and then traverse up the class hierarchy at runtime, looking for the method. In the following example, we see some sample methods that may be associated with each type of student object:

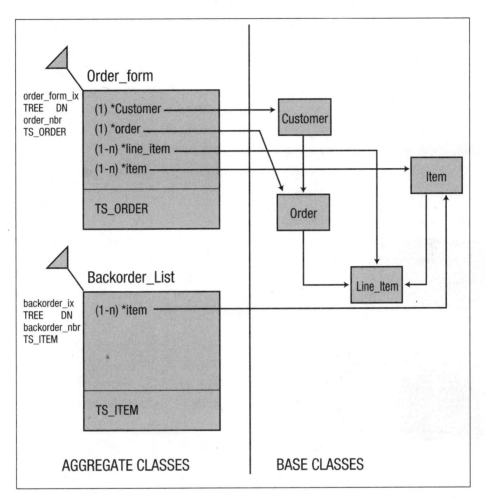

Figure 1.13
The aggregate class diagram for the order processing system.

```
Methods for student;
   display_student();
   compute_tuition();
   enroll_student();
Methods for graduate_student;
   assign_mentor();
   compute_tuition();
   update_thesis_status();
Methods for non_resident_students;
   compute_tuition();
```

```
   record_transfer_statistics();
Methods for foreign_students;
   compute_tuition();
```

Here, you can see that some methods unique to the subclass appear only within the subclass definition. For example, **update_thesis_status** would not have any meaning to an undergraduate student.

This should now provide a general method for the mapping of processes to database objects. As this text repeatedly states, it is critical to the design of an object database that careful planning of methods takes place before a database schema is defined.

Now that we understand the performance implications of the Oracle8 object features on our database design, let's take a look at what we can expect in the next version of Oracle—Oracle8.2.

Database Object Summary

All of these database design tools are very exciting, but it might not be apparent when they should be used. Table 1.1 provides some general guidelines for using the Oracle8 features in a database design. In this table, you can see the type of repeating relationship (i.e., one-to-many relationship), and how it's handled in Oracle7 and Oracle8.

As you can see, in cases where the many sides of a relationship have a fixed number of small data items, **varray**s of data are appropriate. In cases where the many sides of a relationship contain a varying number of large items, an Oracle8 store table can be used to model the relationship. In cases where many sides of a relationship are shared by more than one owner (i.e., the junction table in an n-way many-to-many relationship), then a traditional Oracle7 table with a foreign key is appropriate.

Table 1.1   When to use Oracle design constructs.

Type	Oracle7	Oracle8
Many relationship	Representation	Representation
Fixed number, small	Table	**varray** of data
Variable number, large	Table	Store table
Many owners (i.e., junction table)	Table	Table

There are a set of guidelines that are used to decide when it is appropriate to introduce repeating groups into an Oracle table:

- Attribute sets that have a low, fixed number of occurrences should be placed into **varray**s. (This might not be true if constraints or direct comparisons are required.)

- Attribute sets with many occurrences or sets requiring constraints and value-to-value comparisons should be placed in nested tables.

- Attribute sets that are one-to-one with the main object should be placed in a **TYPE** definition such that the entire object can be defined with one type.

- Always use the **WITH ROWID** and **OIDINDEX** clauses when defining an object table. See Chapter 5, *Tuning Oracle SQL* for details on Oracle8 object creation.

One Step Beyond—Oracle8.2

While Oracle8 has made great strides in incorporating the object-oriented features of user-defined data types, aggregate objects, and coupling of data and methods, there are still more enhancement planned. Oracle8.2 will include support for class hierarchies, which will set the foundation for true inheritance and polymorphism.

Inheritance

Inheritance is defined as the ability of a lower-level object to inherit or access the data structures and behaviors associated with all classes that are above it in the class hierarchy. Multiple inheritance refers to the ability of an object to inherit data structures and behaviors from more than one superclass. Oracle has promised to deliver support for inheritance in version 8.2.

To illustrate inheritance, let's look at an application for a vehicle dealership. Occurrences of **ITEM**s to a dealership are **VEHICLE**s. Beneath the **VEHICLE** class, you might find subclasses for **CAR**s and **BOAT**s. Within **CAR**s, the classes can be further partitioned into classes for **TRUCK**, **VAN**, and **SEDAN**. The **VEHICLE** class would contain the data items unique to vehicles, including the vehicle ID and the year of manufacture. The **CAR** class, because it IS-A **VEHICLE**, would inherit the data items of the **VEHICLE** class. The **CAR** class might contain data items such as the number of axles and the gross weight of the vehicle. Because the **VAN** class IS-A **CAR**, which in turn IS-A **VEHICLE**, objects of the **VAN** class will inherit all data structures and behaviors relating to **CAR**s and **VEHICLE**s.

It is critical to the understanding of inheritance to note that inheritance happens at different times during the life of an object. The following points describe the two things that are inherited inside the database:

- *Inheritance of Data Structures*—At object creation time, inheritance is the mechanism whereby the initial data structure for the object is created. Only data structures are inherited, *never* data. It is a common misconception that data is inherited, such that an order can inherit the data items for the customer who placed the order. Inheritance is only used to create the initial, empty data structures for the object. In the vehicle example, all vehicles would inherit data definitions in the **VEHICLE** class, while an object of a lower-level class (say, **SAILBOAT**) would inherit data structures that apply only to sailboats—as in **sail_size**.

- *Inheritance of Methods*—Inheritance also happens at runtime when a call to a method (stored procedure) is made. For example, assume that the following call is made to **SAILBOAT** object:

```
SAILBOAT.compute_rental_charges();
```

The database would first search for the **compute_rental_charges** in the **SAILBOAT** class. If it is not found, the database would search *up the class hierarchy* until **compute_rental_charges** is located.

Abstraction

Abstraction was promised for Oracle8 but has been deferred until the introduction of Oracle8.2. *Abstraction* is defined as the conceptual (not concrete) existence of classes within a database. For example, a database could have a class hierarchy that includes classes without objects. A military database could contain the conceptual entities of **DIVISION**, **BATTALION**, **SQUADRON**, and **PLATOON**. The function of the database would be to track the platoons, and the entity classes of **DIVISION**, **BATTALION**, and **SQUADRON** might not have any associated objects.

This is not to say that abstract classes have no purpose. When a class is defined, it is associated with behaviors, which in turn are inherited by each object in the **PLATOON** class. From a database perspective, there will be no instances of any objects except **PLATOON**, but higher levels in the class hierarchy will contain behaviors that the **PLATOON** objects inherit.

The IS-A Construct

Oracle is planning to introduce an extension to its Designer/2000 product to allow for the modeling of class hierarchies. This new extension, tentatively dubbed Designer/2001, should allow for object-oriented constructs to be described and modeled. Unfortunately, Oracle8 does not support the IS-A relationship with inheritance, but this feature is promised with Oracle8.2.

Here is a vision of how it might work. After establishing a class hierarchy with the E/R model, the principle of generalization is used to identify the class hierarchy and the level of abstraction associated with each class. *Generalization* implies a successive refinement of a class, allowing superclasses of objects to inherit the data attributes and behaviors that apply to the lower levels of the class. Generalization establishes taxonomy hierarchies, organizing the classes according to their characteristics—usually in increasing levels of detail. Generalization begins at a very general level and proceeds to a specific level, with each sublevel having its own unique data attributes and behaviors.

The IS-A relationship is used to create a hierarchy within the object class with lower-level classes inheriting behaviors. The IS-A relationship models the hierarchy created as the class entity is decomposed into its logical subcomponents. For example, customers can be **preferred_customers** or **new_customers**, and orders can be **cod_orders** or **prepaid_orders**—each with their own data items and behaviors.

Understanding Multidimensional Pointers And Oracle

At this time, Oracle8 only supports one level of OID indirection. In plain English, Oracle8 does not allow for the definition of an OID column that points to a **varray** of OIDs. This is a severe limitation of the Oracle8 architecture, but future releases promise to allow multiple levels of OIDs, such that it would be possible to implement hierarchical structures of pointers.

To understand multidimensional pointers, let's begin with a simple example of a natural hierarchy of data relationships (see Figure 1.14). In this example, you can see that each university has many departments, each department offers many courses, and each course offers many sections. This is a natural descending hierarchy of one-to-many relationships.

As you probably know, there are many options for modeling this type of descending one-to-many data relationship. In a "plain vanilla" relational database, each entity would exist as a table, with the primary key of the owner table copied into the member table. But, there is an alternative to modeling this structure in the object/

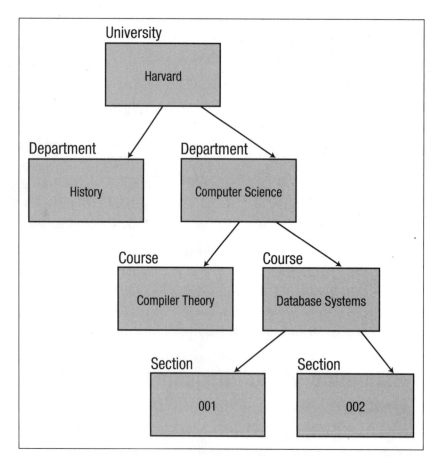

Figure 1.14
A hierarchy of data relationships.

relational model. Listing 1.1 shows how a hierarchical data structure could be implemented in some future release of Oracle8.

Listing 1.1   Implementing a hierarchical data structure.

```
CREATE TYPE full_name (
        first_name    varchar(20),
        MI            char(1),
        last_name     varchar(20));

CREATE TYPE section_type (
    section_number    number(5),
    instructor_name   full_name,
    semester          char(3),
    building          varchar(20),
    room              char(4),
    days_met          char(5),
    time_met          char(20));

CREATE TABLE SECTION OF section_type;

CREATE TYPE section_array AS varray(10) OF section_type;

CREATE TYPE course_type (
    course_ID         number(5),
    course_name       varchar(20),
    credit_hours      number(2),
    section_list      section_array);

CREATE TABLE COURSE OF course_type;

CREATE TYPE course_array AS varray(20) OF course_type;

CREATE TYPE dept_type (
    dept_name           varchar(20),
    chairperson_name    full_name,
    course_list         course_array);

CREATE TABLE DEPARTMENT OF dept_type;
```

Figure 1.15 illustrates the data structure defined in the preceding code.

As you can see in Figure 1.15, pointers allow fast access from owner to member in the hierarchy. But where are the owner pointers? As it turns out, you must first

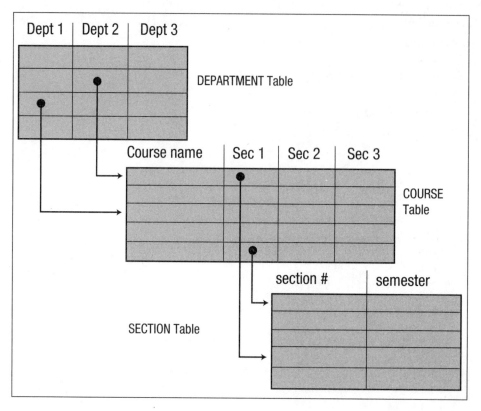

Figure 1.15
An implementation of multidimensional row pointers.

define a hierarchy before you have the necessary definitions to include the pointers. You can add owner pointers using the **ALTER TYPE** statement, as follows:

```
ALTER TYPE section_type
    ADD COLUMN course_owner_pointer        course_type;
ALTER TYPE course_type
    ADD COLUMN department_owner_pointer department_type;
```

A two-way pointer structure has now been created, such that all owner rows in the hierarchy point to their member rows, while all member rows point to their owners. However, you must bear in mind that these are only data structures. It is up to the programmer to assign these pointers when the rows are created.

In a sense, this data structure is the Oracle8 equivalent to the **char data structure of the C language (as mentioned earlier). In our Oracle8 example, the department has an array of pointers to courses, which, in turn, contain arrays of pointers to sections.

The next question, then, is how do you query these pointers with Oracle SQL? In order to accommodate the new object features, most object/relational vendors are implementing the **CAST** and **MULTISET** extensions to SQL. For example, here is what a query to populate the **STUDENT_LIST** internal table looks like:

```
INSERT INTO
   COURSE (STUDENT_LIST)
   (CAST
      (MULTISET
         (SELECT
               student_name,
               student_address,
               grade
            FROM
               GRADE, STUDENT
            WHERE
               GRADE.course_name = 'CS101'
               AND
               GRADE.student_name = STUDENT.student_name
         )
      )
);
```

As you can see, the new SQL extensions are rather foreign to those accustomed to pure relational syntax.

Summary

Now that we have taken a high-level look at the new features of Oracle8, we can begin an in-depth exploration of the internals of Oracle, with an eye toward performance and tuning. While the new object features of Oracle8 promise to add some exciting new opportunities for improving the performance of Oracle8 systems, we must acknowledge that it will be several years before these new features appear in production systems. We will begin the next chapter with a look at logical analysis for performance, followed by a chapter on physical design for performance. Subsequent chapters will explore specific internals of Oracle as they apply to specific internal components of the Oracle8 architecture.

Logical Performance Design

CHAPTER

2

Logical Performance Design

A number of books are offered on today's relational database environment, with tips on the effective design of relational database systems. Unfortunately, many of these texts are purely theoretical and fail to take into account the real-world issues involved in designing a high-performance Oracle database. At the same time, dozens of Computer Aided Systems Engineering (CASE) vendors claim that their tools are indispensable for database design. Real-world experience has no substitute in this realm, especially with all of the exciting new object-oriented constructs introduced with Oracle8. However, this text is the next best thing to real-world experience, since many of the techniques addressed in this chapter are not addressed in any of the Oracle manuals.

This chapter will cover the following topics:

- Database distribution design

- Referential integrity

- Logical design for performance

- Logical design of database objects

It is critical to always keep in mind that the database design is the single most important factor in creating a high-performance system. As such, this chapter will serve as the foundation for the later chapters in this book, which are presented in their order of importance.

Database Distribution Design

It is critical to remember that database distribution is a design issue—not an analysis issue. The structured specification for the systems analysis phase specifies the logical data stores, but it provides no reference to the physical placement or type for the data stores. In the analysis phase, it doesn't matter whether data storage is in a VSAM file on a mainframe, an Oracle database on a VAX, or a Rolodex file on the user's desk. The concern is documenting the data flows among the logical processes and showing how data interacts with the logical data repositories. While it can be very tempting for some analysts to address physical design issues in the middle of an analysis, the disconnection of analysis and design is critical to the development of an effective Oracle system. In fact, this contamination of a logical analysis with a physical design issue is one of the main reasons projects suffer from *analysis paralysis*. Analysis paralysis usually occurs when tasks overwhelm the analysis team, shifting the focus from "How does it function?" to "How can we implement the function?"

If we accept the premise that creating a high-performance database is a physical design issue, it follows that any generally accepted analysis methodology will suffice for documenting the requirements of the system. Structured specifications with data flow diagrams (for example, the popular DeMarco style or Gane and Sarson methods of systems analysis), along with a data dictionary and process logic specifications, represent an excellent starting point for system design.

In the upcoming sections, we'll look at database design from a variety of angles. First, we'll look at the economics of database design issues. Then, we'll move on to review location transparency and distributed database performance and tuning. Finally, to tie the elements together, we'll look at an example of a distributed database design. Let's start at the bottom—the bottom line, that is—and look at the economics of database design.

The Economics Of Database Design

The promise of running open systems with cheaper hardware and software is one of the primary reasons companies abandon centralized mainframes. With the costs of an IBM mainframe data center approaching $500,000 per month, it is not surprising that many top IS managers force organizations to undertake the long march into open, distributed databases. In addition to hardware costs, database software costs are dramatically higher for mainframe systems. A large mainframe DBMS package easily reaches the $250,000 price range, yet a good relational database for a Unix-based midrange computer costs as little as $10,000.

As attractive as these savings may sound, they still must be balanced against the costs of maintaining distributed systems. As processors are added to remote locations, human functions—system administration, LAN management, and database administration—must also be replicated. And while the costs of a database server may be low, many companies lapse into shock when they are ready to attach 1,000 PC workstations to the server and find the cost for PC seats soaring up to $2,000 per database desktop client. PC workstations using a GUI with multiple database connections carry a price tag in excess of $3,000 per PC, a figure that often prompts managers to question the economic justification for downsizing. Performing a valid cost-benefit analysis (see Figure 2.1) requires the identification and quantification of all of the potential costs and savings for hardware, software, and human resources.

Many IS managers do not realize that their staff sizes may more than double, depending on the type of open systems database migration. The open system approach has a tremendous initial cost, and the savings accrue several years after implementation. When a mainframe database is partitioned into 20 remote Oracle servers, the database administration and system administration support staff may actually triple in size.

Saving money is not the only reason for downsizing, however. Companies relying on competitive information are often forced to the new midrange platforms in order to use the most advanced software.

Jumping on the bandwagon of downsizing to keep up with technology, companies are faced with problems not encountered in the mainframe days. Specifically, companies

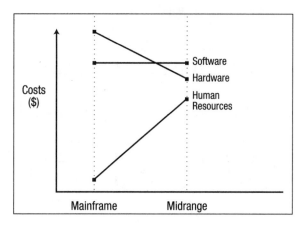

Figure 2.1
Downsizing cost-benefit analysis for database systems.

are forced to find ways to have their networks function and appear as unified systems. When creating distributed databases, it is very important to plan for the locations in order to allow the proper transparency between the remote processors. The following section discusses how this can be best achieved within Oracle.

Location Transparency And Database Design

Location transparency refers to a distributed database's ability to function as a unified whole, appearing to end users as a single unified system. Where the database resides, what type of database is used, and the required database access method are all unimportant to the end user. With Oracle, this type of transparency is definitely possible—but not without expense. Even a distributed system composed entirely of relational databases must deal with different dialects of SQL (see Figure 2.2).

Managing the various dialects of SQL is one of the most pressing problems with distributed databases. Each major database vendor (ostensibly to improve its implementation of SQL) adds its own features and extensions. Oracle is one of the most prolific at adding SQL extensions. It is true that Oracle implements some outstanding and useful extensions, such as the **decode** function, but queries to non-Oracle databases using these features can mean failure.

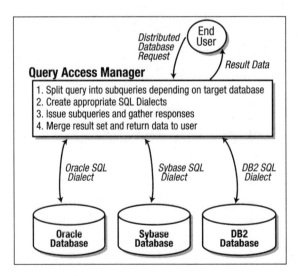

Figure 2.2
An example of single-architecture database queries.

These SQL dialect problems are even more aggravating when a distributed database is composed of databases from nonrelational architectures. In order to achieve transparency, sophisticated techniques are necessary to interrogate the distributed query, identifying which data components reside in what architecture and decomposing the subqueries into the appropriate access language (see Figure 2.3).

To understand the concept of location transparency, consider this example: Assume a parts inventory system has separate databases in Washington, Boise, New York, and Albuquerque. The manager needs to know the number of widgets in stock at all the locations. The manager issues the following SQL command to the distributed database manager:

```
SELECT count(*)
FROM INVENTORY
WHERE partname = 'widget';
```

In the preceding example of **count(*)** with location transparency, the end user has no interest in any individual databases when servicing this request, defining it as a *global transaction*. The transaction manager has the responsibility to query all of the distributed **INVENTORY** tables and collect the counts from each table, merging them into a single result set.

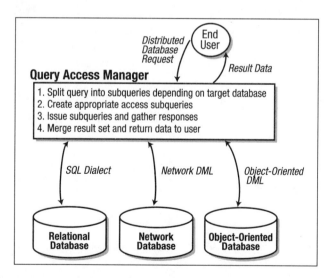

Figure 2.3
An example of multiarchitecture database queries.

In many relational databases, such as Oracle with SQL*Net, creating *database links* to the remote database and assigning a global synonym to the remote tables achieves transparency. A location suffix associated with a Telnet name creates database links in Oracle. At the lowest level, computers are assigned an IP (Internal Protocol) address, which gives the computer a distinct number. An example would be **150.223.90.27**. The Telnet name translates into the IP address for the computer. In the following example, **london_unix** translates into the IP address **143.32.142.3:1**:

```
CREATE PUBLIC DATABASE LINK london.com
     CONNECT TO london_unix USING oracle_user_profile;
```

You can now include any tables from the London site by qualifying the remote site name in the SQL query, as in the following:

```
SELECT     CUSTOMER.customer_name,
           ORDER.order_date
    FROM   CUSTOMER@london.com,
           ORDER
    WHERE
    CUSTOMER.cust_number = ORDER.customer_number;
```

But where is the location transparency? To make the location of the **CUSTOMER** table transparent, the DBA assigns synonyms for the **CUSTOMER** table in London, giving the query the appearance of being local:

```
CREATE SYNONYM CUSTOMER for CUSTOMER@london.com;
```

The query can now run with complete location transparency because the SQL has no need to reference either the IP address of the computer or the name of the database on that computer:

```
SELECT     CUSTOMER.customer_name,
           ORDER.order_date
    FROM   CUSTOMER,
           ORDER
    WHERE
    CUSTOMER.cust_number = ORDER.customer_number;
```

Oracle stored procedures can also be defined for the remote table without any reference to its physical location. For example, the procedure **add_customer** can be called with the following statement:

```
add_customer("Burleson")

CREATE PROCEDURE add_customer (cust_name char(8)) AS
   BEGIN
      INSERT INTO CUSTOMER VALUES(cust_name);
   END;
```

Many sites recognize the need to track the locations of their remote database while providing location transparency to the users and programmers. The concept of database domains and hierarchies of physical locations are especially important in situations of horizontal partitioning, where tables with identical names are kept at numerous locations. Domains establish a logical hierarchy of physical locations for the enterprise. Figure 2.4 shows a sample database that establishes a domain hierarchy for its remote databases.

As you can see in Figure 2.4, the DBA at each node in the network assigns synonyms for all unique tables within the distributed network, creating abbreviated domain names for the duplicate table structures that exist at remote locations. For example, assume both Japan and Ohio have a **CUSTOMER** table that is identical in structure but contains different rows. You could assign Oracle synonyms as follows:

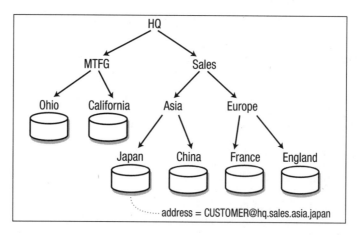

Figure 2.4
A sample hierarchy of database domains.

```
CREATE SYNONYM japan_customer FOR      CUSTOMER@hq.sales.asia.japan;

CREATE SYNONYM ohio_customer  FOR      CUSTOMER@hq.mtfg.ohio;
```

Now that we understand how Oracle synonyms can be used to implement location transparency, let's take a look at how distributed Oracle databases can be configured to maximize performance.

Distributed Database Performance And Tuning Issues

The ability to identify and correct performance problems has plagued distributed database systems since their genesis. Even within the context of a single transaction, distributed query optimization can be a formidable challenge. On a single database, SQL query tuning takes place by running an SQL **EXPLAIN** and performing the appropriate tuning. However, when a single query is split into distributed databases, the overall query tuning becomes far more complex. When a query spans hosts, several distributed database managers are required to take the distributed query and partition it into subqueries, which are then independently optimized and run (sometimes simultaneously) on the distributed databases. The query is considered complete when the last subquery has completed successfully and results are returned to the user. This approach is sometimes dubbed the *weakest link* architecture. The longest running of any number of partitioned subqueries determines the overall performance of the entire query. This is true despite the execution speed of any other partitioned subqueries involved. An excellent example of this approach is Oracle's parallel query facility, which was first introduced in Oracle version 7.3.

Tuning a distributed query requires the user to consider the following:

- Physical location of the database

- Availability of multiple CPUs

Today, tools are available to perform *load balancing*, whereby a processor may borrow CPU cycles from underutilized processors to balance the query and achieve maximum throughput.

Distributed databases need to be able to address information regardless of the hardware platform or the architecture of the database, especially in volatile environments where hardware and network configurations may change frequently. The two types of interoperability that emerge with distributed databases fall into the general categories of database and hardware:

- *Database Interoperability*—The ability of a database to function autonomously, allowing the distributed database to access numerous types of databases within the domain of a unified environment. The UniFace and PowerBuilder tools attempt to serve this market, automatically providing mechanisms for subtasking database queries and merging result sets. Chapter 3, *Physical Performance Design*, discusses how Oracle parallel query techniques partition a single Oracle query into multiple processes.

- *Hardware Interoperability*—The ability of the distributed system to address resources at many locations on an as-needed basis. At the hardware level, a single subquery of a distributed query runs on numerous processors, and load balancing tools assign multiple processors to a single database.

The key to success with distributed servers is very simple. Start small and phase in new servers only after communications with the existing servers have been debugged. Companies choosing a very large or mission-critical system often get mired in technical problems, unable to deliver a finished system. The mastery of distributed databases is achieved through experience, so in the next section, we'll look at an example of distributed database design.

An Example Of A Distributed Database Design

To understand distributed database design issues fully and first hand, perform the following exercise. This exercise requires:

- A small, well-tested Oracle system that resides on a midrange computer or mainframe.

- A PC with Oracle's SQL*Net connectivity software.

- Another database on the same platform as the source system.

Begin with a small existing system that is not mission critical and remove part of the centralized data onto another platform. Assume that we are dealing with a customer-order system running on an Oracle database on a Unix platform. This system is very old and needs replacement, but all components have been fully tested and operational for several years. As you can see from the sample entity/relation (E/R) model shown in Figure 2.5, the database has five tables:

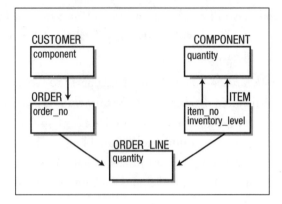

Figure 2.5
A sample customer-order database.

- **CUSTOMER**—Stores information about the customer

- **ORDER**—Stores order information

- **ITEM**—Stores product information

- **COMPONENT**—Stores the bill-of-material structure to indicate component parts within an item

- **ORDER_LINE**—Stores the quantity for each item that participates in an order

A huge difference exists in the amount of effort that will be required to migrate the data depending on the architecture of the target system (see Figure 2.6). With a relational

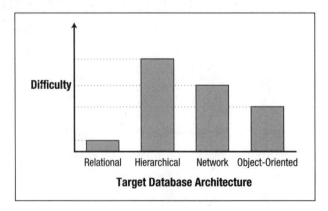

Figure 2.6
The relative difficulty of moving to new database architectures.

target system, extracting the data and reformatting the data for import into other relational tables is relatively simple. Other architectures, such as object or network databases, are far more complicated and require sophisticated load programs.

For this example, simply take the existing **CUSTOMER** table and export the table from Oracle. Next, add the table to the new database on another platform using Oracle's **import** utility. In sum, we have extracted data from a centralized source and created a distributed relational environment. While this exercise may seem trivial and artificial, the industry is moving toward architectures where the data will reside on a multitude of hardware platforms.

Now that we understand how distributed Oracle databases are configured to maximize performance, let's take a look at how business rules are enforced within an Oracle database. The Oracle implementation of these rules is called referential integrity (RI), and the proper use of RI is critical to the performance of the Oracle database.

Referential Integrity

Oracle databases allow for the control of business rules with *constraints*. These referential integrity rules ensure that one-to-many and many-to-many relationships are enforced within the distributed relational schema. For example, a constraint could be used to ensure that orders are not placed for nonexistent customers, or that customers are not deleted until all of their orders have been filled.

Several types of constraints can be applied to Oracle tables to enforce referential integrity, including the following constraints:

- **check**—This constraint validates incoming columns at row **INSERT** time. For example, rather than having an application verify that all occurrences of **region** are North, South, East, or West, a **check** constraint can be added to the table definition to ensure the validity of the region column.

- **NOT NULL**—This constraint is used to specify that a column may never contain a **NULL** value. This is enforced at SQL **INSERT** and **UPDATE** time.

- **primary key**—This constraint is used to identify the primary key for a table. This operation requires that the primary column(s) is unique, and Oracle will create a unique index on the target primary key.

- **references**—This is the foreign-key constraint as implemented by Oracle. A **references** constraint is only applied at SQL **INSERT** and **DELETE** times. For example, assume a one-to-many relationship between the **CUSTOMER** and **ORDER** tables such that each **customer** may place many **orders**, yet each **order** belongs to only one **customer**. The **reference** constraint tells Oracle at **INSERT** time that the value in **ORDER.cust_num** must match the **CUSTOMER.cust_num** in the **customer** row, thereby ensuring that a valid customer exists before the **order** row is added. At SQL **DELETE** time, the **references** constraint can be used to ensure that a **customer** is not deleted if rows still exist in the **ORDER** table.

- **unique**—This constraint is used to ensure that all column values within a table never contain a duplicate entry.

> **Note:** There is a distinction between **unique** and **primary key**. While both of these constraints create a unique index, a table may only contain one **primary key** constraint column—but it may have many **unique** constraints on other columns.

Referential integrity usually needs to be double coded, once for the database and again within the application. For example, in a multipart SQL*Form, you may not become aware of an RI violation until you are many pages into the form and your form attempts to commit.

Now, let's recap and place all of this into perspective: Referential integrity maintains business rules. Relational systems allow control of business rules with constraints, and RI rules form the backbone of relational tables. For example, in Figure 2.7, RI ensures that a row in the **CUSTOMER** table is not deleted if the **ORDER** table contains orders for that customer.

It is clear that enforcing the business rule in Figure 2.7 is a real challenge. While it is relatively simple to tell an Oracle system not to delete a row from its **CUSTOMER** table if rows for that customer exist in the **ORDER** table, it is not simple to enforce this rule when the **CUSTOMER** table resides in a Sybase database and the **ORDER** table resides within Oracle. The solution is to remove the database RI rules from each database, remembering to manually replicate the RI rules using procedural code within the application. This essentially creates your own customized RI within the application.

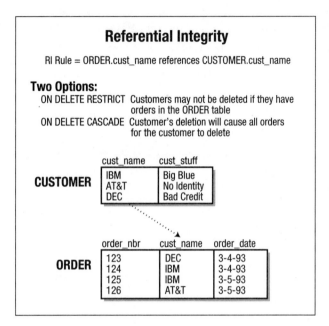

Figure 2.7
An example of referential integrity.

The next step is to import the data into the newly defined table in one of two ways. The easiest method uses Oracle's import/export utility to import the **CUSTOMER** table into SQL **INSERT** statements. The second, and more complicated, way extracts the table into a flat file, adds column delimiters, and then uses Oracle's SQL*Loader to add the data into the new database. Of course, Oracle's **import** utility can only be used when the import file is formatted according to the format required by Oracle's **import** utility.

For example, a flat-file data extract could be manipulated to state the following:

```
INSERT INTO CUSTOMER VALUES ('Burleson','343 State St','Rochester','NY');
INSERT INTO CUSTOMER VALUES ('Joe Chelko','123 4th st.','New York','NY');
```

Let's assume that a **CUSTOMER** table has been added to an instance called *Triton*, and that an **ORDERS** table resides in an instance called *Phobos*. How does the user make these tables function as if they resided in a unified database? When a distributed request is made to tables within different architectures, the query is partitioned into separate subqueries and executed against each database engine. The processor governing the distributed request acts as the consolidator, merging the result sets and performing any postretrieval processes, such as **ORDER BY** or **GROUP BY** clauses that must manipulate all of the returned data.

In our example, we join the tables for a customer, pulling the customer information from Sybase and the order information from Oracle. Directly addressing SQL across different database products generates the query shown in Listing 2.1.

Listing 2.1 Sample query addressing SQL across database products.

```
SELECT          cust_name,
                customer_street_address,
                order_date
FROM
     CUSTOMER@triton,
     ORDERS@phobos
WHERE
     ORDERS.cust_number=CUSTOMER.cust_number        AND
     CUSTOMER.cust_name LIKE 'Burleson';
```

> *Note: This SQL uses node names to identify the physical location of the tables. This is not standard SQL syntax, but it illustrates the need to join diverse tables.*

For a more realistic test, let's retrieve information from all four tables. Listing 2.2 joins the **CUSTOMER** table with the **ORDERS** table where **cust_name LIKE 'Burleson'** and then joins the **ORDERS** table entries with the **ORDER_LINE** table. Finally, the SQL joins **ORDER_LINE** with the **PRODUCT** table, retrieving product information.

Listing 2.2 A sample distributed query.

```
SELECT    CUSTOMER.cust_name,
          CUSTOMER.customer_street_address,
          ORDERS.order_date,
          PRODUCT.product_cost,
          PRODUCT.product_name
FROM
     CUSTOMER@triton,
     ORDERS@phobos,
     ORDER_LINE@phobos,
     PRODUCT@phobos
WHERE
     CUSTOMER.cust_number = ORDERS.cust_number
     AND
     ORDERS.order_number = ORDER_LINE.order_number
     AND
```

```
ORDER_LINE.prod_number = PRODUCT.prod_number
AND
CUSTOMER.cust_name LIKE 'Burleson';
```

This query can be easily issued from a remote PC using the SQL*Net software. Another access route to these tables is an already-defined tool that accesses protocols for each database, such as the popular UniFace tool.

Accessing a remote database node from a PC platform uses similar steps. Simply punch the relational table into a flat file, and transfer this file to the PC using either FTP or some other file transfer utility. At that point, the flat file can be loaded into a PC-based database for local reference.

The steps to populate a relational table on a PC platform differ from the steps for a midrange database. Most PC databases do not support **CREATE TABLE** SQL. The table is defined using the online GUI screens. To define the table to FoxPro, choose File|New, and define the tables using the GUI interface. Now we can manually define a **PRODUCT** table with identical column names and field sizes. Fortunately, adding rows to a FoxPro table is very simple. Using the PC's text editor, insert a delimiter character between each field in the flat file in the PC text editor.

Choose a character that does not exist in the data, such as the caret (^) or at sign (@). If your database supports adding literals to queries, characters can be added at extraction time:

```
SELECT cust_name||"^"||cust_city||"^"||cust_state FROM CUSTOMER;
```

The massaged file appears as follows:

```
Burleson^343 State St^Rochester^NY
Joe Chelko^123 4th st.^New York^ NY
```

This flat file can now be easily imported into FoxPro. From the FoxPro command prompt, enter the following commands:

```
CLOSE DATA
USE PRODUCT
APPEND FROM c:\myfile.dat TYPE SDF DELIMITED with '^'
```

This **APPEND** command takes the data from the flat file and moves it into the FoxPro table. Incidentally, even though FoxPro does not support SQL **INSERT** statements, it is one of the easiest databases for data migration. Also, because FoxPro's Rushmore technology is so fast, many sites move systems directly from mainframes into FoxPro. Systems can move directly from mainframes onto FoxPro data servers and gain improved response time. I have proven this point from personal experience: I migrated from an IBM 3090 to FoxPro, and each SQL query performed faster (on a standalone PC) than its SQL counterpart on the mainframe.

Now that we understand how distributed Oracle database are designed, let's narrow our focus and take a look at how individual Oracle entities are designed to maximize performance.

Logical Database Design For Performance

This section focuses on database server techniques for creating high-performance, client/server Oracle applications. Without an effective database design, no amount of tuning allows the system to achieve optimal performance. Hence, it is critical to a database design that you derive the most from the available servers. To accomplish this task, there are several areas we need to look at. Specifically, this section reviews concepts relating to:

- Data normalization and modeling theory
- Misleading data relationships
- Denormalizing many-to-many data relationships
- Recursive data relationships
- STAR schema design

These issues are commonly overlooked in an Oracle design with disastrous performance implications. A firm understanding of these principles will help ensure improved database performance.

Data Normalization And Modeling Theory

As you probably know, five types of data relationships must be considered when designing any Oracle database:

- One-to-one relationship

- One-to-many relationship

- Many-to-many relationship

- Recursive many-to-many relationship

- IS-A relationship

The role of an effective Oracle database designer is to represent these types of relationships in a sensible way while ensuring that the server performance level remains acceptable. Once the database relationships have been designed, we need to take a look at how the introduction of redundancy can improve performance.

In a hierarchical or CODASYL (network) database, it is possible to define and implement a database design that contains absolutely no redundant information (such as pure Third Normal Form, or 3NF). Hierarchical and network databases can be truly free of redundant information because all data relationships are represented through pointers and not through duplicated foreign keys. Because object-oriented systems use pointers to establish data relationships (more on pointers later in this chapter), many object-oriented systems can also be designed totally free of redundant data. The elimination of redundancy requires embedded pointers to establish the data relationships, so no relational database can ever be totally free of redundant data.

An Oracle database with either one-to-many or many-to-many relationships has redundant foreign keys or objects ids embedded in the tables to establish logical relationships. Redundant foreign keys in the subordinate tables create the data relationships, making it possible to join tables together and relate the contents of the data items in the tables.

As the size of the database increases, redundancy can become a major problem. Today, many users create very large databases, many of which contain trillions of bytes. For databases of this size, a single table can contain more than a billion rows, and the introduction of a single new column to a table can represent thousands of dollars in additional disk expense. Data redundancy is detrimental for two reasons. First and foremost, duplicating the redundant material consumes disk storage space. The second and most ominous reason is that updating redundant data requires extra processing. Redundant duplication of very large and highly volatile data items can cause huge processing bottlenecks.

However, this does not imply that redundancy is always undesirable. Performance is still an overriding factor in most systems. Proper control of redundant information implies that redundant information may be introduced into any structure as long as the performance improvements outweigh the additional disk costs and update problems.

Since the first publication of Dr. E. F. Codd's 1993 research paper *Providing OLAP (Online Analytical Processing) To User-Analysts: An IT Mandate,* database designers have attempted to find an optimum way of structuring tables for low data redundancy. Codd's rules of normalization guide designers to create logically correct table structures with no redundancy, but performance rules often dictate the introduction of duplicated data to improve performance.

This is especially true for distributed Oracle databases. Any node in a distributed database might want to browse a list of customers at other nodes without establishing a connection to that node. The technological problems inherent in the two-phase commit necessitate widespread replication of entire tables or selected columns from tables. However, the distributed database designer does not have free reign to introduce redundancy anywhere in the enterprise. Redundancy always carries a price, whether it is the cost of the disk storage or the cost of maintaining a parallel update scheme. Figure 2.8 shows a strategy for analyzing the consequences of data redundancy.

In Figure 2.8, a boundary line lies within a range between the size of a redundant data item and the update frequency of the data item. The size of the data item relates to the disk costs associated with storing the item, and the update frequency is associated with the cost of keeping the redundant data current, whether by replication techniques or by two-phase commit updates. Because the relative costs are different for each hardware configuration and for each application, this boundary may be quite different depending on the type of application. The rapid decrease in the disk storage costs designates that the size boundary is only important for very large-scale redundancy. A large, frequently changing item (e.g., **street_address**) is not a good candidate for redundancy. But large static items (e.g., **service_history**) or small, frequently changing items (e.g., **product_price**) are acceptable for redundancy. Small static items (e.g., **gender**) represent ideal candidates for redundant duplication.

Now that we understand the basic principles of introducing redundancy, let's look at how redundancy is introduced when relationships exist between Oracle tables.

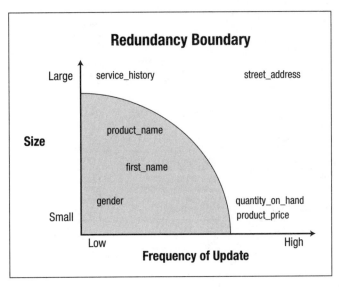

Figure 2.8

A comparison of size versus volatility for redundant data.

Denormalizing One-To-Many Data Relationships

One-to-many relationships exist in many real-world situations. Many entities that possess one-to-many relationships can be removed from the data model, eliminating some join operations. The basic principle is simple: Redundant information avoids expensive SQL joins and yields faster processing. But remember, designers must deal with the issue of additional disk storage and the problems associated with updating the redundant data. For example, consider the E/R model shown in Figure 2.9, where, as you can see, the structure is in pure Third Normal Form. Note that the **CITY** and **STATE** tables exist because each state has many cities and each city has many customers. This model works for most transactions on an online transaction processing (OLTP) system. However, this high degree of normalization would require the joining of the **CITY** and **STATE** tables each time address information is requested, forcing some SQL requests to perform very slowly.

Consider a query to display the **state_bird** for all orders that have been placed for **BIRDSEED**. This is a cumbersome query that requires the joining of numerous tables, since the desired data (**STATE.state_bird**) is many tables away from the boolean criteria (**ITEM.item_name**):

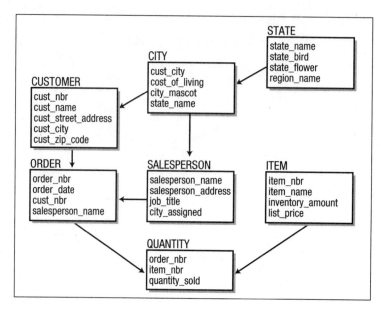

Figure 2.9
A fully normalized E/R model sales database.

```
SELECT state_bird
FROM STATE, CITY, CUSTOMER, ORDER, QUANTITY, ITEM
WHERE
item_name = 'BIRDSEED'
AND
ITEM.item_nbr = QUANTITY.item_nbr
AND
QUANTITY.order_nbr = ORDER.order_nbr
AND
ORDER.cust_nbr = CUSTOMER.cust_nbr
AND
CUSTOMER.cust_city = CITY.cust_city
AND
CITY.state_name = STATE.state_name;
```

With Oracle and the cost-based optimizer, this type of complex join guarantees that at least one table is read front to back using a full-table scan. This is a shortcoming of Oracle's cost-based optimizer because an SQL optimizer should always avoid a full-table scan whenever indexes are present—and full-table scans are very expensive. This situation might be avoided by using Oracle hints with the optimizer to determine the optimal path to this data. A *hint* is an extension of Oracle's SQL that directs the SQL optimizer to change its normal access path. For more detailed information on optimizing full-table scans, see Chapter 7, *Oracle DBA Performance And Tuning.* For more detailed information about using hints for SQL tuning, refer to Chapter 5, *Tuning Oracle SQL.*

What if your goal is to simplify the data structure by removing several of the one-to-many relationships? Adding redundancy poses two problems: You need additional space for the redundant item, as well as a technique to update the redundant item if it changes. One solution is to build a table of columns that roll the **CITY** and **STATE** tables into the **CUSTOMER** table. For example, consider Table 2.1. Assume that the **STATE** table contains 50 rows, the **CITY** table has 2,000 rows, and the **CUS-TOMER** table has 10,000 rows.

In Table 2.1, you can see that the **CITY** and **STATE** tables can be removed entirely for a total savings of 400,000 bytes, as shown in Figure 2.10. What about the **cost_of_living** field? If we choose to eliminate the **CITY** table and duplicate **cost_of_living** in every **CUSTOMER** row, it would be necessary to visit each and every **CUSTOMER** row—which means changing the cost of living 10,000 times. Before this change, the following SQL can be used to update each **CITY** table:

```
UPDATE CITY SET cost_of_living = :var1
WHERE CITY = :var2;
2000 ROWS UPDATED
```

While the management of redundancy seems a formidable challenge, the following SQL **UPDATE** statement makes this change easily, and we can make the change to all affected rows:

Table 2.1 Redundancy matrix to determine optimal normalization.

Column	Size	Duplication	Total Space	Change
state_bird	10	10,000	100,000	Rare
state_flower	10	10,000	100,000	Rare
region_name	2	10,000	20,000	Never
cost_of_living	8	10,000	80,000	Quarterly
city_mascot	10	10,000	100,000	Rare

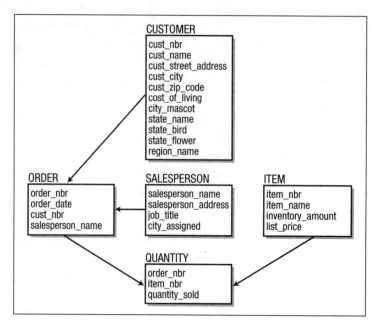

Figure 2.10
A denormalized E/R model sales database.

```
UPDATE CUSTOMER SET cost_of_living = :var1
WHERE CITY = :var2;
100,000 ROWS UPDATED
```

Using the same **state_bird** query as before, you can see how it is simplified by removing the extra tables:

```
SELECT state_bird
FROM  CUSTOMER, ORDER, QUANTITY, ITEM
WHERE
item_name = 'BIRDSEED'
AND
ITEM.item_nbr = QUANTITY.item_nbr
AND
QUANTITY.order_nbr = ORDER.order_nbr
AND
ORDER.cust_nbr = CUSTOMER.cust_nbr;
```

It is still necessary to join three tables, but this query results in a much faster, simpler query than the original five-way table join. You can carry this concept to the point where the model is condensed into a single, highly redundant table.

Misleading Data Relationships

When creating an E/R model, it is often tempting to look at the data model from a purely logical perspective without any regard for the physical implications of the data. The designer strives to recognize and establish all of the logical relationships in the data model while sometimes finding that the relationships are misleading. A relationship can be misleading when the relationship actually exists, but the application may have no need to reference this relationship. Consider the E/R model for a university shown in Figure 2.11.

Now, consider the association of the **hair_color** attribute to the **student** entity. Does a many-to-many data relationship really exist between **hair_color** and **student**? Many students have blonde hair, and blonde hair is common to many students. Why not create a many-to-many relationship between **student** and **hair_color**? The solution depends upon whether any other non-key data items exist within the **hair_color** entity.

If many other data items relating to hair color are present, then it is perfectly appropriate to create another entity called **hair_color**. But in this case, even though a many-to-many relationship exists between **hair_color** and **student**, **hair_color** is a standalone data attribute, so it is unnecessary to create an additional data structure.

Another example is the **zip_code** attribute in the **student** entity. At first glance, it appears that a violation of Third Normal Form (that is, a transitive dependency) has occurred between **city** and **zip_code**. In other words, it appears that a **zip_code** is

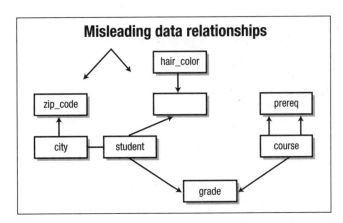

Figure 2.11
An example of misleading data relationships.

paired with the city of residence for the student. If each **city** has many **zip_code**s, while each **zip_code** refers only to one **city**, it makes sense to model this as a one-to-many data relationship (see Figure 2.11). The presence of this data relationship requires creating a separate entity called **zip** with attached **student** entities. However, this is another case where the **zip** entity lacks key attributes, making it impractical. In other words, **zip_code** has no associated data items—creating a database table with only one data column would be nonsense.

This example demonstrates that it is not enough to group together "like" items and then identify the data relationships. A practical test must be made regarding the presence of non-key attributes within an entity class. If an entity has no attributes (that is, the table has only one field), the presence of the entity is nothing more than an index to the foreign key in the member entity. Therefore, it can be removed from the E/R model. This technique not only simplifies the number of entities, but it creates a better environment for a client/server architecture. More data is logically grouped together, resulting in less data access effort. Figure 2.12 shows an example of correct relationships.

Denormalizing Many-To-Many Data Relationships

In many cases, a many-to-many relationship can be condensed into a more efficient structure to improve the speed of data retrieval. After all, less tables need to be joined to get the desired information. To understand how a many-to-many relationship can be collapsed into a more compact structure, consider the relationship between a course and a student, as shown in Figure 2.13.

As you can see in Figure 2.13, a student takes many courses, and each course has many students. This is a classic many-to-many relationship and requires that we

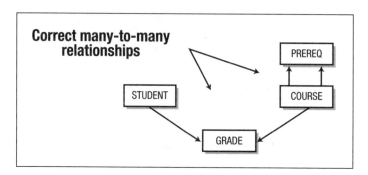

Figure 2.12
An example of correct many-to-many relationships.

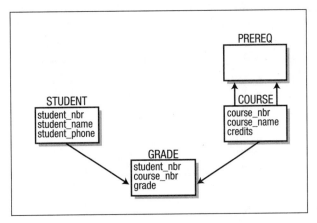

Figure 2.13
A sample university database.

define a junction table between the base entities to establish the necessary foreign keys. Note that the junction table (**GRADE**) contains the following contents:

- **course_nbr**—The primary key for the **COURSE** table

- **student_nbr**—The primary key for the **STUDENT** table

- **grade**—A non-key attribute to both foreign keys

Next, consider the question: In what context does a grade have meaning? Stating that *The grade was A in CS-101* is insufficient, and stating, *Joe earned an A* makes no sense. Only when both the student number and the course number are associated does the grade column have meaning. Stating that *Joe earned an A in CS-101* makes sense.

Recursive Data Relationships

Recursive many-to-many relationships contain an object that also has a many-to-many relationship with other occurrences of the same object. These relationships are often termed *Bill-of-Materials* (BOM) *relationships*, and the graphical representation of the recursive relationship is sometimes termed a *Bill-of-Materials explosion*. These relationships are termed recursive because a single query makes many subpasses through the tables to arrive at the solution (see Figure 2.14).

Bill-of-Materials relationships denote an object with a many-to-many relationship with another object in the same class. In other words, a part may consist of other parts, but at the same time, it is a component in a larger assembly. For example, a

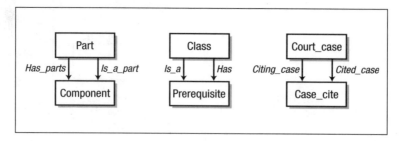

Figure 2.14
An example of recursive many-to-many relationships.

class at a university may have many prerequisites, but at the same time, it is a prerequisite for another class. These courses all have prerequisites of their own, which may also have prerequisites, and so on.

Each occurrence of a **COURSE** object has different topics, and a complete implementation must iterate through all courses until reaching *terminus*, the point where the course has no further prerequisites.

Unfortunately, the recursive many-to-many relationship is very confusing and almost impossible to understand without the aid of a graphical representation. Visualize the recursive many-to-many relationship as an ordinary many-to-many relationship with the owner entity "pulled apart" into **Part1** and **Part2**. Figure 2.15 shows how the junction entity establishes the relationship.

Only graphical representations conceptualize a recursive many-to-many relationship. In the CODASYL model, these are called *set occurrence* diagrams, and they show the pointer chains that link the relationships (see Figure 2.16, which illustrates the rela-

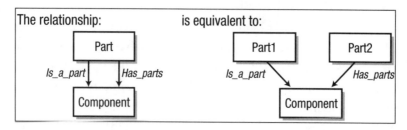

Figure 2.15
Viewing a recursive many-to-many relationship
as an ordinary many-to-many relationship.

tionships among the elements in a **Big_Meal**). Table sketches show that the junction table contains both an implosion and an explosion column in relational databases.

In Figure 2.16, you can navigate the database, determining the components for a **Big_Meal**. To navigate this diagram, start at the object **Big_Meal** and follow the **Has_parts** link to the bubble containing the number 1. This is the quantity for the item. You can now follow the bubbles to the **Is_a_part** link, which shows that one order of fries is included in a **Big_Meal**. Return to the **Has_parts** link for **Big_Meal** and you will find the next bubble. The **Is_a_part** link shows that one soda is included in a **Big_Meal**. Then continue this process until no further entities can be found in the **Has_parts** relationship. In sum, the **Has_parts** relationships indicate that a **Big_Meal** consists of one order of fries, one soda, and one hamburger. In addition, the hamburger consists of two meat patties and one bun.

Continuing with the example shown in Figure 2.16, you can see how a database is navigated to determine which parts use a specific component. For example, if you start at the **Hamburger** bubble and navigate the **Is_a_part** relationships, you see that one hamburger participates in the **Value_Meal** and also in the **Big_Meal**.

Recursive relationships can now be generated from the structure. For example, when listing the components of a **Big_Meal**, all components appear as shown in Table 2.2.

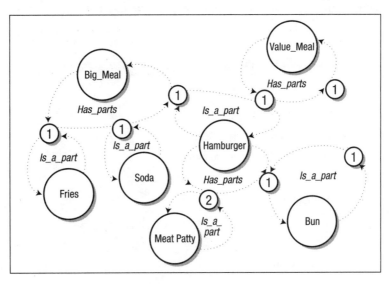

Figure 2.16
A set occurrence diagram for a recursive relationship.

Table 2.2 BOM explosion for **Big_Meal.**

Part1	Part2	Part3	Quantity
Hamburger			1
	Meat Patty		2
		Oatmeal	4 oz.
		Beef	3 oz.
	Bun		
Fries			1 order
	Potato		1
	Grease		1 cup
Soda			1
	Ice		1/2 cup
	Drink		1/3 cup

Conversely, the recursive association can be applied to any item to see its participation in other items. For example, the uses of grease can be seen by running an implosive query, as shown in Table 2.3.

These examples may seem simplistic, but many database systems have items with numerous subassemblies. Recursions may cascade dozens of levels down in a hierarchy.

Table 2.3 BOM implosion for grease.

Part1	Part2	Part3
Fries		
		Big Meal
		Value Meal
Meat Patty		
	Hamburger	
		Big Meal
		Value Meal
	Cheeseburger	
Pies		
		Value Meal

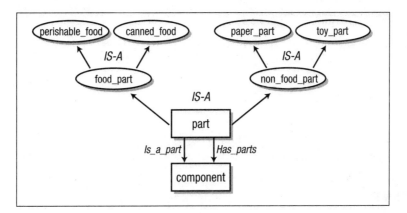

Figure 2.17
Recursive many-to-many relationships with the addition of an ISA hierarchy.

Consider the design of a database that manages fast food items (see Figure 2.17). All non-food items have a *class construct*, which holds all data and behaviors. This class construct is an example of an *abstract class*, with no object of **non_food_part** created. But **non_food_part** does include ordering behaviors and the names of suppliers. These data items cascade to lower-level classes, specifically the **toy_part** and **paper_part** objects. The **toy_part** class is not only next in the class hierarchy, but it also has data and behaviors. Contrasted with the **non_food_part** abstract class, **toy_part** is a *concrete class*.

Clearly, we compound the problem of recursive relationships by adding this additional construct—namely, a class hierarchy. Unfortunately, these types of challenges are very common. While it is true that "parts are parts," the different parts have subtle variations, leading to different data items depending on part type. For example, a food-related part might have a **shelf_life** column, but that column does not apply to a non-food part.

With an understanding of the nature of recursive relationships, the question becomes one of implementation: What is the best way to represent a recursive relationship in Oracle and navigate the structure?

The following Oracle table definitions describe the tables for the part-component example:

```
CREATE TABLE PART (
part_nbr     number,
```

```
part_name    varchar2(10),
part_desc    varchar2(10),
qty_on_hand  number);

CREATE TABLE COMPONENT (
has_parts      number,
is_a_part      number,
qty            number);
```

Look closely at the **COMPONENT** example. Both the **Has_parts** and **Is_a_part** fields are foreign keys for the **part_nbr** field in the **PART** table. Therefore, the **COMPONENT** table is all keyed except for the **qty** field, which tells how many parts belong in an assembly. Look at the following SQL code required to display all components in a **Big_Meal**:

```
SELECT part_name
FROM PART, COMPONENT
WHERE
has_parts = 123
AND
PART.part_nbr = COMPONENT.has_part;
```

This type of Oracle SQL query requires joining the table against itself. Unfortunately, because all items are of the same type (namely, **PART**), no real substitute exists for this type of data relationship.

While the principles of denormalization apply to all Oracle systems, there are special cases of data warehousing where a specific technique is used to introduce redundancy. This is called STAR schema design.

STAR Schema Design

The STAR schema design was first introduced by Dr. Ralph Kimball as an alternative database design for data warehouses. The name *STAR* comes directly from the design form, where a large **FACT** table resides at the center of the model surrounded by various "points," or reference tables. The basic principle behind the STAR query schema is the introduction of highly redundant data for high performance. A more exhaustive discussion of STAR schema design is included in Chapter 10, *Tuning Oracle Data Warehouse And OLAP Applications*.

Returning to the customer-order E/R model shown earlier in this chapter in Figure 2.9, you can see an illustration of a standard Third Normal Form database used to represent the sales of items. Because redundant information is not an issue, salient data (such as the total for an order) is computed from the items comprising the order. In this Third Normal Form database, users need a list of line items to multiply the quantity ordered by the price for all items belonging in order 123. An intermediate table, called **TEMP**, holds the result list, shown in the following example:

```
CREATE TABLE TEMP AS
SELECT (QUANTITY.quantity_sold * ITEM.list_price) line_total
FROM QUANTITY, ITEM
WHERE
QUANTITY.order_nbr = 123
AND
QUANTITY.item_nbr = ITEM.item_nbr;
SELECT sum(line_total) FROM TEMP;
```

The **STATE-CITY-CUSTOMER** hierarchy is very deliberate. To be truly in the Third Normal Form, no redundant information is possible. As such, a user's seemingly simple query is complex to the system. For example, the SQL calculating the sum of all orders for the Western region looks very complex and involves a five-way table join, as follows:

```
CREATE TABLE TEMP AS
SELECT (QUANTITY.quantity_sold * ITEM.list_price) line_total
FROM QUANTITY, ITEM, CUSTOMER, CITY, STATE
WHERE
QUANTITY.cust_nbr = ITEM.item_nbr       /* join QUANTITY and ITEM */
AND
ITEM.cust_nbr = CUSTOMER.cust_nbr       /* join ITEM and CUSTOMER */
AND
CUSTOMER.cust_city = CITY.cust_city    /* join CUSTOMER and CITY */
AND
CITY.state_name = STATE.state_name     /* join CITY and STATE */
AND
STATE.region_name = 'WEST';
```

In reality, sufficient redundancy eliminates the **CITY** and **STATE** tables. The point is clear: A manager who is analyzing a series of complete order totals requires a huge amount of realtime computation. This process arrives at the basic trade-off. For true freedom from redundant data, query time demands a price.

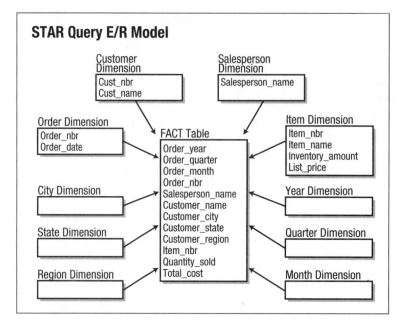

Figure 2.18

The STAR query E/R model.

In practice, the Third Normal Form database generally evolves into a STAR schema as you create a **FACT** table to hold the quantity for each item sold (see Figure 2.18).

At first glance, it's hard to believe Figure 2.18 displays the same data as the normalized database. The new **FACT** table contains one row for each item on each order, resulting in a tremendous amount of redundant key information in the **FACT** table. It should be obvious that the STAR query schema requires far more disk space than a Third Normal Form database. Also, the STAR schema is most likely a read-only database because of the widespread redundancy introduced into the model. Finally, the widespread redundancy makes updating difficult (if not impossible) for the STAR schema.

Notice the dimension tables around the **FACT** table. Some of the dimension tables contain data that is added to queries with joins. Other dimensions, such as **Region Dimension**, contain no data. What purpose, then, does this STAR schema achieve with huge disk space consumption and a read-only restriction?

Using the STAR schema illustrated in Figure 2.18, let's formulate SQL queries for rapid retrieval of desired information. For example, identifying the total cost for an order is simple, as seen in the following code:

```
SELECT sum(total_cost) order_total
FROM FACT
WHERE
FACT.order_nbr = 123;
```

It is clear that this structure makes the realtime query faster and simpler. Consider the result if the goal is to analyze information by aggregate values using this schema. Suppose the manager needs the breakdown of regional sales. The data by region is not available, but the **FACT** table supplies the answer. Obtaining the sum of all orders for the Western region is now simple, as seen in the following code:

```
SELECT sum(total_cost)
FROM FACT
WHERE
REGION = 'WEST';
```

Once the principles of traditional database design are applied to the Oracle table structures, we next need to consider those situations where the new object features of Oracle8 may be appropriate. These new object features present the database designer with many choices, and the following section discusses when it is appropriate to use the object constructs in your logical design.

Logical Design Of Database Objects

There has been a lot of debate regarding the potential benefits of adding objects into mainstream database management systems. For the past decade, a small but highly vocal group of object-oriented zealots preached about object revolution with an almost religious fervor. It is interesting to note that despite the hoopla, object-oriented databases languished until the major relational database vendors, such as Oracle and Informix, made a commitment to incorporate object support into their databases. But supplying the power of objects is only the beginning. Oracle developers are now struggling to understand how the new object extensions change the way their applications are designed and implemented.

Oracle's commitment to objects is not merely an acknowledgment of a fad. The benefits of being able to support objects is very real, and the exciting new extensions of Oracle8 will help administrators create a new foundation for database systems for the 21st century.

If you examine the Oracle8 database engine, you will see that the new features essentially consist of user-defined data types, pointers to rows, and the ability to couple data with behavior, using methods. These new features of Oracle8 carry huge ramifications. They change the way databases are designed and implemented, in ways Oracle developers never imagined.

With Oracle8, database designers no longer need to decompose applications to the most atomic levels. The new *pointer* constructs of Oracle8 allow for the creation of aggregate objects. In addition, Oracle8 no longer requires database administrators to create Oracle views to assemble composite objects at runtime. Many critics of the relational model have noted that relational databases need to be able to model real-world objects.

The object-oriented advocates use an automobile analogy to describe the problems of the relational model. They argue that it does not make sense to dismantle your car when you arrive home each night, only to reassemble your car the next time you want to go for a drive (just like in Oracle7, where you must assemble aggregates using SQL joins every time you want to see aggregate objects). With Oracle8, database designers can model the real world at all levels of aggregation and not just at the highly decomposed Third Normal Form level.

This ability to prebuild real-world objects enables Oracle8 designers to model the world as it exists, without having to re-create objects from their pieces each time they are needed. These real-world objects also have ramifications for Oracle's SQL. Rather than having to join numerous tables together to create an aggregate object, the object will have an independent existence, even if it is composed entirely of pieces from atomic tables (see Figure 2.19).

The ability to use pointers to preassemble objects implies a whole new type of database access. Rather than having to use SQL, Oracle8 databases may be "navigated," going from row to row, chasing the pointer references without ever having to use SQL to join tables. This nondeclarative, navigational data access allows Oracle designers to create faster links between tables, avoiding some of the time-consuming SQL join operations that can plague systems.

Finally, the ability of Oracle8 to tightly couple data and behavior changes the way programs are created. Rather than having your program logic stored in external computer programs, the process code moves with the data into the Oracle database, and

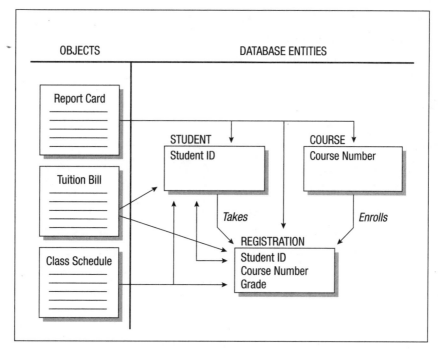

Figure 2.19
Objects made up of atomic relational entities.

the Oracle engine manages both the data and the processes that operate on the data. As mentioned previously, the coupling of data and behavior is achieved by using *methods*.

Methods were first introduced into the object-oriented model to provide encapsulation and code reusability. *Encapsulation* means that all data inside an object can only be modified by invoking one of its methods. By having these pretested and reliable methods associated with the object, an Oracle8 object "knows" how to behave, and the methods will always function in the same manner regardless of the target objects.

A more important feature for Oracle8 is code reusability. Reusability is achieved by eliminating the "code hunt." Before methods were introduced, Oracle programmers had to scan through Pro*C programs or stored procedures to find the code they desired. With methods, a developer only needs to know the name of the class associated with the object, and the list of methods can be displayed easily. The availability of reusable methods changes the role of the Oracle8 programmer from being the creator of hand-crafted code to the role of a code assembler. The Oracle8 programmer will be able to select from prewritten and pretested methods, assembling them to create new methods. Just as the introduction of reusable parts changed the way American manufacturing functioned, the introduction of reusable code changes the way Oracle systems are constructed and maintained.

Reusability does not come without a price. The structure of the aggregate objects must be carefully defined. Oracle developers must give careful consideration to the methods associated with objects at each level of object aggregation, and this requires careful planning.

Now that we have seen the compelling benefits of object/relational databases, let's take a closer look at how Oracle8 has implemented these features. Oracle is implementing the object/relational model in stages, introducing objects in Oracle8, while database inheritance will appear in Oracle8.2. The next few sections will examine the specific object features of Oracle8 and discuss how they can be incorporated into an Oracle design.

Abstract Data Types

The ability of Oracle to support user-defined data types (sometimes called *abstract data types*, or *ADTs*) has profound implications for Oracle8 database design and implementation. User-defined data types extend the basic data types of **char** and **number**, and allow the following:

- *Creation of aggregate data types*—Aggregate data types are defined as data types that contain other data types. For example, an aggregate data type called **FULL_ADDRESS** could contain all of the subfields necessary for a complete mailing address.

- *Nesting of user-defined data types within other data types*—Data types can be placed within other user-defined data types to create data structures that can be easily reused within Oracle tables and PL/SQL. For example, a data type called **ORDER** could be defined that contains a data type called **ORDER_DETAILS**, which, in turn, may contain a data type called **ORDER_HISTORY**, and so on.

For more information on Oracle abstract data types see Chapter 3, *Physical Performance Design.*

Pointers And Oracle8

One of the new user-defined data types in the Oracle8 architecture is a *pointer* data type. Essentially, to Oracle a pointer is implemented as an object ID (OID), which is a unique reference to a row in a relational table. The ability to store OIDs inside a relational table extends the traditional Oracle model and enhances the ability of an Oracle8 database to establish relationships between tables. The new abilities of pointer data types include the following:

- *Referencing sets of related rows in other tables*—It is now possible to violate First Normal Form and have a cell in a table that contains a pointer to repeating table values. Oracle calls this feature *nested tables*. For example, an employee table can contain a pointer called **job_history_set**, which, in turn, contains pointers to all of the relevant rows in a **JOB_HISTORY** table. This technique also allows for aggregate objects to be prebuilt, such that all of the specific rows that comprise an aggregate table can be preassembled.

- *Declaring pointers to non-database objects in a flat file*—In Oracle8, a table cell can contain a pointer to a flat file that contains a non-database object, such as a picture in GIF or JPEG format.

- *Providing the ability to establish data relationships without relational foreign keys*—This feature of Oracle8 alleviates the need for relational **JOIN** operations because table columns can contain references to rows in other tables. By dereferencing these pointers, rows from other tables can be retrieved without ever using the time-consuming SQL **JOIN** operator.

In addition to collecting data types into user-defined data types, Oracle8 allows for the creation of extensions to the base table types.

Basic Object Data Structures

Extensions to the base table types can be used to embed additional information into an object, or they can be used to establish relationships to other objects. In addition, the extensions may be used to create aggregate objects that consist entirely of data inside other objects. These data type extensions fall into several categories:

- Data extensions with user-defined data types
  - Lists of repeating data items
  - Lists of groups of repeating data items
- Pointer extensions to data types
  - Single pointers to other rows

- Lists of pointers to other rows (Oracle **varray**s)

- Lists of pointers to pointers to other rows (Multidimensional Oracle **varray**s)

- A pointer to another whole table (Oracle nested tables)

- Lists of pointers to other whole tables (Multidimensional arrays of OIDs)

As you can see, Oracle8 database designers are presented with many choices of data structures. There are, however, certain rules that an Oracle database designer can follow when choosing a data structure to implement within their model. The next section talks a little bit about how these data structures are represented graphically in our design documentation. For more information on these new constructs, see Chapter 3, *Physical Performance Design*.

A Data Representation Model For Oracle8

One of the confounding problems with the object-oriented extensions of Oracle8 is representing the data structures in a graphic form. While early efforts by modeling diagrams have achieved limited success, the approach taken here aspires to display the components of an object/relational database in a simple, easy-to-understand format. When we add the class hierarchies, methods, aggregate objects, and nested structures to an entity/relationship model, the diagram often becomes a muddle of incomprehensible lines. This diagram technique was developed out of necessity to create a consistent method for documenting object-oriented data models and is quite similar to the model diagrams found in the Oracle Designer product. Let's take a look at some of the components of the model shown in Figure 2.20.

Entity Icon

The Entity icon in Figure 2.20 is the rectangle symbol, and it represents a database entity (just like the boxes on an entity/relation model). Inside the rectangle are the descriptions of all base entities in the data model. Information includes the entity name, the type of entity, length of the data in the entity, primary key for the object, whether duplicate keys are allowed, and the place where the object is stored (usually a tablespace for object/relational databases). In order to more completely describe the characteristics of the entity, the following values have been added to the box:

- **Entity_name**—This is the internal name of the entity as it appears inside the database.

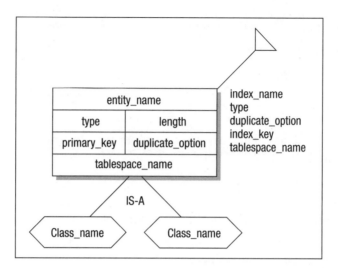

Figure 2.20
The object/relational diagram model.

- **Type**—An entity may be either a table, view, OID table, store table, or aggregate table.

    - **Table**—This is a standard Oracle table.

    - **View**—This is a traditional relational view. A view in most relational databases is stored internally as an SQL statement that joins base tables together to form aggregate views of table data. As such, a view and an aggregate table are very similar in purpose.

    - **OID Table**—This is an object/relational table defined to contain a special column for the object ID for each row in the table.

    - **Store Table**—A store table is an internal representation of a table whereby an owner table may be coupled with another internal table. For more information on this concept, see Chapter 3, *Physical Performance Design*.

    - **Aggregate Table**—An aggregate table is a table that represents assemblies of base-level objects. These tables are usually made up exclusively of pointers to other OID tables within the model.

- **Length**—This is the physical stored length of each row of the entity within the table.

- **Primary_key**—This is the column or OID that may be used to uniquely identify each row within the entity.

- **Duplicate_option**—This describes whether duplicate rows are allowed within the entity. Valid values are **DN** for duplicates not allowed and **DA** for duplicates allowed.

- **Tablespace_name**—This parameter describes the tablespace where the entity resides inside the database.

Index

An index is represented in the object/relational model as a line emanating from the entity rectangle with a triangle at the end of the line. This construct describes all of the information about an index, including the name of the index, type of the index (b-tree or bitmap), duplicate option setting, keys for the index, and the place where the physical index is stored:

- **Index_name**—This is the internal index name as defined within the database management system:

- **Type**—This can have the value of **TREE** for a b-tree index or **BITMAP** for a bitmap structure index.

- **Duplicate_option**—This describes whether duplicate rows are allowed within the index. Valid values are **DN** for duplicates not allowed and **DA** for duplicates allowed.

- **Index_key**—This contains the names of each column within the entity that participates within the index as a key column.

- **Tablespace_name**—This parameter describes the tablespace where the entity resides inside the database.

Class Descriptions

This component of the model uses polygons to represent entities that have attached class hierarchies. While each class name is represented on the diagram, another diagram is used to describe the details about each class hierarchy.

Set

The set includes all information regarding one-to-many relationships between database entities. As you know, there are several ways to represent data relationships among entities in the object relation model:

- *Foreign key relationships*—Foreign key relationships are established by embedding the primary key of one table into another table, becoming a foreign key in that table. The relationship is established at runtime by using the SQL **JOIN** statement to relate the tables together. There are several options available when using foreign key relationships. The relationship can be established in an ad hoc fashion simply by having two matching columns within two tables, or the foreign key relationship can be defined in a more formal way by using referential integrity (RI). When using RI, the database will manage the data relationship and ensure that the constraint is complete. At object insertion time, the RI will check to see that a valid owner key exists before allowing new entities into the model. At object deletion time, the RI will allow two options: **RESTRICT** and **DELETE**. **RESTRICT** will not allow the owner object to be deleted if it has any member objects. You can use **CASCADE** with **DELETE** to delete all member objects when the owner object is deleted.

- *Pointers to rows in other tables*—This construct allows for columns within a table to contain an array of pointers to rows in the member table. This feature can replace the foreign key in the dependent table with an OID, allowing faster access to the parent table. For Oracle8, OIDs are especially useful as "owner" pointers, replacing foreign keys. For example, rather the duplicating a customer number as a foreign key in an order table, an OID of the customer can be stored, allowing for faster retrieval of the customer row.

- *Pointers to other tables*—These are sometimes referred to as *pointers to structures*. In the object/relational model, these pointers can point to many rows in a subordinate table. Oracle8 implements this feature as "nested" tables, whereby a column may contain a pointer to a set of rows in a subordinate table.

Figure 2.21 shows a portion of a complete object/relational diagram. Here, you can see that there are two entities: one for customer and another for order. The customer

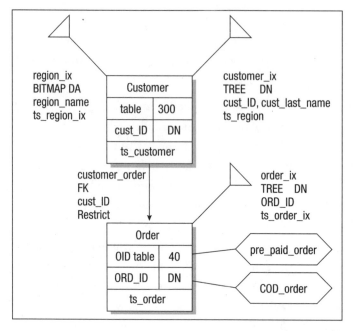

Figure 2.21
A sample object/relational diagram.

is a table type, while the order entity has been defined as the OID table type, meaning that each row contains a unique object identifier.

Note that there are two indexes on the **Customer** entity. The **region_ix** index is a bitmapped structure index, which makes sense because a region has only four distinct values. The **customer_ix** index is a tree index that contains two keys: the **cust_ID** column and the **cust_last_name** column.

You can also see in Figure 2.21 that the **Order** entity has an attached class hierarchy. As you will learn in detail in later chapters, a class hierarchy contains a *base* class (which in this case is the **Order** entity). While the **Order** entity contains all of the base data structures and methods for orders, there are two subtypes of orders: **pre_paid_order** and **COD_order**. Each subtype has its own unique data structures and methods. Instantiations of **COD_order**s and **pre_paid_order**s will inherit the data structures and methods from the **Order** base class. The use of Oracle8 methods can have a dramatic impact on performance, but careful planning is required to successfully implement methods. Now let's move on to discuss one of the most important features of Oracle8: the coupling of data with the behavior of the data.

Benefits Of Methods And Database Objects

If we review the evolution of databases from the earliest hierarchical systems to today's object/relational databases, the single most important new feature is the coupling of data with the behavior of data. The flat-file systems brought us data storage, hierarchical and network databases added the ability to create relationships between data, and relational databases brought declarative data query. Now, we see with Oracle8 the coupling of the data with the behavior of the data.

One of the huge benefits of Oracle's object-relational architecture is the ability to move procedures out of application programs and into the database engine. In addition to providing a more secure repository for the code, the ability to tie data and behavior together also enhances the ability to reuse routines. When combined with the ability to directly represent aggregate objects, we now have a framework for coupling all data processes directly with the object that contains the data to be manipulated.

While this may seem trivial at first glance, there are tremendous ramifications for systems development. Because the process code now moves into the database along with the data, the job of Database Administrators (DBAs) and System Developers will change radically. The DBA, whose exclusive domain was the proprietorship of the data, must now take on additional responsibility for management of the behaviors stored in the database. Systems development also changes. Programmers will no longer have the freedom to write custom-crafted code any time they wish. With the introduction of reusable methods, programmers will change from a custom craftsman to a code assembler. Aside from these factors, some of the most commonly cited reasons for using methods to couple data and behaviors include:

- *Code reusability*—Process code only needs to be written once, and the fully tested and reliable process code can then be included in many different applications.

- *Control over the environment*—By making the database a central repository for process code, all processes are stored in a common format and in a central location. The benefits of this approach include the ability to quickly find code as well as the ability to scan the process code with text-search capability.

- *Proactive tuning*—Because the SQL is present in the database, the DBA can extract and test the access methods used by SQL for an application. This information can be used to identify indexes that need to be created, tables that can benefit from caching in the buffer pool, and other DBA tuning techniques. In addition, developers can use this central repository to tune their SQL, adding hints and changing the SQL in order to obtain an optimal access path to the data.

- *Application portability*—Because the application code resides in a platform-independent language within the database, the application consists exclusively of calls to the methods that invoke the processes. As such, an application front end can easily be ported from one platform to another without the fear that the process code will need to be changed.

- *Cross-referencing of processes*—Because the data dictionary for the database will keep track of all of the programs that call the data, it is very easy to keep track of where a method is used and what methods are nested within other methods. This feature greatly simplifies systems maintenance because all applications that reference a particular entity can be easily and reliably identified.

While the coupling of data with behaviors is a revolutionary concept for database management, the failure to properly plan the implementation can be a disaster. In order to achieve the benefits of using methods, a careful decomposition of the processes must take place.

Planning A Method Hierarchy

As we discussed, there are three types of processes: those that are independent of the database classes, those that are attached to a base-level database class, and those that are attached to aggregate database classes. In addition, any method may have other methods nested within its structure, while at the same time participating as a submethod within another method (see Figure 2.22).

In Figure 2.22, you can see that the **check_credit** method is composed of the subprocesses **check_payment_history** and **check_credit_reference**. At the same time, **check_credit** participates in the **place_order** and **hire_employee** methods. Given this huge array of choices, where do we begin developing the methods? There is a sequence of events that must take place to achieve this mapping of methods to classes:

1. Before the mapping of methods to classes can begin, you should have alread created the following analysis and design documents:

    - *A set of fully decomposed data flow diagrams (DFDs) for your system*—This will be used as the specification for the methods. From the DFDs, you can gather

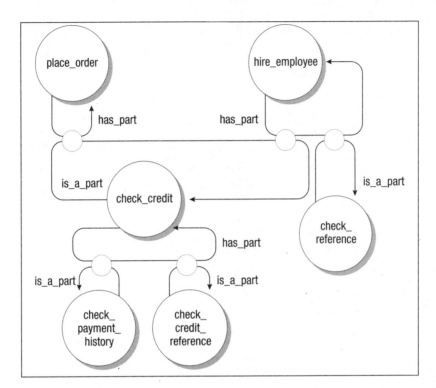

Figure 2.22
The recursive many-to-many nature of method nesting.

the method names, input and output values, and breakdown of nested methods.

- *An entity/relationship diagram of the system*—This diagram will be used to identify the base classes for the system.

- *An aggregate object diagram*—This diagram will be used to associate the higher-level processes with the methods that will be attached to the classes.

2. From the DFD, create a prototype for every process on the data flow diagram. This will formally state the input and output parameters for each process on all levels of the DFD.

3. Identify and prototype all standalone functions in the system.

4. Map the prototypes to the entities.

While this mapping of processes to methods may seem to be a straightforward approach, there are many new concepts that a traditional analyst may not be familiar with. For the purpose of illustration, the next section looks at an example from an order processing system and uses the subprocesses contained within the **fill_order** process as a mapping example.

Data Flow Diagrams And Object Analysis

The generally accepted starting point when creating a data flow diagram is to begin with either a traditional data flow diagram or a functional model. (Remember, a data flow diagram and functional model are almost the same thing.) Let's begin by doing a short review of object analysis.

A functional specification for any system describes the complete logical model and consists of three documents. The data flow diagram is a pictorial description of all of the processes in the system, and it is supplemented with two other documents: the data dictionary, which is used to define all of the data flows and data stores in our system; and the process logic specifications (mini-specs), which are used to describe each process, showing how the data flow is modified within each process.

As you probably know, the data flow diagram is the foundation of any systems analysis. The DFD diagrams the processes, data flows, and data stores. While these documents may be known by different names depending on the chosen analysis methodology, each document should contain a complete description of all of the entities in the system. Let's begin by taking a level one data flow diagram and showing the breakdown of the processes (see Figure 2.23).

Figure 2.23 shows the overall specification for the **fill_order** process, and you can easily see all of the incoming and outgoing data items. In this case, you can see **cust_info** coming in as the input to the **fill_order** process. Of course, **cust_info** does not tells us about the details of this data flow, so we must go to the data dictionary to see the contents of **cust_info**:

```
cust_info =

cust_full_name =
    cust_last_name +
    cust_first_name +
    cust_middle_initial

cust_full_address =
    cust_street_address +
```

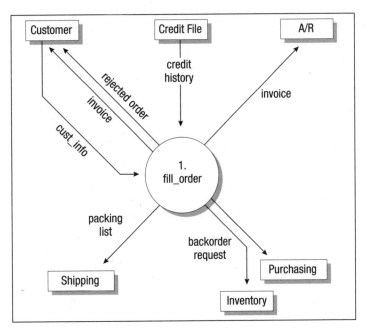

Figure 2.23
A level one data flow diagram for filling orders.

```
     cust_city_name +
     cust_state +
     cust_zip_code +
cust_phone_nbr

1
{ item_ID + item_quantity }
n
```

We will use these data dictionary definitions to gather the data items that are of interest to each process in our data flow diagram. Remember, the purpose of designing methods is to map the incoming and outgoing data flows to clean, well-defined procedures that can be coupled with the database entities.

Now, let's take a look at how the **fill_order** process is decomposed into lower-level DFDs. Looking at the next lowest level DFD (shown in Figure 2.24), you can see that **fill_order** is broken down into three subprocesses: **check_customer_credit**, **check_inventory**, and **prepare_invoice**. This DFD shows all of the input and output data flows for these processes.

In Figure 2.24, you can see another level of detail for the **fill_order** process. The process is broken down into three subprocesses, each with its own data flows and processes. As you might guess, the departitioning of the processes will correspond to the departitioning of the methods for our object database.

Let's complete the foundation for our methods by showing the next level DFD for some of the lower-level processes. To accomplish this, we will use the **check_inventory** process (see Figure 2.25). We can assume that these are *functional primitive* processes, and they will serve as our lowest level methods in our example.

It is important for the mapping of methods to database objects to understand when a process has been departitioned to a level that corresponds with the functions of a database entity. We could continue to departition this DFD, making each process smaller and smaller, but the subprocesses would not easily map to the database ob-

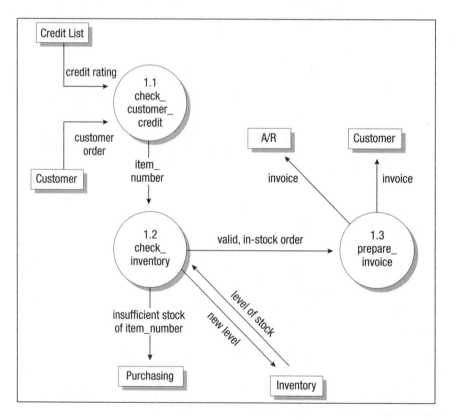

Figure 2.24
A level two data flow diagram for the fill order process.

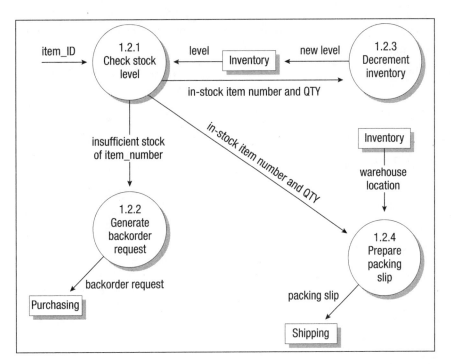

Figure 2.25
The data flow diagram for the **check_inventory** process.

jects. Hence, when you see that a process on your DFD deals with a single function on a single database entity, you will know that you have reached the functional primitive level, and the analysis is complete.

Summary

This chapter demonstrates how a proper logical design can be critical for good performance as a database is analyzed. While far from being an exhaustive description of logical design techniques, it focuses on the basic principles that will help to ensure that your Oracle database functions as quickly as possible. I have come to believe that response time is one of the most critical factors to the success of any database. Regardless of how well a system is analyzed or implemented—no matter now flashy the GUI interface—if the system fails to deliver data in a timely fashion, the project is doomed.

Now that we have reviewed logical database design, let's move on to the physical implementation of Oracle databases. Of course, there is far more to performance and tuning than just design principles. The following chapter referral list provides a general guideline for further exploration:

- Oracle8 object structures—Chapter 3, *Physical Performance Design.*

- Distributed database tuning—Chapter 8, *Performance And Tuning For Distributed Oracle Databases.*

- Database connectivity for client/server—Chapter 9, *Performance And Tuning For Oracle Database Connectivity Tools.*

- STAR schema design—Chapter 10, *Tuning Oracle Data Warehouse And OLAP Applications.*

Physical Performance Design

HIGH PERFORMANCE

CHAPTER

3

Physical Performance Design

Once a good logical model has been created, it is critical to translate the logical model into an Oracle implementation capable of performing at optimal speed. Because Oracle involves so many design issues, this chapter takes a detailed look at how specific physical design tools can be used to exploit client/server performance. Remember, a proper design is the single most important factor in database performance. No amount of tuning can fix a database that is poorly designed.

Database Performance Design Issues

There are many basic design principles that can be applied to improve the performance of your Oracle8 database. These topics are the single most critical factor in ensuring that your database runs at optimal performance. While many of these items can be changed after implementation of the database, careful preplanning in the design stage will help ensure that your database will run properly from the start. Topics discussed in this section include:

- Indexes
- Tables
- Referential Integrity
- Stored Procedures
- Pinning Packages
- Triggers
- Clusters

- Hash Clusters

- Parallel Queries

Indexes

In Oracle, an index is used to speed up the time required to access table information. Internally, Oracle indexes are b-tree data structures in which each tree node can contain many sets of key values and **ROWID**s.

In general, Oracle indexes exist for the purpose of preventing full-table scans. Full-table scans create two problems. The main problem is the time lost in servicing a request as each and every row of a table is read into Oracle's buffer pool. In addition to causing the task performance to suffer, a full-table scan also causes performance degradation at the system level. When this happens, all other tasks on the system might have to incur additional I/O because the buffer block held by competing tasks will have been flushed by the full-table scan. As blocks are flushed from the buffer pool, other tasks are required to incur additional I/Os to reread information that would have remained in the buffer pool if the full-table scan had not been invoked. More information on optimizing full-table scans can be found in Chapter 7, *Oracle DBA Performance And Tuning*.

Almost any Oracle table can benefit from the use of indexes. The only exception to this rule would be a very small table that can be read in less than two-block I/Os. Two-block I/Os are used as a guideline because Oracle will need to perform at least one I/O to access the root node of the index tree and another I/O to retrieve the requested data. For example, assume that a lookup table contains rows of 25 bytes each and you have configured Oracle to use 4K block sizes. Because each data block would hold about 150 rows, using an index for up to 300 rows would not make processing any faster than a full-table scan.

If you plan to use the Oracle parallel query facility, all the tables in the SQL query must cause a full-table scan. If an index exists, the cost-based optimizer must be used with a hint to invalidate the index in order to use parallel query. For the rule-based optimizer, indexes can be turned off by using an Oracle built-in function in the **WHERE** clause. Look for details on this in Chapter 5, *Tuning Oracle SQL*.

One important concept in indexing is the "selectivity" or the uniqueness of the values in a column. To be most effective, an index column must have many unique values. Columns having only a few values (e.g., sex = m/f, status = y/n) are not good candidates for traditional Oracle b-tree indexing, but they are ideal for bitmapped indexes. To see the selectivity for a column, compare the total number of rows in the table with the number of distinct values for the column, as follows:

```
SELECT count(*) FROM CUSTOMER;

SELECT DISTINCT STATUS FROM CUSTOMER;
```

Another concept used in indexing is called *distribution*. Distribution refers to the frequency that each unique value is distributed within a table. For example, let's say you have a **state_abbreviation** column that contains 1 of 50 possible values. This is acceptable to use as an index column, provided that the state abbreviations are uniformly distributed across the rows. However, if 90 percent of the values are for New York, then the index will not be very effective.

Oracle has addressed the index data distribution issue with the **ANALYZE TABLE** command. When using Oracle's cost-based SQL optimizer, **ANALYZE TABLE** looks at both the selectivity and distribution of the column values. If they are found to be out-of-bounds, Oracle can decide not to use the index. Oracle has a view called **DBA_HISTOGRAMS** that tells the cost-based optimizer about the distribution of values within a column. The purpose of a histogram is to provide a clear picture of the distribution of values within a low-cardinality index. Unfortunately, getting the histogram data requires each and every index column to be analyzed, and most Oracle designers favor bitmapped indexes over tree indexes for low-cardinality indexes.

Oracle recommends the following guidelines when considering whether to index a column:

- Columns frequently referenced in SQL **WHERE** clauses are good candidates for an index.

- Columns used to join tables (primary and foreign keys) should be indexed.

- Columns with many unique values should not be indexed using a b-tree. Any column with less than 10 percent of unique values should be indexed as a bitmap index.

- Frequently modified columns are not good candidates for indexing because excessive processing is necessary to maintain the structure of the index tree.

- Columns used in SQL **WHERE** clauses using Oracle functions or operators should not be indexed. For example, an index on **last_name** will not be effective if it is referred to in the SQL as **upper(last_name)**.

- When using referential integrity, always create an index on the foreign key.

Most programmers do not realize that database deadlocks occur frequently within the database indexes. It is important to note that a **SELECT** of a single row in a database can cause more than one lock entry to be placed in the storage pool because all affected index rows are also locked. In other words, the individual row receives a lock, but each index node that contains the value for that row will also have locks assigned (see Figure 3.1). If the "last" entry in a sorted index is retrieved, the database will lock all index nodes that reference the indexed value, in case the user changes that value. Because many indexing schemes always carry the high-order key in multiple index nodes, an entire branch of the index tree can be locked—all the way up to the root node of the index. While each database's indexing scheme is different, some relational database vendors recommend that tables with ascending keys be loaded in descending order, so the rows are loaded from Z to A on an alphabetic key field. Other databases, such as Oracle, recommend indexes be dropped and re-created after rows have been loaded into an empty table.

When an **UPDATE** or **DELETE** is issued against a row that participates in an index, the database will attempt an exclusive lock on the row. This attempt requires the task to check if any shared locks are held against the row as well as any index nodes

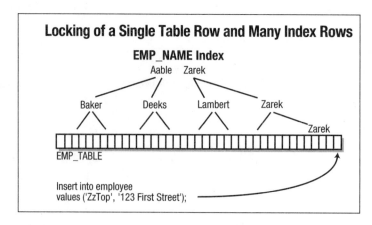

Figure 3.1
An overview of Oracle locking.

that will be affected. Many indexing algorithms allow for the index tree to dynamically change shape, spawning new levels as items are added and condensing levels as items are deleted.

However, for any table of consequential size, indexes are recommended to improve performance. Of course, indexes require additional disk space, and a table with an index on each column will have indexes that consume more space than the table they support. Oracle will update indexes at runtime as columns are deleted, added, or modified—and this index updating can cause considerable performance degradation. For example, adding a row to the end of a table will cause Oracle to adjust the high-key value for each node in the index.

Another guideline for determining when to use an index involves examination of the SQL issued against a table. In general, the SQL can be collected, and each value supplied in each SQL **WHERE** clause could be a candidate for inclusion in an index.

Another common approach for determining where to create indexes is to run an explain plan for all SQL and carefully look for any full-table scans. The Oracle cost-based optimizer operates in such a fashion that Oracle will sometimes perform a full-table scan, even if an index has been defined for the table. This occurs most commonly when issuing complex n-way joins, and techniques for avoiding this problem are discussed in Chapter 5, *Tuning Oracle SQL*. If you are using rule-based optimization in Oracle, the structure of an SQL statement can be adjusted to force the use of an existing index. For Oracle's cost-based optimizer, adding "hints" to the structure can ensure that all indexes are used. The cost-based optimizer sometimes chooses full-table scans when an index scan would be more efficient.

Indexes do much more than speed up an individual query. When full-table scans are performed on a large Oracle table, the buffer pool begins to page out blocks from other queries. This causes additional I/O for the entire database and results in poor performance for all queries—not just the offending full-table scan.

Indexes are never a good idea for long descriptive columns. A column called **customer_description** would be a poor choice for an index because of its length and the inconsistency of the data within the column. Also, a field such as **customer_description** would usually be referenced in SQL by using Oracle extensions, such as **substr**, **LIKE**, and **upper**. Remember, these Oracle extensions invalidate the index. Suppose an index has been created on **customer_last_name**. The following query would use the index:

```
SELECT STATUS
FROM CUSTOMER
WHERE
customer_last_name = 'BURLESON';
```

The following queries would bypass the index, causing a full-table scan:

```
SELECT STATUS
FROM CUSTOMER
WHERE
customer_last_name = lower('burleson');

SELECT STATUS
FROM CUSTOMER
WHERE
customer_last_name LIKE 'BURL%';
```

Unlike other relational databases, such as DB2, Oracle administrators cannot physically load a table in key order. Consequently, administrators can never guarantee that the rows in a table will be in any particular order.

The use of an index can help whenever the SQL **ORDER BY** clause is used. For example, even if there are no complex **WHERE** conditions, the presence of a **WHERE** clause will assist the performance of the query. Consider the following SQL:

```
SELECT customer_last_name, customer_first_name
FROM CUSTOMER
ORDER BY customer_last_name, customer_first_name;
```

Here, building a multivalued index on **customer_last_name** and **customer_first_name** will alleviate the need for an internal sort of the data, significantly improving the performance of the query:

```
CREATE INDEX   cust_name
ON CUSTOMER
(customer_last_name, customer_first_name) ascending;
```

Now that we understand the basics of Oracle indexing, let's move on to take a look at how indexes interact with referential integrity. We'll also examine the performance implications of these features.

Constraints And Indexes

In Oracle, some constraints create an index on your behalf. For example, creating a primary key constraint on the **CUSTOMER** table for the **cust_id** will create an index on the field, and it is not necessary to manually build an index (see Listing 3.1).

Listing 3.1   Creating a primary key constraint.

```
CREATE TABLE CUSTOMER (
        cust_nbr                number
        CONSTRAINT cust_ukey
PRIMARY KEY (cust_nbr)
USING INDEX
PCTFREE  10
INITRANS 2
MAXTRANS 255
TABLESPACE TS1
STORAGE  (
   INITIAL     256000
   NEXT        102400
   MINEXTENTS  1
   MAXEXTENTS  121
   PCTINCREASE 1 ),
        dept_name               char(10)
        CONSTRAINT dept_fk REFERENCES DEPT ON DELETE CASCADE,

        organization_name       char(20)
        CONSTRAINT org_fk REFERENCES ORG ON DELETE RESTRICT,

        region_name             char(2)
        CONSTRAINT state_check
        CHECK region_name IN ('NORTH', 'SOUTH', 'EAST', 'WEST')
);
```

Note that you should always specify the tablespace name when declaring constraints. In the previous example, had the **cust_ukey** constraint been defined without the **STORAGE** clause, the index would have been placed in whatever tablespace is specified by the table owner's **DEFAULT** tablespace, with whatever default storage parameters are in effect for that tablespace.

Listing 3.1 shows some examples of Oracle constraints. The first constraint is on the **cust_nbr** column, the primary key. When you use Oracle's RI to specify a primary key, Oracle automatically builds a unique index on the column to ensure that no duplicate values are entered.

The second constraint in Listing 3.1 is on the **dept_name** column of the **DEPT** table. This constraint tells Oracle that it can not remove a department row if there are existing customer rows that reference that department. **ON DELETE CASCADE** tells Oracle that when the department row is deleted, all customer rows referencing that department will also be deleted.

The next RI constraint on **organization_name** ensures that no organization is deleted if customers are participating in that organization. **ON DELETE RESTRICT** tells Oracle not to delete an organization row if any customer row still references the organization. Only after each and every customer has been set to another organization can the row be deleted from the organization table.

The last RI constraint shown in Listing 3.1 is called a *check constraint*. Using a check constraint, Oracle will verify that the column is one of the valid values before inserting the row, but it will not create an index on the column.

In addition to basic indexes, Oracle8 allows for an index to contain multiple columns. This ability can greatly influence the speed at which certain types of queries function within Oracle.

Using Multicolumn Indexes

When an SQL request is commonly issued using multiple columns, a concatenated or multicolumn index can be used to improve performance. Oracle supports the use of multivalued indexes, but there are some important limitations. Unlike other relational databases, Oracle requires that all columns in an index be sorted in the same order, either ascending or descending. For example, if you needed to index on **customer_last_name** ascending, followed immediately by **gross_pay** descending, you would not be able to use a multivalued index.

Sometimes two columns—each with poor selectivity (i.e., both columns have few unique values)—can be combined into an index that has better selectivity. For example, you could combine a status field that has three values (good, neutral, bad) with another column such as **state_name** (only 50 unique values), thereby creating a multivalued index that has far better selectivity than each column would have if indexed separately.

Another reason for creating concatenated indexes is to speed the execution of queries that reference all the values in an index. For example, consider the following query:

```
SELECT      customer_last_name,
            customer_status,
            customer_zip_code
FROM CUSTOMER
ORDER BY customer_last_name;
```

Now, an index can be created, as follows:

```
CREATE INDEX last_status_zip
ON CUSTOMER
(customer_last_name, customer_status, customer_zip_code) ascending;
```

If this query was issued against the **CUSTOMER** table, Oracle would never need to access any rows in the base table! Because all key values are contained in the index and the high-order key (**customer_last_name**) is in the **ORDER BY** clause, Oracle can scan the index and retrieve data without ever touching the base table.

With the assistance of this feature, the savvy Oracle developer can also add columns to the end of the concatenated index so that the base table is never touched. For example, if the preceding query also returned the value of the **customer_address** column, this column could be added to the concatenated index, dramatically improving performance.

In summary, the following guidelines apply when creating a concatenated index:

- Use a composite index whenever two or more values are used in the SQL where the clause and the operators are **AND**ed together.

- Place the columns in a **WHERE** clause in the same order as in the index, with data items added at the end of the index.

Now that we understand the basic constructs of Oracle indexes, let's take a closer look at the SQL optimizer and examine how it chooses which indexes to use to service SQL requests.

How Oracle Chooses Indexes

It is interesting to note that the fastest execution for an individual task might not always be the best choice. For example, consider the following query against the **CUSTOMER** table:

```
SELECT customer_name
FROM CUSTOMER
WHERE
    credit_rating = 'POOR'
AND
    amount_due > 1000
AND
    state = 'IOWA'
AND
    job_description LIKE lower('%computer%');
```

Here, you can see a query where a full-table scan would be the most efficient processing method. Because of the complex conditions and the use of Oracle extensions in the SQL, it might be faster to perform a full-table scan. However, the fast execution of this task might be done at the expense of other tasks on the system as the buffer pool becomes flushed.

In general, the type of SQL optimizer will determine how indexes are used. As you probably know, the Oracle optimizer can run as either rule-based or cost-based. As a general rule, Oracle is intelligent enough to use an index if it exists, but there are exceptions to this rule. The most notable exception is the n-way join with a complex **WHERE** clause. The cost-based optimizer, especially when the **all_rows** mode is used, will get "confused" and invoke a full-table scan on at least one of the tables, even if the appropriate foreign key indexes exist for the tables. The only remedy to this problem is to use the rule-based optimizer or use the **first_rows** mode of the cost-based optimizer. This problem is discussed at length in Chapter 5, *Tuning Oracle SQL*.

Always remember, Oracle will only use an index when the index column is specified in its "pure" form. The use of the **substr**, **upper**, **lower**, and other functions will invalidate an index. However, there are a few tricks to help you get around this obstacle. Consider the following two equivalent SQL queries:

```
SELECT * FROM CUSTOMER
WHERE
total_purchases/10 > 5000;
```

```
SELECT * FROM CUSTOMER
WHERE
total_purchases > 5000*10;
```

The second query, by virtue of the fact that it does not alter the index column, would be able to use an index on the **total_purchases** column.

While index usage has an impact on database performance, the way that Oracle8 tables are allocated can also influence the system performance, especially tables that are updated frequently. Let's take a look at some of the most important considerations when allocating Oracle8 tables.

Allocating Tables

Several parameters can be used to ensure that all data stored within Oracle tables remains in an optimal configuration. Consider the following Oracle table definition:

```
CREATE TABLE ITEM (
        item_nbr                number,
        item_name               varchar(30),
        item_description        varchar(50))
STORAGE(         INITIAL   50K
                 NEXT      50K
                 PCTFREE   10
                 PCTUSED   60
                 FREELISTS 1
                 INITTRANS 1
                 MAXTRANS  5 );
```

PCTFREE tells Oracle how much space to reserve in each Oracle block for future updates and can have an important impact on the performance of an Oracle database if it is set too low. For example, if a row contains a lot of **varchar** data types and the rows are initially inserted without values, later updates of values into the **varchar** fields will cause the rows to expand on the block. If the target block does not have enough room, Oracle will have to fragment the row and store some row information on the next physical block in the tablespace. If this block is also full, Oracle could create a very long chain until it finds a block with enough room to store the new column data. This condition can lead to many unnecessary I/Os when the row is retrieved because many database blocks must be read to retrieve the row. The rule here is simple: Determine the average row length and predicted growth for each row, then use **PCTFREE** to reserve the proper amount of space on each block. For static read-only tables, it is acceptable to set **PCTFREE** to a very small number in order to fully occupy each database block. Again, the **PCTFREE** parameter is only useful for the SQL **UPDATE** statement—and only when the **UPDATE** will cause the row to grow in size. If this is not the case, then **PCTFREE** should be set to 5, reserving only 5 percent of each database block for updates.

PCTUSED tells Oracle when it is acceptable to insert rows onto a database block. For example, if **PCTUSED** is set to 80, Oracle will not allow rows to be added to any database blocks unless they are less than 80 percent full. Oracle will try to keep a database block at least **PCTUSED** full. As rows are deleted from a table, database blocks that fall below **PCTUSED** will become eligible to receive new rows. The default is 40 percent, so any database block less than 40 percent full could have rows added to that block. **PCTUSED** is a trade-off between efficient table utilization and performance. If **PCTUSED** is set to a large value, Oracle will keep the database blocks more full, making more efficient use of storage. However, it does so at the expense of performance, especially for **INSERT** and **UPDATE** operations. For very high performance, **PCTUSED** could be set to a lower value, say 60 percent. This will keep Oracle from constantly moving database blocks onto the **FREELIST** as rows are deleted, thereby improving performance. Again, **PCTUSED** plays an essential role for very volatile tables with many **DELETE** operations.

PCTFREE and PCTUSED work together. The sum of these values can never equal more than 100, and it is usually wise to sum the values at a limit of 90 because of overhead found on each database block.

FREELIST is the parameter used when more than one concurrent process is expected to access a table. Oracle keeps one **FREELIST** for each table in memory and uses the **FREELIST** in order to determine what database block to use when an SQL **INSERT** occurs. As a row is added, the **FREELIST** is locked. If more than one concurrent process is attempting to insert into your table, one of the processes might need to wait until the **FREELIST** has been released by the previous task. To see if adding a **FREELIST** to a table will improve performance, you will need to evaluate how often Oracle has to wait for a **FREELIST**. Fortunately, Oracle keeps a **V$** table called **V$WAITSTAT** for this purpose. The following query shows how many times Oracle has waited for a **FREELIST** to become available. As you can see, it does not tell you which **FREELISTS** are experiencing the contention problems:

```
SELECT CLASS, COUNT
FROM V$WAITSTAT
WHERE CLASS = 'free list';

    CLASS                        COUNT
    -----                        -----
    free list                    83
```

Here, you can see that Oracle had to wait 83 times for a table **FREELIST** to become available. This could represent a wait of 83 times on the same table or perhaps a single wait for 83 separate tables. While 83 seems to be a large number, remember that Oracle can perform hundreds of I/Os each second, so 83 could be quite insignificant to the overall system. In any case, if you suspect that you know which table's **FREELIST** is having the contention, the table can be exported, dropped, and redefined to have more **FREELISTS**. While an extra **FREELIST** consumes more of Oracle's memory, additional **FREELISTS** can help throughput on tables that have lots of **INSERT**s. Generally, you should define extra **FREELISTS** only on those tables that will have many concurrent **UPDATE** operations.

INITTRANS specifies the initial number of transactions allocated within each block. **MAXTRANS** is a value that specifies the maximum number of concurrent transactions that can update a block.

Now, let's take a look at the table definitions shown in Listings 3.2 and 3.3. Let's see if you can infer the type of activity that will be taking place against the tables.

Listing 3.2   Table definition one.

```
CREATE TABLE ORDER (
       order_nbr          number,
       order_date         date)
STORAGE ( PCTFREE  10 PCTUSED  40 FREELISTS 3);
```

Here, you can infer the table has very few **UPDATE**s that cause the row length to increase because **PCTFREE** is only 10 percent. You can also infer that this table will have a great deal of **DELETE** activity because **PCTUSED** is at 40 percent, thereby preventing immediate reuse of database blocks as rows are deleted. This table must also have a lot of **INSERT** activity because **FREELISTS** is set to 3, indicating that up to three concurrent processes can be inserting into the table. Let's look at the second example.

Listing 3.3 Table definition two.

```
CREATE TABLE ITEM (
        item_nbr                    number,
        item_name                   varchar(20),
        item_description            varchar(50),
        current_item_status         varchar(200) )
STORAGE ( PCTFREE  40 PCTUSED  60 FREELISTS 1);
```

In Listing 3.3, you can infer that **UPDATE** operations are frequent and will prob-ably increase the size of the varchar columns because **PCTFREE** is set to reserve 40 percent of each block for row expansion. You can also infer that this table has few **DELETE**s because **PCTUSED** is set to 60, making efficient use of the database blocks. Assuming that there will not be very many **DELETEs**, these blocks would become constantly re-added to the **FREELISTS**.

Now that the basic table and index structures have been designed, we can move on to take a look at how referential integrity is used from a performance perspective.

Referential Integrity And Performance

Before most relational databases supported referential integrity, it was the responsi-bility of the programmer to guarantee the maintenance of data relationships and business rules. While this was fine for the applications, the risk came into play when ad hoc updated SQL commands were issued using Oracle's SQL*Plus. With these ad hoc update tools, the programmatic SQL could be bypassed easily, skipping the business rules and creating logical corruption.

Relational database systems, such as Oracle, allow for the control of business rules with *constraints*. In general, RI rules are used to enforce one-to-many and many-to-many relationships within relational tables. For example, RI would ensure that a row in a **CUSTOMER** table could not be deleted if orders for that customer exist in an **ORDER** table. (See Figure 3.2.)

Referential integrity has earned a bad reputation in Oracle because of overhead cre-ated when enforcing business rules. In almost every case, it will be faster and more efficient to write your own rules to enforce RI instead of having Oracle do it for you. Provided that your application does not allow ad hoc query, it is relatively easy to attach a trigger with a PL/SQL routine to enforce RI on your behalf. In fact, this is

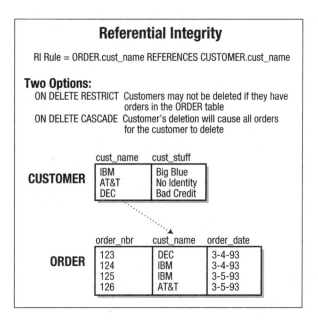

Referential Integrity

RI Rule = ORDER.cust_name REFERENCES CUSTOMER.cust_name

Two Options:
ON DELETE RESTRICT Customers may not be deleted if they have orders in the ORDER table
ON DELETE CASCADE Customer's deletion will cause all orders for the customer to delete

CUSTOMER

cust_name	cust_stuff
IBM	Big Blue
AT&T	No Identity
DEC	Bad Credit

ORDER

order_nbr	cust_name	order_date
123	DEC	3-4-93
124	IBM	3-4-93
125	IBM	3-5-93
126	AT&T	3-5-93

Figure 3.2
An overview of referential integrity.

one of the best uses of a trigger because the DML **DELETE** event will not take place if the RI rules are invalid. Consider the following foreign key constraint that protects a customer from being deleted if they have outstanding orders:

```
CREATE TABLE CUSTOMER (
    cust_id                 number
    CONSTRAINT cust_ukey unique (cust_id),
    cust_name               varchar(30),
    cust_address            varchar(30);)

CREATE TABLE ORDER (
    order_id                number,
    order_date              date,
    cust_id                 number
    CONSTRAINT cust_fk REFERENCES CUSTOMER ON DELETE RESTRICT
);
```

To ensure SQL*Plus has no ad hoc updates, it can be configured to disallow update operations. This is accomplished with the **PRODUCT_USER_PROFILE** table. Issuing the following row into this table will disable any ad hoc updates with SQL*Plus:

```
INSERT INTO PRODUCT_USER_PROFILE (product, user_id, attribute)
VALUES (
        'SQL*Plus',
        '%',
        'UPDATE');
```

Are you now free to write your own procedural RI without fear of accidental corruption? Actually, there is another way that users can access ad hoc queries, thereby bypassing your business rules. A user on a PC (with SQL*Net installed) can access Oracle using ODBC without ever entering SQL*Plus. So beware, and be sure that all ad hoc holes have been plugged before attempting to write your own RI rules.

Another problem with RI occurs when two tablespaces (TS1 and TS2) contain tables (Table A and Table B) that have foreign key rules into the other tablespace. The DBA must commonly drop and rebuild the tablespaces as a part of routine database compression. For example, when trying to drop tablespace TS1 that has RI into another tablespace, the **DROP TABLESPACE CASCADE** will fail because foreign key references are contained in Table B in tablespace TS2. Conversely, the DBA cannot drop tablespace TS2 because it has references into tablespace TS1. This turns DBA maintenance into a nightmare because all constraints must be identified and disabled from tablespace TS2 in order to drop tablespace TS1.

Oracle8 methods now provide a way to keep PL/SQL code inside the database. As more code moves out of the external database and into Oracle, there will be less resource consumption within the System Global Area (SGA) and faster performance.

Stored Procedures

As objects such as stored procedures and triggers become more popular, more application code will move away from external programs and into the database engine. Oracle has been encouraging this approach in anticipation of the object-oriented features introduced in Oracle version 8. However, the Oracle DBA must be conscious of the increasing memory demands of stored procedures, and carefully plan for the days when all database access code resides within the database.

Today, most Oracle databases have only a small amount of code in stored procedures—but this is rapidly changing. Many compelling benefits can be derived by placing all Oracle SQL inside stored procedures, including:

- *Better Performance*—Stored procedures are loaded once into the System Global Area (SGA) and remain there unless they become paged out. Subsequent executions of the stored procedure are far faster than external code.

- *Coupling Of Data With Behavior*—Relational tables can be coupled with the behaviors associated with them by using naming conventions. In Oracle8, you have the ability to define *methods*, which are stored procedures directly associated with the database table. For example, if all behaviors associated with the **EMPLOYEE** table are prefixed with the table name (e.g., **EMPLOYEE.hire**, **EMPLOYEE.give_raise**), then the data dictionary can be queried to list all behaviors associated with a table (for instance, **SELECT * FROM DBA_OBJECTS WHERE OWNER = 'EMPLOYEE'**), and code can be readily identified and reused.

- *Isolation Of Code*—All SQL is moved out of the external programs and into stored procedures, so application programs are nothing more than calls to stored procedures or methods. As such, it becomes very simple to swap out one database and swap in another.

One of the foremost reasons why stored procedures and triggers function faster than traditional code is because of Oracle's SGA. After a procedure has been loaded into the SGA, it remains in the library cache until it is paged out of memory. Items are paged out of memory based on a least-recently-used algorithm. Once loaded into the RAM memory of the shared pool, the procedure will execute very quickly. The trick is to prevent pool-thrashing during the period when many procedures are competing for a limited amount of library cache within the shared pool memory.

When tuning Oracle, two init.ora parameters emerge as more important than all other parameters combined. These are the **db_block_buffers** and the **shared_pool_size** parameters. These two parameters define the size of the in-memory region that Oracle consumes on startup and determines the amount of storage available to cache data blocks, SQL, and stored procedures.

Oracle also provides a construct called a *package*. Essentially, a package is a collection of functions and stored procedures that can be organized in a variety of ways. For example, functions and stored procedures for employees can be logically grouped together in an employee package as follows:

```
CREATE PACKAGE EMPLOYEE AS

    FUNCTION compute_raise_amount (percentage number);
    PROCEDURE hire_employee();
    PROCEDURE fire_employee();
    PROCEDURE list_employee_details();

END EMPLOYEE;
```

Here, all employee "behaviors" have been captured into a single package that will be added into Oracle's data dictionary. If you force your programmers to use stored procedures, the SQL moves out of the external programs and into the database, reducing the application programs into nothing more than a series of calls to Oracle stored procedures.

As systems evolve and the majority of process code resides in stored procedures, Oracle's shared pool will become very important. The shared pool consists of the following subpools:

- Dictionary cache
- Library cache
- Shared SQL areas
- Private SQL areas (these exist during cursor open/cursor close)
- Persistent area
- Runtime area

As mentioned, the shared pool utilizes a least-recently-used algorithm to determine which objects are paged out of the shared pool. As this paging occurs, fragments, or discontiguous chunks of memory, are created within the shared pool.

This means a large procedure that initially fits into memory might not fit into contiguous memory when it's reloaded after paging out. Consider the problem that occurs when the body of a package has been paged out of the instance's SGA because of other, more recent (or more frequent) activity. Fragmentation will occur, and the server might not find enough contiguous memory to reload the package body, thereby resulting in an ORA-4031 error. In Oracle, you can avoid paging by *pinning* packages in the SGA.

Pinning Packages In The SGA

To prevent paging, packages can be marked as nonswappable. Marking a package as nonswappable tells a database that after the package is initially loaded, the package must always remain in memory. This is called *pinning* or *memory fencing*. Oracle provides a procedure called **dbms_shared_pool.keep** to pin a package. Packages can be unpinned with **dbms_shared_pool.unkeep**.

> **Note:** *Only packages can be pinned. Stored procedures cannot be pinned unless they are placed into a package.*

The choice of whether to pin a package in memory is a function of the size of the object and the frequency of its use. Very large packages that are called frequently might benefit from pinning, but any difference might go unnoticed because the frequent calls to the procedure have kept it loaded into memory anyway. Therefore, because the object never pages out in the first place, pinning has no effect. Also, the way procedures are grouped into packages can have some influence. Some Oracle DBAs identify high-impact procedures and group them into a single package, which is pinned in the library cache.

In an ideal world, the **shared_pool** parameter of the init.ora should be large enough to accept every package, stored procedure, and trigger that can be used by the applications. However, reality dictates that the shared pool cannot grow indefinitely, and wise choices must be made in terms of which packages are pinned.

Because of their frequent usage, Oracle recommends that the **standard**, **dbms_standard**, **dbms_utility**, **dbms_describe**, and **dbms_output** packages always be pinned in the shared pool. The following snippet demonstrates how a stored procedure called **sys.standard** can be pinned:

```
CONNECT INTERNAL;

@/usr/oracle/rdbms/admin/dbmspool.sql

EXECUTE dbms_shared_pool.keep('sys.standard');
```

A standard procedure can be written to pin all of the recommended Oracle packages into the shared pool. Here is the script:

```
EXECUTE dbms_shared_pool.keep('DBMS_ALERT');
EXECUTE dbms_shared_pool.keep('DBMS_DDL');
EXECUTE dbms_shared_pool.keep('DBMS_DESCRIBE');
EXECUTE dbms_shared_pool.keep('DBMS_LOCK');
EXECUTE dbms_shared_pool.keep('DBMS_OUTPUT');
EXECUTE dbms_shared_pool.keep('DBMS_PIPE');
EXECUTE dbms_shared_pool.keep('DBMS_SESSION');
EXECUTE dbms_shared_pool.keep('DBMS_SHARED_POOL');
EXECUTE dbms_shared_pool.keep('DBMS_STANDARD');
EXECUTE dbms_shared_pool.keep('DBMS_UTILITY');
EXECUTE dbms_shared_pool.keep('STANDARD');
```

Automatic Re-Pinning Of Packages

Unix users might want to add code to the /etc/rc file to ensure that the packages are re-pinned after each database startup, guaranteeing that all packages are re-pinned with each bounce of the box. A script might look like this:

```
[root]: more pin
ORACLE_SID=mydata
export ORACLE_SID
su oracle -c "/usr/oracle/bin/svrmgrl /<<!
connect internal;
select * from db;
   @/usr/local/dba/sql/pin.sql
exit;
!"
```

The database administrator also needs to remember to run pin.sql whenever restarting a database. This is done by reissuing the **PIN** command from inside SQL*DBA immediately after the database has been restarted.

How To Measure Pinned Packages

Listing 3.4 shows a handy script to look at pinned packages in the SGA. The output from this listing should show those packages that are frequently used by your application.

Listing 3.4   Looking at pinned packages in the SGA using memory.sql.

```
memory.sql - Display used SGA memory for triggers, packages, & procedures

SET PAGESIZE 60;
```

```
COLUMN EXECUTIONS FORMAT 999,999,999;
COLUMN Mem_used   FORMAT 999,999,999;

SELECT substr(owner,1,10) Owner,
       substr(type,1,12)  Type,
       substr(name,1,20)  Name,
       executions,
       sharable_mem       Mem_used,
       substr(kept||' ',1,4)  "Kept?"
 FROM V$DB_OBJECT_CACHE
 WHERE TYPE IN ('TRIGGER','PROCEDURE','PACKAGE BODY','PACKAGE')
 ORDER BY EXECUTIONS DESC;
```

Listing 3.5 shows the output of memory.sql.

Listing 3.5 The output of memory.sql.

```
SQL> @memory
```

OWNER	TYPE	NAME	EXECUTIONS	MEM_USED	KEPT?
SYS	PACKAGE	STANDARD	867,600	151,963	YES
SYS	PACKAGE BODY	STANDARD	867,275	30,739	YES
SYS	PACKAGE	DBMS_ALERT	502,126	3,637	NO
SYS	PACKAGE BODY	DBMS_ALERT	433,607	20,389	NO
SYS	PACKAGE	DBMS_LOCK	432,137	3,140	YES
SYS	PACKAGE BODY	DBMS_LOCK	432,137	10,780	YES
SYS	PACKAGE	DBMS_PIPE	397,466	3,412	NO
SYS	PACKAGE BODY	DBMS_PIPE	397,466	5,292	NO
HRIS	PACKAGE	S125_PACKAGE	285,700	3,776	NO
SYS	PACKAGE	DBMS_UTILITY	284,694	3,311	NO
SYS	PACKAGE BODY	DBMS_UTILITY	284,694	6,159	NO
HRIS	PACKAGE	HRS_COMMON_PACKAGE	258,657	3,382	NO
HRIS	PACKAGE BODY	S125_PACKAGE	248,857	30,928	NO
HRIS	PACKAGE BODY	HRS_COMMON_PACKAGE	242,155	8,638	NO
HRIS	PACKAGE	GTS_SNAPSHOT_UTILITY	168,978	11,056	NO
HRIS	PACKAGE BODY	GTS_SNAPSHOT_UTILITY	89,623	3,232	NO
SYS	PACKAGE	DBMS_STANDARD	18,953	14,696	NO
SYS	PACKAGE BODY	DBMS_STANDARD	18,872	3,432	NO
KIS	PROCEDURE	RKA_INSERT	7,067	4,949	NO
HRIS	PACKAGE	HRS_PACKAGE	5,175	3,831	NO
HRIS	PACKAGE BODY	HRS_PACKAGE	5,157	36,455	NO
SYS	PACKAGE	DBMS_DESCRIBE	718	12,800	NO
HRIS	PROCEDURE	CHECK_APP_ALERT	683	3,763	NO
SYS	PACKAGE BODY	DBMS_DESCRIBE	350	9,880	NO

```
SYS       PACKAGE        DBMS_SESSION          234     3,351    NO
SYS       PACKAGE BODY   DBMS_SESSION           65     4,543    NO
GIANT     PROCEDURE      CREATE_SESSION_RECOR   62     7,147    NO
HRIS      PROCEDURE      INIT_APP_ALERT          6    10,802    NO
```

This is an easy way to tell the number of times a non-pinned stored procedure is swapped out of memory and required a reload. To effectively measure memory, two methods are recommended. The first is to regularly run the estat-bstat utility (usually located in ~/rdbms/admin/utlbstat.sql and utlestat.sql) to measure SGA consumption over a range of time. Another handy method is to write a snapdump utility to interrogate the SGA and note any exceptional information relating to the library cache. This would include the following measurements:

- Data dictionary hit ratio

- Library cache miss ratio

- Individual hit ratios for all namespaces

Also, be aware that the relevant parameter, **shared_pool_size**, is used for other objects besides stored procedures. This means that one parameter fits all, and Oracle offers no method for isolating the amount of storage allocated to any subset of the shared pool.

Listing 3.6 is a sample report for gathering information relating to **shared_pool_size**. As you can see, the data dictionary hit ratio is above 95 percent, and the library cache miss ratio is very low. However, you can see over 125,000 reloads in the SQL area namespace, which means the DBA might want to increase the **shared_pool_size**. When running this type of report, always remember statistics are gathered from startup, and the numbers could be skewed. For example, for a system that has been running for six months, the data dictionary hit ratio will be a running average over six months. Consequently, data from the **V$** structures is meaningless if you want to measure today's statistics.

Some DBAs run utlbstat.sql, wait one hour, and run utlestat.sql. This produces a report, shown in Listing 3.6, that shows the statistics over the elapsed time interval.

Listing 3.6   The generated report showing statistics.

```
=============================
DATA DICT HIT RATIO
=============================
```

(should be higher than 90 else increase shared_pool_size in init.ora)

Data Dict. Gets	Data Dict. cache misses	DATA DICT CACHE HIT RATIO
41,750,549	407,609	99

```
============================
LIBRARY CACHE MISS RATIO
============================
```

(If > 1 then increase the shared_pool_size in init.ora)

executions	Cache misses while executing	LIBRARY CACHE MISS RATIO
22,909,643	171,127	.0075

```
===========================
LIBRARY CACHE SECTION
===========================
```

hit ratio should be > 70, and pin ratio > 70 ...

NAMESPACE	Hit ratio	pin hit ratio	reloads
SQL AREA	84	94	125,885
TABLE/PROCEDURE	98	99	43,559
BODY	98	84	486
TRIGGER	98	97	1,145
INDEX	0	0	
CLUSTER	31	33	
OBJECT	100	100	
PIPE	99	99	52

Let's take a look Listing 3.7, which shows the SQL*Plus script used to generate the statistical report shown in Listing 3.6.

Listing 3.7 The script that generates the report shown in Listing 3.6.

```
PROMPT
PROMPT
PROMPT            ============================
PROMPT            DATA DICT HIT RATIO
PROMPT            ============================
PROMPT (should be higher than 90
PROMPT  else increase shared_pool_size in init.ora)
```

```
PROMPT
COLUMN "Data Dict. Gets"              FORMAT 999,999,999
COLUMN "Data Dict. cache misses"      FORMAT 999,999,999
SELECT sum(gets) "Data Dict. Gets",
       sum(getmisses) "Data Dict. cache misses",
       trunc((1-(sum(getmisses)/sum(gets)))*100)
       "DATA DICT CACHE HIT RATIO"
FROM V$ROWCACHE;

PROMPT
PROMPT             ==============================
PROMPT             LIBRARY CACHE MISS RATIO
PROMPT             ==============================
PROMPT (If > 1 then increase the shared_pool_size in init.ora)
PROMPT
COLUMN "LIBRARY CACHE MISS RATIO"        FORMAT 99.9999
COLUMN "executions"                      FORMAT 999,999,999
COLUMN "Cache misses while executing"    FORMAT 999,999,999
SELECT sum(pins) "executions", sum(reloads)
                "Cache misses while executing",
    (((sum(reloads)/sum(pins)))) "LIBRARY CACHE MISS RATIO"
FROM V$LIBRARYCACHE;

PROMPT
PROMPT             ==============================
PROMPT             LIBRARY CACHE SECTION
PROMPT             ==============================
PROMPT hit ratio should be > 70, and pin ratio > 70 ...
PROMPT

COLUMN "reloads" FORMAT 999,999,999
SELECT namespace, trunc(gethitratio * 100)
       "Hit ratio",
trunc(pinhitratio * 100) "pin hit ratio",
       reloads "reloads"
FROM V$LIBRARYCACHE;
```

Just as the wisdom of the 1980s dictated that data should be centralized, the 1990s is an era where SQL is centralized and managed. With the centralization of SQL, many previously impossible tasks have become trivial. For instance:

- SQL can easily be identified and reused.

- SQL can be extracted by a DBA, allowing the DBA to run **EXPLAIN PLAN** utilities to determine the proper placement of table indexes.

- SQL can be searched, allowing for fast identification of "where used" information. For example, when a column changes definition, all SQL referencing that column can be quickly identified.

As memory becomes less expensive, it will eventually become desirable to have all of an application's SQL and code loaded into the Oracle library cache. In this way, code will be quickly available for execution by any external applications regardless of its platform or host language. The most compelling reasons to put SQL within packages are portability and code management. If applications become "SQL-less" with calls to stored procedures, then entire applications can be ported to other platforms without touching a single line of the application code.

As the cost of memory drops, 500MB Oracle regions will not be uncommon. Until that time, however, the DBA must carefully consider the ramifications of pinning a package in the SGA.

Whenever there are behaviors that are directly tied to DML events, such as inserts into a table, an Oracle trigger can be used. Triggers, just like stored procedures, contain PL/SQL, but a trigger is tightly coupled with an SQL operation on a specific table.

Triggers

Many database systems now support the use of *triggers* that can be fired at specific events. The insertion, modification, or deletion of a record can fire a trigger, or business events, such as **place_order**, can initiate a trigger. Oracle Corporation claims that the design of its triggers closely follows the ANSI/ISO SQL3 draft standard (ANSI X3H6), but Oracle triggers are more robust in functionality than the ANSI standard. Triggers are defined at the schema level of the system, and they will "fire" whenever an SQL **UPDATE**, **DELETE**, or **INSERT** command is issued. Remember, a trigger is always associated with a single DML event.

The choice of when to use a trigger and when to use a stored procedure can have a profound impact on the performance of a system.

Deciding When To Use A Trigger

In general, triggers are used when additional processing is required as a row is inserted into a table. For example, assume that whenever a **customer** row is added, the system is required to look for the customer in the **BAD_CREDIT** table. If the customer appears in the **BAD_CREDIT** table, then its **shipping_status** column is set to **COD**. In this case, a trigger on **INSERT OF CUSTOMER** can fire the PL/SQL procedure to do the necessary lookup and set the **shipping_status** field to its appropriate value.

Oracle triggers have the ability to call procedures, and triggers can include SQL statements. This combination provides the ability to nest SQL statements. Oracle triggers are stored as procedures that can be parameterized and used to simulate object-oriented behavior.

As we can see from Figure 3.3, there will be cases where a single process may be associated with several SQL events, and the trick is to "map" the behavior to the appropriate tables. For example, we see that the **compute_order_total** process selects appropriate rows from the **LINE_ITEMS** table, and then updates the **ORDER** table to reflect the total amount of the order.

For example, assume you want to perform a behavior called **CHECK_TOTAL_INVENTORY** whenever an item is added to an order. The trigger definition would be:

```
CREATE TRIGGER CHECK_TOTAL_INVENTORY
          BEFORE INSERT OF LINE_ITEM
FOR EACH ROW LOOP
    ......
IF :count < ITEM.TOTAL THEN
    ......
END IF;
```

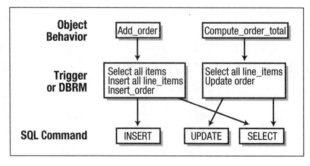

Figure 3.3
The relationships among objects, triggers, and SQL.

Triggers can be combined to handle multiple events, such as the reordering of an **ITEM** when the quantity on hand falls below a predefined level, as follows:

```
CREATE TRIGGER REORDER BEFORE UPDATE ON ITEM
    FOR EACH ROW WHEN (new.reorderable = 'Y')
        BEGIN
                IF new.qty_on_hand + old.qty_on_order < new.minimum_qty
                THEN
                        INSERT INTO REORDER VALUES (item_nbr,
                        reorder_qty);
                        new.qty_on_order := old.qty_on_order +
                        reorder_qty;
                END IF;
END;
```

Now that we understand triggers and stored procedures, we can take a look at some of the more advanced performance features. These include the design for Oracle clusters and hash clusters, which can radically improve Oracle database performance.

Clusters

Clustering is a very important concept for improving client/server performance. When traversing a database, reducing I/O always improves throughput. The concept of clustering is very similar to the use of the **VIA** set in the CODASYL Network database model, where member records are stored physically near their parent records. For Oracle, clusters can be used to define common one-to-many access paths, and the member rows can be stored on the same database block as their owner row. For example, assume you have a one-to-many relationship between customers and orders. If your application commonly accesses the data from customer to order, you can cluster the order rows on the same database block as the customer row. In this way, you'll receive the list of all orders for a customer in a single I/O. (See Figure 3.4.) Of course, you'll need to size the database blocks with **db_block_size** so that an entire order will fit onto a single database block. For more information on **db_block_size**, refer to Chapter 7, *Oracle DBA Performance And Tuning*.

You should note one important issue, however: While a cluster tremendously improves performance in one direction, queries in the other direction will suffer. Consider the many-to-many relationship between customers and orders. In addition, let's say you have a junction table, **ORDER_LINE**, at the intersection of this many-to-many

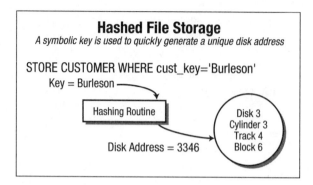

Figure 3.4
A sample Oracle cluster.

relationship and you need to decide which owner, **ORDER** or **ITEM**, will be the anchor for your cluster. If you commonly traverse from **ORDER** to **ITEM** (e.g., displaying an order form), it would make sense to cluster the **ORDER_LINE** records on the same database block as their **ORDER** owner. If, on the other hand, you commonly traverse from **ITEM** to **ORDER** (e.g., requesting the details for all orders containing widgets), you would cluster the **ORDER_LINE** rows near their **ITEM** owner. If you cluster on the **ORDER** owner, database queries that display order forms will be very fast, while queries in the other direction will have to perform additional I/O.

Many Oracle neophytes do not understand the difference between Oracle clusters and Oracle hash clusters. The following section describes these differences and shows how hash clusters are used to improved performance.

Hash Clusters

Starting with Oracle7, Oracle has supported the concept of hash clusters. A *hash cluster* is a construct that works with Oracle clusters and uses the **HASHKEYS** command to allow fast access to the primary key for the cluster. Oracle relies on a *hashing algorithm*, which takes a symbolic key and converts it into a **ROWID**. The hashing function ensures that the cluster key is retrieved in a single I/O, which is faster than reading multiple blocks from an index tree. Because a hashing algorithm always produces the same key each time it reads an input value, duplicate keys have to be avoided. In Oracle, these "collisions" result when the value of **HASHKEYS** is less than the maximum number of cluster key values. For example, if a hash cluster uses the **customer_nbr** field as the key, and you know there will be 50,000 unique

customer_nbr values, then you must be sure that the value of **HASHKEYS** is set to at least 50,000. Also, you should always round up your value for **HASHKEYS** to the next highest prime number. Here is an example of a hash cluster:

```
CREATE CLUSTER my_cluster (customer_nbr    varchar(10))
    TABLESPACE user1
        STORAGE (INITIAL 50K NEXT 50K PCTINCREASE 1)
        SIZE 2K
        HASH IS customer_nbr HASHKEYS 50000;
```

Now, a table can be defined within the cluster:

```
CREATE TABLE CUSTOMER (
        customer_nbr  number primary key )
CLUSTER my_cluster (customer_nbr);
```

The **SIZE** parameter is usually set to the average row size for the table. Oracle recommends the following guidelines when using hash clusters:

- Use hash clusters to store tables commonly accessed by **WHERE** clauses that specify equalities.

- Only use hash clusters when you can afford to keep plenty of free space on each database block for updates. This value is set by the **PCTFREE** statement in the **CREATE TABLE** parameter.

- Only use hash clusters if you are absolutely sure that you will not need to create a new, larger cluster at a later time.

- Do not use a hash cluster if your table is commonly accessed by full-table scans, especially if a great deal of extra space from future growth has been allocated to the hash cluster. In a full-table scan, Oracle will read all blocks of the hash cluster, regardless of whether or not they contain any data rows.

- Do not use a hash cluster if any of the hash cluster keys are frequently modified. Changing the value of a hash key causes the hashing algorithm to generate a new location, and the database will migrate the cluster to a new database block if the key value is changed. This is a very time-consuming operation.

Keep in mind that the total size of the index columns must fit inside a single Oracle block. If the index contains too many long values, additional I/O will be required, and **UPDATE**s and **INSERT**s will cause serious performance problems. Note the sample hashing routine shown in Figure 3.5.

When using Oracle hash clusters, you can choose to make buffer blocks large to minimize I/O if your application clusters records on a database page. If a customer record is only 100 bytes, you will not gain by retrieving 32,000 bytes in order to get the 100 bytes you need. However, if you cluster the orders physically near the customer (on the same database page), and if I/O usually proceeds from customer to order, then you won't need further I/O to retrieve orders for the customer. They will already reside in the initial read of 32,000 bytes.

Now that we have covered Oracle clusters, we can take a look at some of the new parallel features of Oracle. We will begin by taking a look at Oracle's parallel query facility.

Parallel Query

One of the more exciting performance features of Oracle8 was actually introduced in Oracle7.3. The performance feature I'm talking about is the ability to partition an SQL query into subqueries and dedicate separate processors to concurrently service each subquery. At this time, parallel query is only useful for queries that perform full-table scans on long tables, but the performance improvements can be dramatic. Here's how it works.

Instead of having a single query server manage the I/O against a table, parallel query allows the Oracle query server to dedicate many processors to simultaneously access the data, as shown in Figure 3.6.

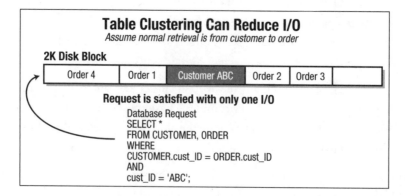

Figure 3.5
A sample hashing routine.

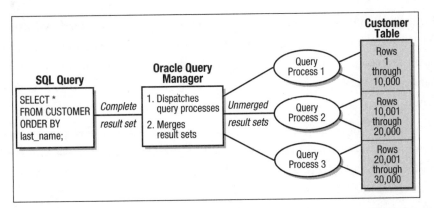

Figure 3.6
A sample parallel query.

In order to be most effective, the table should be partitioned onto separate disk devices, such that each process can do I/O against its segment of the table without interfering with the other simultaneous query processes. However, the client/server environment of the 1990s relies on RAID or a logical volume manager (LVM), which scrambles data files across disk packs in order to balance the I/O load. Consequently, full utilization of parallel query involves *striping* a table across numerous data files, each on a separate device.

Even if your system uses RAID or LVM, some performance gains are still available with parallel query. In addition to using multiple processes to retrieve a table, a query manager can also dedicate numerous processes to simultaneously sort a result set. (See Figure 3.7.)

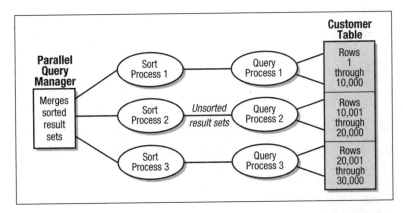

Figure 3.7
A sample parallel sort.

However, parallel query works best with symmetric multiprocessor (SMP) boxes, which have more than one internal CPU. Also, it is important to configure the system to maximize the I/O bandwidth, either through disk striping or high-speed channels. Because of the parallel sorting feature, it is also a good idea to beef up the memory on a processor.

While sorting is no substitute for using a presorted index, the parallel query manager services requests far faster than a single process. While the data retrieval will not be significantly faster because all of the retrieval processes are competing for a channel on the same disk, each sort process has its own sort area (as determined by the **sort_area_size** init.ora parameter), which speeds along the sorting of the result set. In addition to full-table scans and sorting, the parallel query option also allows for parallel processes for merge joins and nested loops.

Invoking the parallel query option requires that all indexing is bypassed. Hence, the most important consideration is that the execution plan for the SQL query specifies a full-table scan. If the output of the explain plan does not indicate a full-table scan, the query can be forced to ignore the index by using query hints or adding built-in functions to items in the **WHERE** clause of the SQL.

The number of processors dedicated to servicing an SQL request is ultimately determined by Oracle's query manager, but the programmer can specify the upper limit on the number of simultaneous processes. When using the cost-based optimizer, the **PARALLEL** hint can be embedded into the SQL to specify the number of processes. For example:

```
SELECT /*+ FULL(EMPLOYEE_TABLE) PARALLEL(EMPLOYEE_TABLE,  4) */
       employee_name
       FROM
       EMPLOYEE_TABLE
       WHERE
       emp_type = 'SALARIED';
```

If you are using SMP with many CPUs, you can issue a parallel request and leave it up to each Oracle instance to use their default degree of parallelism. For example:

```
SELECT /*+ FULL(EMPLOYEE_TABLE)
       PARALLEL(EMPLOYEE_TABLE,  DEFAULT, DEFAULT) */
       employee_name
       FROM
```

```
EMPLOYEE_TABLE
WHERE
emp_type = 'SALARIED';
```

Several important init.ora parameters have a direct impact on parallel query, including the following:

- **sort_area_size**—The higher the value, the more memory available for individual sorts on each parallel process. Note that the **sort_area_size** parameter allocates memory for every query on the system that invokes a sort. For example, if a single query needs more memory and you increase the **sort_area_size**, all Oracle tasks will allocate the new amount of sort area, regardless of whether or not they will use all of the space.

- **parallel_min_servers**—The minimum number of query servers that will be active on the instance. System resources are involved in starting a query server, so having the query server started and waiting for requests will speed up processing. Note that if the actual number of required servers is less than the value of **parallel_min_servers**, the idle query servers will be consuming unnecessary overhead, and the value should be decreased.

- **parallel_max_servers**—The maximum number of query servers allowed on the instance. This parameter will prevent Oracle from starting so many query servers that the instance is unable to service all of them properly.

To see how many parallel query servers are busy at any given time, the following query can be issued against the **V$PQ_SYSSTAT** table:

```
SELECT * FROM V$PQ_SYSSTAT
       WHERE STATISTIC = 'Servers Busy';


STATISTIC               VALUE
-------                 ------
Servers Busy            30
```

In this case, you can see that 30 parallel servers were busy at the moment the query was run. Do not be misled by this number. Parallel query servers are constantly accepting work or returning to idle status, so it is a good idea to issue the query many times over a one-hour period. Only then will you have a realistic measure of how many parallel query servers are being used.

Summary

This completes our discussion on Oracle8's physical design issues. Now, we can begin to look at tuning Oracle. Tuning is much more than guaranteeing that your applications have a good design. You must also ensure that Oracle has enough system resources to properly service your requests.

HIGH PERFORMANCE

Tuning The Oracle Architecture

CHAPTER

4

HIGH PERFORMANCE

Tuning The Oracle Architecture

A holistic approach to the tuning of the overall Oracle architecture is paramount to the development of effective client/server systems. Regardless of how slick and well-tuned the client performs, poor response time at the server level can cause an entire development effort to fail. Whether your server is private to your application or shared among many client applications, the optimal usage of Oracle resources can ensure that the system performs at an acceptable level. Topics in this chapter include:

- The Oracle architecture

- Oracle's internal structures

- Oracle memory

- I/O-based tuning

Before you can tune a system, you need to know what elements make up the system. So, let's start this chapter with a quick review of the fundamentals of Oracle's architecture. The Oracle architecture lays the foundation for understanding Oracle performance and tuning, since the architecture determines how Oracle interacts with the operating environment.

The Oracle Architecture

Oracle is the world's leading relational database, continuing to dominate the marketplace for midrange computer platforms. Since Oracle's inception in 1971, it has evolved to the point where Oracle8 bears little resemblance to Oracle's original offering. While Oracle has many extensions, the base product consists of the following 26 components:

- *Con Text*—Allows access to text-based data stored in Oracle.

- *Designer-2000*—Allows a developer to maintain logical table definitions and create a physical model from the logical structure. This utility is part of the Oracle family of CASE tools.

- *Developer-2000*—Provides for the generation of forms reports and 3GL code based on the inputs to Designer-2000.

- *Enterprise Backup*—Provides automated backup and recovery options for Oracle.

- *Enterprise Manager*—Provides the capability to manage multiple instances across your entire enterprise.

- *Express*—Oracle Express is a multidimensional database for supporting data warehouses and online analytical processing (OLAP). This product has yet to be integrated with the standard Oracle engine, and communications with relational databases are usually accomplished either by extracting data from Oracle8 and loading it into Oracle Express (OLAP) or extracting and aggregating the relational data in realtime (ROLAP).

- *Import/Export*—Allows a developer to dump table data into a flat file and allows the flat file to be restored to the database.

- *ORA*Reports*—Serves as Oracle's standard report writer. This report writer is GUI based and includes menuing.

- *Oracle*Graphics*—Allows the graphic representation of query results.

- *PL/SQL*—Provides Oracle's proprietary implementation of the ANSI SQL standard. PL/SQL can be used within Oracle applications tools, called SQL*Forms, or embedded into remote tools, such as C programs or PC GUIs. A fully functional programming language by itself, PL/SQL adds extensions to the SQL to allow sophisticated processing.

- *Precompilers*—Provides an interface to most major 3GL languages.

- *Procedure Builder*—Provides an easy-to-use interface for the development of Oracle procedures.

- *RDBMS Kernel*—Serves as the database engine—the workhorse of Oracle.

- *Server Manager*—Serves as the visual reporting component for Oracle. Server Manager provides a graphical interface to online reports that give fast, visual access to a database. Server Manager can be run with Windows using Oracle SQL*Net for communications to the database, or it can be run on the individual server using Motif.

- *SQL*DBA*—Provides an interface to Oracle for a database administrator. SQL*DBA allows a DBA to create databases, tablespaces, tables, clusters, indexes, and a sundry of other Oracle constructs.

- *SQL*Forms*—Serves as an online system generator that allows easy access to data, reports, and procedures.

- *SQL*Loader*—Allows delimited flat files to be loaded into Oracle tables. For example, an extract from a DB2 database could be created with commas delimiting each table column. Then, SQL*Loader could be used to import this flat file into an Oracle table.

- *SQL*Menu*—Serves as the menu builder for Oracle, allowing individual SQL*Forms screens to be linked together.

- *SQL*Net*—Serves as the communications protocol that allows remote database servers to communicate with each other. SQL*Net is described extensively in Chapter 8.

- *SQL*Plus*—Provides an online interface to the Oracle database. Like SPUFI for DB2 and IDD for CA-IDMS, SQL*Plus is used to allow ad hoc queries and updates to be issued against a database.

- *SQL*Report*—Serves as Oracle's first report writer language.

- *Structured Query Language (SQL)*—SQL is the common data access and update language for relational databases.

- *SVRMGR*—Serves as Oracle's replacement tool for SQL*DBA.

- *System Global Area (SGA)*—Creates the in-memory region for all of the Oracle buffers and caches. The SGA is created when Oracle is started.

- *Video Server*—Allows for the storage and management of video clips.

- *WebServer*—Allows Web pages to interface with Oracle databases and developer tools.

As you can see, Oracle8 offers a wealth of products and tools to serve the data management market. Now that we've looked at the basic Oracle products, let's move on to the individual process components of a running Oracle system.

When a running Oracle instance is viewed from the operating system, you can see that it consists of numerous programs that continue to run until the database is shut down. These programs are called *background processes*, and there are new background processes for Oracle8 that weren't around in Oracle7. Table 4.1 displays Oracle's background processes (background processes new to Oracle8 are denoted with asterisks). The background processes run as separate processes inside the operating system and appear to the operating system as programs that are executing.

Table 4.1   Oracle's background processes.

Feature	Process	Description
Advanced Queuing*	Aq_tn*xx*	These are the Oracle8 advanced queuing processes used to thread processes through the Oracle8 instance.
Archive Monitor	ARCHMON	This is a process on Unix that monitors the archive process and writes the redo logs to the archives.
Archiver Process	ARCH	This process is only active if archive logging is in effect. This process writes the redo log data files tha are filled into the archive log data files.
Callout Queues*	EXTPROC	There will be one callout queue for each session performing callouts. It was hoped that Oracle8 would multithread these processes, but this feature remains "in the works" for multithreaded environments. As of Oracle8.0.2 beta, callout queues were not working with environments where a multithreaded server was enabled.
Checkpoint Processes	CKP*xx*	These are the checkpoint processes that can be started to optimize the checkpoint operation for Oracle logging.
Database Writer	DBWR	This process handles data transfer from the buffers in the SGA to the database files.
Dispatcher	D*nnn*	This process allows multiple processes to share a finite number of Oracle servers. It queues and routes process requests to the next available server.

(continued)

Table 4.1   Oracle's background processes *(continued)*.

Feature	Process	Description
Distributed Recoverer	RICO	This is an Oracle process that resolves failures involving distributed transactions.
Listener (SQL*Net v1)	ORASRV	If you are running SQL*Net version 1, this process will be running to service **TWO_TASK** requests.
Listener (SQL*Net v2)	TNSLSNR	If you are running TCP/IP, this process, known as the TNS listener process, will be running.
Lock Processes	LCK*n*	These processes are used for interinstance locking in an Oracle Parallel Server environment.
Log Writer	LGWR	This process transfers data from the redo log buffers to the redo log database files.
Process Monitor	PMON	This process recovers user processes that have failed and cleans up the cache. This process also recovers the resources from a failed process.
Server	S*nnn*	This process makes all the required calls to the database to resolve user requests. It returns results to the D*nnn* process that calls it.
Snapshot Queues*	Snp*xx*	These are snapshot process queues.
System Monitor	SMON	This process performs instance recovery on instance startup and is responsible for cleaning up temporary segments. In a parallel environment, this process recovers failed nodes.

* Denotes the background process is new for Oracle8.

Now that we have reviewed Oracle's major products and processes, let's take a look at the internal structures that make up an Oracle instance.

Oracle's Internal Structures

When Oracle is started, a region of memory is configured according to the initialization parameters. Oracle initialization is governed by a file called the init.ora file. In

Oracle7, there was a second file called config.ora, but these two files have been combined in Oracle8. The init.ora file tells the database software how to configure the system global area (SGA), which is the term used to describe a running Oracle. The init.ora file may be made to contain all of the necessary information to start an Oracle instance.

Because the SGA resides within an operating system, it is dependent upon the operating environment (see Figure 4.1). In Unix, Oracle must share memory space with many other memory regions, competing for the limited memory and processing resources. As shown in Figure 4.2, we see that the Oracle instance occupies an area of memory (the SGA), while external Oracle applications, also in a memory space, communicate with Oracle to service their data needs.

The SGA consists of the following main components, each of which is configured at database startup time:

- Buffer cache

- Log buffer

- Shared pool and large pool

- Program Global Areas (PGAs)

- The in-memory **V$** tables

In addition, Oracle's internal structure includes the use of **V$** tables. In the next few sections, we'll look at each component of the SGA.

Buffer Cache

The buffer cache is the in-memory area of the SGA where incoming Oracle data blocks are kept. On standard Unix databases, the data is read from disk into the Unix buffer where it is then transferred into the Oracle buffer. The size of the buffer cache can have a huge impact on Oracle system performance; the larger the buffer cache, the greater the likelihood that data from a prior transaction will reside in the buffer, thereby avoiding a physical disk I/O. At the internal level, each Oracle instance has predefined interfaces to the hardware to allow it to communicate with the physical devices. Being a database software product, Oracle must be able to communicate with disk devices and CD-ROMs, retrieving and storing information from these devices. When the DBA defines a tablespace, a physical data file is associated with the

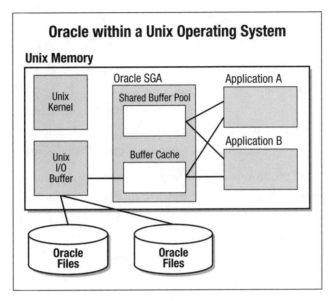

Figure 4.1
A sample Oracle instance in Unix.

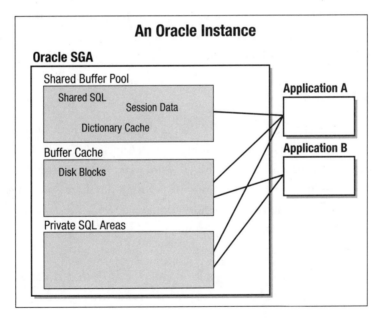

Figure 4.2
The relationships between Oracle and applications.

tablespace, and Oracle will manage the addressing to this file. In other words, Oracle manages all of the mapping of the logical tablespaces to the physical data files.

The configuration of the SGA is critical to designing high-performance client/server applications. The sizes allocated to the program pool and the buffer pools have a direct impact on the speed at which Oracle retrieves information. Remember, most business applications are I/O bound—the single greatest delay being the time required to access data from disk. As such, tuning for I/O becomes a critical consideration.

An Oracle instance contains several buffer areas, including a buffer area for the redo logs and the database buffer for incoming Oracle data. The single most important component for tuning an Oracle database is the size of the database buffer. The database buffer is where Oracle holds blocks that have already been retrieved by a prior database request. Whenever a new request for data is made, Oracle will first check this buffer. If the block is in memory, Oracle can deliver the block to the user 10,000 times faster than if Oracle had to perform an I/O to go to the external disk for information. Access time on disks now reaches impressive speeds—between 10 and 25 milliseconds. However, data that already resides in the RAM area of Oracle SGA can be retrieved in nanoseconds. The parameter controlling the size of the buffer is called **db_block_buffers** and is one of the parameters in the init.ora file. We'll talk more about **db_block_buffers** later in this chapter.

Shared Pool

The second important region of the SGA is the shared pool, which stores a number of subareas. One of the confounding problems with Oracle is that all of these subareas are sized by only one parameter: **shared_pool_size**. It is impossible to dedicate separate regions of memory for the components within the shared pool. The shared pool is normally the second largest memory component within the SGA, depending upon the size of the **db_block_size** parameter. The shared pool holds memory for the following purposes:

- *Library Cache*—Stores the plan information for SQL that is currently being executed. This area also holds stored procedures and trigger code.

- *Dictionary Cache*—Stores environmental information, including referential integrity, table definitions, indexing information, and other metadata stored within Oracle's internal tables.

- *Session Information*—Stores session information for systems that are using SQL*Net version 2 with Oracle's multithreaded server. See Chapter 8 for details on using the multithreaded server.

The Oracle multithreaded server (MTS) is also important to the tuning of **shared_pool_size**. When using the MTS, it is possible to define a new parameter called **large_pool_size** in the init.ora file. The **large_pool_size** parameter defines a storage area for the exclusive use of Oracle sorting. Without the MTS, all Oracle sorting is done in the **shared_pool_size** region of memory and this can often cause conflicts with other objects in the shared pool, especially when heavy sorting of data is taking place. With the MTS and the **large_pool_size** defined, we have segregated the sort area into a separate memory buffer, giving the Oracle DBA more control over the memory allocation.

We'll talk more about the shared pool later in this chapter in the section entitled *Tuning The Shared Pool Size*.

PGA

The SGA is not the only memory structure used by Oracle. Each application that accesses Oracle receives a *program global area*, or PGA. The PGA contains private SQL areas that are used by individual programs to hold application-specific database information. A private SQL area can store the current values of cursors and other program-dependent information.

Oracle Metadata—The V$ Structures

V$** tables are internal structures built into memory when an Oracle instance is started. Although they appear to be tables, they are really internal memory structures implemented in the C language. Therefore, **V$ tables only exist during the execution of an instance and are destroyed at shutdown. **V$** tables are used by Oracle to capture information about the overall status of a database, and information from **V$** tables can provide tremendous insight into the internal operations of an Oracle database. While dozens of **V$** tables exist, only a handful can be used for Oracle performance and tuning. Instead of offering an exhaustive list of all the Oracle **V$** tables, this text includes only relevant queries against **V$** tables.

V$** tables have limited use for measuring time-dependent information because they accumulate information from the moment an Oracle instance is started up until the present time. As such, measurements such as the buffer hit ratio are normalized, presenting only the average for the entire time the instance has been running. Now that we understand the purpose of the **V$ structures, let's take a closer look at the other things that are found inside Oracle's memory region.

Oracle Memory

The memory size of the SGA is commonly called the Oracle region. The way Oracle memory is managed can have a huge impact on performance, and each SGA can be tuned according to the needs of the application. However, you must remember that the SGA faces dynamic forces, and one transaction can cause problems for other transactions accessing Oracle. Hundreds of transactions can be serviced concurrently, each requesting different data. Tuning the memory for the activity at one point in time might not be suitable for another time. Because of the dynamic nature of Oracle databases, only general tuning is possible.

This general approach works well because of Oracle's high level of sophistication. Tuning Oracle's memory involves a number of parameters and features, including:

- Sizing the SGA

- Tuning the Oracle PGA

- Tuning Oracle sorting

- Tuning the data buffer

- Tuning the shared pool and large pool sizes

- Tuning memory cache

- Simulating pinned database rows

- Batch processing Oracle instances

We'll take a look at each of these memory elements in the upcoming sections. The first task of the Oracle DBA is to determine the appropriate size for the Oracle instance. While only the **db_block_size**, **log_buffer**, **large_pool_size**, and **shared_pool_size** have an impact on the size of the SGA, there are dozens of other Oracle parameters that influence the performance of the Oracle instance.

Sizing The SGA

The init.ora file not only determines the overall size of the SGA, but also which Oracle constructs get a specified amount of memory. Oracle8 contains 184 initialization parameters.

To see the size of the SGA, you can issue the **show SGA** command from SQL*DBA. The output of the **show SGA** command appears below:

```
SQLDBA> show sga

Total System Global Area         8252756 bytes
Fixed Size                       48260 bytes
Variable Size                    6533328 bytes
Database Buffers                 1638400 bytes
Redo Buffers                     32768 bytes
```

Fortunately, only the following five parameters are of paramount importance to the overall performance of Oracle, although there are other important parameters that influence performance:

- **db_block_buffers**—This parameter determines the number of database block buffers in the Oracle SGA and represents the single most important parameter to Oracle memory.

- **db_block_size**—The size of the database blocks can make a huge improvement in performance. While the default value is 2,048 bytes, databases that have large tables with full-table scans will see a tremendous improvement in performance by increasing **db_block_size** to a larger value.

- **log_buffer**—This parameter determines the amount of memory to allocate for Oracle's redo log buffers. If there is a high amount of update activity, the **log_buffer** should be allocated more space.

- **shared_pool_size**—This parameter defines the pool that is shared by all users in the system, including SQL areas and data dictionary caching.

- **large_pool_size**—This parameter defines a memory pool that is used exclusively for Oracle sorting. It is only valid when the multithreaded server is defined, but it has a great impact on shared memory usage because it segregates Oracle sorting memory from the memory for the SQL areas and data dictionary cache.

Note: For more information on tuning with the init.ora parameters, see Chapter 7, Oracle DBA Performance And Tuning.

Now that we have reviewed the Oracle initialization par ameters, let's take a look at how the Oracle PGA interacts with the Oracle instance and how the PGA can be tuned.

Tuning The Oracle PGA

As mentioned earlier, the SGA is not the only memory area available to programs. The PGA is a private memory area allocated to external tasks. The PGA is used for keeping application-specific information, such as the values of cursors, and allocating memory for internal sorting of result sets from SQL queries. The following two init.ora parameters influence the size of the PGA:

- **open_links**—This parameter defines the maximum number of concurrent remote sessions that a process can initiate. Oracle's default is four, meaning that a single SQL statement can reference up to four remote databases within the query.

- **sort_area_size**—This defines the maximum amount of PGA memory that can be used for disk sorts. For very large sorts, Oracle will sort data in its temporary tablespace, and the **sort_area_size** memory will be used to manage the sorting process. When using the multithreaded server, the sort area will be taken from another memory pool, as defined by the **large_pool_size** parameter.

In addition to the SGA and PGA, Oracle must provide resources for sorting intermediate and result sets from Oracle queries. SQL operations such as **JOIN, ORDER BY**, and **GROUP BY** clauses may invoke Oracle sorting, and memory must be devoted for Oracle to perform this task.

Tuning Oracle Sorting

As a small but very important component of SQL syntax, sorting is a frequently overlooked aspect of Oracle tuning. In general, an Oracle database will automatically perform sorting operations on row data as requested by a **CREATE INDEX** or an SQL **ORDER BY** or **GROUP BY** statement. In Oracle, sorting occurs under the following circumstances:

- Using the **ORDER BY** clause in SQL

- Using the **GROUP BY** clause in SQL

- When an index is created

- When a **MERGE SORT** is invoked by the SQL optimizer because inadequate indexes exist for a table join

At the time a session is established with Oracle, a private sort area is allocated in memory for use by the session for sorting. Unfortunately, the amount of memory must be the same for all sessions—it is not possible to add additional sort areas for tasks that are sort intensive. Therefore, the designer must strike a balance between allocating enough sort area to avoid disk sorts for the large sorting tasks, keeping in mind that the extra sort area will be allocated and not used by tasks that do not require intensive sorting.

The size of the private sort area is determined by the **sort_area_size** init.ora parameter. The size for each individual sort is specified by the **sort_area_retained_size** init.ora parameter. Whenever a sort cannot be completed within the assigned space, a disk sort is invoked using the temporary tablespace for the Oracle instance. As a general rule, only index creation and **ORDER BY** clauses using functions should be allowed to use a disk sort.

Disk sorts are expensive for several reasons. First, they consume resources in the temporary tablespaces. Oracle must also allocate buffer pool blocks to hold the blocks in the temporary tablespace. In-memory sorts are always preferable to disk sorts, and disk sorts will surely slow down an individual task, as well as impact concurrent tasks on the Oracle instance. Also, excessive disk sorting will cause a high value for free buffer waits, paging other tasks' data blocks out of the buffer. You can see the amount of disk and in-memory sorts by issuing the following query against the **V$SYSSTAT** table:

```
sorts.sql - displays in-memory and disk sorts
SPOOL /tmp/sorts
COLUMN VALUE FORMAT 999,999,999
SELECT NAME, VALUE FROM V$SYSSTAT
  WHERE NAME LIKE 'sort%';
SPOOL OFF;
```

Here is the output:

```
SQL> @sorts

NAME                        VALUE
----                        -----
sorts (memory)              7,019
sorts (disk)                   49
sorts (rows)            3,288,608
```

Here, you can see that there were 49 sorts to disk. Out of a total of 7,019 memory sorts, this is well below 1 percent and is probably acceptable for the system.

The value "sorts (memory)" is the total number of in-memory sorts, and this value can be compared to the number of disk sorts to see the percentage of overall sorts that were too large to be done in memory.

> **Note:** *For tips on avoiding disk sorts, see Chapter 5,* Tuning Oracle SQL, *where we'll take a look at specific techniques for ensuring in-memory sorts.*

Oracle version 7.2 added several new parameters to the init.ora file for use in allocating a new in-memory sort area, including **sort_write_buffer_size**, **sort_write_buffers**, and **sort_direct_writes**. The **sort_write_buffer_size** parameter defines the size of the in-memory sort area, and the **sort_write_buffers** defines the number of buffer blocks. You must also set the parameter **sort_direct_writes=true** to use the disk sort area feature. Setting this parameter will allows disk sorts in the temporary tablespace to use a direct write buffer area. Writing sorts to this buffer bypasses the need for the sort to contend for free blocks in the buffer cache, thereby improving sorting performance by up to 50 percent. Of course, this is done at the expense of additional memory with the SGA. This movement towards segmenting the buffer into individual components can dramatically improve response times in Oracle. The size of **sort_write_buffers** × **sort_write_buffer_size** should not be more than 1/10th the size allocated in **sort_area_size**.

At the risk of being redundant, let me emphasize again that the single most important factor in the performance of an Oracle database is the minimization of disk I/O. Hence, the tuning of the Oracle data buffer remains one of the most important considerations in the tuning of any Oracle database. Let's explore some of the tuning issues.

Tuning The Data Buffer

When a request is made to Oracle to retrieve data, Oracle will first check the internal memory structures to see if the data is already in the buffer. In this fashion, Oracle avoids doing unnecessary I/O. It would be ideal if you could create one buffer for each database page, ensuring that Oracle would read each block only once. However, the costs of memory in the real world makes this prohibitive.

At best, you can only allocate a small number of real-memory buffers, and Oracle will manage this memory for you. Oracle utilizes a least-recently-used algorithm to determine which database pages are to be flushed from memory. Another related memory issue emerges that deals with the size of the database blocks. In most Unix environments, database blocks are sized to only 2K. Unlike the mainframe ancestors that allowed blocks of up to 16,000 bytes, large Unix blocks are not always desirable because of the way Unix handles its page I/O. Remember, I/O is the single most important slowdown in a client/server system, and the more relevant the data that can be grabbed in a single I/O, the better the performance. The cost of reading a 2K block is not significantly higher than the cost of reading an 8K block. However, the 8K block read will be of no benefit if you only want a small row in a single table. On the other hand, if the tables are commonly read front-to-back, or if you make appropriate use of Oracle clusters (as described in Chapter 3), you can reap dramatic performance improvements by switching to large block sizes.

For batch-oriented reporting databases, very large block sizes are always recommended. However, many databases are used for online transaction processing during the day, while the batch reports are run in the evenings. Nevertheless, as a general rule, 8K block sizes will benefit most systems.

Fortunately, Oracle allows for large block sizes, and the **db_block_size** parameter is used to control the physical block size of the data files. Unlike other relational databases, Oracle allocates the data files on your behalf when the **CREATE TABLESPACE** command is issued. One of the worst things that can happen to a buffer cache is the running of a full-table scan on a large table.

In order to optimize performance, Oracle allows for several extensions to the basic parameters. One of the most important interactions is between the **db_block_size** parameter and **db_file_multiblock_read_count**.

Using The db_block_size Parameter With db_file_multiblock_read_count

As we'll discuss in Chapter 7, the **db_block_size** parameter can have a dramatic impact on system performance. In general, **db_block_size** should never be set to less than 8K, regardless of the type of application. Even online transaction processing systems (OLTP) will benefit from using 8K blocks, while systems that perform many full-table scans will benefit from even larger block sizes. Depending on the operating system, Oracle can support up to 16K block sizes. Systems that perform full-table scans can benefit from this approach.

In addition, note the relationship between **db_block_size** and the **db_file_multiblock_read_count** parameter. At the physical level in Unix, Oracle always reads in a minimum of 64K blocks. Therefore, the values of **db_file_multiblock_read_count** and **db_block_size** should be set such that their product is 64K. For example:

```
8K blocks     db_block_size=8192     db_file_multiblock_read_count=8
16K blocks    db_block_size=16384    db_file_multiblock_read_count=4
```

Note that the block size for Oracle is not immutable. Eventually, all small Oracle databases should be compressed (export/import) to reduce fragmentation. At that point, it becomes trivial to alter the value of **db_block_size**. Of course, very large databases cannot easily be re-created through an export since it may take days to complete. Hence, predetermining the **db_block_size** for very large Oracle databases is very important.

Remember, increasing the size of **db_block_size** will increase the size of the Oracle SGA. The values of **db_block_size** are multiplied by the value of **db_block_buffers** to determine the total amount of memory to allocate for Oracle's I/O buffers.

In order to make an intelligent decision about the optimal number of buffers to have in your data cache, Oracle provides a utility for predicting the benefit from adding more buffers. Remember, adding memory to the buffers will decrease the available pool of memory in your host for other programs, and this decision should always be given careful consideration.

Predicting The Benefit Of Additional Block Buffers

As database blocks are retrieved from disk into the database, they are stored in RAM memory in a buffer. The block remains in the buffer until it is overwritten by another database request. At read time, the database first checks to see if the data already resides in the buffer before incurring the overhead of a disk I/O (see Figure 4.3).

The size of the buffer is determined by the database administrator—and for some databases, separate buffers can be created for different tables. The method for maximizing the use of buffers is to perform a check on the *buffer hit ratio*. The buffer hit ratio is the ratio of logical requests to physical disk reads. A logical read is a request from a program for a record, while a physical read is real I/O against a database. A 1:1 correspondence does not always exist between logical and physical reads because some records might have been fetched by a previous task and still reside in the buffer. In other words, the buffer hit ratio is the probability of finding the desired record in the memory buffer. The equation for finding the buffer hit ratio is:

```
Hit Ratio = Logical Reads - Physical Reads / Logical Reads
```

Listings 4.1 and 4.2 show two scripts for calculating the buffer hit ratio.

Listing 4.1   Method 1: Calculating the buffer hit ratio.

```
buffer1.sql - displays the buffer hit ratio
PROMPT ***********************************************************
PROMPT  HIT RATIO SECTION
PROMPT ***********************************************************
PROMPT
PROMPT          ===========================
PROMPT          BUFFER HIT RATIO
PROMPT          ===========================
PROMPT (should be > 70, else increase db_block_buffers in init.ora)

SELECT trunc((1-(sum(decode(name,'physical reads',value,0))/
              (sum(decode(name,'db block gets',value,0))+
              (sum(decode(name,'consistent gets',value,0)))))
          )* 100) "Buffer Hit Ratio"
FROM V$SYSSTAT;
```

Listing 4.2   Method 2: Calculating the buffer hit ratio.

```
buffer2.sql - displays the buffer hit ratio

PROMPT ***********************************************************
PROMPT  HIT RATIO SECTION
```

```
PROMPT  *********************************************************
PROMPT
PROMPT            ==========================
PROMPT            BUFFER HIT RATIO
PROMPT            ==========================
PROMPT (should be > 70, else increase db_block_buffers in init.ora)

COLUMN "logical_reads" FORMAT 99,999,999,999
COLUMN "phys_reads"    FORMAT 999,999,999
COLUMN "phy_writes"    FORMAT 999,999,999
SELECT A.value + B.value   "logical_reads",
       C.value             "phys_reads",
       D.value             "phy_writes",
       round(100 * ((A.value+B.value)-C.value) / (A.value+B.value))
          "BUFFER HIT RATIO"
FROM V$SYSSTAT A, V$SYSSTAT B, V$SYSSTAT C, V$SYSSTAT D
WHERE
    A.statistic# = 37
AND
    B.statistic# = 38
AND
    C.statistic# = 39
AND
    D.statistic# = 40;
```

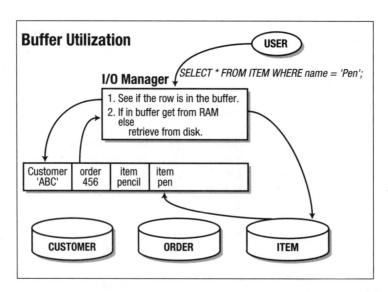

Figure 4.3
Oracle's data buffer operation.

Listing 4.3 shows the output from the second method.

Listing 4.3   Method 2 output.

```
SQL> @t3
************************************************************
HIT RATIO SECTION
************************************************************


===============================
BUFFER HIT RATIO
===============================
(should be > 70, else increase db_block_buffers in init.ora)

Fri Feb 23                                                    page    1
                            dbname Database
                       Data Dictionary Hit Ratios

    logical_reads    phys_reads       phy_writes    BUFFER HIT RATIO
    -------------    ----------       ----------    ----------------
     18,987,002       656,805           87,281             97

1 row selected.
```

Be aware that the buffer hit ratio (as gathered from the **V$** tables) measures the overall buffer hit ratio of the system since the Oracle instance was started. Because the **V$** tables keep their information forever, your current buffer hit ratio could be far worse than the 97 percent shown in Listing 4.3. To get a measure of the buffer hit ratio over a specific time period, use Oracle's bstat-estat utility, as described in Chapter 9.

While some mainframe databases allow individual buffers for each record type, midrange databases, such as Oracle, provide only one databasewide buffer for all database I/O. In general, the buffer hit ratio is a function of the application and size of the buffer pool. For example, an application with a very large customer table is not likely to benefit from an increase in buffers because the I/O is widely distributed across the tables. However, smaller applications will often see an improvement as the buffer size is increased because this also increases the probability that frequently requested data will remain in the buffer. For example, the high-level nodes of an index are generally used by all applications, and response time can be improved if these blocks can be kept in the buffers at all times. Oracle does allow small tables to be specified as cached when they are created.

Databases that allow segmented buffer pools (such as the CA-IDMS) can be configured such that small indexes will be kept in the buffer at all times. This is accomplished by allocating an index to a separate area and assigning the area to a separate buffer in the Device Media Control Language (DMCL). Oracle has a **_small _ table_ threshold** initialization value that allows specification of the size of tables (or indexes) to be cached in the buffer space, this is usually set to 10 percent of the total SGA size.

If the hit ratio is less then 70 percent (i.e., two-thirds of data requests require a physical disk I/O), you might want to increase the number of blocks in the buffer. In Oracle, a single buffer pool exists and is controlled by the **db_block_buffers** parameter in the init.ora process.

To estimate statistics, the following init.ora parameters must be set, and the database must be bounced:

```
db_block_lru_statistics = true
db_block_lru_extended_statistics = #buffers
```

#buffers is the number of buffers to add. Be aware that the SGA will increase in size by this amount, such that a value of 10,000 would increase an SGA by 80MB (assuming an 8K block size). Ensure that your host has enough memory before trying this. Also, note that performance will be degraded while these statistics are running. It is a good idea to choose a noncritical time for this test.

Oracle uses two system tables called **SYS.X$KCBRBH** (to track buffer hits) and **SYS.X$KCBCBH** (to track buffer misses). Note that these are temporary tables and must be interrogated before stopping Oracle. An SQL query can be formulated against the **SYS.X$KCBRBH** table to create a chart showing the size of the buffer pool and the expected buffer hits, as shown in Listing 4.4.

Listing 4.4   Creating a chart showing the buffer pool size.

```
REM morebuff.sql - predicts benefit from added blocks to the buffer

SET LINESIZE 100;
SET PAGES 999;
```

```
COLUMN "Additional Cache Hits" FORMAT 999,999,999;
COLUMN "Interval"              FORMAT a20;
 SELECT 250*trunc(indx/250)+1
                 ||' to '||250*(trunc(indx/250)+1) "Interval",
                   sum(count) "Additional Cache Hits"
FROM SYS.X$KCBRBH
GROUP BY trunc(indx/250);
```

The SQL in Listing 4.4 creates a result that shows the range of additional buffer blocks that can be added to the cache and the expected increase in cache hits. Listing 4.5 displays the results of running the SQL in Listing 4.4.

Listing 4.5 Results of the code in Listing 4.4.

```
SQL> @morebuff

Interval                Additional Cache Hits
--------                ---------------------
1 to 250                         60
251 to 500                       46
501 to 750                       52
751 to 1000                     162
1001 to 1250                    191
1251 to 1500                    232
1501 to 1750                    120
1751 to 2000                     95
2001 to 2250                     51
2251 to 2500                     37
2501 to 2750                     42
```

In Listing 4.5, you can see that the number of cache hits peaks at 232 with the addition of 1,500 buffer blocks. Additionally, you can see a decreasing marginal benefit from adding more buffers. This is very typical of online transaction processing databases in which the majority of end users frequently reference common information.

The following sample is from a database that primarily performs reports that invoke full-table scans:

```
SQL> @morebuff

Interval                Additional Cache Hits
--------                ---------------------
```

1 to 250	60
251 to 500	46
501 to 750	52
751 to 1000	62
1001 to 1250	51
1251 to 1500	24
1501 to 1750	28
1751 to 2000	35
2001 to 2250	31
2251 to 2500	37
2501 to 2750	42

Here, you can see no peak and no marginal trends with the addition of buffers. This is very typical of databases that read large tables front-to-back. Doing a full-table scan on a table that is larger than the buffer will cause the first table blocks to eventually page out as the last table rows are read. Consequently, there is no specific "optimal" setting for the **db_block_buffers** parameter.

As a general rule, all available memory on the host should be tuned, and Oracle should be given **db_block_buffers** up to a point of diminishing returns. There is a point where the addition of buffer blocks will not significantly improve the buffer hit ratio, and these tools give the Oracle DBA the ability to find the optimal amount of buffers.

The general rule is simple: As long as marginal gains can be achieved from adding buffers and you have the memory to spare, you should increase the value of **db_block_buffers**. Increases in buffer blocks increase the amount of required RAM memory for the database, and it is not always possible to "hog" all of the memory on a processor for the database management system. Therefore, a DBA should carefully review the amount of available memory and determine the optimal amount of buffer blocks.

If you overallocate SGA memory on a Unix system, such as with Oracle user's sign-on, the Unix kernel will begin to swap out chunks of active memory in order to accommodate the new users and cause a huge performance problem.

Today, many databases reside alone on a host. When this is the case, you can predict the amount of "spare" memory and run your Oracle SGA up to that amount. For example, assume you have a host machine with 350MB of available memory. The

Unix kernel consumes 50MB, leaving 300MB available for your Oracle database. Each online user will need to allocate a PGA when accessing the application, and the largest share of the PGA is determined by the value of the **sort_area_size** init.ora parameter. Therefore, assuming that you have a **sort_area_size** of 20MB and 10 online users, you can assume that about 200MB of real memory must be reserved for end user sessions, leaving 100MB for the Oracle SGA.

In many cases, you will see conditions where memory can be subtracted from the SGA without causing any serious performance hits. Oracle provides the **X$KCBCBH** table for this purpose, and you can query this table to track the number of buffer misses that would occur if the SGA was decreased in size, as shown in Listing 4.6.

Listing 4.6   Querying the **X$KCBCBH** table.

```
REM lessbuff.sql - predicts losses from subtracting db_block_buffer
REM values

SET LINESIZE 100;
SET PAGES 999;

COLUMN "Additional Cache Misses" FORMAT 999,999,999;
COLUMN "Interval"                FORMAT a20;

SELECT 250*trunc(indx/250)+1
       ||' To '||250*(trunc(indx/250)+1) "Interval",
       sum(count) "Additional Cache Misses"
FROM X$KCBCBH
WHERE indx > 0
GROUP BY trunc(indx/250);
```

Listing 4.7 shows an example of how the output from querying the **X$KCBCBH** table might appear.

Listing 4.7   Sample output from querying the **X$KCBCBH** table.

```
SQL>@lessbuff

Interval                 Additional Cache Misses
--------                 -----------------------
1 To 250                       3,895,959
251 To 500                        35,317
501 To 750                        19,254
```

751 To 1000	12,159
1001 To 1250	9,853
1251 To 1500	8,624
1501 To 1750	7,035
1751 To 2000	6,857
2001 To 2250	6,308
2251 To 2500	5,625
2501 To 2750	5,516
2751 To 3000	5,343
3001 To 3250	5,230
3251 To 3500	5,394
3501 To 3750	4,965

As you can see, this database has some shared information, with nearly 4 million cache hits in the first 250 buffer blocks. From 250 on up, you can see a slowly decreasing downward trend, indicating that this application is doing some full-table scans or is not referencing a lot of common information.

For more sophisticated databases, you can control not only the number of buffer blocks, but also the block size for each buffer. For example, on an IBM mainframe, you might want to make the buffer blocks very large so that you can minimize I/O contention. An I/O for 32,000 bytes is not a great deal more expensive than an I/O for 12,000 bytes. A database designer might choose to make the buffer blocks large to minimize I/O if the application "clusters" records on a database page. If a customer record is only 100 bytes, you will not gain by retrieving 32,000 bytes to get the 100 bytes that you need. However, if you cluster orders physically near the customer (i.e., on the same database page), and if I/O usually proceeds from customer to order, you won't need further I/O to retrieve orders for the customer. They will already reside in the initial read of 32,000 bytes, as shown in Figure 4.4.

Now that we understand the issues involved in adding more block buffers, we can move on to the next most important parameter for memory sizing, the **shared_pool_size** parameter.

Tuning The Shared Pool Size

The shared pool component of the Oracle SGA is primarily used to store shared SQL cursors, stored procedures, and session information, and to function as a cache for the dictionary cache and library cache. Let's take a look at tuning each component of the shared pool.

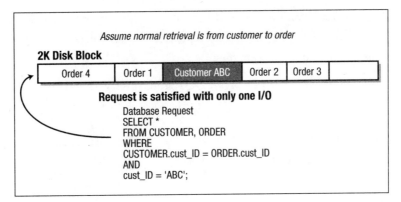

Figure 4.4
Using table clusters to reduce I/O.

Tuning The Library Cache

The shared SQL areas and the PL/SQL areas are called the library cache, which is a subcomponent of the shared pool. The library cache miss ratio tells the DBA whether or not to add space to the shared pool, and it represents the ratio of the sum of library cache reloads to the sum of pins. In general, if the cache miss ratio is over 1, you should consider adding to the **shared_pool_size**. Library cache misses occur during the compilation of SQL statements. The compilation of an SQL statement consists of two phases: the parse phase and the execute phase. When the time comes to parse an SQL statement, Oracle first checks to see if the parsed representation of the statement already exists in the library cache. If not, Oracle will allocate a shared SQL area within the library cache and then parse the SQL statement. At execution time, Oracle checks to see if a parsed representation of the SQL statement already exists in the library cache. If not, Oracle will reparse and execute the statement.

Within the library cache, hit ratios can be determined for all dictionary objects that are loaded. These include tables/procedures, triggers, indexes, package bodies, and clusters. If any of the hit ratios fall below 75 percent, you should add to the **shared_pool_size**.

The table **V$LIBRARYCACHE** is the **V$** table that keeps information about library cache activity. The table has three relevant columns: **namespace**, **pins**, and **reloads**. The first is the **namespace**, which indicates whether the measurement is for the SQL area, a table or procedure, a package body, or a trigger. The second value in this table is **pins**, which counts the number of times an item in the library cache is executed. The **reloads** column counts the number of times the parsed representation did not exist in the library cache, forcing Oracle to allocate the private SQL areas in order to parse and execute the statement.

Listing 4.8 shows an example of an SQL*Plus query that interrogates the **V$LIBRARYCACHE** table to retrieve the necessary performance information.

Listing 4.8   An example of an SQL*Plus query interrogating the **V$LIBRARYCACHE** table.

```
library.sql - lists the library cache
PROMPT
PROMPT             ==========================
PROMPT             LIBRARY CACHE MISS RATIO
PROMPT             ==========================
PROMPT (If > 1 then increase the shared_pool_size in init.ora)
PROMPT
COLUMN "LIBRARY CACHE MISS RATIO"        FORMAT 99.9999
COLUMN "executions"                      FORMAT 999,999,999
COLUMN "Cache misses while executing"    FORMAT 999,999,999
SELECT sum(pins) "executions", sum(reloads)
       "Cache misses while executing",
       (((sum(reloads)/sum(pins)))) "LIBRARY CACHE MISS RATIO"
FROM V$LIBRARYCACHE;

PROMPT
PROMPT             ==========================
PROMPT             LIBRARY CACHE SECTION
PROMPT             ==========================
PROMPT hit ratio should be > 70, and pin ratio > 70 ...
PROMPT

COLUMN "reloads" FORMAT 999,999,999
SELECT namespace, trunc(gethitratio * 100) "Hit ratio",
       trunc(pinhitratio * 100) "pin hit ratio", RELOADS "reloads"
FROM V$LIBRARYCACHE;
```

Listing 4.9 shows the output of the SQL query displayed in Listing 4.8.

Listing 4.9   The output of the query in Listing 4.8.

```
SQL> @temp


==========================
LIBRARY CACHE MISS RATIO
==========================
```

```
(If > 1 then increase the shared_pool_size in init.ora)
```

```
   executions Cache misses while executing LIBRARY CACHE MISS RATIO
---------- ---------------------------- ------------------------
   251,272                    2,409                        .0096
```

```
==============================
LIBRARY CACHE SECTION
==============================
hit ratio should be > 70, and pin ratio > 70 ...
```

```
NAMESPACE                Hit ratio    pin hit ratio    reloads
---------                ---------    -------------    -------
SQL AREA                        90               94      1,083
TABLE/PROCEDURE                 93               94      1,316
BODY                            96               95          9
TRIGGER                         89               86          1
INDEX                            0               31          0
CLUSTER                         44               33          0
OBJECT                         100              100          0
PIPE                           100              100          0
```

```
8 rows selected.
```

One of the most important measures a developer can take to reduce the use of the library cache is to ensure that all SQL is written within stored procedures. For example, Oracle library cache will examine the following SQL statements and conclude that they are not identical:

```
SELECT * FROM customer;
```

```
SELECT * FROM Customer;
```

While capitalizing a single letter, adding an extra space between verbs, or using a different variable name might seem trivial, the Oracle software is not sufficiently intelligent to recognize that the statements are identical. Consequently, Oracle will reparse and execute the second SQL statement, even though it is functionally identical to the first SQL statement.

Another problem occurs when values are hard coded into SQL statements. For example, Oracle considers the following statements to be different:

```
SELECT count(*) FROM CUSTOMER WHERE status = 'NEW';
```

```
SELECT count(*) FROM CUSTOMER WHERE status = 'PREFERRED';
```

This problem is easily alleviated by using an identical bind variable, such as:

```
SELECT count(*) FROM CUSTOMER WHERE status = :var1;
```

The best way to prevent reloads from happening is to encapsulate all SQL into stored procedures, bundling the stored procedures into packages. This removes all SQL from application programs and moves them into Oracle's data dictionary. This method also has the nice side effect of making all database calls appear as functions. As such, a layer of independence is created between the application and the database. Again, by efficiently reusing identical SQL, the number of reloads will be kept at a minimum and the library cache will function at optimal speed.

The **cursor_space_for_time** parameter can be used to speed executions within the library cache. Setting **cursor_space_for_time** to **FALSE** tells Oracle that a shared SQL area can be deallocated from the library cache to make room for a new SQL statement. Setting **cursor_space_for_time** to **TRUE** means that all shared SQL areas are pinned in the cache until all application cursors are closed. When set to **TRUE**, Oracle will not bother to check the library cache on subsequent execution calls because it has already pinned the SQL in the cache. This technique can improve the performance for some queries, but **cursor_space_for_time** should not be set to **TRUE** if there are cache misses on execution calls. Cache misses indicate that the **shared_pool_size** is already too small, and forcing the pinning of shared SQL areas will only aggravate the problem.

Another way to improve performance on the library cache is to use the init.ora **session_cached_cursors** parameter. As you probably know, Oracle checks the library cache for parsed SQL statements, but **session_cached_cursors** can be used to cache the cursors for a query. This is especially useful for tasks that repeatedly issue parse calls for the same SQL statement—for instance, where an SQL statement is repeatedly executed with a different variable value. An example would be the following SQL request that performs the same query 50 times, once for each state:

```
SELECT sum(sale_amount)
FROM SALES
WHERE
state_code = :var1;
```

Tuning The Dictionary Cache

The data dictionary cache is used to hold rows from the internal Oracle metadata tables, including SQL stored in packages. Based on my experience, I highly recommend that you store all SQL in packages. So, let's take a look at how packages interact with the dictionary cache.

When a package is invoked, Oracle first checks the dictionary cache to see if the package is already in memory. Of course, a package will not be in memory the first time it is requested, and Oracle will register a *dictionary cache miss*. Consequently, it is virtually impossible to have an instance with no dictionary cache misses, because each item must be loaded once.

The **V$ROWCACHE** table is used to measure dictionary cache activity. Three columns are of interest: **Data Dict.**, **gets**, and **getmisses**. The first column, **Data Dict.**, describes the type of dictionary object that has been requested. The second parameter, **gets**, provides the total number of requests for objects of that type. The last column, **getmisses**, counts the number of times Oracle had to perform a disk I/O to retrieve a row from its dictionary tables.

The data dictionary cache hit ratio is used to measure the ratio of dictionary hits to misses. Bear in mind, however, that this ratio is only good for measuring the average hit ratio for the life of the instance. If the data dictionary hit ratio is too low, the remedy is to increase the value of the **shared_pool_size** init.ora parameter.

The data dictionary cache hit ratio can be measured by using the script shown in Listing 4.10.

Listing 4.10   Measuring the dictionary cache hit ratio.

```
dict.sql - displays the dictionary cache hit ratio
PROMPT
PROMPT
PROMPT              ==========================
PROMPT              DATA DICT HIT RATIO
PROMPT              ==========================
PROMPT (should be higher than 90 else increase shared_pool_size in
```

```
PROMPT init.ora)
PROMPT

COLUMN "Data Dict. Gets"          FORMAT 999,999,999
COLUMN "Data Dict. cache misses"  FORMAT 999,999,999
SELECT sum(gets) "Data Dict. Gets",
       sum(getmisses) "Data Dict. cache misses",
       trunc((1-(sum(getmisses)/sum(gets)))*100)
       "DATA DICT CACHE HIT RATIO"
FROM V$ROWCACHE;

SQL> @t2
```

Listing 4.11 displays the output of the script presented in Listing 4.10.

Listing 4.11 Sample output of the script measuring the dictionary cache hit ratio.

```
============================
DATA DICT HIT RATIO
============================
(should be higher than 90 else increase shared_pool_size in init.ora)


Fri Feb 23                                              page    1
                          dbname Database
                      Data Dictionary Hit Ratios

Data Dict. Gets Data Dict. cache misses DATA DICT CACHE HIT RATIO
------------------------ ------------ -------------------------
409,288                       11,639                  97

1 row selected.
```

Listing 4.12 measures the contention for each dictionary object type.

Listing 4.12 A script that measures the contention for dictionary object types.

```
ddcache.sql - Lists all data dictionary contention
REM SQLX SCRIPT
SET PAUSE OFF;
SET ECHO OFF;
SET TERMOUT OFF;
SET LINESIZE 78;
```

```
SET PAGESIZE 60;
SET NEWPAGE 0;
TTITLE "dbname Database|Data Dictionary Hit Ratios";
SPOOL /tmp/ddcache
SELECT   substr(PARAMETER,1,20) PARAMETER,
         gets,getmisses,count,usage,
         round((1 - getmisses / decode(gets,0,1,gets))*100,1) HITRATE
FROM     V$ROWCACHE
ORDER BY 6,1;
SPOOL OFF;
```

Listing 4.13 shows a sample output of the script presented in Listing 4.12.

Listing 4.13 Sample output of the script measuring the contention for dictionary object types.

```
SQL> @t1
```

```
Fri Feb 23                                                      page    1
                            dbname Database
                       Data Dictionary Hit Ratios
```

PARAMETER	GETS	GETMISSES	COUNT	USAGE	HITRATE
dc_object_ids	136	136	12	0	0
dc_free_extents	1978	1013	67	48	48.8
dc_used_extents	1930	970	63	5	49.7
dc_database_links	4	2	3	2	50
dc_sequence_grants	101	18	121	18	82.2
dc_synonyms	527	33	34	33	93.7
dc_objects	18999	947	389	387	95
dc_columns	163520	6576	2261	2247	96
dc_segments	8548	314	127	117	96.3
dc_constraint_defs	7842	250	218	210	96.8
dc_table_grants	26718	792	772	763	97
dc_sequences	4179	75	11	7	98.2
dc_users	1067	14	20	14	98.7
dc_tables	49497	261	272	271	99.5
dc_tablespace_quotas	957	4	5	4	99.6
dc_indexes	59548	172	329	328	99.7
dc_tablespaces	1162	3	7	3	99.7
dc_tablespaces	1201	4	27	4	99.7
dc_user_grants	9900	14	24	14	99.9
dc_usernames	18452	18	20	18	99.9
dc_users	14418	17	18	17	99.9

dc_column_grants	0	0	1	0	100
dc_constraint_defs	0	0	1	0	100
dc_constraints	0	0	1	0	100
dc_files	0	0	1	0	100
dc_histogram_defs	0	0	1	0	100
dc_profiles	0	0	1	0	100
dc_rollback_segments	18560	6	17	7	100

28 rows selected.

Now that we have completed our survey of Oracle's in-memory structures, let's expand our scope and take a look at some of the other Oracle processes and see how they influence the overall performance of the database. We will begin with a discussion of Oracle's multithreaded server as an alternative to the single-threaded server environment, and discuss the relative benefits of each approach.

Multithreaded Server Tuning

Remember, if you are using SQL*Net version 2 with the multithreaded server, Oracle will allocate storage in the library cache to hold session information.

Using MTS To Segregate Memory

*One of the major shortcomings of the Oracle8 architecture is the requirement that each transaction must allocate a Program Global Area (PGA) with space defined in the **sort_area_size**. In a real-world environment, there may only be a few transactions that require a large sort area, but Oracle8 forces all transactions to always allocate the same size local sort area, regardless of the sorting requirements of each transaction. When using the MTS, you can segregate the memory that is allocated for SQL sorting and create a shared memory area that is dedicated for sorts. Without the MTS, the **sort_area_size** is taken from the storage allocated in the PGA for each session, often leading to a memory shortage for the other objects on the processor. With the MTS, the **large_pool_size** init.ora parameter can be used to define new storage for the exclusive use of Oracle sorts, thereby segregating sorting into a globally available buffer area, and reducing the size of the PGA for all transactions on the database.*

There are many benefits to using the MTS, including:

- *Better allocation of memory*—The MTS allows for the definition of a global sort area (as defined by **large_pool_size**), thereby reducing the size of each transaction's PGA and making better use of available memory.

- *Faster execution of parallel queries*—Because the MTS preallocates the database connections through its dispatchers, Oracle parallel queries will execute far faster than with a traditional listener process that spawns database connections at runtime.

- *Less system resource consumption*—In addition to memory savings, the MTS also reduces the load on the operating system, since new connections are multiplexed through a dispatcher process rather than allocating separate OS processes for each and every transaction.

As new connections are established through the multithreaded server, Oracle will allocate memory, and the amount of memory can be measured with the **V$SESSSTAT** table. Listing 4.14 shows a sample query that displays the memory high-water mark for all sessions.

Listing 4.14 A sample query for session memory usage.

```
SELECT sum(VALUE) || ' bytes' 'Total memory for all sessions'
   FROM V$SESSSTAT, V$STATNAME
WHERE
NAME = 'session memory'
AND
V$SESSSTAT.statistics# = V$STATNAME.statistic#;

SELECT sum(VALUE) || ' bytes' 'Total maximum memory for all sessions'
   FROM V$SESSSTAT, V$STATNAME
WHERE
NAME = 'max session memory'
AND
V$SESSSTAT.statistics# = V$STATNAME.statistic#;
```

Listing 4.15 shows how the output of the query shown in Listing 4.14 might appear.

Listing 4.15 Sample output of the query shown in Listing 4.14.

```
Total memory for all sessions
-----------------------------
203460 bytes
```

```
Total maximum memory for all sessions
-------------------------------------
712473 bytes
```

Based on an instant in time, the report in Listing 4.15 shows that 203K is allocated to sessions, while the maximum memory for all sessions is 712K. When deciding whether or not to increase the **shared_pool_size** parameter, the total memory for all sessions is the best guideline because it is unlikely that all sessions will reach maximum memory allocation at the same moment in time.

Getting back to our central theme of minimizing database disk I/O, there are tools and tricks that can be used within Oracle to help ensure that frequently referenced data is kept inside Oracle's data buffer. The next section will explore some of these techniques.

Simulating Pinned Database Rows

Unfortunately, unlike the pinning of packages in the library cache, Oracle does not yet support the pinning of database blocks within its buffer cache. If it were possible to keep specific data blocks from swapping out, commonly used blocks, such as common reference tables and the high-level nodes of indexes, could be kept in memory. However, while pinning is not yet possible in Oracle, tricks have been devised to simulate this type of buffer pinning. Introduced in Oracle7.2, read-only tablespaces allow for the creation of separate instances that concurrently access the same tablespace. For example, assume your application has a common set of lookup tables, commonly referenced by every user. This table could be placed inside a separate instance, sized only for the lookup tables. Because the instance has its private buffer pool, you can ensure that the reference tables will always reside in memory. This type of architecture is beneficial for systems that must do full-table scans. This alleviates the buffer flushing that occurs when an online transactions system is slowed by a single task that is required to do a full-table scan on a large table. But what if the table is read both by the online transaction processing and by the full-table scan request? Again, Oracle version 7.2 and above offers read-only tablespaces.

There is also the **TABLE CACHE** option. For small, frequently referenced tables, the **TABLE CACHE** option will place the incoming rows onto the most-recently used end of the buffer cache. The default for full-table scans is to place the rows onto the least-recently used end of the data buffer.

With read-only tablespaces, a tablespace can be in update mode for the online transactions processing instance, while a separate instance handles read-only full-table scans (see Figure 4.5). The Oracle DBA should make every possible effort to identify and isolate read-only tables into a read-only tablespace because performance is dramatically faster in read-only processing mode.

> **Note:** *For details on read-only tablespaces, refer to Chapter 7,* Oracle DBA Performance And Tuning.

When configuring Oracle, it is important to remember that it is possible to create several init.ora files, each one suited to the type of processing that the Oracle instance will perform. The following section discusses this technique.

Batch Processing Oracle Instances

In some cases, widely differing applications can access the same tables. An excellent example of this scenario is a banking application that processes fast online transactions during the day and long-running background tasks in the evening.

A fundamental difference exists between the database resources required for transaction processing and batch processing. Online transactions are usually small and re-

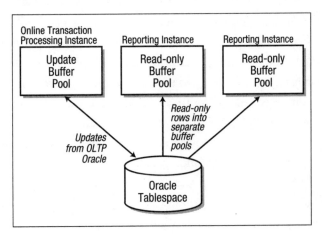

Figure 4.5
Oracle's read-only tablespaces.

quire few resources from the database lock manager. Batch processes are generally lock intensive, sweeping a table in a linear fashion.

Oracle's buffer pool offers a finite amount of RAM storage within the region. This storage can be allocated to lock pools or buffer pools, but it is impossible to reallocate these resources as the applications change, unless the system is brought down and then restarted with a new configuration (called bouncing). For online transaction systems with hundreds of concurrent users, the demands on the database buffer pool are much more intensive than with systemwide updates. Conversely, batch updates make very little use of large buffers but require a lot of room in the lock pools to hold row locks between commit checkpoints.

One simple solution to these application-specific requirements is to create two database configurations, each with a different configuration of buffers and lock pools. At the end of the online transaction day, the online system can be brought down and a batch version of the database can be started with a different memory configuration.

Now that we see how the configuration of Oracle will affect performance, let's take a look at some techniques for I/O-based tuning of Oracle, and how tuning the I/O subsystem can improve data throughput.

I/O-Based Oracle Tuning

In a distributed database environment, it is important to understand that the overall distributed system is only going to perform as well as the weakest link. Therefore, most distributed database tuning treats each remote node as an independent database, individually tuning each one and thereby improving overall distributed system requests. In addition, several tricks are available to reduce I/O time from disk, including disk allocation, disk striping, cache memory, buffer expansion, and file placement. There have been some impressive advances in disk technology in the past few years, including optical disks, redundant arrays of inexpensive disks (RAID), and writable CD-ROM devices. Oracle can take advantage of many of the new disk technology features. This section explores some of the guidelines for designing disk layouts for Oracle, including disk allocation, disk striping, RAID, and optical disks.

Disk Allocation

In order to be compliant with Oracle's Flexible Architecture (OFA), Oracle recommends that an Oracle instance should have at least five separate disk devices. Using five disks allows OFA compliance and permits maximum spread of I/O load across the devices. Following is a sample Oracle configuration for five disk devices. Note that the data files and the index are segregated onto separate devices to relieve I/O contention:

- Disk 1—Archive log files

- Disk 2—Rollback segment data files, export files

- Disk 3—Executables, a copy of the control file, redo logs, the SYSTEM data files

- Disk 4—Data files, temporary user data files, a copy of the control file

- Disk 5—Index data files, a copy of the control file

Of course, the more disks the better, because relieving I/O contention is largely dependent on spreading the I/O across as many disks as possible. In light of this requirement to spread the load across multiple disks, let's explore some other methods used in Oracle8 to spread the database I/O. Specifically, let's look at disk striping and RAID.

Disk Striping

Striping involves taking a very large or very busy data table and distributing it across many disks. When a performance problem occurs on a regular basis, it is most often the result of disks waiting on I/O. By distributing a file across many physical devices, the overall system response time will improve. Disk striping is generally done for tables that are larger than the size of a disk device, but striping can be equally effective for small, heavily accessed tables (see Figure 4.6).

Note in Figure 4.6 that the data files appear to the database management system as a single logical file. This technique avoids any I/O problems from within the database when doing table striping. As rows are requested from the table, the SQL I/O module

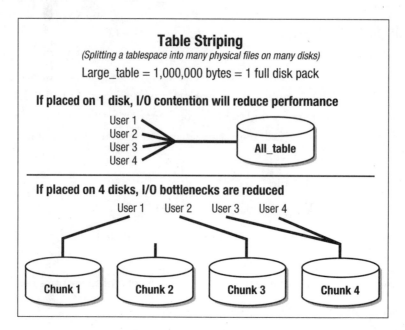

Figure 4.6
Striping a table across many disks.

will request physical data blocks from the disk—one at a time—unaware that the logically continuous table is actually comprised of many physical data files.

In an Oracle database, disk striping is done in a similar fashion. Consider the following Oracle syntax:

```
CREATE TABLESPACE TS1
  DATA FILE "/usr/disk1/bigfile1.dbf"  SIZE 30M
  DATA FILE "/usr/disk2/bigfile2.dbf"  SIZE 30M;

CREATE TABLE BIG_TABLE (
  big_field1     char(8)
  big_field2     varchar(2000))
TABLESPACE TS1
STORAGE (INITIAL 25M   NEXT 25M   MINEXTENTS 2   PCTINCREASE 1);
```

Here, you can see that a tablespace is created with two data files—bigfile1 and bigfile2. Each file is 30MB. When you are ready to create a table within the tablespace, you need to size the extents (or extra storage) of the table such that the database is forced to allocate the table's initial extents into each data file. As the table is created in the empty tablespace, the **MINEXTENTS** parameter tells the database to allocate two extents, and the **INITIAL** parameter tells the database that each extent is to be 25MB. The database then goes to bigfile1 on disk1 and allocates a 25MB extent. It then tries to allocate another 25MB extent on bigfile1, but only 5MB of free space are available. The database must move to bigfile2 to allocate the final extent of 25MB, as shown in Figure 4.7. Of course, we have 5MB of unallocated space in bigfile1, but this could be allocated to a small table.

After a table has been initially created, the value for the **NEXT** extent should be changed to a smaller value than the **INITIAL** extent, as follows:

```
ALTER TABLE BIG_TABLE
STORAGE (NEXT 1M);
```

Some database administrators recommend striping all tables across each and every physical disk. If a system has 10 tables and the CPU is configured for two disks, then each of the 10 tables would be striped into each disk device.

It is unfortunate that the relational databases require a DBA to "trick" the database allocation software into striping files rather than allowing direct control over the file placement process. This lack of control can be a real problem when tables are com-

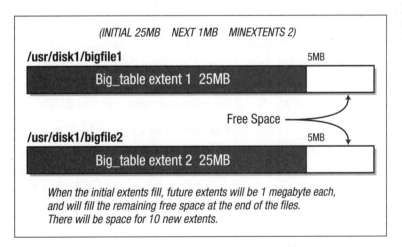

Figure 4.7
Allocating an Oracle table with striped extents.

pressed. Luckily, Oracle8 allows physical partitioning of individual table partitions into multiple tablespaces by range of values.

There are several methods to ensure that the tables are striped across the disks. Many databases with a sophisticated data dictionary allow queries that reveal the striping of files. Oracle relies on the following script:

```
striping.sql - displays striped file names
SELECT DISTINCT file_name,
FROM    DBA_DATA_FILES A, DBA_EXTENTS B
WHERE
        A.file_id = B.file_id
AND
        segment_name = :striped_table_name;

(WHERE :striped_table_name = 'BIG_TABLE')
```

Other databases offer utilities that report on the physical file utilization for a specific table or database record type.

RAID Technology And Oracle

Advances in disk technology are making some of the traditional database recovery mechanisms obsolete. Disk memory schemes such as RAID now offer a very high degree of reliability and availability. As a consequence of RAID, there are many new distributed object-oriented database offerings that do not contain the traditional roll-forward and roll-back utilities. Unlike traditional database recovery mechanisms where a disk crash causes the application to go offline while the disk is restored and rolled forward, RAID offers almost instantaneous recovery from disk failure.

RAID technology was the brainchild of three researchers at the University of California who found that by creating an array of small disks, they could create software to duplicate all write operations, and quickly recover if of one of the disks in an array fails. Essentially, RAID consists of the following three components (see Figure 4.8):

- An array of small disk devices

- A controller to manage the I/O against the disks

- Software to distribute the data across the disk array and manage recovery

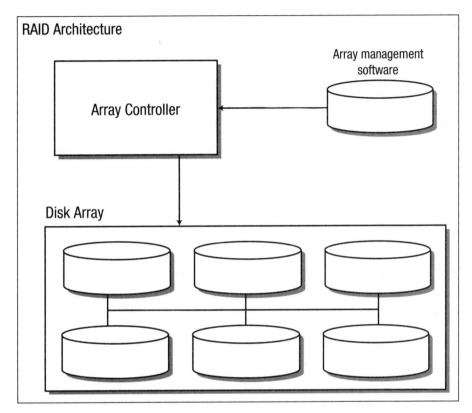

Figure 4.8
The RAID 5 architecture.

The most complex component of RAID is the array management software. The algorithms for RAID differ widely, and, as of 1994, there are seven RAID levels, or types of RAID software, that can be used with the array management software. These levels are depicted with numbers that range from zero through six, and new vendors continue to add new RAID level numbers as they develop new algorithms to improve data availability. The RAID levels are as follows:

- *RAID 0*—Disk striping

- *RAID 1*—Disk mirroring

- *RAID 2*—Block interleaf with check disk

- *RAID 3*—Byte interleaf

- *RAID 4*—Byte interleaf with error correcting code
- *RAID 5*—Byte interleaf with parity checking
- *RAID 6*—Byte interleaf with double parity checking

RAID is a software technique, and the array controller and the disks are purchased from standard industry hardware vendors. As such, you only need to purchase the RAID level software of your choice, and purchase the disk and controllers separately.

When evaluating disk recovery methods, there are two acronyms worth noting: MTBF and MTTR. MTBF is an acronym for Mean Time Between Failures, and MTTR is an acronym for Mean Time To Recovery. MTBF is a statistic that can be provided by the disk vendor, and MTTR is a function of the recovery software. With RAID, several disks would have to fail within the same hour to get a failure. For a five-disk array, this can mean astounding improvements in the MTBF. If each disk in a five-disk array has a MTBF of 150,000 hours, RAID 5's redundancy will increase the MTBF of the disk array to 46 million hours! (Assuming, of course, that individual disk failures are promptly replaced with new disks.)

When a disk failure occurs, the RAID software redirects any new write operations to temporary storage, and once the bad disk is replaced, the RAID software resynchronizes the new disk automatically. This is a huge improvement over the traditional disk failure, when application users sat idly by while a new disk was initialized, restored to the last backup, and rolled forward from archived log tapes.

Optical Disk And Oracle

Optical disks come in two varieties: WORM (Write Once, Read Many) and MWMR (Multiple Write, Multiple Read). Optical disks are relatively immune to disk failures and provide a very reliable means for storing data. On the other hand, optical disks are far slower than traditional disks. Consequently, their main use within Oracle is to store information that is not frequently accessed, such as the Oracle archived redo logs, Oracle export files, and in some cases, read-only tablespaces. Optical drives have also been used successfully with large image files (BLOBS) or large document files. Usually, unless you have a rewritable CD system, the tablespaces placed on a CD-ROM will be read only. Due to their reliability, optical disks are rapidly replacing magnetic tapes as the media of choice for backups, exports, and archived redo logs.

Using Raw Devices With Oracle

Raw devices are generally used when an Oracle database must get the maximum performance on a server. Oracle has two methods for writing to disk: through Oracle I/O buffers or directly to the raw devices. Bypassing traditional disk writing can increase performance of Oracle I/O by up to 30 percent, and there will not be a loss of data integrity. However, there is some debate about whether raw devices are worth the extra work because raw devices have some serious drawbacks over traditional disks. The Oracle data file names are restricted to a specific syntax, and a DBA does not have a lot of flexibility in naming data files on the raw devices. A more concerning limitation is that the entire raw partition must be used for only one Oracle file. This can lead to wasted space if planning is poor. Finally, DBAs must keep maps of the raw partitions so they know which partitions are used for which tablespaces.

There are conditions such as the use of Oracle Parallel Server where Oracle forces a DBA to use raw devices so that the files can be shared between servers. In sum, the administrative headaches generally outweigh the performance gains from raw devices, and you can see that only the most I/O-intensive Oracle applications use the raw option. Raw devices are also required for any parallel configuration that uses a shared disk architecture.

Now that we have reviewed the issues related to disk I/O, let's take a look at how data fragmentation within the Oracle blocks can affect performance.

Tuning Data Fragmentation

Fragmentation occurs when the preallocated space for a data area or table has been exceeded. In relational databases, tables are allocated into tablespaces, and each table is given several storage parameters. The storage parameters include **INITIAL**, **NEXT**, **PCTINCREASE**, and **MAXEXTENTS**.

As tables grow, they automatically allocate extents at a size determined by the **NEXT** parameter. If a table reaches its maximum number of extents, all processing against that table will stop, causing major performance interruptions. In Oracle, the maximum number of extents can range from 121 extents for a 2K block size through 505 for an 8K block size, and increases according to the value of the **db_block_size** init.ora parameter. See your Oracle installation and configuration guide for the exact values for max extents on your operating system. When using Oracle8, you might want to consider using **MAXEXTENTS UNLIMITED**.

Even before data tables fill, performance against a table might degrade as the amount of extents increases. An operating system such as Unix is forced to chase the **inode** chains to scan the entire table, and the increased I/O translates into performance delays (see Figure 4.9).

Several SQL queries can be used to detect table fragmentation. These queries are unique to the database system tables, but most databases allow for table fragmentation to be measured. These reports are generally incorporated into a periodic report, and those files that are fragmenting are then scheduled for export-import to unfragment the tables.

As the initial extents of a table fill, the database manager should allocate additional spaces on the disk to allow the table to expand. These fragments eventually create a performance problem, and the tables will need to be compressed to remove the extents. Table compression is achieved by performing the following five steps:

1. Determine the level of fragmentation and the new table sizes.

2. Offload all table data using an export utility.

3. Drop the old tables.

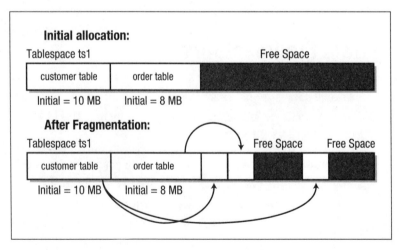

Figure 4.9
Free space allocation in an Oracle table space.

4. Reallocate the new tables at their new sizes.

5. Import the data to repopulate the tables.

Disk Issues With Other System Resources

Most databases have other high-impact resources such as the recovery logs and transaction logs. Most systems have several recovery logs, and it is a good idea to locate these logs on different disk devices as well as devices that do not have any other high-impact data tables.

Summary

Now that we have discussed how Oracle functions at the system level, we are ready to take a closer look at how individual SQL can be tuned to get the most from the available database resources. As you have learned, a myriad of factors can degrade performance. Fortunately, many techniques are available for diagnosing and correcting performance problems, from tuning Oracle locks and/or the client application, to performance and tuning for distributed servers.

The ability to identify and correct performance problems has plagued distributed systems from their genesis. Even within the context of a single transaction, distributed query optimization can be a formidable challenge. On a single database, query tuning takes place by running an SQL **EXPLAIN** and performing the appropriate tuning. However, when a query is split into distributed databases, the overall query tuning becomes much more complex. Many distributed database managers take a distributed query and partition it into subqueries, which are then independently optimized and run (sometimes simultaneously) on the distributed databases. The query is considered complete when the last subquery has completed successfully and the results are returned to the user. As mentioned previously, this approach is sometimes called the weakest link architecture. If a distributed query partitions into four subqueries, for example, the longest running of the four subqueries determines the overall performance for the entire query, regardless of how fast the other three subqueries execute. We'll look at tuning SQL queries in the next chapter.

HIGH PERFORMANCE

Tuning
Oracle SQL

CHAPTER

5

HIGH PERFORMANCE

Tuning Oracle SQL

While several books on the market are devoted to the efficient use of Oracle SQL, there are only a few general rules and guidelines that are actually effective in guaranteeing optimal performance from your Oracle systems. This chapter focuses on the basic techniques for quickly achieving the maximum SQL performance with the least amount of effort. SQL tuning has more influence on database performance than any other activity except the initial design of the database tables. Figure 5.1 illustrates how tuning SQL can impact Oracle performance. As you will see in this chapter, there are many opportunities to dramatically tune an application by tuning the SQL. In this chapter, we'll look at the following concepts in relation to SQL tuning in an Oracle environment:

- SQL syntax

- Indexes

- Explain plan facility

- Oracle optimizers

- Stored procedures and triggers

- ODBC as a server interface

- Simulating object-orientation with SQL

- Oracle8 objects

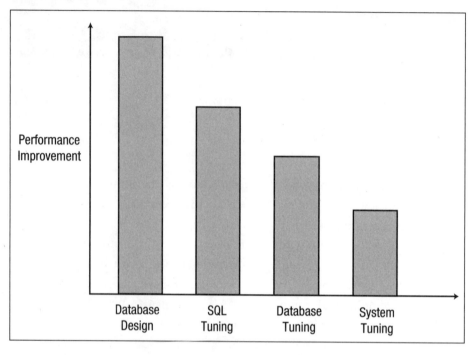

Figure 5.1
The impact of tuning on Oracle performance.

Tuning Oracle SQL Syntax

SQL is a declarative language, so queries can be written in many ways. While identical results can be obtained from a number of queries, the execution time can vary dramatically. To illustrate this concept, let's say you have a small employee table with only 15 rows and an index on **sex** and **hiredate**. You issue the following query to retrieve all female employees who have been hired within the last 90 days (this example assumes that you are using Oracle's rule-based optimizer):

```
SELECT emp_name
FROM EMPLOYEE
WHERE
sex = 'F'
AND
hiredate BETWEEN SYSDATE-90 AND SYSDATE;
```

Because the table has only 15 rows, the most efficient way to service this request would be to use a full-table scan. However, Oracle will walk through the existing index, even though it would be faster to perform a full-table scan. This causes extra I/Os as it reads the index tree to access the rows in the table. While this is a simplistic example, it serves to illustrate the concept that the execution time of SQL is heavily dependent on the structure of a query statement, as well as the internal index structures within Oracle.

Entire books are devoted to some of the more subtle nuances of SQL behavior, most notably Joe Celko's bestselling book *SQL for Smarties,* by Morgan Kaufman Publishers. For Oracle tuning, the upcoming book *Oracle8 SQL Programming and Tuning,* written by the noted Oracle SQL expert Peter Cassidy and published by The Coriolis Group, promises to be even more popular than Cassidy's *Oracle Cookbook for SQL*Plus,* which has become a classic in the Oracle arena.

For the purposes of this chapter, we'll omit discussion of tuning some of the more obscure queries, such as outer joins and nullable foreign key queries. Instead, we'll concentrate on tuning some of the common SQL queries that rely on Oracle's cost-based and rule-based optimizers. And while these guidelines are no substitute for the SQL explain plan facility, they can reduce the chances that a database query will consume large amounts of system resources.

In the next few sections, we'll look at the cost considerations relevant to SQL tuning decisions and the use of boolean operators when tuning your SQL. In addition, I'll provide you with some general rules designed to help you make the most of your SQL, regardless of your choice of optimizers.

Cost Considerations

The first step in tuning Oracle SQL is to look at the relative costs for each type of SQL access. Oracle has published the cost list shown in Table 5.1 that describes the relative cost of each type of row access.

As you can see, the fastest way to retrieve a row is by knowing its row ID. A row ID (called a **ROWID** in Oracle) is the number of the database block followed by the "displacement" or position of the row on the block. For example, 1221:3 refers to

Table 5.1   Costs for SQL access.

Cost	Type of Operation
1	Single row by row ID (**ROWID**)
2	Single row by cluster join
3	Single row by hash cluster key with unique or primary key
4	Single row by unique or primary key
5	Cluster join
6	Hash cluster key
7	Indexed cluster key
8	Use of a multi-column index
9	Use of a single-column index
10	Bounded range search on indexed columns
11	Unbounded range search on unindexed columns

the third row on block number 1221. Many savvy programmers capture the **ROWID** for a row if they plan to retrieve it again. In Oracle, **ROWID** is a valid column statement, such that you can select the **ROWID** along with your data in a single statement, as follows:

```
SELECT ROWID FROM EMPLOYEE INTO :myvar;
```

On the other end of the cost spectrum is the full-table scan. As noted earlier in this book, a full-table scan is desirable for small tables, but it can wreak havoc on Oracle when a full-table scan is invoked against a large table. Therefore, more than any other SQL tuning technique, avoiding full-table scans is a primary consideration. In short, full-table scans on large tables can *always* be avoided by the proper placement of indexes and the use of index hints. However, another issue must be considered. While a full-table scan might be the fastest technique for an individual query with many complex **WHERE** conditions, the full-table scan is done at the expense of other SQL on the system. The question then becomes: Do you tune an individual query for performance, or do you tune the database as a whole? The answer to this question is not simple because each SQL statement must be tuned individually, but individual tuning cannot be done at the expense of other queries on the database. Let's begin our exploration of SQL performance by discussing how **WHERE** conditions can influence performance.

SQL Boolean Operators

One confounding problem with Oracle SQL is that the "improper" specification of **WHERE** conditions can cause inefficient table access, regardless of whether the rule-based or the cost-based optimizer is used. An *improper* SQL statement is one that can be made to run more efficiently by restructuring the query. To illustrate, consider the following query:

```
SELECT
    student_name
FROM
    STUDENT
WHERE
     (student_nbr = :host_student
   OR
     :host_student IS NULL)
AND
     (social_security_nbr = :host_social
   OR
     :host_social IS NULL);
```

Here, you can see a query where the SQL is formulated to query either by **student_nbr** or by **social_security_nbr**, depending on the value supplied by the end user. This is a very useful way to specify an SQL query because the user of the application can use the same SQL, regardless of whether they are accessing students by **student_nbr** or **social_security_nbr**. From a programming perspective, this SQL is very terse and concise, specifying the operating rules in a clear fashion. Unfortunately, as you shall see, this query does not run at optimum efficiently.

This underscores a very important point about SQL tuning. The "elegance" of an SQL statement often has an adverse impact on the performance of a query. Unfortunately, many SQL programmers are taught in college to write SQL booleans in the most compact form, assuming that the optimizer will be able to parse the query and get the fastest access path. But, in Oracle, a compact query such as

```
TABLE ACCESS       FULL         STUDENT
```

could cause a full-table scan of the **STUDENT** table.

For Oracle, the solution to this dilemma is to rewrite the SQL as four separate queries, each with different boolean conditions. The first part will query if a **student_nbr** is provided, the second part will be executed if a **social_security_nbr** is provided, the third part will be executed if both **student_nbr** and **social_security_nbr** are provided, and the fourth part of the query will be executed only if neither value is provided. The query would be written as follows:

```
SELECT
    student_name
FROM
    STUDENT
WHERE
    student_nbr = :host_student
    AND
    :host_student IS NOT NULL
    AND
    :host_social  IS     NULL
UNION
SELECT
    student_name
FROM
    STUDENT
WHERE
    social_security_nbr = :host_social
    AND
    :host_social  IS NOT NULL
    AND
    :host_student IS     NULL
UNION
SELECT
    student_name
FROM
    STUDENT
WHERE
    student_nbr = :host_student
    AND
    social_security_nbr = :host_social
    AND
    :host_social  IS NOT NULL
```

```
   AND
      :host_student IS NOT NULL
UNION
SELECT
   student_name
FROM
   STUDENT
WHERE
      :host_social   IS NULL
      AND
      :host_student IS NULL
;
```

Now, it might seem like this is a very verbose and confusing way to specify the conditions for a query, especially as the results of the queries are identical. But the last query, even though it is far more verbose, has a far faster execution time than the first two queries, as noted in the following **EXPLAIN PLAN**:

```
PROJECTION
   SORT                        UNIQUE
      UNION-ALL
         FILTER
            TABLE ACCESS       BY ROWID      STUDENT
               INDEX           RANGE SCAN    STU_NBR_SOC_SEC_IDX
         FILTER
            INDEX              RANGE SCAN    SOC_SEC_STU_NBR_IDX
         TABLE ACCESS          BY ROWID      STUDENT
            INDEX              RANGE SCAN    STU_NBR_SOC_SEC_IDX
         FILTER
            TABLE ACCESS       FULL          STUDENT
```

Here, you can see that the original query has been partitioned into separate queries and concatenated together with the SQL **UNION** operator. The first part of the query uses a concatenated index on **student_nbr** and **social_security_nbr** to service the query. The second and third queries also use an index, and the fourth query performs a full-table scan whenever both input variables are null. While rewriting a query in this fashion might seem like a lot of effort, if this is a query for an online application that is executed thousands of time each day, the performance improvements can be huge. While Oracle's SQL is inherently complex, there are a few general guidelines that can be applied. We'll take a look at these rules in the next section.

General Rules For Efficient SQL

Fortunately, some general rules are available for writing efficient SQL in Oracle regardless of the optimizer that is chosen. These rules might seem simplistic, but following them in a diligent manner will relieve more than half of the SQL tuning problems you are likely to encounter:

- Never do a calculation on an indexed column (e.g., **WHERE salary*5 > :myvalue**).

- Whenever possible, use the **UNION** statement instead of **OR** conditions.

- Avoid the use of **NOT IN** or **HAVING** in the **WHERE** clause. Instead, use the **NOT EXISTS** clause.

- Always specify numeric values in numeric form and character values in character form (e.g., **WHERE emp_number = 565, WHERE emp_name = 'Jones'**).

- Avoid specifying **NULL** in an indexed column.

- Avoid the **LIKE** parameter if = will suffice. Using any Oracle function will invalidate the index, causing a full-table scan.

- Never mix data types in Oracle queries, as it will invalidate the index. If the column is numeric, do not use quotes (e.g., **salary = 50000**). For **char** index columns, always use quotes (e.g., **name = 'BURLESON'**).

- Remember that Oracle's rule-based optimizer looks at the order of table names in the **FROM** clause to determine the driving table. Always make sure that the last table specified in the **FROM** clause is the table that will return the smallest number of rows. In other words, specify multiple tables with the largest result set table specified first in the **FROM** clause.

- Avoid using subqueries when a **JOIN** will do the job.

- Use the Oracle **decode** function to minimize the number of times a table has to be selected.

- To turn off an index that you do not want to use (only with cost-based), concatenate a null string to the index column name (e.g., **name||''**) or add zero to a numeric column name (e.g., **salary+0**). With the rule-based optimizer, this allows you to manually choose the most selective index to service your query.

- If your query will return more than 20 percent of the rows in the table, use a full-table scan rather than an index scan.

- Always use table aliases when referencing columns.

Simple queries can be written in many different ways. For example, a simple query such as "What students received an A last semester?" can be written in three ways, as shown in Listings 5.1, 5.2, and 5.3, each returning an identical result.

Listing 5.1 A standard join.

```
SELECT *
FROM STUDENT
WHERE
    STUDENT.student_id = REGISTRATION.student_id
AND
    REGISTRATION.grade = 'A';
```

Listing 5.2 A nested query.

```
SELECT *
FROM STUDENT
WHERE
    student_id =
    (SELECT student_id
        FROM REGISTRATION
        WHERE
        grade = 'A'
    );
```

Listing 5.3 A correlated subquery.

```
SELECT *
FROM STUDENT
WHERE
    0 <
    (SELECT count(*)
        FROM REGISTRATION
        WHERE
        grade = 'A'
        AND
        student_id = STUDENT.student_id
    );
```

The three queries shown in Listings 5.1, 5.2, and 5.3 will return identical results but with varying response times.

It is important to note that several steps are required to understand how SQL is used in a distributed database. Distributed SQL queries function in the same way as queries within a single database, with the exception that cross-database joins and updates can utilize indexes that reside on different databases. Regardless, a basic understanding of the behavior of SQL can lead to dramatic performance improvements.

Now that we understand the basic characteristics of the SQL syntax and execution, let's examine the influence of indexes on the performance of SQL queries.

Tuning SQL With Indexes

As a general rule, indexes will always increase the performance of a database query. In some databases, such as DB2, in situations where a query intends to "sweep" a table in the same sequence that the rows are physically stored, index usage could actually hinder performance. For Oracle, indexes are recommended for two reasons: to speed the retrieval of a small set of rows from a table and to "pre-sort" result sets so that the SQL **ORDER BY** clause does not cause an internal sort.

In order to use an index, the SQL optimizer must recognize that a column has a valid value for index use. This is called a *sargeable predicate*, and it is used to determine the index access. Listing 5.4 shows some valid predicates, and Listing 5.5 shows some invalid predicates.

Listing 5.4   Valid predicates.

```
SELECT * FROM EMPLOYEE WHERE emp_no = 123;

SELECT * FROM EMPLOYEE WHERE dept_no = 10;
```

Listing 5.5   Invalid predicates.

```
SELECT * FROM EMPLOYEE WHERE emp_no = "123";

SELECT * FROM EMPLOYEE WHERE salary * 2 < 50000;

SELECT * FROM EMPLOYEE WHERE dept_no != 10;
```

Whenever a transformation to a field value takes place, an Oracle database will not be able to use an index for that column.

Some databases, such as DB2, will recognize a linear search and invoke a *sequential prefetch* to look ahead, and Oracle uses the **DB_FILE_MULTIBLOCK_READ_COUNT** init.ora parameter for read-ahead functionality. As a general rule, an SQL query that retrieves more than 15 percent of the table rows in a table will run faster if the optimizer chooses a full-table scan than if it chooses to use an index.

For example, assume that a student table has 1,000 rows, representing 900 undergraduate students and 100 graduate students. A nonunique index has been built on the **student_level** field that indicates **UNDERGRAD** or **GRAD**. The same query will benefit from different access methods depending on the value of the literal in the **WHERE** clause. The following query will retrieve 90 percent of the rows in the table and will run faster with a full-table scan than it will if the SQL optimizer chooses to use an index:

```
SELECT * FROM STUDENT WHERE student_level = 'UNDERGRAD';
```

This next query will only access 10 percent of the table rows and will run faster by using the index on the **student_level** field:

```
SELECT * FROM STUDENT WHERE student_level = 'GRAD';
```

Unfortunately, the Oracle database cannot predict in advance the number of rows that will be returned from a query. Many SQL optimizers will invoke an index access even though it might not always be the fastest access method.

To remedy this problem, Oracle SQL allows users to control index access. This is a gross violation of the declarative nature of theoretical SQL: The user does not control access paths. But in practice, these extensions can improve performance. Oracle, for example, allows the concatenation of a null string to the field name in the **WHERE** clause to suppress index access. The previous query could be rewritten in Oracle SQL to bypass the **student_level** index, as follows:

```
SELECT * FROM STUDENT WHERE student_level||'' = 'UNDERGRAD';
```

The concatenation (II) of a null string to the field tells the Oracle SQL optimizer to bypass index processing for this field and invoke a faster-running full-table scan, instead.

This a very important point. While the Oracle8 SQL optimizer is becoming more intelligent about their databases, they still cannot understand the structure of the data and will not always choose the best access path.

In addition to single-column indexes, Oracle allows indexes to contain the values of several columns. These are commonly referred to as multi-column or *concatenated* indexes, and they provide the Oracle professional with a very powerful tool to increase the performance of certain types of SQL queries.

Concatenated Indexes

A concatenated index is created on multiple columns. This type of index can greatly speed up a query where all the index columns are specified in the query's SQL **WHERE** clause. For example, assume the following index on the **STUDENT** table:

```
CREATE INDEX idx1
ON STUDENT
(student_level, major, last_name) ascending;
```

The following concatenated index could be used to speed up queries that reference both **student_level** and **major** in the **WHERE** clause:

```
SELECT student_last_name FROM STUDENT
WHERE
    student_level = 'UNDERGRAD'
AND
    major = 'computer science';
```

However, some queries using **major** or **student_level** will not be able to use this concatenated index. In this example, only the **major** field is referenced in the query:

```
SELECT * FROM STUDENT
WHERE
    major = 'computer science';
```

In this example, even though **student_level** is the high-order index key, it will not be used because there are other index keys following **student_level**. Because **major** is the second column in the index, Oracle will conclude that the index cannot be used. Here's another example:

```
SELECT last_name FROM STUDENT
WHERE
    student_level = 'PLEBE'
ORDER BY last_name;
```

In this instance, because **student_level** is the first item in the index, the leading portion of the index can be read, and the SQL optimizer will invoke an index scan. Why have I chosen to add the **last_name** to the index, even though it is not referenced in the **WHERE** clause? Because Oracle will be able to service the request by reading only the index, the rows of the **STUDENT** table will never be accessed, and the **ORDER BY** clause asks to sort by **last_name**, Oracle will not need to perform a sort on this data.

The NOT Operator

The **NOT** (!) operator will cause an index to be bypassed and the following query to "show all undergrads who are **NOT** computer science majors" will cause a full-table scan:

```
SELECT * FROM STUDENT
WHERE
    student_level = 'UNDERGRAD'
AND
    major != 'computer science';
```

Here, the **not** condition isn't a sargeable predicate and will cause a full-table scan.

Now that we understand the ramifications of indexes on Oracle SQL, let's move deeper into SQL and take a look at how Oracle's explain plan facility can allow us to see exactly how a query is accessing the database.

Using Oracle's Explain Plan Facility

Tools exist within most implementations of SQL that allow the access path to be interrogated. To see the output of an explain plan, you must first create a plan table. Oracle provides a script in $ORACLE_HOME/rdbms/admin called utlxplan.sql. Execute utlxplan.sql, and create a public synonym for the **PLAN_TABLE**, as follows:

```
sqlplus > @utlxplan
table created.

sqlplus > CREATE PUBLIC SYNONYM PLAN_TABLE FOR SYS.PLAN_TABLE;
synonym created.
```

Most relational databases use an explain utility that takes SQL statements as input, runs the SQL optimizer, and outputs the access path information into a **PLAN_TABLE**, which can then be interrogated to see the access methods. Listing 5.6 uses an explain utility to run a complex query against a database.

Listing 5.6   A sample database query.

```
EXPLAIN PLAN SET statement_id = 'test1' FOR
SET statement_id = 'RUN1'
INTO PLAN_TABLE
FOR
SELECT    'T'||PLANSNET.terr_code, 'P'||DETPLAN.pac1 || DETPLAN.pac2 ||
          DETPLAN.pac3, 'P1', sum(PLANSNET.ytd_d_ly_tm),
                              sum(PLANSNET.ytd_d_ty_tm),
                              sum(PLANSNET.jan_d_ly),
                              sum(PLANSNET.jan_d_ty),
FROM PLANSNET, DETPLAN
WHERE
    PLANSNET.mgc = DETPLAN.mktgpm
AND
    DETPLAN.pac1 in ('N33','192','195','201','BAI',
    'P51','Q27','180','181','183','184','186','188',
    '198','204','207','209','211')
GROUP BY 'T'||PLANSNET.terr_code, 'P'||DETPLAN.pac1 || DETPLAN.pac2 ||
                                  DETPLAN.pac3;
```

The syntax shown in Listing 5.6 is piped into the SQL optimizer, which will analyze the query and store the plan information in a row in the plan table identified by **RUN1**. Please note that the query will not execute—it will only create the internal access information in the plan table. The plan table contains the following fields:

- **operation**—The type of access being performed. Usually table access, table merge, sort, or index operation.

- **options**—Modifiers to the operation, specifying a full table, range table, or join.

- **object_name**—The name of the table being used by the query component.

- **process ID**—The identifier for the query component.

- **parent_ID**—The parent of the query component. Note that several query components can have the same parent.

Now that the **PLAN_TABLE** has been created and populated, you can interrogate it to see your output by running the following query:

```
plan.sql - displays contents of the explain plan table
SET PAGES 9999;
SELECT  lpad(' ',2*(level-1))||operation operation,
        options,
        object_name,
        position
FROM PLAN_TABLE
START WITH id=0
AND
statement_id = 'RUN1'
CONNECT BY prior_id = parent_id
AND
statement_id = 'RUN1';
```

Listing 5.7 shows the output from the query shown in Listing 5.6.

Listing 5.7   The plan table's output.

```
SQL> @list_explain_plan

OPERATION
---------
OPTIONS                 OBJECT_NAME            POSITION
-------                 -----------            --------
SELECT STATEMENT

  SORT
GROUP BY                                              1

    CONCATENATION                                     1

      NESTED LOOPS                                    1

      TABLE ACCESS FULL     PLANSNET                  1
```

```
        TABLE ACCESS BY ROWID  DETPLAN                      2

            INDEX RANGE SCAN     DETPLAN_INDEX5              1

    NESTED LOOPS
```

From this output, you can see the dreaded **TABLE ACCESS FULL** on the **PLANSET** table. To diagnose the reason, return to the SQL, and look for any **PLANSNET** columns in the **WHERE** clause. There, you can see that the **PLANSNET** column called **mgc** is being used as a join column in the query, indicating that an index is necessary on **PLANSNET.mgc** to alleviate the full-table scan.

While the plan table is useful for determining the access path to the data, it does not tell the entire story. The configuration of the data is also a consideration. While the SQL optimizer is aware of the number of rows in each table (the cardinality) and the presence of indexes on fields, the SQL optimizer is not aware of certain factors, such as the number of expected rows returned from each query component.

The other tool that is used with the plan table is an SQL trace facility. Most database management systems provide a trace facility that shows all of the resources consumed within each query component. The trace table will show the number of I/Os that were required to perform the SQL, as well as the processor time for each query component.

Some other relational databases, such as DB2, allow a DBA to specify the physical sequence for storing rows, and this can also be simulated in Oracle8. Generally, this sequence will correspond to the column value that is most commonly used when a table is read sequentially by an application. If a customer table is frequently accessed in customer ID order, then the rows should be physically stored in customer ID sequence.

The explain plan output will display many database access methods. The major access techniques include:

- **AND-EQUAL**—This indicates that tables are being joined and that Oracle will be able to use the values from the indexes to join the rows.

- **CONCATENATION**—This indicates an SQL **UNION** operation.

- **COUNTING**—This indicates the use of the SQL **count** function.

- **FILTER**—This indicates that the **WHERE** clause is removing unwanted rows from the result set.

- **FIRST ROW**—This indicates that a cursor has been declared for the query.

- **FOR UPDATE**—This indicates that returned rows were write locked (usually by using the **SELECT . . . FOR UPDATE OF . . .**).

- **INDEX (UNIQUE)**—This indicates that an index was scanned for a value specified in the **WHERE** clause.

- **INDEX (RANGE SCAN)**—This indicates that a numeric index was scanned for a range of values (usually with the **BETWEEN LESS_THAN** or **GREATER_THAN** specified).

- **INTERSECTION**—This indicates a solution set from two joined tables.

- **MERGE JOIN**—This indicates that two result sets were used to resolve a query.

- **NESTED LOOPS**—This indicates that the last operation will be performed *n* times, once for each preceding operation. For example, below the **INDEX (UNIQUE)**, these operations will be performed for each row returned by **TABLE ACCESS (FULL): NESTED LOOPS, TABLE ACCESS (FULL) OF 'CUSTOMER'**, and **INDEX (UNIQUE) OF SY_01_IDX**.

- **PROJECTION**—This indicates that only certain columns from a selected row are to be returned.

- **SORT**—This indicates a sort, either into memory or the **TEMP** tablespace.

- **TABLE ACCESS (ROWID)**—This indicates a row access by **ROWID** that is very fast.

- **TABLE ACCESS (FULL)**—This is a full-table scan and is usually cause for concern unless the table is very small.

- **UNION**—This indicates that the **DISTINCT** SQL clause was probably used.

- **VIEW**—This indicates that an SQL view was involved in the query.

Database statistics packages can be made to capture this information, but they tend to be very resource intensive. Turning on SQL trace statistics for a very short period of time during processing is a good practice to follow in order to gather a representative sample of the SQL access.

There are many tricks used by Oracle professionals to help speed their queries. One of the best tricks for certain types of queries is the use of temporary tables. The following section discusses the rules for using temporary tables within Oracle queries.

Temporary Tables

The prudent use of temporary tables can dramatically improve Oracle performance. Consider the following example: You want to identify all users who exist within Oracle, but have not been granted a role. So, you formulate the following query:

```
SELECT USERNAME FROM DBA_USERS
WHERE USERNAME NOT IN
(SELECT GRANTEE FROM DBA_ROLE_PRIVS);
```

This query runs in 18 seconds. Now, let's say you rewrite the same query to utilize temporary tables, as follows:

```
CREATE TABLE TEMP1 AS
   SELECT DISTINCT USERNAME FROM DBA_USERS;

CREATE TABLE TEMP2 AS
   SELECT DISTINCT GRANTEE FROM DBA_ROLE_PRIVS;

SELECT USERNAME FROM TEMP1
WHERE USERNAME NOT IN
(SELECT GRANTEE FROM TEMP2);
```

This query runs in less than three seconds. While it is not completely evident why the second query runs faster that the first, part of the reason is that the second query is interrogating a small, temporary table, while the original query was against a very large view, which was, in turn, composed of large tables that had to be joined together at runtime.

Now, let's take a look at how the Oracle optimizers can be manipulated to ensure the fastest response time.

Tuning With Oracle Optimizers

The goal of SQL tuning is quite simple, but the process of tuning SQL can be very challenging. Tuning SQL involves choosing the appropriate default SQL optimizer, and then evaluating all reoccurring SQL statements on an individual basis to ensure that an optimal path is being taken to access Oracle.

There is also debate concerning what the "best plan" for an SQL query might be. To most, the best plan is the one that results in the fastest response time (the **first_rows** hint). To others, the best plan is the plan that uses the minimum amount of database resources (the **all_rows** hint). In general, common goals of SQL tuning include:

- Alleviating full-table scans by creating indexes whenever the cost of the index is smaller than the cost of waiting for the full-table scan.

- Ensuring that the Oracle SQL optimizer is using all index resources properly.

- Using bitmapped indexes whenever appropriate.

- Using cost-based hints to improve the performance of SQL queries.

In terms of tuning SQL, the following section is the most important in this chapter. We will review the nature of Oracle cost-based and rule-based SQL optimizers, and then move on to look at how "hints" can be embedded into SQL to improve performance. Finally, we will review an overall strategy for SQL tuning that maximizes the productivity of the Oracle professionals.

SQL Optimizers

Oracle offers two methods of tuning SQL. If you are running Oracle7.2 or above, you can use the cost-based optimizer, while releases of Oracle7.1 and below recommend the rule-based optimizer. The rule-based method was the only method available in version 6. When using the rule-based optimizer, the indexing of tables and order of clauses within an SQL statement control the access path. The cost-based optimizer automatically determines the most efficient execution path, and the programmer is given *hints* that can be added to a query to alter the access path. As of Oracle7.3.3, the cost-based optimizer and rule-based optimizer can be set in the init.ora file by setting the **optimizer_mode** to **rule**, **all_rows**, **first_rows**, or **choose**, as follows:

- **optimizer_mode=rule**—This will invoke the rule-based optimizer regardless of the presence of statistics on tables and indexes.

- **optimizer_mode=all_rows** or **optimizer_mode=first_rows**—This will use the cost-based optimizer and will estimate statistics at runtime if table and index statistics do not exist.

- **optimizer_mode=choose**—The cost-based optimizer will be invoked whenever statistics exist for any of the tables in a query. The rule-based optimizer will be used to service a query if all the tables in the query do not contain statistics.

Be careful when using the **choose** option. When you give Oracle the ability to choose the optimizer mode, Oracle will favor the cost-based approach if *any* table in a query has statistics. (Statistics are created with the **ANALYZE TABLE** command.) For example, if a three-table join is specified in **choose** mode and statistics exist for one of the three tables, Oracle will decide to use the cost-based optimizer and will issue an **ANALYZE TABLE ESTIMATE STATISTICS** at runtime. This will dramatically slow down a query.

The optimizer option (rule versus cost) can be controlled at the database level or at the program level. Prior to version 7.0.16, the cost-based analyzer had significant problems, and Oracle recommended the use of the rule-based optimizer. With the rule-based optimizer, table names are read from right to left. Hence, the last table in the **FROM** clause should be the table that returns the smallest number of rows. This is the exact opposite of the cost-based optimizer, which reads table names from left to right. Despite the best efforts of Oracle, the rule-based optimizer remains the best choice for many applications, especially applications where the SQL syntax is static and can be altered to accommodate the rule-based optimizer.

It should be noted that the cost-based optimizer has made tremendous headway over the past five years. As of Oracle8, the Oracle cost-based optimizer supports many new features that cannot compete with the rule-based optimizer, especially in the area of data warehousing. For data warehouses, the cost-based optimizer offers the use of bitmapped indexes and STAR query hints. For Oracle8, the bitmapped index and STAR query hints have been combined into a new hint that dramatically reduces execution times for certain types of warehouse queries.

But, despite all the enhancements to the cost-based optimizer, the rule-based optimizer continues to be a better choice for many systems. For example, the cost-based optimizer will often perform full-table scans when more than three tables are being joined—even when indexes exist to service the query. Hence, the rule-based optimizer continues to be supported in Oracle8, and it continues to be a good choice for some applications.

There are cases where it is not always possible to alter Oracle SQL. Let's now take a look at a popular approach within ad hoc Oracle query tools, whereby a tool generates SQL on behalf of the end user.

The Problem Of Ad Hoc SQL Generators

In Oracle applications where the end-user community has tools that automatically generate SQL, there can be some serious performance issues. Many ad hoc SQL generation tools generate SQL without any regard for the rule-based optimizer, which means the tools can formulate queries that are not ideal for the rule-based optimizer. For instance, an SQL generation tool might not specify the proper "driving" table (as determined by the order of the table names in the **FROM** clause).

Also, these ad hoc SQL generator tools do not always allow for the addition of hints. If hints cannot be added, all queries submitted through the tool will be forced to use the default optimizer mode as specified in the init.ora parameter file. For example, even if you determined that a query would run 10 times faster with a hint, you would be unable to use this hint because the SQL generator does not allow additions. This problem forces an Oracle developer to choose a default SQL optimizer mode, and this mode will be used by all queries that originate from the SQL generator. The issue is aggravated when the SQL generator tool is used for many types of SQL queries. For example, 50 percent of the queries might access a single table and would run best with the rule-based optimizer, while the other 50 percent might join four or more large tables and would run best with the cost-based optimizer.

Assuming that we have the freedom to alter our SQL, we can now take a look at the internal workings of Oracle's cost-based optimizer.

Tuning Oracle's Cost-Based Optimizer

To execute SQL, an optimizer must create an execution plan that tells Oracle the order in which to access the desired tables and indexes. The cost-based optimizer works by weighing the relative "costs" for different access paths to the data, and choosing the path with the smallest relative cost.

The cost-based optimizer uses statistics derived from tables and indexes, and, in Oracle7.3 and above, column value distribution statistics can also be gathered. In Oracle applications predating the release of Oracle7.3, column values are assumed to be evenly distributed. Consequently, a query might access an index to get table rows, when a full-table scan might be more efficient. In Oracle7.3 and above, once the statistics have been collected, there are three ways to invoke the cost-based optimizer:

- Set the init.ora parameter **optimizer_mode = all_rows** or **first_rows**

- **ALTER SESSION SET OPTIMIZER_GOAL=all_rows** or **first_rows**

- Use cost-based hints **/*+ all_rows */** or **--+ all_rows**

These "costs" for a query are determined with the aid of table and index statistics that are computed with the **ANALYZE** command in Oracle, as follows:

- *Tables*—**ANALYZE TABLE xxx ESTIMATE STATISTICS SAMPLE 10%;**

- *Indexes*—**ANALYZE INDEX xxx COMPUTE STATISTICS;**

It is important that the statistics are refreshed periodically, especially when the distribution of data changes frequently. The SQL shown in Listing 5.8 can be used to run the **ANALYZE** statements for tables and indexes. It is not always a good idea to use Oracle's **dbms_utility.analyze_schema** or the **dbms_ddl.analyze_object** packages to perform this task because a failure on one of the statements can affect the results of subsequent statements. The script shown in Listing 5.8 will generate the proper SQL syntax.

Listing 5.8 A script to analyze tables and indexes for the cost-based optimizer.

```
Spool runstat.sql;
SELECT
'ANALYZE TABLE '|| owner ||'.' || table_name || '
    ESTIMATE STATISTICS SAMPLE 20%;'
FROM
```

```
    DBA_TABLES
WHERE
    owner NOT IN ('SYS','SYSTEM');

SELECT
'ANALYZE INDEX '|| owner ||'.' || index_name || '
    COMPUTE STATISTICS;'
FROM
    DBA_INDEXES
WHERE
    owner NOT IN ('SYS','SYSTEM');

SPOOL OFF;
@runstat
```

In Oracle7.3 and above, the **DBA_HISTOGRAMS** view is provided for keeping information on the distribution of column values. Oracle uses height-balanced histograms as opposed to width-balanced histograms, meaning that each bucket of the histogram will contain the same number of elements. The purpose of a histogram is to provide a clear picture of the distribution of values within a low-cardinality index. Unfortunately, getting histogram data requires each and every index column to be analyzed. However, it is recommended that histograms should never be used. Bitmapped indexes are a far better choice for low-cardinality column values and they don't require histograms. In short, bitmapped indexes are a much better choice than b-tree indexes for columns that have less than 20 distinct values. The bitmapped index will consume up to 80 times less space than a b-tree index, and the bitmapped index will provide far better response time.

While bitmapped indexes can be of great help, there are things that can be done to alter Oracle SQL to change the access path to the data. Now let's take a look at the use of SQL hints with Oracle's cost-based optimizer.

Using Hints In SQL Queries

There are several hints that can be directly embedded into Oracle SQL. These hints serve the purpose of changing the optimizer path to the data. Remember, hints override all settings for **optimizer_mode** and **optimizer_goal**.

Hints are always specified immediately after the **SELECT** statement in either of two forms:

- **SELECT /*+ all_rows */ customer_name FROM CUSTOMER;**

- **SELECT --+ all_rows customer_name FROM CUSTOMER;**

Following is a summary of the most common hints that can be added to SQL:

- **ALL_ROWS**—Provides the best overall throughput and minimum resource consumption for the cost-based approach.

- **AND_EQUAL(table_name index_name1)**—Causes merge scans for two to five single-column indexes.

- **CACHE**—Causes any table in a full-table scan within the size of the **cache_size_threshold** init.ora parameter to be treated as if the table cache option is specified.

- **CLUSTER(table_name)**—Requests a cluster scan of the **table_name**.

- **FIRST_ROWS**—Provides the best response time.

- **FULL**—Requests the bypassing of indexes, doing a full-table scan.

- **HASH(table_name)**—Causes a hash scan of **table_name**.

- **HASH_AJ**—Performs a hash anti-join when placed in a **NOT IN** subquery.

- **INDEX(table_name index_name)**—Requests the use of the specified index against the table. If no index is specified, Oracle will choose the best index.

- **INDEX_ASC(table_name index_name)**—Requests to use the ascending index on a range scan operation.

- **INDEX_COMBINE(table_name index_name)**—Requests that the specified bitmapped index be used.

- **INDEX_DESC(table_name index_name)**—Requests to use the descending index on a range scan operation.

- **MERGE_AJ**—Performs an anti-join when placed in a **NOT IN** subquery.

- **NO_EXPAND**—Requests a query to not perform **OR** expansion (i.e., **OR** concatenation).

- **NO_MERGE**—Prevents a view from being merged into a parent query.

- **NOCACHE**—Causes the table cache option to be bypassed.

- **NOPARALLEL**—Turns off the parallel query option.

- **ORDERED**—Requests that tables be joined in the order that they are specified (left to right). For example, if you know that a **STATE** table has only 50 rows, you might want to use this hint to make **STATE** the driving table.

- **PARALLEL(table_name degree)**—Requests that the **table_name** query in full-table scans be executed in parallel mode with "degree" processes servicing the table access.

- **PUSH_SUBQ**—Causes all subqueries in the query block to be executed at the earliest possible time.

- **ROWID**—Requests a **ROWID** scan of the specified table.

- **RULE**—Indicates that the rule-based optimizer has been invoked (sometimes to the absence of table statistics).

- **STAR**—Forces the use of a STAR query plan, provided that there are at least three tables in the query and a concatenated index exists on the fact table.

- **USE_CONCAT**—Requests that a **UNION ALL** be used for all **OR** conditions.

- **USE_HASH(table_name1 table_name2)**—Requests a hash join against specified tables.

- **USE_MERGE**—Requests a sort merge operation.

- **USE_NL(table_name)**—Requests a nested loop operation with the specified table as the driving table.

Because hints are coded into queries as comments, SQL will not indicate an error if a hint is improperly entered. So, be very careful to ensure that hints are properly stated within your queries.

Oracle has published a table that describes the precedence hierarchy for hints, **optimizer_goal**, and **optimizer_mode** settings, as shown in Listing 5.9.

Listing 5.9 Oracle's precedence hierarchy for hints, **optimizer_goal**, and **optimizer_mode** settings.

Hint	A table has Statistics	Optimizer_Goal	Optimizer_Mode	Actual Mode
RULE	Irrelevant	Irrelevant	Irrelevant	RULE
ALL_ROWS	Irrelevant	Irrelevant	Irrelevant	ALL_ROWS
FIRST_ROWS	Irrelevant	Irrelevant	Irrelevant	FIRST_ROWS
None	Irrelevant	RULE	Irrelevant	RULE
Other	Irrelevant	RULE	Irrelevant	ALL_ROWS
None	Irrelevant	ALL_ROWS	Irrelevant	ALL_ROWS
Other	Irrelevant	ALL_ROWS	Irrelevant	ALL_ROWS
None	Irrelevant	FIRST_ROWS	Irrelevant	FIRST_ROWS
Other	Irrelevant	FIRST_ROWS	Irrelevant	FIRST_ROWS
None	Irrelevant	Not Set	RULE	RULE
Other	Irrelevant	Not Set	RULE	ALL_ROWS
None	Irrelevant	Not Set	ALL_ROWS	ALL_ROWS
Other	Irrelevant	Not Set	ALL_ROWS	ALL_ROWS
None	Irrelevant	Not Set	FIRST_ROWS	FIRST_ROWS
Other	Irrelevant	Not Set	FIRST_ROWS	FIRST_ROWS

As you can see in Listing 5.9, a hint overrides all optimizer settings, while **optimizer_goal** overrides **optimizer_mode** settings. **optimizer_mode** settings only take effect when neither **optimizer_goal** settings nor hints are present.

Beware when using the **ALTER SESSION SET OPTIMIZER_GOAL** inside Pro*C programs. While the Pro*C precompiler allows this statement, it will not have any effect on subsequent SQL inside the Pro*C program. The only solution is to physically embed hints into SQL statements.

When issuing the ALTER SESSION SET OPTIMIZER_GOAL command, it is important to remember that the command will not take effect on SQL that is already in Oracle's shared pool because Oracle will directly load the plan from the shared pool, ignoring the new setting for OPTIMIZER_GOAL. There are two ways to get around this problem. The first method is to issue the ALTER SYSTEM FLUSH SHARED POOL command to remove all SQL statements from the shared pool. A more reliable alternative is to slightly alter the SQL statement to make it different from the one in the shared pool. This can be done by adding spaces or changing the capitalization of some of the verbs. Oracle recognizes that SQL starting with Select is not the same statement as SQL starting with select.

There are several general facts to remember about hints:

- All hints except **rule** invoke the cost-based optimizer.

- The **all_rows** hint tends to favor full-table scans.

- The **first_rows** hint tends to favor index access.

By default, the cost-based optimizer uses **all_rows** costing, which minimizes Oracle resources (**first_rows** maximizes response time). Remember, the cost-based optimizer will only be as accurate as the statistics that are computed from the tables. Your DBA will need to create a periodic **cron** job (a Unix-based job scheduling utility) to reestimate statistics for all tables that are volatile and change columns frequently. While a full **ANALYZE TABLE xxx ESTIMATE STATISTICS** will interrogate every row of the table, a faster method can be used by issuing **ANALYZE TABLE ESTIMATE STATISTICS SAMPLE nn ROWS**. By taking a sample of the rows within the table, the statistics generation will run much faster. Keep in mind that one of the things that the **ANALYZE** command reviews is the selectivity and distribution of values within an index. As such, care should be taken to sample at least 100 rows from each table. Listing 5.10 shows the results of a test that created a set of three tables—**DEPT**, **DEPT1**, **DEPT2**—each with an index on **deptno** and set **optimizer_goal** as **rule** in the init.ora.

Listing 5.10   The results of the test query.

```
SELECT /*+ INDEX(DEPT DEPT_PRIMARY_KEY) INDEX(DEPT2 i_dept2)
INDEX(DEPT1 i_dept1)*/
DEPT.deptno, DEPT1.dname, DEPT2.loc
FROM DEPT, DEPT1, DEPT2
WHERE DEPT.deptno=DEPT1.deptno AND
DEPT1.deptno=DEPT2.deptno

Misses in library cache during parse: 1
Optimizer hint: RULE
Parsing user id: 48  (DON)

Rows      Execution Plan
-----     --------------
    0   SELECT STATEMENT   OPTIMIZER HINT: RULE
    4     MERGE JOIN
    4       SORT (JOIN)
    4         NESTED LOOPS
    5           INDEX (RANGE SCAN) OF 'DEPT_PRIMARY_KEY' (UNIQUE)
    4           TABLE ACCESS (BY ROWID) OF 'DEPT1'
```

```
8              INDEX (RANGE SCAN) OF 'I_DEPT1' (NON-UNIQUE)
4        SORT (JOIN)
4          TABLE ACCESS (BY ROWID) OF 'DEPT2'
5            INDEX (RANGE SCAN) OF 'I_DEPT2' (NON-UNIQUE)
```

Listing 5.11 shows what is received if the test query is run without any hints.

Listing 5.11   The test query results without hints.

```
SELECT DEPT.deptno, DEPT1.dname, DEPT2.loc
FROM DEPT, DEPT1, DEPT2
WHERE DEPT.deptno=DEPT1.deptno AND
DEPT1.deptno=DEPT2.deptno

Misses in library cache during parse: 1
Optimizer hint: RULE
Parsing user id: 48   (JACK)


Rows     Execution Plan
----     --------------------
   0   SELECT STATEMENT   OPTIMIZER HINT: RULE
   4    NESTED LOOPS
   4      NESTED LOOPS
   4        TABLE ACCESS (FULL) OF 'DEPT2'
   4        TABLE ACCESS (BY ROWID) OF 'DEPT1'
   8          INDEX (RANGE SCAN) OF 'I_DEPT1' (NON-UNIQUE)
   4        INDEX (UNIQUE SCAN) OF 'DEPT_PRIMARY_KEY' (UNIQUE)
```

If you add a hint for the **DEPT2** index, the full-table scan would be on **DEPT1**, and so on.

While hints are invaluable tuning with the cost-based optimizer, they are of no help when using the rule-based optimizer. The next section will take a look at how to tune rule-based Oracle SQL.

Tuning With Oracle's Rule-Based Optimizer

In Oracle's rule-based optimizer, the ordering of the table names in the **FROM** clause determines the driving table. The driving table is important because it is retrieved first, and the rows from the second table are then merged into the result set from the first table. Therefore, it is essential that the second table return the least amount of rows based on the **WHERE** clause. *This is not always the table with the least amount of*

Table 5.2   New York and London **EMP** tables.

	Rows	Dept 100	Dept 200
New York	1,000	100	900
London	200	150	50

rows (i.e., the smallest cardinality). For example, consider two **EMP** tables—one in London and another in New York, as shown in Table 5.2.

In this example, a total **SELECT** from the **EMP TABLE** should specify the New York table first because London has the least amount of returned rows:

```
SELECT *
FROM EMP@new_york, EMP@london;
```

If the SQL specifies a **WHERE** condition to include only Department 100, the order of table names should be reversed, as follows:

```
SELECT *
FROM EMP@london, EMP@new_york
WHERE
    dept = 100;
```

It is not always known what table will return the least amount of rows, so procedural code should be used to interrogate tables and specify the tables in their proper order. This type of SQL generation can be very useful for ensuring optimal database performance, as shown in Listing 5.12.

Listing 5.12   Automatic generation of optimal rule-based SQL.

```
SELECT count(*) INTO :my_london_dept
    FROM EMP@london
    WHERE dept = :my_dept;

SELECT count(*) INTO :my_ny_dept
    FROM EMP@new_york
    WHERE dept = :my_dept;

IF my_london_dept >= my_ny_dept
{
    TABLE_1 = EMP@london
    TABLE_2 = EMP@new_york
```

```
ELSE
    TABLE_1 = EMP@new_york
    TABLE_2 = EMP@london
};

/* Now we construct the SQL */

SELECT *
FROM :TABLE_1, :TABLE_2
WHERE
    dept = :my_dept;
```

Let's look at another rule-based optimizer example. Consider the following query:

```
SELECT
    customer_name,
    sum(order_amount)
FROM
    ORDER, CUSTOMER
WHERE
    customer_id = 98765;
```

Here, you can expect that there will be a single row returned from the **CUSTOMER** table, while there might be hundreds of orders for this customer. Consequently, the query properly specifies the **CUSTOMER** table as the last table in the **FROM** clause. There are three ways to invoke the rule-based optimizer:

- Set the init.ora parameter **optimizer_mode = rule**.

- **ALTER SESSION SET OPTIMIZER_GOAL=rule**.

- Use cost-based hints **/*= rule */** or **--+ rule**.

Tips For The Rule-Based Optimizer

Here are some tips for effectively tuning Oracle's rule-based optimizer:

- *Try changing the order of the tables listed in the **FROM** clause. Joins should be driven from tables returning fewer rows rather than tables returning more rows. In other words, the table that returns the fewest rows should be listed last. This usually means that the table with the most rows is listed first. If the tables in the statement have indexes, the driving table is determined by the indexes. One Oracle developer recently slashed processing in half by changing the order of the tables in* the **FROM** clause! Another developer had a process shift from running for 12 hours to running in 30 minutes by changing the **FROM** clause.

- Try changing the order of the statements in the **WHERE** clause. Here's the idea: Assume that an SQL query contains an **IF** statement with several boolean expressions separated by **AND**s. Oracle parses the SQL from the bottom of the SQL statement, in reverse order. Therefore, the most restrictive boolean expression should be on the bottom. For example, consider the following query:

```
SELECT
     last_name
FROM
     STUDENT
WHERE
eye_color = 'BLUE'
AND
national_origin = 'SWEDEN';
```

- Here, you can assume that the number of students from Sweden will be smaller than the number of students with blue eyes. To further confound matters, if an SQL statement contains a compound **IF** separated by **OR**s, the rule-based optimizer parses from the top of the **WHERE** clause. Therefore, the most restrictive clause should be the first boolean item in the **IF** statement.

- Analyze the existence/nonexistence of indexes. Understand your data. Again, unlike the cost-based optimizer, the rule-based optimizer only recognizes the existence of indexes and does not know about the selectivity or the distribution of the index column. Consequently, use care when creating indexes, especially when using rule-based optimization. Consider all programs that use a field in a **WHERE** clause of a **SELECT**. A field should only be indexed when a very small subset (less than 5 to 10 percent) of the data will be returned.

- Is the target table fragmented? For example, a table could be fragmented if it constantly has a large number of rows inserted and deleted. This is especially true in **PCTFREE** because the table has been set to a low number. Regular compression of the table with Oracle's export/import utility will re-store a table row and remove fragmentation.

- Always run questionable SQL through **EXPLAIN PLAN** to examine the access path.

- *Understand which query paths are the fastest. For example, accessing a table by ROWID is the fastest access method available where a full-table scan is 17 out of 18 for the ranking of query paths. (Reference Table 5.1, shown earlier in this chapter, for the complete list of relative costs.)*

- *Avoid joins that use database links into Oracle6 tables.*

- *Make effective use of arrays. Array processing significantly reduces database I/O. Consider the following example: A table has 1,000 rows to be selected. The records are manipulated and then updated in the database. Without using array processing, the database receives 1,000 reads and 1,000 updates. With array processing (assuming an array size of 100), the database receives 10 reads (1,000/100) and 10 updates. According to Oracle, increasing the array size to more than 100 has little benefit.*

When The Rule-Based Optimizer Fails

There are cases in which the rule-based optimizer fails to choose the best index to service a query. This is because the rule-based optimizer is not aware of the number of distinct values in an index.

Let's look at an example. Assume there are 100,000 retired employees, 20,000 employees in the personnel department, and 500 employees who are both retired and belong to the personnel department. Let's also assume that you have created a non-unique index on both the status and the department columns of your employee table. In this example, you would expect that the most efficient way to service this query would be to scan the most selective index (in this case, the department index), scanning the 20,000 retired employees to get the 500 in the personnel department. It would be far less efficient to scan the status index, reading through 100,000 retired employees to find those who work in the personnel department. Therefore, the more efficient query would appear as follows:

```
SELECT
    count(*)
FROM
    EMPLOYEE
WHERE
    department = 'PERSONNEL'
AND
    status = 'RETIRED';
```

Using the rule-based optimizer, you can see the following plan:

```
SELECT STATEMENT
    SORT AGGREGATE
        SELECT BY ROWID EMPLOYEE
            NON-UNIQUE INDEX NON-SELECTIVE RANGE SCAN status_ix(status)
```

Even reversing the order of the items in the **WHERE** clause does not change the fact that the rule-based optimizer is choosing to scan through all 100,000 retired employees looking for the 500 that belong to the Personnel department. With the cost-based optimizer, you can see that the selectivity of the indexes is known and that the most efficient index is used to service the request, as follows:

```
SELECT STATEMENT
    SORT AGGREGATE
        SELECT BY ROWID EMPLOYEE
            NON-UNIQUE INDEX NON-SELECTIVE RANGE SCAN dept_ix(department)
```

In sum, you need to pay careful attention to the indexes that are chosen by the rule-based optimizer, and either disable the indexes that you do not want to be used in a query or force the use of the index that you want. To review, indexes can be explicitly specified with the **INDEX** hint, or unwanted indexes can be disabled by mixing data types on the index (i.e., **WHERE numeric_column_value = 123||'**).

Now, let's put all of this information together and take a look at an overall strategy for tuning with the Oracle optimizers. While no single strategy works for every database, with a little analysis you can determine a systemwide strategy based on the SQL characteristics of your database.

A Strategy For Optimizer Tuning

When planning an overall strategy for SQL tuning, you must take into consideration the shortcomings of Oracle optimizers, as well as the nature of your data and the types of queries that are issued against the data. This section will take a look at how you can develop an overall plan for the prudent use of the appropriate optimizers within your databases.

Unfortunately, there are numerous anomalies with the Oracle cost-based optimizer, even as of release 8. For example, the **ALTER SESSION SET OPTIMIZER_GOAL=**

rule statement does not always guarantee that subsequent SQL is run with the rule-based optimizer.

There is also the issue of bitmapped indexes, which can dramatically speed up certain queries. Bitmapped indexes will not be used with the rule-based optimizer. Consequently, it appears that the best overall approach is to tune queries on an individual basis. Every database is different, both in the types of queries and the structures of the data. However, following are some general rules that can be applied:

- Queries that join three or more large tables will generally benefit from the rule-based optimizer or the **first_rows** hint.

- Queries that access bitmapped indexes will benefit from the cost-based optimizer.

- Queries that use STAR query hints need the cost-based optimizer.

Given that any Oracle environment can benefit from both optimizers, there are a couple of choices a DBA must make, including setting a default optimizer.

Setting A Default Optimizer

A DBA can choose to make the cost-based optimizer the default and use rule hints when required, or a DBA can make the rule-based optimizer the default and use cost hints and statistics when desired. It has been the experience of many Oracle DBAs that the best approach for most systems is to make rule-based SQL optimization the default for a system, and then use the **/*+ ALL_ROWS */** hint in conjunction with table statistics to use the cost-based optimizer for queries that contain bitmapped indexes.

 TIP

If there are situations where SQL*Plus queries would benefit from an ***optimizer_mode*** *that is different from SQL in application programs and PL/ SQL, then the* ***ALTER SESSION SET OPTIMIZER GOAL*** *statement can be placed in the SQL*Plus global login script to ensure that all SQL*Plus queries use the same optimizer. The global login script can be found in $ORACLE_HOME/sqlplus/admin/glogin.sql.*

Let's take a look at how we can set the default optimizers for either cost-based or rule-based optimization.

Setting The Cost-Based Optimizer As The Default

To set the cost-based optimizer as the default, follow the steps presented below:

1. Set one of the following init.ora parameters: **optimizer_mode=all_rows** or **optimizer_mode=first_rows**.

2. Bounce the database.

3. Collect statistics of all tables and indexes with the **ANALYZE** command.

4. Use rule hints or **ALTER SESSION SET OPTIMIZER_GOAL** statements to invoke rule-based optimization, as required.

To invoke cost-based optimization, you need to create statistics for all indexes and tables participating in the query (using the **ANALYZE** command), use cost hints, or **ALTER SESSION SET OPTIMIZER_GOAL** statements to invoke rule-based optimization as required.

When using the cost-based optimizer, you can be assured that the order of items in the **FROM** and **WHERE** clauses will not affect the access paths. However, there could be circumstances where the rule-based optimizer will generate the fastest path to the data, such as a case where the rule-based optimizer chooses a nonselective index instead of a selective index.

Setting The Rule-Based Optimizer As The Default

To set the rule-based optimizer as the default, follow the steps presented below:

1. Set the following init.ora parameter: **optimizer_mode=rule**.

2. Bounce the database.

To default to rule-based SQL optimization, the init.ora parameter **optimizer_ mode** must be set to **rule**. You can then use hints to invoke the cost-based optimizer for queries that require bitmapped indexes or STAR query joins. However, you should be wary of the rule-based approach. The order that tables appear in the SQL **FROM** clause might affect the access path. Hence, the rule-based default is best for systems that do not have SQL generation tools, such as the GQL product, which will generate SQL that is not always optimally structured for the rule-based optimizer.

There are cases in the real world where a complex query demands a complex SQL statement. In such cases, we must pay careful attention to the proper formulation of the query, especially when SQL subqueries are involved.

Tuning SQL Subqueries

Whenever possible, the use of a subquery within Oracle should be avoided. In most cases, the subquery can be replaced with a standard **JOIN** operation and thereby avoid the overhead associated with subqueries. However, there are circumstances where the use of an Oracle subquery is unavoidable, and this section describes the rules for determining the best way to specify a subquery.

As you probably know, Oracle SQL (and all other SQL) only allows one table to be specified in the **FROM** clause of an SQL **UPDATE** or **DELETE** statement. As a consequence, the only way to specify values from another table is to place the reference to the other table into a subquery. There is a question about the most efficient way to specify a subquery to update or delete from a table when the operation depends on the values of rows inside other tables. For example, the only way to update **TABLE1** based on corresponding rows in **TABLE2** would be to write a subquery to specify the **TABLE2** condition, as follows:

```
UPDATE
    TABLE1
    set attribute = 'y'
WHERE
    key IN
    (SELECT key from TABLE2);
```

As mentioned earlier, one of the shortcomings of the SQL language is that there are numerous ways to write most SQL statements, and each will return identical results (although they will access radically different paths and execute at different speeds). Also, while the Oracle SQL optimizer will often detect complex queries and decompose them into equivalent join operations (taking a subquery and converting it into a nested loop join), you cannot always count on the optimal access path to service a query.

In cases where you must use subqueries, there are several options for you to consider. You have the choice of using a correlated or a noncorrelated subquery, and you also have the choice of using either the **IN** clause or the **EXISTS** clause as the comparison condition for the subquery. Hence, a subquery has the following four possible forms:

```
UPDATE TABLE1 . . SET . WHERE key IN (non-correlated sub-query);
UPDATE TABLE1 . . SET . WHERE key IN (correlated sub-query);

UPDATE TABLE1 . . SET . WHERE EXISTS (non-correlated sub-query);
UPDATE TABLE1 . . SET . WHERE EXISTS (correlated sub-query);
```

Let's examine each of these possibilities and see what the possible options are for the most efficient processing in Oracle SQL.

Correlated Vs. Noncorrelated Subqueries

You have the choice of using a correlated or a noncorrelated subquery. In essence, a *correlated* subquery references the outer table inside a subquery while a *noncorrelated* subquery does not reference the outer table. A correlated subquery is evaluated once per row processed by the parent query, while a noncorrelated subquery is only executed once and the result set is kept in memory, if the result set is small, or in an Oracle temporary segment, if the result set is large. A noncorrelated subquery that returns a single row is called a *scalar* subquery. When a subquery returns one row, the Oracle optimizer will reduce the result to a constant and only execute the subquery once.

Listings 5.13 and 5.14 show identical queries except that one is written as a correlated subquery and the other is written as a noncorrelated subquery. Both subqueries will return the same result set.

Listing 5.13   A noncorrelated subquery.

```
SELECT
    count(*)
FROM
    TABLE1
WHERE
    key IN
    (SELECT key FROM TABLE2);
```

Listing 5.14 A correlated subquery.

```
SELECT
   count(*)
FROM
   TABLE1
WHERE
   key IN
   (SELECT key FROM TABLE2 WHERE TABLE1.key = TABLE2.key);
```

For the purposes of this discussion, let's call the main query—**SELECT count(*)**—the parent query, as opposed to the subquery, which is enclosed in parentheses. Given that both of these queries will return the same result, which query is the most efficient? As it turns out, the answer to this question depends on the number of rows that are returned by the parent query and the subquery. So, let's begin our answer to this question by exploring the number of rows that you get back from the query.

Issues Of Scale And Subqueries

In practice, the choice between a correlated and noncorrelated subquery depends on the number of rows expected to be returned by both the parent query and the subquery. Our goal is to balance the overhead associated with each type of subquery. Following is a brief summary of the overhead accompanying each type of subquery:

- *Correlated subquery overhead*—The subquery will be re-executed once for each row returned by the outer query. Hence, you must ensure that the subquery uses an index whenever possible.

- *Noncorrelated subquery overhead*—The subquery is executed once, and the result set is usually sorted and kept in an Oracle temporary segment where it is referenced as each row is returned by the parent query. In cases where a subquery returns a large number of rows, there will be a significant overhead involved with sorting this result set and storing the temporary segment.

In sum, your choice depends wholly on the number of rows returned by a parent query. If your parent query only returns a few rows, the overhead of re-executing the subquery is not so great. On the other hand, if the parent query returns a million rows, the subquery would be executed a million times. The same concept applies to the number of rows returned by the subquery. If your subquery only returns a few rows, then there is not much overhead in keeping the result set in memory for the parent query. If the subquery returns a million rows, then Oracle would need to store this result set as a temporary segment on disk, and then sort the segment in order to service each row of the parent query. Now, let's take a look at how we would tune an Oracle subquery with the explain plan utility.

A Real-World Test Of Subquery Execution

To see the difference between the execution plan for correlated and noncorrelated subqueries, let's design an experiment where a DBA replaces **UPDATE** with **count(*)** and take a look at the explain plan for the queries to see which is the most efficient.

In this test, Table1 has 14,000 rows and Table2 has 7,000 rows. A nonunique index was created on the key for both tables, and the DBA used Oracle's rule-based optimizer to generate paths to the data. The DBA expects that each of the **count(*)** queries will return 7,000 rows—one row for each row in Table1 that is found in Table2. To factor out variances in elapsed times, the DBA ran each query three times, and the total elapsed time for the queries was recorded.

Based on our previous discussion on issues of scale, you probably expect the parent query to return 14,000 rows and the subquery to return 7,000 rows. Consequently, the correlated subquery would need to execute the inner query 14,000 times to service all the rows in the parent table. The noncorrelated subquery will need to store 7,000 rows in a temporary segment, but the result set is small enough that the sort can take place in memory, and the DBA will only need to execute the subquery once. Therefore, the noncorrelated subquery would probably run faster because there will be fewer fetches. Using the SQLab product from Quest software, the DBA executed the queries and generated explain plans for each query.

Following is the output and the explain plan (shown in Figure 5.2) for the noncorrelated subquery using the **IN** clause:

```
COUNT(*)
-----
     7000

Elapsed: 00:00:01.09
Elapsed: 00:00:01.46
Elapsed: 00:00:01.30
```

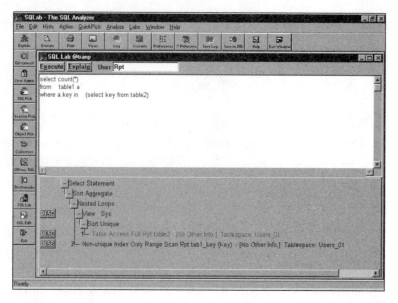

Figure 5.2

An example of a noncorrelated subquery.

Here, you can see that the query completed in slightly more than one second. The noncorrelated subquery begins by performing a full-table scan on Table2 and sorting the table in memory, storing the sorted result in a system view (temporary segment). Next, Oracle moves into nested loops where the index on Table1 is used to retrieve the key for Table1. This key is looked up in the temporary segment. As noted earlier, the subquery is only executed once, and the result set is kept and used for each test from the parent query.

Following is the output and the explain plan (shown in Figure 5.3) for a correlated subquery using the **IN** clause:

```
COUNT(*)
-----
    7000

Elapsed: 00:00:02.82
Elapsed: 00:00:04.72
Elapsed: 00:00:04.83
```

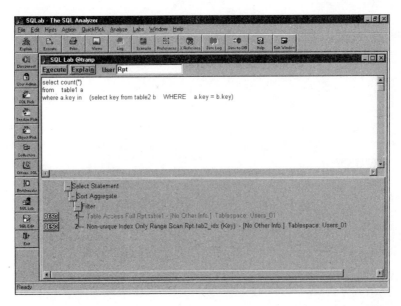

Figure 5.3
An example of a correlated subquery.

Here, you can see that the execution time is roughly twice as long as the noncorrelated subquery execution time. As discussed earlier, the correlated subquery is executed once for each row that is returned from the parent query. Hence, if 14,000 rows are returned from a parent query, the inner query would be executed once for each row. As you can see from the execution plan, a full-table scan is invoked for Table1. As each row is fetched, the key column from Table1 is used in an index-only merge scan to return the counts from the query.

As we noted earlier in this chapter, SQL provides a host of syntax for joining subordinate tables, and the subquery syntax has many permutations. Let's take a look at the performance implications of the SQL **EXISTS** clause.

Using The EXISTS Clause With Oracle Subqueries

The **EXISTS** clause can sometimes be used instead of the **IN** clause for subqueries, but there are some important differences in the behavior of the queries. When using **EXISTS** with a subquery, the boolean operator in the parent statement becomes **TRUE** if *any* rows are returned by the subquery, and this might not provide the desired result. Consequently, the following query would fail to count the 7,000 matching rows:

```
SELECT
    count(*)
FROM
    TABLE1
WHERE
    EXISTS
    (SELECT key FROM TABLE2);
```

Here is the output (shown in Figure 5.4) for a query as a noncorrelated subquery using the **EXISTS** clause:

```
COUNT(*)
-------
   14000

Elapsed: 00:00:00.12
Elapsed: 00:00:00.11
Elapsed: 00:00:00.13
```

Note that using the **EXISTS** clause in a noncorrelated subquery gives us the wrong number of rows. In this noncorrelated subquery, using the **EXISTS** clause results in

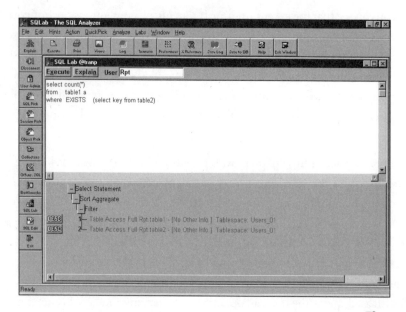

Figure 5.4
An example of a noncorrelated subquery using the **EXISTS** clause.

returning the number of rows from the parent table (Table1, in this case), and the subquery seems to be disregarded.

But, what about using the **EXISTS** clause as a part of a correlated subquery? Because the correlated subquery is executed once for each row in the parent table, you would expect that the following approach would work in identifying the 7,000 rows:

```
SELECT
    count(*)
FROM
    TABLE1
WHERE
    EXISTS
    (SELECT key FROM TABLE2 WHERE TABLE1.key = TABLE2.key);
```

Following is the execution listing and the explain plan (shown in Figure 5.5) for a correlated subquery using the **EXISTS** clause:

```
COUNT(*)
------
    7000
```

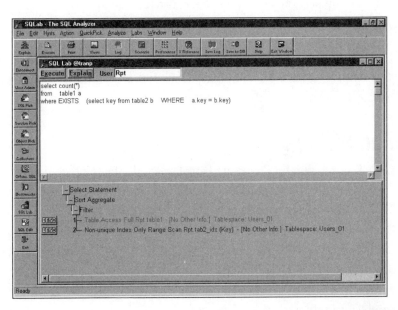

Figure 5.5

An example of a correlated subquery using the **EXISTS** clause.

```
Elapsed: 00:00:03.73
Elapsed: 00:00:03.36
Elapsed: 00:00:03.36
```

Note that the explain plan for the **EXISTS** clause is identical to the explain plan used in the **IN** clause and that the result set is the same as when the **IN** clause was used.

Conclusions About Subqueries

The overriding conclusion about subqueries is that each SQL subquery must be evaluated on an individual basis, with an emphasis on the number of expected rows to be returned. Let's review some other conclusions that can be drawn about subqueries:

- When using a correlated subquery, the explain plans and results are identical for both the **IN** clause and the **EXISTS** clause.

- The **EXISTS** clause is inappropriate for a noncorrelated subquery.

- When a parent query returns a relatively small number of rows, a correlated subquery will perform faster than a noncorrelated subquery.

- When a subquery returns a small number of rows, a noncorrelated subquery will run faster than a correlated subquery.

Now that we have reviewed the tuning of subqueries, let's take a look at tuning SQL as it exists within Oracle's PL/SQL language.

Tuning PL/SQL

PL/SQL is the acronym for Procedure Language/SQL, the standard procedural language for online Oracle applications. PL/SQL is commonly used within Oracle's SQL*Forms application framework, but the popularity of PL/SQL for non-SQL*Forms applications has reemerged because of the benefits of using Oracle stored procedures (which must be written with PL/SQL). PL/SQL offers the standard language constricts, including looping, **IF** statement structures, assignment statements, and error handling. There are several problems with PL/SQL. We'll look at some of those problems in this section.

PL/SQL offers two types of SQL cursors, the *explicit* cursor and the *implicit* cursor. Explicit cursors are manually declared in PL/SQL as follows:

```
DECLARE
CURSOR c1 IS
SELECT last_name
FROM CUSTOMER
WHERE
cust_id = 1234;
```

However, it is possible to issue the SQL statement directly in PL/SQL without specifying the cursor name. When this happens, Oracle opens an implicit cursor to handle the request. Implicit cursors create a tremendous burden for Oracle, as the implicit cursor must always reissue a **FETCH** command to ensure that only a single row is returned by the query. This will double the amount of **FETCH** statements for a query. The moral is simple: Always declare all cursors in your PL/SQL.

PL/SQL allows certain types of correlated subqueries to run much faster than a traditional Oracle SQL query. Consider a situation where a bank maintains a general ledger table and a transaction table. At the end of the banking day, the check transaction table is applied to the **GENERAL_LEDGER** table, making the requisite deductions from the **account_balance** column. Let's assume that the **GENERAL_LEDGER** table contains 100,000 rows and 5,000 daily checks need to be processed. A traditional SQL query issued to accomplish the updating of **account_balance** would involve a correlated subquery, as illustrated in Listing 5.15.

Listing 5.15 Using a traditional SQL query to update account_balance.

```
UPDATE GENERAL_LEDGER
SET account_balance = account_balance -
   (SELECT check_amount FROM TRANSACTION
     WHERE
     TRANSACTION.account_number = GENERAL_LEDGER.account_number)
WHERE
EXISTS
(SELECT 'x' FROM TRANSACTION
 WHERE
 TRANSACTION.account_number = GENERAL_LEDGER.account_number);
```

As you might recall, a correlated subquery involves executing the subquery first and then applying the result to the entire outer query. In this case, the inner query will execute 5,000 times, and the outer query will execute once for each row returned from the inner query. This Cartesian product has always been a problem for correlated subqueries. Now, consider the identical query written in PL/SQL, as shown in Listing 5.16.

Listing 5.16 Query updating **account_balance** using PL/SQL.

```
DECLARE
  CURSOR c1 is
  SELECT account_number,
    check_amount
  FROM TRANSACTION;

    keep_account_number       number;
    keep_check_amount         number;

BEGIN

    OPEN c1;
    LOOP
            FETCH c1 INTO keep_account_number, keep_check_amount;
    EXIT WHEN c1%NOTFOUND;

    UPDATE GENERAL_LEDGER
    SET account_balance = account_balance - keep_check_amount
    WHERE account_number = keep_account_number;
    END LOOP;
END;
```

Here, you can see that each check amount is retrieved in a separate transaction and fetched into cursor **c1**. For each **check_amount**, the balance is applied to the **general_ledger** row, one at a time.

While entire books have been written to discuss the performance of PL/SQL with Oracle, we must always remember that PL/SQL is nothing more than a procedural language that accepts embedded SQL. As such, it is the presence of the SQL that determines the execution time for a PL/SQL procedure, and the tuning of SQL will always have the most dramatic impact on the execution time of a PL/SQL procedure.

Let's now take a look that the use of the Open Database Connectivity (ODBC) tool as a vehicle for executing Oracle8 SQL.

Using Oracle Stored Procedures And Triggers

Many excellent benefits can be derived from using stored procedures and triggers for all database access code. Stored procedures and triggers offer many database management enhancements to Oracle DBAs, including:

- *Encapsulation*—With stored procedures and triggers, code resides within a database instead of in external programs. With the proper use of Oracle packages, stored procedures can be logically grouped together into a cohesive framework of SQL statements.

- *Performance*—Stored procedures and triggers are cached into the shared pool, making repeated calls to a procedure very fast.

- *Flexibility*—By keeping all database access inside Oracle packages, applications contain no SQL, becoming little more than a set of calls to the stored procedures. As such, the application is insulated from the database and becomes very easy to migrate to another platform or database product.

Certain rules apply in deciding when to use a trigger or stored procedure. The choice revolves around the nature of the desired SQL, and whether it is specific to a DML event or is global in nature. In general, the validation of input data is ideally suited to an **INSERT** trigger, especially when it involves accessing another Oracle table. If you are writing your own referential integrity, **DELETE** triggers are appropriate. Triggers are generally associated with SQL that is closely tied to a single DML event, such as the insertion, deletion, or updating of a row.

Stored procedures are generally used when an SQL query creates an aggregate object, which accesses rows from many tables to create a single result set. The creation of an invoice, an order form, or a student's schedule are examples of these types of queries.

One of the problems with using Oracle stored procedures and triggers is keeping track of the SQL once it has been entered into a database. Unlike the object database products, Oracle7 did not provide a mechanism for directly associating a stored procedure with the tables that it touches. Fortunately, Oracle8 makes this less of a problem. But client/server programmers must be able to identify and reuse queries that have already been written and tested.

To achieve reusability, you can use naming conventions to ensure that all SQL is logically associated with any pertinent tables. For example, the action of SQL inserting a row into a customer table could be given a meaningful name, say **customer_insert()**. This way, the data dictionary can be interrogated to identify all existing SQL that touched a table. The use of naming conventions is tricky when a single SQL statement joins many tables, but prudent use of naming conventions can help ensure that your SQL can be located easily.

Oracle triggers have the ability to call stored procedures, and a trigger can include many SQL statements, thus providing the ability to nest SQL statements. Oracle triggers are stored as procedures that can be parameterized and used to simulate object-oriented behavior. For example, assume that you want to perform a behavior called **CHECK_TOTAL_INVENTORY** whenever an item is added to an order. The trigger definition would be:

```
CREATE TRIGGER CHECK_TOTAL_INVENTORY
         BEFORE INSERT OF LINE_ITEM
         DECLARE my_count INT;
         BEGIN
FOR EACH ROW

   SELECT count(*) INTO :my_count
   FROM QUANTITY WHERE ITEM_# = :myitem:

IF :my_count < ITEM.total THEN
    ......
END IF;
```

Triggers can also be combined to handle combined events, such as the reordering of an **ITEM** when the quantity on hand falls below a predefined level. For example:

```
CREATE TRIGGER REORDER BEFORE UPDATE ON ITEM
    FOR EACH ROW WHEN (new.reorderable = 'Y')
      BEGIN
        IF NEW.qty_on_hand + OLD.qty_on_order < NEW.minimum_qty
        THEN
            INSERT INTO REORDER VALUES (item_nbr, reorder_qty);
            NEW.qty_on_order := OLD.qty_on_order + reorder_qty;
        END IF;
      END
```

As you see, Oracle triggers are a step in the direction of coupling data with behavior, but they still have a long way to go. Now let's take a look at how the ODBC product is used as an interface between objects and Oracle.

Using ODBC As A Server Interface

The Open Database Connectivity (ODBC) product was initially developed by Microsoft as a generic database driver. Its architecture, shown in Figure 5.6, has been generalized, and many vendors are offering open database connectivity products based on Microsoft's ODBC. ODBC is the predominant common-interface approach to database connectivity and is part of Microsoft's Windows Open Service Architecture (WOSA). ODBC and WOSA define a standard set of data access services that can be used by a variety of other products when interfacing with MS-Windows applications.

ODBC consists of more than 50 functions that are invoked from an application using a call-level API. The ODBC API does not communicate with a database di-

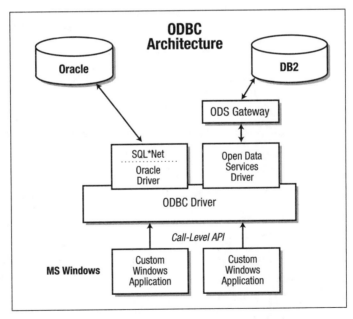

Figure 5.6
A look at the ODBC architecture.

rectly. Instead, it serves as a link between the application and a generic interface routine. The interface routine, in turn, communicates with the database drivers via a Service Provider Interface (SPI), as illustrated in Figure 5.6. Each custom application within Windows will have call-level API calls to the ODBC database driver, which then directs the request to the appropriate database driver for execution. The database driver manages the communication between the databases and handles all returning data and messages, passing them back to the ODBC driver—which passes them back to the invoking application.

As ODBC becomes more popular, database vendors are creating new ODBC drivers that will allow ODBC to be used as a gateway into their database products. It should be noted that most programmers are successful with ODBC in a simple application, but effective use of ODBC in multidatabase environments is a very difficult task. Programmers are not only faced with all the different dialects of SQL, but they must also be aware of the native API to the database engines. However, despite the steep learning curve, a few tips can ease the effort with ODBC.

Essentially, ODBC serves as the traffic cop for all data within the client/server system. When a client requests a service from a database, ODBC receives the request and manages the connection to the target database. ODBC manages all of the database drivers, checking all of the status information as it arrives from the database drivers.

It is noteworthy that the database drivers should be able to handle more than just SQL. Many databases have a native API that requires ODBC to map the request into a library of functions—for example, an SQL-server driver that maps ODBC functions to database library function calls. Databases without a native API (i.e., non-SQL databases) can also be used with ODBC, but they go through a much greater transformation than the native API calls.

When accessing multiple databases with ODBC, an API programmer has to manage the multiple database connections and the multiple SQL requests that are being directed to the connections. In ODBC, *handles* are used to point to each database connection. Handles are usually pointers into the database, and the value of a handle is a record key, a row ID, or an object ID.

Most people associate ODBC with SQL. While SQL is now the single most common access method for databases, many important non-SQL databases are widely used. Popular non-SQL databases include IMS, CA-IDMS, Basis Plus, and almost all of the new object-oriented databases. It is a misconception that a database that does not support SQL cannot use ODBC.

Now that we see how ODBC is used to allow communication between databases, let's take a look at how SQL is evolving to handle objects.

The Evolution Toward Object-Oriented SQL

When discussing the movement toward object-orientation with SQL, we need to remember that Oracle is only one of many database vendors that are adding extensions to SQL to support objects. On one side, of this market, you'll find the "pure" ODBMSs developing SQL interfaces to their object architectures, and on the other side of the market, you'll see relational vendors creating object layers for their table structures. On one side, we see the Object Management Group's Object Database Management Group (ODMG) developing a standard object query language (OQL) for SQL access to object databases. On the other side, we see the ANSI X3H7 committee developing a standard called SQL3 to incorporate objects into relational SQL. While neither approach is ideal from the perspective of an MIS manager, great progress has been made in both directions. The time has arrived when programmers who have mastered SQL also need to understand its object-oriented dialects. These products include SQL++ by Objectivity Inc., Object SQL by ONTOS, and sqlX by UniSQL. Many proponents of the relational model state that the ad hoc query capability of SQL is inconsistent with the object-oriented principle of encapsulation, but the sheer popularity of these tools has led to many attempts to reconcile SQL with object-oriented databases.

The object/relational hybrids promise to allow users to keep their existing relational technology while gaining object features. Unlike traditional relational databases, these hybrids allow cells within a table to contain multiple values or even another entire table. This nesting of tables within tables allows far more flexibility than traditional database systems, even though it appears to toss away even the most fundamental principles of normalization. As you might recall from earlier chapters, Codd's definition of First Normal Form (1NF) does not allow for repeating data items within a field, much less an Oracle8 nested table! Consequently, the extension of SQL to provide for objects presents a real challenge.

Using SQL to access nonrelational architectures is not limited to the object databases. In the early 1980s, when SQL became popular, many database vendors wrote SQL "umbrellas" over their hierarchical and network database products. Some companies even renamed their products to reflect the changing times. For example, CA's CA-IDMS was renamed to IDMS/R, proudly proclaiming that they were relational because they supported SQL queries. Of course, it takes much more than SQL to make a database relational, and great debate continues to rage about how relational an object database becomes when it allows SQL access.

The basic operators for SQL are **SELECT**, **INSERT**, **UPDATE**, and **DELETE**. Mapping these to an object database requires first matching the context of the data involved, then the semantics of the operation. For instance, the SQL engine maps:

- Relational tables to object classes

- Rows to objects

- Row identifiers to object identifiers

- Columns to object data members

In addition, SQL **SELECT** operations enable table and attribute information to identify accessible table and column names.

While originally specified in the ANSI X3H2 SQL syntax, SQL3 has promised object extensions for invoking object methods, navigating relationships between objects, and accessing nested structures. Furthermore, extents and virtual object identifiers are supported. But, SQL3 has failed to create a usable standard, so, for the time being, the database community will have to come up with a de facto standard for accessing object databases with SQL.

The upcoming sections explore how client/server developers can adapt their SQL programming to deal with objects. The sections include comments from actual users of SQL++ and discuss how programmers can prepare for this new SQL paradigm.

> **Note:** For details about the Oracle8 object layer, refer to Chapter 3, Physical Performance Design.

SQL And Oracle8 Objects

If you make a careful comparison of the relational model and the object model, you will find several constructs within object technology for which SQL must be extended to address:

- *Inheritance*—Some or all objects within a class hierarchy can be selected.

- *Abstraction*—Selecting from "composite" objects.

- *Pointer-Based Navigation*—Non-key-based data retrieval.

- *Invoking Methods in SQL*—Addressing data behaviors and functions.

Many of the characteristics of SQL for relational databases contradict some of the new features of the object/relational implementations of Oracle8 SQL. One of the most confounding problems in the database arena today is the reconciliation of objects with SQL. This problem was addressed by Christopher Stone, President of the Object Management Group:

> What the object database community needs—excuse me, what the object community needs—is an agreement on a data model and how to pinpoint it for design. How do you build applications that are free from specific Data Manipulation Languages (DMLs)? Does that mean that you extend SQL...to be object-oriented? Does it mean you develop an entirely new object query language? Probably not. Does it mean you just extend C++ and pray the marriage of a programming language and a database is really going to happen? I don't think that is going to happen.

When attempting to reconcile object-orientation and relational databases, it is very important to recognize that the object-oriented approach deals with data at a much higher level than relational databases. Whereas relational databases deal with data at the column and row level, an object-oriented system deals with objects. Objects can be any number of collections of data items. An object can be an order, an inventory list, or any real-world representation of a physical object. For example, consider an object called **ORDER_FORM**. **ORDER_FORM** is a logical object to the object-oriented system, and each **ORDER_FORM** could have associated data items and behaviors. Behaviors might include **place_order**, **change_order**, and so on.

In a relational database, an **ORDER_FORM** is really a consolidation of many different columns from many different tables. The customer name comes from the

CUSTOMER table, order date comes from the **ORDER** table, quantity from the **LINE_ITEM** table, and item description from the **ITEM** table (see Figure 5.7). Hence, a single behavior for an object could cause changes to many tables within the relational database.

One of the major shortcomings of the relational database model is its inability to represent aggregate objects. All data must be decomposed into tables, and the display of an aggregate object requires a join of the component tables at runtime. Codd suggested the use of relational views to represent this higher level of abstraction. For example, an SQL statement could create an SQL view called **ORDER_FORM**, as follows:

```
CREATE OR REPLACE VIEW
ORDER_FORM
AS
SELECT
    customer_name,
    customer_address,
    customer_phone,
    order_nbr,
    order_date,
    item_name,
    qty_ordered
FROM
    CUSTOMER,
    ORDER,
    LINE_ITEM,
    ITEM
WHERE
order_nbr = :hostvar
AND
CUSTOMER.customer_name = ORDER.customer_name
AND
ORDER.order_nbr = ORDER_LINE.order_nbr
AND
ORDER_LINE.item_nbr = ITEM.item_nbr
;
```

The view could then be used to produce an order form in a single SQL statement without requiring the SQL syntax for joining the tables together. For example:

```
SELECT *
FROM
```

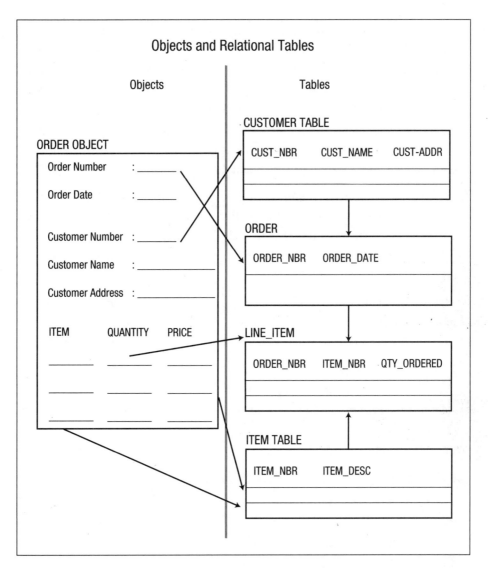

Figure 5.7
The mapping of objects to relational tables.

```
ORDER_FORM
WHERE
order_nbr = 999;
```

The Oracle7 relational **VIEW** construct still missed the basic advantage of pre-built aggregate objects. The whole idea about data aggregation is that higher-level objects should have an independent existence instead of being rebuilt each time a view is used. Also, unlike Oracle8 aggregate objects, Oracle7 relational views cannot be used for update operations. In Oracle7, the row ID could not be maintained within the subordinate tables, and consequently, **UPDATE** and **INSERT** operations were not allowed. Object behaviors such as **PLACE_ORDER** and **CHANGE_ORDER** could not use relational views. Some researchers have suggested methods for creating "updatable" views within the relational database model, but no commercial databases have implemented support for updatable views.

This "build it now" versus "build it later" debate has had a direct impact on the architecture of Oracle8. It is a popular opinion that a major shortcoming of all relational databases is their requirement that all data is modeled at its smallest, most atomic level. What is lost is the ability to create "real-world" objects with an independent existence.

The most important feature of Oracle8 aggregate objects is performance. If you pre-assemble aggregate objects using the object IDs (OIDs) of the components, retrieval of the objects will be far faster than reconstructing an aggregate at runtime each time it is requested.

Let's now take a look at the paradigm mismatch between declarative SQL and the navigational nature of objects. This problem is commonly referred to as the impedance mismatch.

SQL And The Impedance Mismatch

Impedance mismatch refers to the performance setbacks associated with translations between object and relational models. One of the early vendors to address the problems associated with impedance mismatch is Persistence Software. Persistence's object-to-relational mapping product is distinguished by its strong in-memory object caching capabilities.

In an online object-oriented application, such as a C++ program, the impedance mismatch between object and relational models requires encapsulated data to be mapped into a relational table for persistent storage and then reassembled at runtime. Most implementations of this type of mapping of in-memory objects to rows in relational tables results in substantial overhead and performance degradation. But some products alleviate this problem with large object caches that retain highly used business objects (along with their encapsulated data) in memory, thereby avoiding the overhead associated with the reassembly of objects from the underlying relational tables (as well as the delays associated with repeatedly rereading from disk).

However, there are other differences between objects and tables. One of the premises of the database object model is that object data may only be accessed via its methods, and no ad hoc object data access can be allowed. This principle is called encapsulation, and the following section discusses how SQL has been adapted to provide for encapsulation.

SQL And Encapsulation Violation

Encapsulation is defined as the ability to access objects only via their behaviors. Encapsulation is used in nondatabase object-oriented applications to ensure that all operations are performed through the programmer-defined interface, and that data will never be modified outside of the application shell. But what about ad hoc query and update? It appears that any declarative database language that allows external retrievals and updates (such as SQL), does not follow the dictates of encapsulation, and is therefore inconsistent with object-oriented database management.

At first glance, it seems that encapsulation and data independence cannot be reconciled, because it would be impossible to have data tables that are independent of an application when, at the same time, they support encapsulation, which tightly couples objects and their behaviors. However, these concepts are not contradictory. Because behaviors are stored in the database, they are not external and will not jeopardize the independence of applications from data.

For example, let's say you could only access the **credit_rating** field in the **CUSTOMER** table by invoking the **place_order** behavior. The SQL language, of course, would allow access and update to any data items that are allowed within the system security tables. Any authorized user could view the credit rating of a customer without ever invoking an object-oriented method.

Another conceptual limitation of SQL that has legitimate ramifications for object-oriented databases is the inability of SQL to associate a behavior with a data item. The properties of an object and its operational semantics must be coded within an external entity (the application program), and SQL has no built-in method for incorporating behaviors into tables. However, there is a solution to this problem, and many of the object/relational database vendors have created *methods* for database objects that have a one-for-one correspondence with SQL operators. For example, a database might automatically create a method called **insert_customer**, which would invoke the appropriate SQL statement to insert a row into a customer table. A database might automatically create methods to insert, update, and delete rows from the target table, much as C++ allows for constructors and destructors for objects. While this works fine for a simple operation, there are still problems for more sophisticated methods that access and alter more than one data column.

Many of the built-in functions of SQL also violate the encapsulation rule. For example, instead of writing a method to compute the gross pay for an employee, you could directly use SQL to perform this operation, thereby bypassing the method. For example:

```
SELECT
     hours_worked*payrate
FROM
     TIMESHEET, PAYRATES
WHERE
     emp_id = 123
AND
     week = '03/98';
```

The same is true when using **sum**, **avg**, and any other SQL function offered by the major relational database vendors.

Because encapsulation and SQL are incompatible, the only conclusion that can be reached is that encapsulation, does not apply to object-oriented databases because declarative languages violate the principle. In addition, declarative languages cannot be used within a true object-oriented database because all objects must use their pre-defined methods to gain access to the object's data.

Now that we know the nature of encapsulation, let's take a closer look at other conflicts between SQL and objects.

Conflicts Between Oracle SQL And Objects

There are several constructs within the SQL language that conflict with object-oriented databases. The most obvious is the requirement that SQL serves as an ad hoc query facility. These problems fit into the categories of :

- Abstract data typing (Oracle user-defined types)

- Encapsulation and methods

- Pointers

All of these constructs are very foreign to SQL and special extensions have been created to allow for the implementation of these constructs. Now let's take a look at how abstract data types are defined within the Oracle8 object model.

SQL And User-Defined Data Types

Oracle8 allows the concept of abstract data typing, and a programmer can create data types that are indistinguishable from system-defined data types. Oracle8 calls abstract data types user-defined types, or UDTs. For example, an Oracle8 programmer could define a data type of **boolean**, which would be treated by the system like a **char** or **integer** data type. Relational technology does not have a facility for self-defining new data types, but the new object/relational databases allow for data items to be created and used with the **CREATE TYPE** constructs discussed in earlier chapters.

Of course, there are also SQL extensions to allow for the creation and implementation of these user-defined data types. Listing 5.17 shows SQL used to create a **CUSTOMER** table. Note that two of the components, **full_name** and **full_address**, are user-defined data types, and the entire **CUSTOMER** table has been encapsulated into a UDT called **customer_stuff**.

Listing 5.17 Using SQL to create a **CUSTOMER** table.

```
CREATE TYPE
   full_address (
        street_address    varchar(20),
        city_name         varchar(20),
        state_name        char(2),
        zip_code          number(9));

CREATE TYPE
   full_name (
        first_name        varchar(20),
        MI                char(1),
        last_name         varchar(30));
```

```
CREATE TYPE
     customer_stuff AS OBJECT (
        customer_ID       number(6),
        cust_full_name    full_name,
        cust_full_address full_address));

CREATE TABLE CUSTOMER OF  customer_stuff;
```

Once the UDTs have been defined, Oracle8 SQL can be extended to allow for the use of subtyping to address data components that are nested within larger data types. For example, the following SQL selects the ZIP code for a particular customer:

```
SELECT
   customer_stuff.full_address.zip_code
FROM
   CUSTOMER
WHERE
customer_ID = 764645;
```

While dealing with UDTs is a relatively trivial extension to SQL, there are many other new constructs that need to be addressed. Let's take a detailed look at how Oracle8 objects are created and manipulated.

Creating And Manipulating Oracle8 Objects

As illustrated in a number of previous examples, Oracle8 allows for object tables to be defined. Let's now take a detailed look at some object table definitions and see how objects work in the world of Oracle8. Consider Listing 5.18, which shows the object definitions for a customer object, an order object, and an item object. In this example, the customer object is freestanding. The order object contains an owner **OID** to the customer who placed the order, as well as a nested table that will contain the item information for each order.

Listing 5.18 Defining a customer order, order object, and item object.

```
CREATE TYPE customer_stuff AS OBJECT (
    customer_nbr       number(6),
    customer_name      full_name_type,
```

```
        customer_address    address);

CREATE TYPE item_stuff AS OBJECT (
     item_nbr              number(5),
     item_desc             varchar(20),
     item_color            varchar(10),
     quantity_ordered      number(3));

CREATE TABLE ITEM_LIST AS TABLE OF item_stuff;

CREATE TYPE order_stuff AS OBJECT (
     order_date            date,
     customer_nbr          number(5),
     customer_oid          REF customer_stuff,
     order_items           item_list_type);

CREATE TABLE CUSTOMER OF customer_stuff;

CREATE TABLE ORDER OF order_stuff
    (customer_oid WITH ROWID
     SCOPE IS CUSTOMER)
     OIDINDEX oid_customer_nbr (TABLESPACE MY_INDEX)
     NESTED TABLE ORDER_ITEMS STORE AS item_stuff
       PCTFREE 10
       PCTUSED 80
       INITRANS 5
       MAXTRANS 255
       TABLESPACE MY_DATA;
```

Let's take a closer look at the data structure that Listing 5.18 is defining. Essentially, there are three entities: **customer**, **order**, and **item**. Each customer places many orders, but each order is placed by only one customer. Also, each order is for many items, and each item can participate in many orders.

The heart of the object structure is found by closely examining the order object. Here, you can see a foreign key (**customer_nbr**) is used to allow traditional joins of customers to orders, but you can also see the **customer_oid** column in the order object. The **customer_oid** is a **REF** column and is designed to contain the OID of the customer that placed the order. Finally, you can also see that the **ORDER** object contains a nested table of all of the items in the order.

Now, let's take a closer look at the SQL used to define the order object. Note the following:

```
(customer_oid WITH ROWID
     SCOPE IS CUSTOMER)
OIDINDEX oid_customer_nbr (TABLESPACE MY_INDEX)
```

Essentially, the **customer_oid** is an *owner pointer*, containing the OID of the customer that placed this order. The **WITH ROWID** command allows the **ROWID** pseudocolumn to be stored with the OID from the **REF**ed object table, in this case the **CUSTOMER** table. The storing of the **ROWID** and OID speeds the **DEREF** commands but consumes more space in the index than a standard **OIDINDEX**. Also, note that the **SCOPE** command restricts all **REF**s from this column to the customer, thereby enforcing "strong data typing" for this OID and ensuring that only customer OIDs are added into this column. This practice reduces the space requirements for the **REF** column value and speeds access.

Finally, note that the **OIDINDEX** clause creates an index on the OID that can be used to speed **REF**-type queries against tables. The **OIDINDEX** clause specifies an index on the hidden object identifier column and/or the storage specification for the index. In sum, the following principles should be applied to Oracle8 object table definition:

- If a type is going to be referenced by its OID, the object must be created using the **AS OBJECT** clause.

- All **REF** clauses in a **TYPE** declaration must be finished via an **ALTER TABLE** command on the final object table if scoping or **ROWID** storage is required.

These new pointer-based structures provide huge performance improvements over traditional SQL, but they require careful planning to ensure that the data structures are implemented properly.

Let's now take a look at the Oracle8 SQL that is used to display the contents of abstract data types.

Displaying User-Defined Data Types With SQL

There is more to user-defined data types than the ability to define them within a relational table. For instance, another useful feature of data types is that you can reference them from within an SQL query. Because data types are normally comprised of subparts, SQL must be extended to allow for an entire data type to be referenced as a single unit, and the SQL will automatically format all of the subcomponents. For example, the following SQL would display **full_address** data without the need to select each subtype:

```
SELECT DISTINCT full_address FROM CUSTOMER;
```

The preceding SQL would produce a listing like this:

```
STREET_ADDRESS        CITY_NAME     STATE_ABBR    ZIP_CODE
123 First Street      Minot         ND            77363
44 West Avenue        Albuquerque   NM            87112
8337 Glenwood Drive   Fairport      NY            14450
3 Wedgewood Avenue    Denver        CO            63533
```

Note that you would also have to alter your SQL if you wanted to select a component of **full_address**. This is generally accomplished by specifying the subcomponent by inserting a period between the higher-level data type and the data item that you wish to display. For example:

```
SELECT full_address.street_address
WHERE
full_address.zip_code LIKE '144%';
```
This SQL would produce the following listing:

```
STREET_ADDRESS
8337 Glenwood Drive
```

Now that you understand how SQL has been extended for selecting rows that contain user-defined data types, let's move on to look at how user-defined data types are updated with SQL.

Updating User-Defined Data Types With SQL

User-defined data types contain subentities, so special extensions need to be added to relational SQL to allow for these aggregate data types to be updated. This involves partitioning the SQL **UPDATE** statement to allow for the subtypes to be specified. For example, the SQL to update a customer address might look like this:

```
UPDATE CUSTOMER
     (full_address
        (
        VALUES (
                      '422 East Avenue',
                      'Northwest Lake',
                      'NM',
                      83733
                      )
        )
     );
```

As you can see, the **UPDATE** statement is referencing only the **full_address** data type, but because it consists of subtypes, you must specify each of the subtypes separately in the update statement. Now that we understand the basics of UDTs, let's take a look at how OIDs are used to enhance Oracle8 performance.

Oracle SQL And Object Identifiers

One of the greatest mismatches with SQL and objects lies in the arena of pointers, which are know in Oracle as object IDs, or OIDs. The introduction of pointers into Oracle8 has led to a situation where the declarative nature of SQL is changing radically.

For example, the use of the **DEREF** operator in the Oracle8 SQL allows an SQL statement to dereference a row pointer, essentially navigating from one table to the next. Rather than relying on the SQL optimizer to take care of the database access, the developer now has the option of embedding SQL statements into their programs that will allow them to navigate through the database, visiting tables that have been linked together with pointers. This is a very foreign idea for most SQL developers, but it is now a reality.

For example, the following SQL could be used to navigate from a customer to the order rows for the customer:

```
SELECT
   DEREF(order_list)
FROM
   CUSTOMER
```

```
WHERE
    customer_id = 'JONES';
```

This would be the equivalent to the following traditional SQL:

```
SELECT
    order_stuff
FROM
    CUSTOMER, ORDER
WHERE
    customer_id = 'JONES'
AND
customer_ID = order_ID;
```

The SQL becomes even more confounding when it deals with the more abstract uses of pointers in a relational/object model. As you might recall from earlier chapters, OIDs include some very abstract data structures, including:

- Pointers to individual rows in other tables (**REF** columns)

- Repeating groups of data values (table **varray**s)

- Repeating groups of pointers to rows (table **varray**s of OIDs)

- Pointers to arrays of pointers to rows (multidimensional **varray**s)

- Pointers to whole tables (nested tables)

Oracle8 has extended its SQL syntax to provide the following constructs to deal with pointers by using the **DEREF** operator, as follows:

```
SELECT
    DEREF(order_oid)
FROM
    CUSTOMER;
```

This SQL operator accepts an OID and returns the contents of the row that the OID points to.

Oracle8 has also included the **CAST** and **MULTISET** SQL statements. These SQL operators cast a multiple input data stream into the appropriate data types for the SQL operation. Remember, OIDs can be typed, such that a **student** OID is not the same as a **course** OID. Following is an example of an SQL **INSERT** that places a student list into an Oracle8 **COURSE** object:

```
INSERT INTO
   COURSE (STUDENT_LIST)
   (CAST
      (MULTISET
         (SELECT
               student_name,
               student_address,
               grade
            FROM
               GRADE, STUDENT
            WHERE
               GRADE.course_name = 'CS101'
               AND
               GRADE.student_name = STUDENT.student_name
         )
      )
);
```

While this SQL may seem cumbersome when compared to the elegance of a declarative SQL statement, Oracle objects linked with OIDs will have superior performance to traditional relational structures. Let's take a look at some tips for using Oracle8 objects.

Tips For Object SQL

With all of these new pointer constructs and extensions to SQL, it will be several years before the mainstream programming community arrives at a general consensus about the use of pointer-based navigation within SQL programming. Until then, the following guidelines apply to the use of the Oracle8 object extensions in SQL:

- A **varray** or nested table cannot contain a **varray** or nested table as an attribute. This means that it is not possible to nest nested tables and you can only go down one level.

- A table column specified as a **varray** cannot be indexed.

- Default values cannot be specified for **varray**s.

- A table using **varray**s or nested tables cannot use partitioned tables.

- **varray**s cannot be directly compared in SQL.

- **varray** and nested table subattributes cannot be indexed directly from the parent table.

- When using nested tables, you must specify a store table in which to store the records.

- Constraints (even **NOT NULL**) cannot be used in type definitions (they must be specified using the **ALTER TABLE** command, after the type definition has been placed inside the table).

- Store tables inherit the physical attributes of their parent table.

- Nested table store table attributes can be indexed.

If we want to use the object layer of Oracle8 to improve performance, we must remember the nature of OIDs. Oracle8 with OIDs provides the ability to "pre-join" tables, thereby removing the system overhead of doing SQL join operations. In this fashion, we could place "owner" OIDs into rows to remove the overhead of a table join when we want to access the owner of a one-to-many relationship. For example, we could place the customer OID in each order row, such that we could dereference the customer OID to get the customer row. This dereferencing will be faster than joining the order table with the customer table to get the customer information.

In addition, placing OIDs within tables provides the ability to pre-sort access to other objects, such that dereferencing the OIDs will produce the data from the objects in the order that the OIDs were originally stored. For example, a **CUSTOMER** object could contain a **varray** of OIDs to the orders that were placed by that customer—the OIDs could be stored in the **varray** in order according to their order date. In this fashion, we predetermine the sequencing of the orders for each customer, and the display of orders for a customer will take place without the overhead of doing a SQL join into the order table, and without the overhead of sorting the orders into date sequence.

Summary

Now that you understand how individual SQL queries can be tuned to make efficient use of database resources, we can move on to look at the other considerations for effective client/server implementation. Topics we'll discuss include Oracle lock management, database connectivity issues, and tuning a distributed Oracle server environment.

Tuning Oracle Locking

CHAPTER

6

HIGH PERFORMANCE

Tuning Oracle Locking

While most commercial database products provide mechanisms for locking and concurrency control, new issues emerge when using a relational database such as Oracle. This problem is especially prevalent when a single Oracle task updates multiple remote servers, which is becoming increasingly common with distributed Oracle systems. The real nightmare begins when the remote servers are of differing architectures—for example, a distributed update to a relational and a network database. In these cases, the concurrency control is generally turned off for each database and is provided for inside the application program because neither database can be expected to manage the internals of the other database.

In addition to the technical issues, the popularity of client/server interfaces has also changed how concurrency is handled. Many client/server systems disable their Oracle database locking and rely on procedural tricks to maintain data integrity at the server level. We'll discuss how to avoid contention by disabling Oracle locks.

This chapter explains the basic features of Oracle's access control and describes the issues involved when concurrency and database integrity must be maintained in a distributed Oracle server environment. Topics in this chapter include:

- The problem of cohesive updating
- Database locking and granularity
- Oracle locking
- Database deadlocks
- Lock escalation with non-Oracle servers
- Alternative locking mechanisms for Oracle
- Locking and distributed databases

273

- Measuring Oracle locks

- Oracle Parallel Server and locking

The Problem Of Cohesive Updating

To ensure that an Oracle transaction properly retrieves and updates information, it is important to understand the differences between two processing modes: conversational and pseudoconversational. In a conversational scenario, the unit of work is extended to include the entire wall-clock time that a user spends in a transaction. In pseudoconversational mode, the unit of work is partitioned. The duration of the task begins when the user requests a database service and ends when the database delivers the response to the user. The system then stands idle, releasing any locks that might have been held by the previous transaction. (See Figure 6.1.)

Conversational processing is usually associated with a pessimistic locking scheme—that is, the transaction manager assumes that the transaction is going to be "interfered with" during the session, and the locks are held for the entire time that the record is being viewed. Pseudoconversational processing mode is associated with an optimistic locking scheme, whereby the system hopes that the transaction will remain isolated.

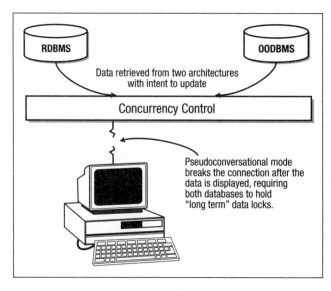

Figure 6.1
Locking and pseudoconversational processing.

As a point of illustration, consider a user who displays a customer's information, waits five minutes, and then issues an update of the customer information. If you process in fully conversational mode, a problem of database corruption never arises because "exclusive" record locks are held for the entire terminal session. However, the resources required to hold the locks could cause a burden on the database, and the lock could impede other transactions that desire to retrieve (and possibly update) the information being held by the session.

The solution to the locking problem is to create your application structure in the pseudoconversational mode, releasing the row locks after the screen is mapped out to the user. In fact, for Oracle client/server, this approach is highly recommended. However, this processing mode can lead to a variety of problems. Releasing locks in the client/server environment can be very desirable from a performance perspective. But, there are many side effects that must be addressed by the application, including dirty reads, nonreproducible results, and database corruption.

Dirty Reads

A dirty read is a situation where a row has been retrieved while it is held by another transaction with intent to update the row. Assume that a transaction begins by grabbing customer ABC with intent to update. The information for ABC is displayed on the screen, and the user changes the value of the **CUSTOMER_STATUS** field. At this time, the change has been written to the database, but the information is not made permanent until either a **COMMIT** or an **ABORT** statement is issued. During the original transaction, the change can be nullified with an **ABORT** statement. Unfortunately, a transaction might have read the value of **CUSTOMER_STATUS** for ABC before the transaction was aborted, thereby reading incorrect information.

Nonreproducible Results

Nonreproducible results most commonly occur when a report is being run against an Oracle database that is actively being updated. The report can be run in local mode. Local mode is a processing mode that uses read-only tablespaces and bypasses the services of the database manager, ignores all database locks, and reads the database files directly from the disk. The local mode report sweeps the database pages to obtain requested information, but it also reports on information that is in the process of being changed. This can result in *phantom rows* because the report can display rows that are in the process of being deleted or added.

False Database Corruption In Non-Oracle Databases

False database corruption can occur when local mode reports are run against a system that is being updated. The report attempts to retrieve a row (usually via an index) while the index nodes are readjusting after an insert or delete. This results in a report terminating with a message that indicates a bad pointer. Many DBAs have gone into a panic over this scenario until they realize that the "bad" pointer is not really corrupt and their database is intact. Because Oracle maintains read consistency, this is not an issue. Oracle will read any changed data from its rollback segments, guaranteeing that the report receives a picture of the database as it exists at the time the report started execution.

To recap, conversational processing is usually associated with a pessimistic locking scheme—that is, the transaction manager assumes that the transaction is going to be "interfered with" during the duration of the session, and the locks are held the entire time that a record is being viewed. Pseudoconversational processing mode is associated with an optimistic locking scheme, whereby the system hopes that the transaction will remain isolated. Whether you use conversational or pseudoconversational locking methods, database locking can take place at many levels.

Now that we understand the processing mode influence on locks, the next section looks at locking and granularity issues within the Oracle engine.

Database Locking And Granularity

For some relational databases, locks can be set for the entire database, a tablespace within the database, a table within the tablespace, or a row within a table, as shown in Figure 6.2. Some relational databases also offer page-level locking. A database *page* is a unit of storage, usually associated with a physical block, upon which rows are stored. For example, a page in an Oracle database defaults to 4K, and the CA-IDMS database allows page sizes to range from 2K up to 32K, depending on the size of the records.

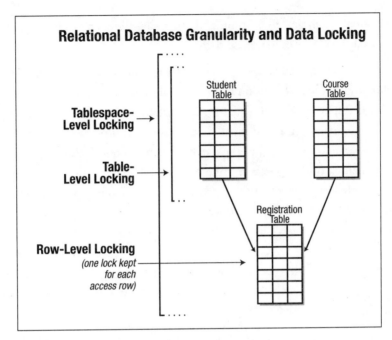

Figure 6.2
The different levels of database locking.

In object-oriented databases, locking can take place in the database, the "container" within the database, or the object within the container. The concept of a container is new to object-oriented databases. A container is defined as a partition of disk memory of arbitrary size that is used to hold objects. A container can be thought of as analogous to the pages that are used within CA-IDMS and DB2. In commercial object-oriented databases, most vendors only support locking at the container level, although most of the vendors recognize the necessity of providing object-level locking mechanisms. As a general rule, as the locking level becomes finer, the demands on resources on the lock manager increase while the potential for database deadlocks decreases.

In some databases, a programmer has some control over whether a database lock is issued. In CODASYL databases, such as CA-IDMS, a programmer can issue a **GET EXCLUSIVE** command to expressly hold a record lock for the duration of the transaction, and some relational databases allow for locks to be controlled with SQL.

Most relational databases offer commands that can allow an application to hold shared or exclusive locks on database rows.

Most commercial relational databases, such as Oracle, offer two types of locks: shared and exclusive. The most common type of locks are shared locks that are issued with SQL **SELECT** statements, and exclusive locks that are issued with **DELETE** and **UPDATE** statements. In shared locking, whenever a unit of data is retrieved from the database, an entry is placed in the database storage pool. This entry records the unit ID (usually a row or database page number). The usual size of a lock ranges from 4 through 16 bytes, depending on the database. This lock will be held by the database until a **COMMIT**, **END**, or **ABORT** message releases the lock. Most locking schemes use a *coexistence* method. For example, many clients can have shared locks against the same resource, but shared locks cannot coexist with exclusive locks. Whenever an update event occurs, the database attempts to post an exclusive lock against the target row. The exclusive lock will wait if any other tasks hold a shared lock against the target row (see Figure 6.3).

Now that we understand the basics of Oracle locking, we can take a more in-depth look at the internal mechanisms of Oracle locks.

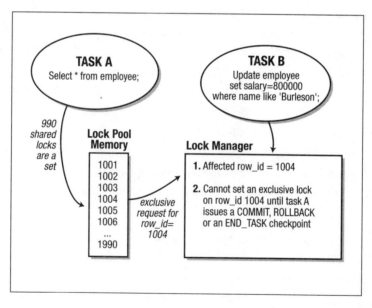

Figure 6.3
Exclusive versus shared locks.

Oracle Locking

Oracle maintains locks at either the row level or the table level. Unlike other databases, such as DB2, Oracle will never escalate locks to the table level if the database detects that a majority of the rows in a table are being locked. Consequently, an Oracle programmer must decide in advance whether to lock the entire table or allow each row of the table to be locked individually.

Two init.ora parameters control locking: **serializable=false** and **row_locking=always**. These default values should never be changed except in very rare cases.

As mentioned, Oracle supports two types of locks: row locks and table locks. These locks can be subdivided into the following categories:

- *Row Share Table Locks (RS)*—These locks are issued when an SQL transaction declares its intent to update a table in row-share mode. This type of lock will allow other queries to update rows in the **CUSTOMER** table. For example:

```
LOCK TABLE CUSTOMER IN ROW SHARE MODE;

SELECT customer_name
FROM CUSTOMER
FOR UPDATE OF CUSTOMER;
```

- *Row Exclusive Table Locks (RX)*—These locks are issued automatically against a table when an **UPDATE, DELETE**, or **INSERT** statement is issued against a table.

- *Table Share Locks (S)*—This type of lock is issued when the **LOCK TABLE** command is issued against a table. This indicates that the transaction intends to perform updates against some rows in the table and prevents any other tasks from execution until **LOCK TABLE xxx IN SHARE MODE** has completed.

- *Share Row Exclusive Table Locks (SRX)*—These locks are issued with the **LOCK TABLE xxx IN SHARE ROW EXCLUSIVE MODE** command. This prevents any other tasks from issuing any explicit **LOCK TABLE** commands until the task has completed, and it also prevents any row-level locking on the target table.

- *Exclusive Table Locks (X)*—This is the most restrictive table lock. This lock prevents everything except queries against the affected table. Exclusive locks are used when a programmer desires exclusive control over a set of rows until their operation has completed. The following command is used to lock the **CUSTOMER** table for the duration of the task:

```
LOCK TABLE CUSTOMER IN ROW EXCLUSIVE MODE NOWAIT;
```

In order to understand how the different types of locks interact with one another, you can reference Table 6.1, which describes how each lock type interacts with other locks. A NO value indicates that the locks cannot be simultaneously held.

Now that we see how locks interact with different lock types, let's take a look at a special case of database locking that can cause tremendous problems for highly interactive systems.

Database Deadlocks

The shared locking scenario of Oracle8 ensures that all database integrity is maintained and that updates do not inadvertently overlay prior updates to the database. However, a penalty has to be paid for maintaining shared locks. In Oracle, each lock requires 4 bytes of RAM storage within the Oracle instance storage pool, and large SQL **SELECT** statements can create S.O.S. (Short On Storage) conditions that can cripple an entire database. For example, a **SELECT** statement that retrieves 1,000 rows into the buffer will require 4,000 bytes of lock space. This condition can also cause the *deadly embrace*, or a database deadlock. A deadlock condition occurs when two tasks are waiting on resources that another task has locked, as depicted in Figure 6.4.

Table 6.1 Lock mode compatibility.

	NULL	SS	SX	S	SSX	X
NULL	YES	YES	YES	YES	YES	YES
RS	YES	YES	YES	YES	YES	NO
RX	YES	YES	YES	NO	NO	NO
S	YES	YES	NO	YES	NO	NO
SRX	YES	YES	NO	NO	NO	NO
X	YES	NO	NO	NO	NO	NO

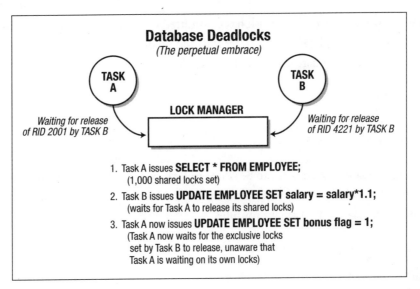

Figure 6.4
A database deadlock.

The majority of Oracle programmers do not realize that database deadlocks occur most commonly within a table index. It is important to note that a **SELECT** of a single row from a database might cause more than one lock entry to be placed in the storage pool. The individual row receives a lock, but each index node that contains the value for that row will also have locks assigned.

When an **UPDATE** or **DELETE** is issued against a row that participates in the index, the database will attempt to secure an exclusive lock on the row. This requires the task to check if any shared locks are held against the row, as well as check on any index nodes that will be affected. Many indexing algorithms allow for the index tree to dynamically change shape, spawning new levels as items are added and condensing levels as items are deleted.

Because most commercial databases only issue automatic locks against a row when they need to lock a row, programmatic solutions can be used to minimize the amount of locking used for very large update tasks. For example, in Oracle SQL, a programmer can use the **SELECT...FOR UPDATE** clause to explicitly lock a row or a set of rows prior to issuing the **UPDATE** operation. This will cause the database to issue exclusive locks (sometimes called pre-emptive locks) at the time of retrieval and hold these exclusive locks until the task has committed or ended. In the following SQL, an exclusive lock is placed on the target row, and no other task will be able to retrieve that row until the update operation has completed:

```
SELECT *
    FROM EMPLOYEE
    WHERE emp_name = 'Burleson'
    FOR UPDATE OF salary;
```

For large updates, statements can be issued to lock an entire table for the duration of an operation. This is useful when all rows in the table are going to be affected, as in the following salary adjustment routine:

```
LOCK TABLE EMP_TABLE IN EXCLUSIVE MODE NOWAIT;

UPDATE EMP_TABLE
    SET salary = salary * 1.1;
```

Sometimes an application will need to update all the rows in a table, but it is not practical to lock the entire table. An alternative to the exclusive update is to use Oracle's SQL **FETCH** statement to lock a small segment of the table, perform an update, and then release the locks with a **COMMIT** statement, as shown in Listing 6.1.

Listing 6.1   Using the **FETCH** statement.

```
DECLARE     CURSOR total_cursor IS
    SELECT emp_name FROM EMP_TABLE;

DECLARE CURSOR update_cursor IS
    SELECT ROWID
    FROM EMP_TABLE
    WHERE emp_name = :my_emp_name
    FOR UPDATE OF salary;

BEGIN
    count = 0;
    OPEN total_cursor;

    begin_loop;

        OPEN update_cursor;
```

```
        FETCH total_cursor INTO :my_emp_name;

        FETCH update_cursor INTO :my_rowid;

        IF (update_cursor%found) THEN
        {
            UPDATE EMP_TABLE
                SET salary = salary * 1.1
            WHERE
                ROWID = :my_rowid;

            count=count+1

            IF (count = 20) THEN
            {
                COMMIT;
                count = 0;
            }
        }
}
CLOSE update_cursor;
CLOSE total_cursor;
END;
```

As you can see in Listing 6.1, the locks are set as the rows are fetched, 20 at a time, and then released with a **COMMIT**. This technique consumes less memory in the lock pool and also allows other SQL statements to access other rows in the table while the update is in progress. Of course, if this code should fail, it will need to be restarted from the point of the last **COMMIT** statement. This requires additional logic to be inserted into the update program to record the row ID of the last **COMMIT**ted row and to restart the program from that row.

Now that we have seen how Oracle handles update locking under different situations, let's look at some of the different types of locking schemes that are used by other relational vendors.

Lock Escalation With Non-Oracle Servers

Some databases attempt to alleviate locking problems by performing *lock escalation*. Lock escalation increases the granularity of a lock in an attempt to minimize the impact on the database lock manager. In a relational database, the level of locking is directly proportional to the type of update that is being executed. Remember, for row-level locking, a lock must be placed in the lock storage pool for every row that an SQL statement addresses. This can lead to very heavy resource consumption, especially for SQL statements that update numerous records in many tables. For example, an SQL query that selects many (but not all) of the records in the **REGISTRATION** table might state:

```
SELECT *
FROM REGISTRATION
    WHERE
    REGISTRATION.grade = 'A';
```

Depending on the number of students affected, this type of query will begin to hold row locks until the task has successfully completed or until the SQL statement terminates because of a lack of space in the lock pool. However, if the database supports lock escalation, the database will set a single lock for the entire table, even if only a portion of the rows in **REGISTRATION** are affected.

In databases such as DB2, a statement such as **SELECT * FROM REGISTRATION**, used to return all rows in the **REGISTRATION** table, will cause DB2 to escalate from row-level locking to page-level locking. If the **REGISTRATION** table resides in a single tablespace, some database engines will escalate to tablespace-level locking. This strategy can greatly reduce strain on the lock pool, but some lock mechanisms will escalate locks (even if it means that some rows will be locked even though they are not used by the large task). For example,

```
SELECT * FROM EMPLOYEE WHERE department = 'MARKETING'
```

might cause the entire **EMPLOYEE** table to lock, preventing updates against employees in other departments.

Whenever possible, large SQL updates should be run using table-level locks, thereby reducing resource consumption and improving the overall speed of the query. Some implementations of SQL provide extensions that allow for the explicit specification of the locking level and granularity. This mechanism could allow exclusive locks to be placed on a result set if the user intends to update the rows, or to turn off shared locks if the rows will never be updated.

In all relational databases, the engine must be sure that a row is "free" before altering any values within the row. The database accomplishes this by issuing an exclusive lock on the target row. The exclusive lock mechanism will then sweep the internal *lock chain* to see if shared locks are held by any other tasks for any rows in the database. If shared locks are detected, the update task will wait for the release of the shared locks until they are freed or until the maximum wait time has been exceeded. While a task is waiting for other tasks to release their locks, it is possible that one of these tasks issues an update. If this update affects the original task's resources, a database deadlock will occur, and the database will abort the task that is holding the least amount of resources.

Unlike object, network, or hierarchical databases that update a single entity at a time, a relational database can update hundreds of rows in a single statement. For example:

```
UPDATE REGISTRATION
SET REGISTRATION.grade = 'A'
WHERE
course_id = 'CS101'
    AND
    COURSE.instructor_id = 'BURLESON';
```

This single statement can update many rows, and the concurrency manager must check for contention (i.e., shared locks). If any other tasks are viewing any other rows in the database, the engine will set as many exclusive locks as possible and put the statement into a wait state until the shared locks from other tasks have been released. Only after all the desired rows are free will the transaction be completed.

Alternative Locking Mechanisms For Oracle

The problems of lock pool resources and database deadlocks have lead to some creative alternatives to Oracle's shared and exclusive locks. Locking can be turned off in Oracle by issuing a **COMMIT** statement immediately after the **SELECT**. Without long-term shared locks, lock pool utilization is reduced and the potential for database deadlocks is eliminated. But DBAs still must deal with the problem of ensuring that updates are not overlaid. Consider Figure 6.5, which is an example of updates without locking.

Both tasks have selected Burleson's employee record and issued **COMMIT** statements to release the locks. Task B now changes Burleson's performance rating to a 12 and issues an **UPDATE** that writes the column back to the database. Task B, which is now looking at an obsolete copy of Burleson's **performance_flag**, changes the salary to $21,000, improperly assigning Burleson's raise. This is a type of *logical* corruption, whereby a user might rely on outdated values in other rows, updating the target column based on the obsolete information.

Some databases, such as SQL/DS and Oracle, allow **SELECT FOR UPDATE** commands. With **SELECT FOR UPDATE**, the before image of the row is compared with the current image of the row before the update is allowed. If you must communicate with non-Oracle databases that do not support **SELECT FOR UPDATE**, several clever techniques are available to release locks while maintaining database integrity. We'll look at two techniques here: using the **WHERE** clause and the date-time stamp.

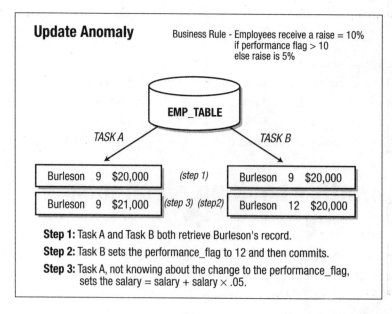

Figure 6.5
Accidental overlaying of data.

The WHERE Clause

If Burleson's row contains the fields shown in Figure 6.6, each of the fields will be specified in the **UPDATE** command, even if the user has not changed the item. If any of the values have changed since the row was initially retrieved, the database will reject the transaction with a "not found" SQL code. Then, the application could interpret the code, re-retrieve the updated record, and present it to the user with its new value.

*It is very important to run the **EXPLAIN** utility with this type of **UPDATE** statement to be sure that the SQL optimizer uses the employee index to locate the row. With more than two items in the **WHERE** clause, some optimizers might become confused and service the request by using a full-table scan, causing significant performance delays. With Oracle SQL, the programmer can specify which index to use to service the query, although other implementations of SQL require that the indexed field be specified first in the **WHERE** clause. Regardless, it is important to run an **EXPLAIN PLAN** on the SQL to be sure that the additions to the **WHERE** clause do not impede performance.*

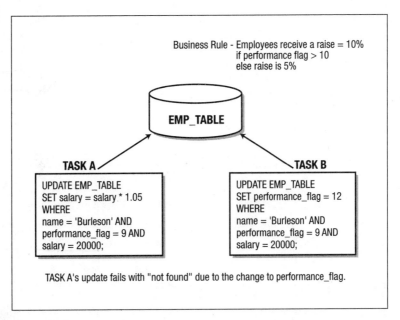

Figure 6.6
A solution to the update anomaly.

As demonstrated in Chapter 5, *Tuning Oracle SQL*, Oracle has SQL hints that can explicitly turn off unwanted indexes. For example, indexes can be turned off by altering the key field used in the **WHERE** clause.

Assume that the **EMP_TABLE** has the following definition:

```
CREATE TABLE EMP_TABLE (
    emp_name            char(20),
    sex                 char(1),
    performance_flag    number,
    salary              decimal(8,2) );
```

Let's further assume that **emp_name** has a unique index, and the field's **sex**, **performance_flag**, and **salary** have nonunique indexes. To ensure that the index on **emp_name** is used, the index key fields will be "altered" by concatenating a null string to the end of the **char** columns and adding a zero to the end of each numeric column.

Hence, the following SQL update would read:

```
UPDATE EMP_TABLE
    SET salary              = salary*1.05
WHERE
    emp_name                = 'Burleson'
AND
    performance_flag+0      = 9
AND
    sex || ''               = 'M'
AND
    salary+0                = 20000;
```

Another method can guarantee the use of the **emp_name** index. You could alter the **emp_name** index to include the nonunique fields of **performance_flag**, **sex**, and **salary**, creating a large concatenated index on every column in the table. A slight index overhead will occur, but you can be assured that all index updates perform efficiently without relying on the SQL programmers to alter their SQL.

The Date-Time Stamp Solution

This solution requires that a date-time stamp column be added to each table that might be updated. All applications are required to select this column and include it in the **WHERE** clause when issuing any **UPDATE** SQL. Of course, if the row has changed, the date-time stamps will not match, and the transaction will fail with a "not found" SQL code.

For example, we could issue the following SQL to re-fetch a row before issuing an update:

```
SELECT date_stamp
FROM CUSTOMER
WHERE
    customer_id = 123
AND
    date_stamp = :old_date_stamp;
```

Now that we have explored alternatives to Oracle's locking mechanisms, let's turn our attention to the use of Oracle locks in a distributed environment.

Locking And Distributed Databases

Whether a manager chooses to purchase an Application Programming Interface (API) or to create a custom API, it is very important to realize that the nature of data access can tremendously impact the processing complexity. For read-only databases, API processing is relatively simple. However, processing problems increase exponentially for systems that require cohesive updating. In fact, it is impossible to implement any cohesive updating scheme with 100 percent reliability.

Distributed databases have an inherent updating problem that is common to all systems. This exposure occurs when a federated database attempts to simultaneously update two distributed databases. Commonly known as the *two-phase commit* (2PC), the procedure is illustrated in the following example:

```
APPLY UPDATE A
APPLY UPDATE B
IF A-OK And B-OK
    COMMIT A
            < ====   "Here is the deadly exposure"
    COMMIT B
  ELSE
    ROLLBACK A
    ROLLBACK B
```

As you can see, updates A and B get posted to the database. If the SQL code indicates that the transactions have completed successfully, the system will issue **COMMIT** statements to A and B. The point of exposure occurs when a failure happens after the **COMMIT** of A and before the **COMMIT** of B. Of course, the exposure can only happen when the failure occurs exactly between the **COMMIT** of A and the **COMMIT** of B. However, it is an exposure that has the potential to cause a major loss of integrity within the federation, and an exposure for which there is no automated recovery. The only remedy is to notify the DBA that the transaction has terminated and manually roll back the updates to A and B. This type of corruption has a *very* small probability, and most databases do not worry about this exposure.

Now that we see the basic dynamics of a two-phase commit, let's take a detailed look at how two-phase commit processing is implemented in Oracle8.

Understanding The Two-Phase Commit

Following the receipt of a message from each remote server stating that a transaction was successful, the initiating Oracle instance begins the two-phase commit. The commit itself consists of several steps: the prepare phase, the commit phase, and the forget phase. To demonstrate, here is an SQL query that simultaneously updates all rows in a horizontally partitioned table residing in London and Paris. Assume that the SQL originates from a remote database in Denver, and that the Denver database will manage the two-phase commit:

```
UPDATE  EMPLOYEE@london,
        EMPLOYEE@paris
SET salary = salary * 1.1;
```

The initiating database in Denver is elected to manage the transaction, and will direct all stages of the two-phase commit, as follows:

1. *Prepare phase*—The prepare phase ensures that none of the remote databases will inadvertently issue a **COMMIT** or a **ROLLBACK** unless the initiating transaction directs the remote database to do so. In Oracle, the remote databases "promise" to allow the initiating request to govern the transaction at the remote database. The initiating request then converts its own locks to "in-doubt" locks that prevent either read or write operations against the data in question.

2. *Commit phase*—The initiating database commits and then instructs each remote database to commit. Each remote database then informs the initiating database that its commit transaction has been executed.

3. *Forget phase*—After all remote databases have committed, the initiating database "forgets" about the transaction and releases all in-doubt locks. Each remote database then, in turn, releases its transaction locks.

Some of the more sophisticated databases allow a database administrator to manually recover any in-doubt transactions that remain after a failure in a distributed database network. For example, a common reason distributed database transactions fail is due to problems with communications lines. These failures can cause an update against several remote databases to fail during any point of the prepare, commit, or forget phases. The database will detect the lost connection, and, depending on the state of the transaction, it will direct the online component to either **COMMIT** or **ROLLBACK** its part of the update. The remaining transaction piece will be posted to an in-doubt system table. When the remote database returns online, the database will direct the failed node to either **COMMIT** or **ROLLBACK**. In the meantime, the DBA might wish to manually direct the operation of the in-doubt transactions.

Now that we have seen how Oracle locks function within an Oracle8 instance, let's take a look at some of the tools that can be applied to measure locking within Oracle.

Measuring Oracle Locks

While Oracle locking mechanisms appear to be very complex on the surface, some useful scripts are available that can quickly identify lock resources. In Oracle, once a lock has been issued, only one of the following can be used to release the lock:

- Ask the holder to **COMMIT** or **ROLLBACK**.
- Kill the session that holds the lock.
- **ALTER SESSION KILL SESSION** sid, serial#.
- Use the **KILL USER SESSION** menu found in the SQL*DBA form.
- Kill the Unix shadow process, which is not recommended. When killing the Unix shadow process, please be careful of shared servers in a multithreaded environment.
- **ROLLBACK FORCE** or **COMMIT FORCE** if it is a two-phase commit transaction.

While many tools can be used to measure Oracle locks, Listing 6.2 will show all locking activity.

Listing 6.2   A locking script.

```
locks.sql - shows all locks in the database.
SET LINESIZE 132
SET PAGESIZE 60
COLUMN OBJECT HEADING 'Database|Object'         FORMAT a15 truncate
COLUMN lock_type HEADING 'Lock|Type'            FORMAT a4 truncate
COLUMN mode_held HEADING 'Mode|Held'            FORMAT a15 truncate
COLUMN mode_requested HEADING 'Mode|Requested'  FORMAT a15 truncate
COLUMN sid HEADING 'Session|ID'
COLUMN username HEADING 'Username'              FORMAT a20 truncate
COLUMN image HEADING 'Active Image'             FORMAT a20 truncate


SPOOL /tmp/locks
SELECT
        C.sid,
        substr(object_name,1,20) OBJECT,
        C.username,
        substr(C.program,length(C.program)-20,length(C.program)) image,
        decode(B.type,
                'MR', 'Media Recovery',
                'RT', 'Redo Thread',
                'UN', 'User Name',
                'TX', 'Transaction',
                'TM', 'DML',
                'UL', 'PL/SQL User Lock',
                'DX', 'Distributed Xaction',
                'CF', 'Control File',
                'IS', 'Instance State',
                'FS', 'File Set',
                'IR', 'Instance Recovery',
                'ST', 'Disk Space Transaction',
                'TS', 'Temp Segment',
                'IV', 'Library Cache Invalidation',
                'LS', 'Log Start or Switch',
                'RW', 'Row Wait',
                'SQ', 'Sequence Number',
                'TE', 'Extend Table',
                'TT', 'Temp Table',
                b.type) lock_type,
        decode(B.lmode,
                0, 'None',                  /* Mon Lock equivalent */
                1, 'Null',                  /* NOT */
                2, 'Row-SELECT (SS)',       /* LIKE */
                3, 'Row-X (SX)',            /* R */
```

```
                4, 'Share',                /* SELECT */
                5, 'SELECT/Row-X (SSX)',   /* C */
                6, 'Exclusive',            /* X */
                to_char(b.lmode)) mode_held,
        decode(B.request,
                0, 'None',                 /* Mon Lock equivalent */
                1, 'Null',                 /* NOT */
                2, 'Row-SELECT (SS)',      /* LIKE */
                3, 'Row-X (SX)',           /* R */
                4, 'Share',                /* SELECT */
                5, 'SELECT/Row-X (SSX)',   /* C */
                6, 'Exclusive',            /* X */
                to_char(b.request)) mode_requested
FROM SYS.dba_objects A, SYS.v_$lock B, SYS.v_$session C WHERE
A.object_id = B.id1 AND B.sid = C.sid AND OWNER NOT IN ('SYS','SYSTEM');
```

Listing 6.3 shows the output of the locking script.

Listing 6.3   The output of the locking script.

```
Database        Lock          Mode    Mode                  Session      Active
Object          Type          Held    Requested             ID  Username Image
-------         ----          ----    ---------             --- -------- -----
102 BANK        OPS$MCACIAT   @xdc (Pipe Two-Task DML Row-SELECT (SS)    None
57 INVOICE      OPS$DMAHTROB  @xdc (Pipe Two-Task DML Row-X      (SX)    None
57 LINE_ITEM    OPS$DMAHTROB  @xdc (Pipe Two-Task DML Row-X      (SX)    None
70 LINE_ITEM    OPS$JCONVICK  @xdc (Pipe Two-Task DML Row-X      (SX)    None
29 LINE_ITEM    OPS$NUMNUTS   @xdc (Pipe Two-Task DML Row-X      (SX)    None
70 LINE_ITEM    OPS$JKONV     @xdc (Pipe Two-Task DML Row-X      (SX)    None
57 LINE_ITEM    OPS$DMAHTROB  @xdc (Pipe Two-Task DML Row-X
```

You can also use Oracle Monitor within SQL*DBA to look at locks. Listings 6.4 and 6.5 show some sample screens.

Listing 6.4   SQL*DBA—MONITOR SESSION.

Session ID	Serial Number	Process ID	Status	Username	Lock Waited	Current Statement
6	35	28	ACTIVE	BURLESON	C4D2B7A4	UPDATE
8	70	19	INACTIVE	PECK		SELECT
12	15	25	INACTIVE	JONES		INSERT
14	17	27	ACTIVE	PAPAJ	C3D2B638	DELETE
15	30	26	ACTIVE	ODELL		UNKNOWN

Listing 6.5 SQL*DBA—MONITOR LOCK.

Username	Session ID	Serial Number	Lock Type	Res ID 1	Res ID 2	Mode Held	Mode Requested
BURLESON	5	23	TM	23294	0	RX	NONE
BURLESON	5	23	TM	22295	0	RX	NONE
BURLESON	5	23	TX	266654	87	NONE	X
BURLESON	5	23	TX	3276482	97	X	NONE
PECK	14	13	TM	2211	0	RX	NONE
PECK	14	13	TM	2223	0	RX	NONE
PECK	14	13	TX	266654	87	X	NONE
GASTON	19	47	TM	2334	0	RX	NONE
GASTON	19	47	TM	2233	0	R	
GASTON	19	47	TX	266654	87	NONE	X
GASTON	19	47	TX	193446	87	X	NONE

In Listing 6.4, the **Lock Waited** column displays the address of a lock that is being waited for. In this example, you can see that Burleson and Gaston are waiting on a lock held by Peck.

In Listing 6.5, the following four types of locks can be displayed under the **Lock Type** column:

- *TX (Transaction)*—Decimal representation of a rollback segment number "wrap" number (the number and slot number of times a rollback slot has been reused).

- *TM (Table Locks)*—Object ID of a table being modified (always 0).

- *RW (Row Wait)*—Decimal representation of a file number and of a row within a block.

- *UL (User Defined Locks)*—A complete list can be found in the *Oracle8 Concepts* Manual or in the Appendix of the *Oracle8 Admin Guide*.

The users with an **X** in the **Mode Requested** column are waiting for a lock release. The following users are waiting for lock 266654:

```
BURLESON    5    23   TX    266654    87   NONE    X
MANSFIELD   19   47   TX    266654    87   NONE    X
```

You can look for this lock ID and see that the following resource is holding the lock:

```
PECK        14   13   TX    266654    87   X    NONE
```

Often, user(s) can modify many tables within a single transaction. At times, this will make it difficult to find out which resource the "waiter" is contending from the "holder." This is easily resolved by looking at a combination of two monitors: **MONITOR SESSION**, which will tell you which user is waiting on a lock, and **MONITOR LOCK**, which will tell you the table that a user is currently trying to modify.

One very important part of Oracle lock management is the ability to quickly identify lock conflicts where several tasks compete for the same data resources. The next section will explore how to identify these conflicts.

Identifying Conflicts

If you suspect a situation where one task is stopping another task from completing, Listing 6.6 shows a query you can run to find the objects that are involved in the locking conflict.

Listing 6.6 Finding a locking conflict.

```
waiters.sql - shows waiting tasks
COLUMN username       FORMAT a10
COLUMN lockwait       FORMAT a10
COLUMN sql_text       FORMAT a80
COLUMN object_owner   FORMAT a14
COLUMN object         FORMAT a15

SELECT  B.username username,
        C.sid sid,
        C.owner object_owner,
        C.object object,
        B.lockwait,
        A.sql_text SQL
FROM V$SQLTEXT A, V$SESSION B, V$ACCESS C
WHERE
    A.address=B.sql_address
    AND
    A.hash_value=B.sql_hash_value
    AND
    B.sid = C.sid
    AND
    C.owner != 'SYS';
```

Listing 6.7 shows the sample output.

Listing 6.7 The locking conflict query's output.

```
USERNAME SID OBJECT_OWNER OBJECT    LOCKWAIT  SQL
----     --  ----------   -----     --------  ----------
BURLESON 36  EMP          EMPLOYEE  C4D450F9  update employee set status
                                              = 'Fired' where
                                              emp_nbr=16152

PAPAJ    15  EMP          EMPLOYEE  C3D320C8  delete from employee where
                                              emp_nbr=16152

PECK     11  EMP          EMPLOYEE  D3D4F9E0  update employee set salary
                                              = salary*.01 lock table
                                              customer in exclusive mode
```

Here, you can see a situation where Burleson and Papaj are waiting for Peck's update on the **EMPLOYEE** table to complete.

Now that we have seen how to identify conflicts, let's move on and look into the general tools for viewing Oracle locks.

Viewing Locks

Several locks scripts within $ORACLE_HOME/rdbms/admin can be used to view locks. To install the scripts, first enter SQL*DBA and then run catblock.sql followed by utllockt.sql.

catblock.sql creates the following views:

- dba_waiters
- dba_blockers
- dba_dml_locks
- dba_ddl_locks
- dba_locks

Listing 6.8 can be used whenever you suspect that locks are impeding performance. This script interrogates all of the views created in catblock.sql:

Listing 6.8 Using alllocks.sql.

```
REM alllocks.sql - shows all locks in the database.
REM written by Don Burleson
```

```
SET LINESIZE 132
SET PAGESIZE 60

SPOOL /tmp/alllocks

COLUMN owner           FORMAT a10;
COLUMN name            FORMAT a15;
COLUMN mode_held       FORMAT a10;
COLUMN mode_requested  FORMAT a10;
COLUMN type            FORMAT a15;
COLUMN lock_id1        FORMAT a10;
COLUMN lock_id2        FORMAT a10;

PROMPT Note that $ORACLE_HOME/rdbma/admin/catblock.sql

PROMPT must be run before this script functions . . .

PROMPT Querying dba_waiters . . .
SELECT
 waiting_session,
 holding_session,
 lock_type,
 mode_held,
 mode_requested,
 lock_id1,
 lock_id2
FROM SYS.dba_waiters;
PROMPT Querying dba_blockers . . .
SELECT
 holding_session
FROM SYS.dba_blockers;

PROMPT Querying dba_dml_locks . . .
SELECT
 session_id,
 owner,
 name,
 mode_held,
 mode_requested
FROM SYS.dba_dml_locks;

PROMPT Querying dba_ddl_locks . . .
SELECT
 session_id,
 owner,
```

```
 name,
 type,
 mode_held,
 mode_requested
FROM SYS.dba_ddl_locks;

PROMPT Querying dba_locks . . .
SELECT
 session_id,
 lock_type,
 mode_held,
 mode_requested,
 lock_id1,
 lock_id2
FROM SYS.dba_locks;
```

Listing 6.9 shows the output of alllocks.sql.

Listing 6.9   The output of alllocks.sql.

```
SQL> @alllocks
Note that $ORACLE_HOME/rdbma/admin/catblock.sql
must be run before this script functions . . .
Querying dba_waiters . . .

no rows selected

Querying dba_blockers . . .

no rows selected

Querying dba_dml_locks . . .

SESSION_ID OWNER      NAME         MODE_HELD MODE_REQUE
-----      ---        -----        -----     -----
19         RPT        RPT_EXCEPTIONS Row-X (SX) None

Querying dba_ddl_locks . . .

SESSION                                      MODE_    MODE_
  _ID    OWNER  NAME          TYPE           HELD     REQUE
-----    ---    -----         ----           ----     ----
    13   RPT    SHP_PRE_INS   Table/Procedure Null    None
                _UPD_PROC
    13   SYS    STANDARD      Body           Null     None
```

14	SYS	STANDARD	Body	Null	None
13	SYS	DBMS_STANDARD	Table/Procedure	Null	None
14	SYS	DBMS_STANDARD	Table/Procedure	Null	None
13	SYS	DBMS_STANDARD	Body	Null	None
14	SYS	DBMS_STANDARD	Body	Null	None
13	SYS	STANDARD	Table/Procedure	Null	None
14	SYS	STANDARD	Table/Procedure	Null	None

9 rows selected.

Querying dba_locks . . .

SESSION_ID	LOCK_TYPE	MODE_HELD	MODE_REQUE	LOCK_ID1	LOCK_ID2
2	Media Recovery	Share	None	32	0
2	Media Recovery	Share	None	31	0
2	Media Recovery	Share	None	30	0
2	Media Recovery	Share	None	29	0
2	Media Recovery	Share	None	28	0
2	Media Recovery	Share	None	27	0
2	Media Recovery	Share	None	26	0
2	Media Recovery	Share	None	25	0
2	Media Recovery	Share	None	24	0
2	Media Recovery	Share	None	23	0
2	Media Recovery	Share	None	22	0
2	Media Recovery	Share	None	21	0
2	Media Recovery	Share	None	20	0
2	Media Recovery	Share	None	19	0
2	Media Recovery	Share	None	18	0
2	Media Recovery	Share	None	17	0
2	Media Recovery	Share	None	16	0
2	Media Recovery	Share	None	15	0
2	Media Recovery	Share	None	14	0
2	Media Recovery	Share	None	13	0
2	Media Recovery	Share	None	12	0
2	Media Recovery	Share	None	11	0
2	Media Recovery	Share	None	10	0
2	Media Recovery	Share	None	9	0
2	Media Recovery	Share	None	8	0
2	Media Recovery	Share	None	7	0
2	Media Recovery	Share	None	6	0
2	Media Recovery	Share	None	5	0
2	Media Recovery	Share	None	4	0
2	Media Recovery	Share	None	3	0
2	Media Recovery	Share	None	2	0

```
2              Media Recovery   Share       None   1      0
3              Redo Thread      Exclusive   None   1      0
14             PS               Null        None   0      0
14             PS               Null        None   0      1
19             DML              Row-X (SX)  None   1457   0
```

```
36 rows selected.
```

The utllockt.sql script creates a view called **LOCK_HOLDERS** that can be queried to see the waiting sessions information. Be aware, however, that this view creates a temporary table and can run slowly. Listing 6.10 is an example query.

Listing 6.10   Using the **LOCK_HOLDERS** view to display waiting session information.

```
COLUMN waiting_session FORMAT a8

SELECT lpad(' ',3*(level-1)) || waiting_session waiting_session,
   lock_type,
   mode_requested,
   mode_held,
   lock_id1,
   lock_id2
FROM LOCK_HOLDERS
CONNECT BY  PRIOR waiting_session = holding_session
START WITH holding_session IS NULL;
```

Listing 6.11 shows the output.

Listing 6.11   Sample output.

```
WAITING_  LOCK_TYPE      MODE_REQUE MODE_HELD  LOCK_ID1  LOCK_ID2
-----     -----          -----      -----      -----     -----
   34     None
   65     Transaction    Exclusive  Exclusive  662534    11291
   44     Transaction    Exclusive  Exclusive  662534    11291
```

Here, you can see that sessions 65 and 44 are waiting on session 34 to complete and release its locks.

We must always remember that locking becomes even more complex when we are operating in a massively parallel environment. The following section explores locking within Oracle8's Parallel Server Product (OPS), and looks at issues that are germane to lock measurement with parallel servers.

Oracle Parallel Server And The DLM

Many parallel server novices are confused by the Distributed Lock Manager (DLM) because the DLM was not a component of the Oracle manufactured software. In Oracle8, the DLM is an Oracle locking facility used in conjunction with the Oracle parallel server to synchronize concurrent processes. For Oracle7, the DLMs are operating-system specific, and there are numerous DLM vendors for Solaris, AIX, and HP-UX implementations of Unix. At the most basic level, the DLM keeps track of concurrent Oracle tasks executing on each CPU and keeps track of lock requests for resources.

With Oracle Parallel Server, the limitation of one instance to one database has been lifted. You can now configure many Oracle instances to share the same databases. Of course, all the Oracle instances are running in the same shared memory, and the DLM is used to provide locking between instances.

 You can tell if your system is running a DLM by checking for the LCK process. Just as the RECO process indicates that distributed transactions are enabled, the presence of an LCK process indicates that a DLM is active. Traditional distributed systems do not have a DLM because they are not sharing the same databases.

While the DLM plays an important role, the amount of freelists on each database block also can cause contention within Oracle Parallel Server. The following section explores how to properly set freelists for parallel access.

Freelists And Oracle Parallel Server Contention

Freelists are especially important for Oracle databases that experience a high volume of localized update activity. A freelist is the parameter used when more than one concurrent process is expected to access a table. Oracle keeps one freelist for each table in memory, and uses the freelist in order to determine what database block to use when an SQL **INSERT** occurs. When a row is added, the freelist is locked. If more than one concurrent process is attempting to insert into your table, one of the processes might need to wait until the freelist has been released by the previous task. To see if adding a freelist to a table will improve performance, you need to evaluate how often Oracle has to wait for a freelist. Fortunately, Oracle keeps a **V$** table called **V$WAITSTAT** for this purpose. The following query example tells you how many times Oracle has waited for a freelist to become available. As you can see, Oracle does not tell you which freelists are experiencing the contention problems:

```
SELECT CLASS, COUNT
FROM V$WAITSTAT
    WHERE CLASS = 'free list';


   CLASS                          COUNT
   -----                          -----
   free list                      83
```

Here, you can see that Oracle had to wait 83 times for a table freelist to become available. This could represent a wait of 83 times on the same table or perhaps a single wait for 83 separate tables. You have no idea. While 83 might seem to be a large number, remember that Oracle can perform hundreds of I/Os each second, so 83 could be quite insignificant to the overall system. In any case, if you suspect that you know which table's freelist is having the contention, the table can be exported, dropped, and redefined to have more freelists. While an extra freelist consumes more of Oracle's memory, additional freelists can help the throughput on tables that have lots of inserts. Generally, you should define extra freelists only on tables that have many concurrent update operations. Now, let's take a look at some table definitions and see if you can infer the type of activity that will be taking place against the tables. Listings 6.12 and 6.13 each present a table definition.

Listing 6.12   Table definition—Example 1.

```
CREATE TABLE ORDER (
    order_nbr        number,
    order_date       date)
STORAGE ( PCTFREE  10 PCTUSED  40 FREELISTS 3);
```

Here, you can infer that the table has very few updates that cause the row length to increase because **PCTFREE** is only 10 percent. You can also infer that this table will have a great deal of delete activity, because **PCTUSED** is set at 40 percent, thereby preventing immediate reuse of database blocks as rows are deleted. This table must also have a lot of insert activity because **FREELISTS** is set to **3**, indicating that up to three concurrent processes can be inserting into the table.

Listing 6.13 Table definition—Example 2.

```
CREATE TABLE ITEM (
    item_nbr                    number,
    item_name                   varchar(20),
    item_description            varchar(50),
    current_item_status         varchar(200) )
STORAGE ( PCTFREE  10 PCTUSED  90 FREELISTS 1);
```

Here, you can infer that update operations are frequent and will probably increase the size of the **varchar** columns because **PCTFREE** is set to reserve 10 percent of each block for row expansion. You can also infer that this table has few deletes because **PCTUSED** is set to 90, making efficient use of the database blocks. Assuming that there will not be very many deletes, these blocks would be constantly re-added to the freelist.

Now that we understand freelists, let's take a look at two Oracle8 views that can be used to view lock activity when using OPS.

The V$LOCK_ACTIVITY View

The **V$LOCK_ACTIVITY** view is a very good way to determine if you have reached the maximum lock convert rate for your DLM. Because the maximum lock convert rate is unique to each vendor's DLM, you need to compare the results from **V$LOCK_ACTIVITY** with the maximum values in your OS vendor's documentation for their DLM. Regardless, if the maximum lock convert rate has been reached, you will need to repartition the application to balance alike transactions into common instances. Here is an example of a query against this table:

```
SELECT * FROM V$LOCK_ACTIVITY;

FROM TO_V ACTION_VAL                                      COUNTER
---- ---  ----------------                               -------
NULL S    Lock buffers for read                               68
NULL X    Lock buffers for write                             156
S    NULL Make buffers CR (no write)                         195
S    X    Upgrade read lock to write                         436
X    NULL Make buffers CR (write dirty buffers)              247
X    S    Downgrade write lock to read (write dirty buffers) 178
X    SSX  Write transaction table/undo blocks                 54
SSX  X    Rearm transaction table write mechanism             54

8 rows selected.
```

The V$SYSSTAT View

The **V$SYSSTAT** view can be used to determine whether lock converts are being performed too often. Excessive lock convert rates usually mean there is contention for a common resource within the database. This resource could be a commonly updated table. For example, inventory management systems often utilize one-of-a-kind (OOAK) rows. An OOAK row could be used to keep the order number of the last order, and all application tasks must increment this row when a new order is placed. This type of architecture forces each parallel instance to single-thread all requests for this resource. But how do you identify these types of database resources?

The lock hit ratio can be used to identify excessive lock conversion by the DLM. The lock hit ratio should generally be above 90 percent, and, if it falls below 90 percent, you should look for sources of data contention. Here is the SQL to determine the lock hit ratio for Oracle parallel server:

```
SELECT
    (A.value - B.value)/(A.value)
FROM
    V$SYSSTAT A, V$SYSSTAT B
WHERE
    A.name = 'consistent gets'
AND
    B.name = 'global lock converts (async)';
```

If you suspect that there is data contention, there are several remedies, including:

- If you identify a specific table as a source of contention, try increasing the freelists for the table.

- If you identify an index as the source of contention, try localizing all access to the index on a single instance.

But how can you identify the source of contention? Oracle parallel server provides a view called **V$PING** to show lock conversions. You start by querying the **V$PING** view to see if there are any data files experiencing a high degree of lock conversions, as follows:

```
SELECT
    substr(name,1,10),
    file#,
```

```
    class#,
    max(xnc)
FROM
    V$PING
GROUP BY 1, 2, 3
ORDER BY 1, 2, 3;
```

You will receive an output that looks similar to Listing 6.14.

Listing 6.14   Querying the **V$PING** view.

Name	File #	Class #	Max (XNC)
Customer	13	1	556
Customer	13	4	32
Item	6	1	11
Item	3	4	32
Order	16	1	33456

Here, you can see that File 16 might have a problem with excessive lock conversions. To further investigate, return to **V$PING**, and get the sums for File 16, as follows:

```
SELECT *
FROM
    V$PING
WHERE
    file#=16
ORDER BY block#;
```

Now, you can see more detail about the contents of File 16, as shown in Listing 6.15.

Listing 6.15   Viewing additional file details.

File #	Block #	Stat	XNC	Class #	Name	Kind
16	11	XCUR	5	1	ORDER	Table
16	12	XCUR	33456	1	ORDER	Table
16	13	XCUR	12	1	ORDER	Table

From this output, you can clearly see that Block 12 is the source of contention.

The following query against the **ORDER** table will reveal the contents of the rows in the data block, as shown in Listing 6.16. Remember, data blocks are numbered in hex, so Block 12 must be converted to a hex(c):

```
SELECT
   rowid,
   order_number,
   customer_number
FROM
   ORDER
WHERE
chattorowid(rowid) LIKE '0000000C%';
```

Listing 6.16   Viewing row contents.

ROWID	ORDER_NUMBER	CUSTOMER_NUMBER
0000000C.0000.0008	1212	73
0000000C.0000.0008	1213	73
0000000C.0000.0008	1214	73

In Listing 6.16, you can see that the lock conversion relates to orders placed by customer number 73. Other than a random coincidence, you can assume that there might be freelist contention in the **ORDER** table as new orders are added to the database. Adding new freelists will allow more concurrency during SQL **INSERT** operations, and the value for freelists should be reset to the maximum number of end users who are expected to be inserting an **ORDER** row at any given time. Unfortunately, Oracle does not allow the dynamic modification of freelists because they are physically stored in each data block. So, the only alternative is to drop and re-create the table with more freelists in each block header. Following is the SQL used to drop and re-create the **ORDER** table:

```
CREATE TABLE ORDER_DUMMY
STORAGE (FREELISTS 10)
AS
SELECT * FROM ORDER;

DROP TABLE ORDER;

RENAME ORDER_DUMMY TO ORDER;
```

Summary

Oracle locking and concurrency control has become a pressing issue because of the increasing popularity of Oracle systems, and it becomes especially important for

Oracle Parallel Server (OPS), where a Distributed Lock Manager is required. As client/server and Oracle technology mature, we will begin to see concurrency methods that can automatically manage updates to distributed databases. In the meantime, developers must decide which updated control mechanisms are best suited to the operation of their distributed databases.

It's time now to look at tuning the client side of the application. In the next chapter, you'll see how a distributed server environment impacts the performance of Oracle8 databases.

Oracle DBA
Performance
And Tuning

CHAPTER

7

Oracle DBA Performance And Tuning

Aside from the basic features for applications programmers, an Oracle database administrator can benefit immensely from an understanding of the Oracle performance features. These features can be especially useful for routine database administration tasks, such as exports/imports, index creation, and table replication. Topics in this chapter include:

- Using Oracle's unrecoverable option
- Using read-only tablespaces
- Determining where to place indexes
- Using bitmapped indexes
- Using Oracle's table cache option
- Using clustered indexes
- Determining when to rebuild indexes

Using The UNRECOVERABLE Option

At specific times, Oracle allows its internal transaction logging mechanism to be turned off. With Oracle, the software maintains a read-consistent image of the data for long-running queries, while at the same time providing rollback capability for each update transaction. Of course, this level of recoverability carries a price, and significant performance improvements can be achieved with the prudent use of the "unrecoverable" option. In practice, use of the **UNRECOVERABLE** clause can improve response time from 40 to 60 percent. Care must be taken, of course, to synchronize the use of the **UNRECOVERABLE** clause with the traditional procedures used when taking backups of the archived redo logs.

You can use **UNRECOVERABLE** for any of the following operations:

- **CREATE TABLE . . . AS SELECT . . . UNRECOVERABLE**—This type of operation is generally performed when a table is *cloned* or replicated from a master table, usually with a subset of columns and rows. For example, you would use this command to create a subset of a customer table, containing only those customers in a specific region. Of course, a failure during the creation of the table would leave a half-built table in the destination tablespace, and the table would need to be manually dropped.

- **CREATE INDEX . . . UNRECOVERABLE**—This is the most common use of the **UNRECOVERABLE** clause, and, certainly, the one that makes the most sense from an Oracle perspective. Regardless of any transaction failures, an index can always be re-created by dropping and redefining the index, so having an incomplete or corrupt index would never be a problem.

- **ALTER TABLE . . . ADD CONSTRAINT . . . UNRECOVERABLE**—As you probably know, when a referential integrity constraint is added to a table, Oracle sometimes creates an index to enforce the constraint. Primary key, foreign key, and unique constraints can cause Oracle to create an index that is built in unrecoverable mode.

- **SQL*Loader**—SQL*Loader is generally used when initially populating Oracle tables from external flat files. For very large numbers of inserts, it is best to leave the default. You already know that in the unlikely event of an abnormal termination, the incomplete tables must be dropped and SQL*Loader run again.

Now that we have reviewed the **UNRECOVERABLE** option, let's take a look at another feature of Oracle that allows read-only data to be treated in a different fashion than updatable data.

Using Read-Only Tablespaces

In a busy environment where many different applications require access to a tablespace, it is sometimes desirable to use the read-only tablespace feature that was introduced with Oracle7.3. With read-only tablespaces, separate instances can be mapped to the same tablespaces, each accessing the tablespace in read-only mode. Of course, sharing a tablespace across Oracle instances increases the risk that I/O against the shared

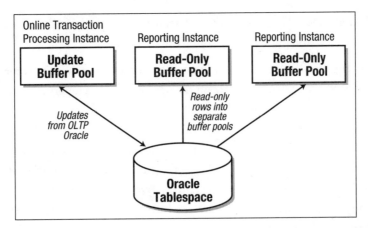

Figure 7.1
Oracle read-only tablespaces.

tablespaces might become excessive. As you can see in Figure 7.1, a read-only tablespace does not have the same overhead as an updatable tablespace.

This approach has some advantages:

- *Buffer pool isolation*—The foremost advantage is the isolation of the buffer pools for each instance that is accessing the tablespace. If user A on instance A flushes the buffer by doing a full-table scan, user B on instance B will still have the blocks needed in memory.

- *Easy sharing of table data*—Read-only tablespaces offer an alternative to table replication and the update problems associated with replicated tables. Because a read-only tablespace can only be defined as updatable by one instance, updates are controlled at the system level.

In addition to moving table data into different storage vehicles, we can also tune our Oracle database through the prudent use of index placement. The following section reviews the rules used to determine when it is appropriate to add an index into an Oracle schema.

Determining Where To Place Indexes

One of the primary responsibilities of an Oracle DBA is ensuring that Oracle indexes are present when they are needed to avoid full-table scans. In order to achieve this goal, the Oracle DBA needs to understand the types of indexes that Oracle provides as well as the proper time to create a table index.

Unfortunately, the Oracle dictionary does not gather statistics about how many times an index is used, so a DBA must rely on the application developers to provide guidance regarding index placement. As more professionals adopt the Oracle8 object option, we will have a new way to tell when Oracle indexes are used because the SQL will be stored as methods within the Oracle dictionary. While Oracle does not yet have a utility for extracting the SQL from Oracle8 methods, many Oracle8 DBAs can extract SQL from the library cache and analyze the access paths. With all of the SQL inside the database, it's possible for the DBA to extract and analyze the explain plan output for all of the SQL within the methods. This is done by selecting the **text** column from the **DBA_SOURCE** view. However, until Oracle provides an SQL extraction utility, the best that an Oracle DBA can hope for is to keep the existing indexes clean and functioning optimally.

Listing 7.1 is a script that can be run to view SQL that has been loaded into the SGA shared pool.

Listing 7.1   The sqltext.sql shows all SQL in the SGA shared pool.

```
REM Written by Don Burleson

SET PAGESIZE 9999;
SET LINESIZE 79;
SET NEWPAGE 0;
SET VERIFY OFF;

BREAK ON ADDRESS SKIP 2;

COLUMN ADDRESS FORMAT 9;

SELECT
        ADDRESS,
        sql_text
FROM
        V$SQLTEXT
ORDER BY
ADDRESS, PIECE;
```

Listing 7.2 shows the output from sqltext.sql.

Listing 7.2 The output for sqltext.sql.

```
D09AFC4C    SELECT DECODE(object_type, 'TABLE', 2,  'VIEW', 2, 'PACKAGE',
            3, 'PACKAGE BODY', 3, 'PROCEDURE', 4, 'FUNCTION', 5, 0) FROM
            ALL_OBJECTS WHERE object_name = upper('V_$SQLTEXT')  AND
            object_type IN ('TABLE', 'VIEW', 'PACKAGE', 'PACKAGE BODY',
            'PROCEDURE', 'FUNCTION') AND owner = upper('SYS')


D09B653C    SELECT OWNER, table_name, table_owner, db_link FROM
            ALL_SYNONYMS WHERE synonym_name = upper('V_$SQLTEXT') AND
            owner = upper('SYS')


D09BC5AC    SELECT OWNER, table_name, table_owner, db_link FROM
            ALL_SYNONYMS WHERE synonym_name = upper('V$SQLTEXT') AND
            (owner = 'PUBLIC' OR owner = USER)


D09C2D58    SELECT DECODE(object_type, 'TABLE', 2,  'VIEW', 2, 'PACKAGE',
            3,'PACKAGE BODY', 3, 'PROCEDURE', 4, 'FUNCTION', 5, 0)
            FROM USER_OBJECTS WHERE object_name = upper('V$SQLTEXT')
            AND  object_type IN ('TABLE', 'VIEW', 'PACKAGE', 'PACKAGE
            BODY', 'PROCEDURE', 'FUNCTION')


D09CFF4C    UPDATE SHPMT SET
            amt_sum_ili=:b1,pmt_wght_sum_ili=:b2,cust_pmt_wght_sum_ili=
            :b3 WHERE shpmt_id = :b4  AND shpmt_sys_src_cd = :b5
```

Of course, this script could be extended to feed the SQL statements into Oracle's explain plan utility, where long-table full-table scans could be detected and indexes created for these queries.

> **Note:** *Oracle's bstat/estat utility also provides information on the number of full-table scans incurred by the database as a whole. Please see Chapter 11, Oracle Application Monitoring, for more information.*

Part of the job of an Oracle DBA is to detect badly out-of-balance indexes and schedule their reconstruction. Unfortunately, very dynamic tables (i.e., those with high **INSERT** and **UPDATE** activity) will always have some issues with out-of-balance indexes. As Oracle indexes grow, two things happen—splitting and spawning:

- *Splitting*—Describes what happens when an index node is filled with keys and a new index node is created at the same level as the full node. Splitting widens a b-tree horizontally.

• *Spawning*—Describes the process of adding a new level to an index. As a new index is populated, it begins life as a single-level index. As keys are added, a spawn takes place, and the first-level node reconfigures itself to have pointers to lower-level nodes. It is important to understand that spawning takes place at specific points within the index and not for the entire index. For example, a three-level index might have a node that experiences heavy insert activity. This node could spawn a fourth level without the other level-three nodes spawning new levels.

Six Oracle dictionary values are used to describe indexes:

• **blevel**—Indicates the number of levels that an index has spawned. Even for very large indexes, there should never be more than four levels. Each **blevel** represents an additional I/O that must be performed against the index tree.

• **leaf_blocks**—References the total number of leaf blocks.

• **distinct_keys**—References the cardinality of the index. If this value is less than 10, consider redefining the index as a bitmapped index.

• **avg_data_blocks_per_key**—This is a measure of the size and cardinality of the index. A low cardinality index (e.g., sex or region) will have high values, as will very large indexes.

• **clustering_factor**—This is the most important measure in this report because it measures how balanced an index is. If the clustering factor is greater than the number of blocks in the index, then the index is out of balance due to a large volume of insert or delete operations. If the clustering factor is more than 50 percent of the number of rows in the table that it is indexing, you should consider dropping and re-creating the index. (We'll talk more about clustering later in this chapter.)

• **avg_leaf_blocks_per_key**—This value is always 1, with the exception of non-unique indexes.

Now that you understand the basic constructs of indexes, let's look at a dictionary query (shown in Listing 7.3) that will tell you the structure of your indexes. Note that this query assumes that your Oracle database is using the cost-based optimizer, and that your tables have been analyzed with the **ANALYZE TABLE** command.

Listing 7.3 index.sql shows the details for indexes.

```
SET PAGESIZE 999;
SET LINESIZE 100;

COLUMN c1 HEADING 'Index'       FORMAT a19;
COLUMN c3 HEADING 'S'           FORMAT a1;
COLUMN c4 HEADING 'Level'       FORMAT 999;
COLUMN c5 HEADING 'Leaf Blks'   FORMAT 999,999;
COLUMN c6 HEADING 'Dist. Keys'  FORMAT 99,999,999;
COLUMN c7 HEADING 'Bks/Key'     FORMAT 99,999;
COLUMN c8 HEADING 'Clust Ftr'   FORMAT 9,999,999;
COLUMN c9 HEADING 'Lf/Key'      FORMAT 99,999;

SPOOL index.lst;

SELECT
  owner||'.'||index_name     c1,
  substr(status,1,1)         c3,
  blevel                     c4,
  leaf_blocks                c5,
  distinct_keys              c6,
  avg_data_blocks_per_key    c7,
  clustering_factor          c8,
  avg_leaf_blocks_per_key    c9
FROM DBA_INDEXES
WHERE
OWNER NOT IN ('SYS','SYSTEM')
ORDER BY blevel desc, leaf_blocks desc;

SPOOL OFF;
```

Listing 7.4 shows the output of index.sql.

Listing 7.4 The output of index.sql.

Index	S	Level	Leaf Blks	Dist. Keys	Bks/ Key	Clust Ftr	Lf/ Key
DON.LOB_SHPMT_PK	V	2	25,816	3,511,938	1	455,343	1
DON.SHP_EK_CUST_INV	V	2	23,977	2,544,132	1	1,764,915	1
DON.SHP_FK_GLO_DEST	V	2	23,944	22,186	112	2,493,095	1

DON.LSH_FK_SHP	V	2	22,650	1,661,576	1	339,031	1
DON.SHP_FK_ORL_ORIG	V	2	21,449	404	806	325,675	53
DON.LSA_FK_LSH	V	2	21,181	2,347,812	1	996,641	1
DON.LSH_FK_LOB	V	2	19,989	187	4,796	896,870	106
DON.SHPMT_PK	V	2	19,716	3,098,063	1	1,674,264	1
DON.SHP_FK_CAR	V	2	18,513	689	390	268,859	26
DON.SHP_EK_ROLE_TY_	V	2	17,847	10	24,613	246,134	1,784
DON.SHP_FK_SPT	V	2	16,442	4	46,872	187,489	4,110
DON.INV_EK_INV_NUM	V	2	16,407	2,014,268	1	518,206	1
DON.SHP_FK_ORL_DEST	V	2	15,863	385	692	266,656	41
DON.SHP_FK_SRC	V	2	15,827	10	17,469	174,694	1,582
DON.INV_LINE_ITEM_P	V	2	14,731	2,362,216	1	102,226	1

Here, you can see that there are no indexes more than two levels deep. Note also that there are two indexes with a clustering factor of more than 1 million. Should either of these tables have less than 3 million rows (clustering factor greater than 50 percent of rows), you will want to schedule a time to drop and re-create the index.

While index placement is important, the type of index can also have a huge impact on Oracle performance. One of the most exciting new features of Oracle is support for bitmapped indexes.

Bitmapped Indexes

Prior to the introduction of bitmapped indexes with Oracle7.3, it was never recommended that a DBA create an index on any fields that were not "selective" and had less than 50 unique values. Imagine, for example, how a traditional b-tree index would appear if a column such as **region** were indexed. With only four distinct values in the index, the SQL optimizer would rarely determine that an index scan would speed up a query; consequently, the index would never be accessed. Of course, the only alternative would be to invoke a costly full-table scan of the table. Today, designers are able to use bitmapped indexes for low cardinality indexes.

It is interesting to note that bitmapped indexes have been used in commercial databases since Model 204 was introduced in the late 1960s. However, their usefulness had been ignored until the data warehouse explosion of 1994 made it evident that a new approach to indexing was needed to resolve complex queries against very large tables.

Bitmapped indexes allow for very fast boolean operations against low cardinality indexes. Complex **AND** and **OR** logic is performed entirely within the index—the base table need never be accessed. Without a bitmapped index, some decision support queries would be impossible to service without a full-table scan.

Bitmaps are especially important for data warehouse/decision support systems, where ad hoc, unanticipated queries make it impractical for an Oracle DBA to index on all possible combinations of columns. Assume that a manager wants to know the average income for all college-educated customers who drive red or blue cars in Wyoming or Nevada. Furthermore, assume that there are 1 million rows in the **CUSTOMER** table. The following query would be very hard to service using traditional indexing:

```
SELECT avg(yearly_income)
FROM CUSTOMER
WHERE
    education IN ('B','M','D')
AND
    car_color IN ('RED','BLUE')
AND
    state_residence IN ('WY','NV')
ORDER BY avg(yearly_income);
```

In a bitmapped index, it is not necessary to read all 1 million rows in the **CUSTOMER** table. Instead, the query manager will build row ID lists for all 1 values for **education**, **car_color**, and **state_residence**, and then match up the row IDs for those that appear in all three columns. When the query is ready to access the rows, it already has a list of row IDs for all rows that meet the selection criteria.

To understand bitmapped indexes, imagine a very wide, fat table with only a few rows. In a bitmapped index, each unique value has one row, such that our **region** index contains only four rows. Across the bitmap, each row in the base table is represented by a column, with a 1 in the bitmap array if the value is **TRUE**, and a 0 if it is **FALSE**. Because of the high amount of repeating ones and zeros, bitmapped indexes can be effectively compressed and expanded at runtime. In fact, the lower the cardinality, the better the compression, such that you can expect a higher compression of a **gender** index with 2 distinct values than with a **state** index with 50 distinct values. Uncompressed, the **state** index would be 48 times larger than the **gender** bitmap, because one row in the bitmap array is required for each unique value.

Oracle bitmapped indexes can consume far less space than a traditional b-tree Oracle index. In fact, their size can easily be computed as follows:

```
bitmap size = (cardinality_of_column * rows_in_table)/8
```

For example, suppose that the **region** index has four distinct values with 800,000 rows. The entire index would only consume 100,000 bytes uncompressed—and with Oracle's compression, the index would be far smaller than 100,000 bytes. In fact, it could probably be read entirely into the Oracle buffer with a few I/Os.

As you can see in the diagram displayed in Figure 7.2, Oracle bitmapped indexes can dramatically reduce I/O for certain types of operations. For example, assume that you are interested in knowing the number of corporations in the western region. Because all of this information is contained entirely within the bitmapped indexes, you have no need to access the table. In other words, the query can be resolved entirely within the index.

How do you identify candidates for bitmapped indexes? Your existing database is the starting place. Listing 7.5 shows a script that can check your b-tree indexes and provide you with a list of candidates in ascending order of cardinality.

Listing 7.5   bitmap.sql identifies low cardinality indexes for bitmapped indexes.

```
REM  Written by Don Burleson

PROMPT Be patient. This can take a while . . .

SET PAUSE OFF;
SET ECHO OFF;
SET TERMOUT OFF;
```

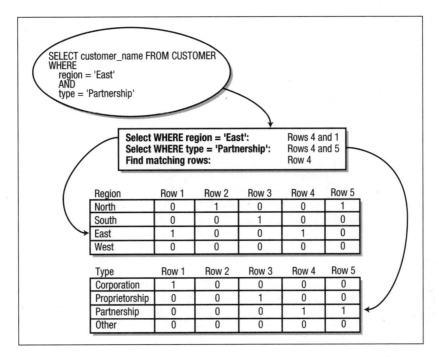

Figure 7.2
Oracle bitmapped indexes.

```
SET LINESIZE 300;
SET PAGESIZE 999;
SET NEWPAGE 0;
SET FEEDBACK OFF;
SET HEADING OFF;
SET VERIFY OFF;


REM  First create the syntax to determine the cardinality . . .


SPOOL idx1.sql;

SELECT 'set termout off;' FROM DUAL;
SELECT 'spool idx2.lst;' FROM DUAL;
SELECT 'column card format 9,999,999;' FROM DUAL;

SELECT 'select distinct count(distinct '
     ||A.column_name
     ||') card, '
     ||''' is the cardinality of '
```

```
        ||'Index '
        ||A.index_name
        ||' on column '
        ||A.column_name
        ||' of table '
        ||A.table_owner
        ||'.'
        ||A.table_name
        ||''' from '
        ||index_owner||'.'||A.table_name
        ||';'
FROM DBA_IND_COLUMNS A, DBA_INDEXES B
WHERE
  A.index_name = B.index_name
AND
  tablespace_name NOT IN ('SYS','SYSTEM')
;

SELECT 'spool off;' FROM DUAL;
SPOOL OFF;

SET TERMOUT ON;


@idx1

!SORT idx2.lst
```

Listing 7.6 shows an example of results generated by the script shown in Listing 7.5.

Listing 7.6   The results of bitmap.sql.

```
     3   is the cardinality of Index GEO_LOC_PK on column GEO_LOC_TY_CD of
         table DON.GEM_LCC
     4   is the cardinality of Index REGION_IDX on column REGION of table
         DON.CUSTOMER
     7   is the cardinality of Index GM_LCK on column GEO_LC_TCD of table
         DON.GEM_LCC
     8   is the cardinality of Index USR_IDX on column USR_CD of table
         DON.CUSTOMER
    50   is the cardinality of Index STATE_IDX on column STATE_ABBR of
         table DON.CUSTOMER
  3117   is the cardinality of Index ZIP_IDX on column ZIP_CD of table
         DON.GEM_LCC
71,513   is the cardinality of Index GEO_LOC_PK on column GEO_LOC_CD of
         table DON.GEM_LCC
```

```
83,459   is the cardinality of Index GEO_KEY_PK on column GEO_LOC_TY_CD of
         table DON.GEM_LCC
```

Of course, columns such as **gender** and **region** should be made into bitmaps—but what about **state** with 50 values, or **area_code** with a few hundred values? Intuition tells us that the benefits of bitmapped indexes are a function of the cardinality and the number of rows in the table, but no hard-and-fast rules exist for identifying what type of index is always best. A heuristic approach is called for, and it is relatively easy for a DBA to create a b-tree index, run a timed query, re-create the index with the **BITMAP** option, and re-execute the timed query.

Regardless, bitmapped indexes are critical to the performance of decision support systems, especially those that are queried in an ad hoc fashion against hundreds of column values. See Chapter 10, *Tuning Oracle Data Warehouse And OLAP Applications*, for a discussion of the applications of bitmapped indexes.

Moving on through our bag of tricks, we'll take a look at a relatively new feature of Oracle that allows small, frequently referenced tables to remain in the buffer cache for a longer period of time. The table cache option can make a huge difference in system performance, as long as you can identify the proper tables for caching.

Oracle's Table Cache Option

The table cache option is a major benefit of the Oracle architecture for databases, and it deserves designers' complete attention. While the term *cache* is a misnomer in the sense that an Oracle table is not permanently stored in memory, the table cache option dramatically improves the buffer hit ratio for small, frequently accessed tables. When a request is made for Oracle to retrieve a row from a table, Oracle performs the following steps:

1. Checks the buffer pool to see if a record is already in the Oracle buffer.

2. Issues an I/O to retrieve the desired data block, if necessary.

3. Fetches the data block from the Unix buffer into the Oracle buffer.

First, Oracle checks the data buffer to see if the database block that contains the row already resides in Oracle's data buffer (see Figure 7.3).

This scan is made from the most-recently used end to the least-recently used end of the buffer, and because this buffer is in the SGA as RAM memory, the check

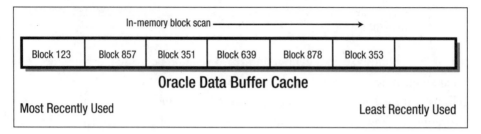

Figure 7.3
The Oracle data buffer.

happens very quickly. Only after Oracle has determined that the database block is not already in the buffer does Oracle perform a physical I/O to fetch the data block, and finally transfer the data block from the Unix buffer into the Oracle buffer.

Many of the new disk array devices contain very large RAM buffers. Therefore, all I/O rquests from Oracle do not always result in a disk I/O because it is possible that the block resides in the local disk cache, even when it is not in the Oracle buffer cache.

When Oracle manages I/O against the database, it uses two strategies to place new data blocks in the buffer cache. For all I/Os except full-table scans, rows are read into the most-recently used section of the Oracle buffer pool. As new data blocks are fetched, the older blocks work their way down to the least-recently used end of the buffer, where they are eventually erased from the buffer to make room for newly acquired data blocks (see Figure 7.4).

The exception to this rule involves data blocks acquired by using full-table scans. As data blocks are read into the buffer during a full-table scan, blocks are placed on the opposite end of the buffer, in the least-recently used section. In this fashion, full-table scans will not interfere with buffers on the most-recently used end of the buffer (i.e., rows from non-full-table scan transactions). Because these rows are already at the least-recently used end of the buffer, they will be flushed quickly as new rows are fetched as part of the full-table scan (see Figure 7.5). Full-table scan data blocks are physically read into Oracle's buffer in chunk sizes

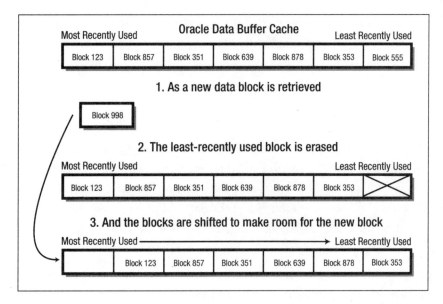

Figure 7.4
Aging blocks from the Oracle buffers.

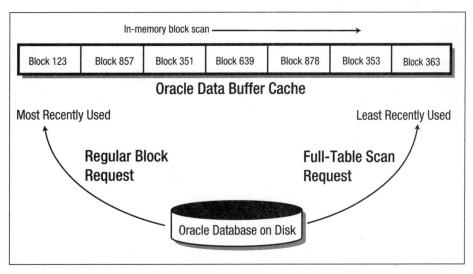

Figure 7.5
Different ends of the buffer cache can be used for different tables.

specified by the init.ora parameter **db_file_multiblock_read_count**. For example, assume that the **db_block_size** is set to 8192 bytes (8K) and the **db_file_multiblock_read_count** is set to 8. When Oracle detects a full-table scan, Oracle will perform reads of four physical blocks at a time, pulling in 64K with each I/O. Remember, physical I/O is very time consuming, and anything that can be done to reduce I/O will improve Oracle performance.

The table cache option was introduced with Oracle7.2 to change the behavior of full-table scan reads. When a table is created using the cache option, full-table scan fetches against a table are treated as if they are not full-table scans, and they are placed at the most-recently used end of the data buffer. Once the data blocks have been read to the buffer cache, they "age-out" and move toward the least-recently used side of the buffer, just like any other data block in Oracle.

In this sense, the term *cache* is somewhat misleading (as I hinted at earlier). For example, when Oracle packages are cached in the library cache, they are *pinned* (i.e., ineligible for being aged-out), and the packages remain in the library cache for the life of the Oracle instance. Data blocks, on the other hand, are not pinned into the data buffer with the cache option, and the data blocks age-out of the buffer at the same rate as other data blocks. Of course, the data blocks remain in the buffer for a much longer period than data blocks fetched with full-table scans, but they do not stay in the buffer indefinitely. At this time, the only way to pin a data block in an Oracle buffer is to utilize Oracle's parallel server to dedicate an Oracle instance for a particular table and make the buffer large enough to hold the entire contents of the table.

Table Caching Setup

The **cache_size_threshold** init.ora parameter must be set to use the table cache option. This parameter controls the space in the buffer cache that is used exclusively for full-table scans. The Oracle documentation falsely implies that the **cache_size_threshold** parameter is used exclusively with Oracle parallel server. In reality, this parameter applies to all Oracle databases.

Also, note that the **cache_size_threshold** parameter must be smaller than the table size. The default for this value is (**.10 * db_block_buffers**), such that any table larger than 10 percent of the buffer pool will not be affected by the cache option.

Turning On The Table Cache Option

There are two ways to activate the table cache option. The option can be specified permanently with a **CREATE TABLE** or **ALTER TABLE** command, or a cache hint can be used with the cost-based SQL optimizer to direct the data blocks. A create and alter table example follows:

```
SQL> CREATE TABLE CUSTOMER
   > STORAGE (NEXT . . . )
   > CACHE;

Table Created.

SQL > ALTER TABLE ORDERS CACHE;

Table Altered.
```

If you use the cost-based optimizer, the second method of invoking table caching is accomplished by adding cache hints. A cache hint is generally used in conjunction with the **FULL** hint to ensure that a full-table scan is being performed against the target table. In the following example, a reference table called **ZIP_CODE** is cached into the buffer:

```
SELECT /*+ FULL(ZIP_CODE) CACHE(ZIP_CODE)  */
zip_code, city_name, county_name, state_name
FROM
   ZIP_CODE;
```

The main purpose of the cache option is to allow small tables that are always read from front to back to remain in the data buffer. These types of tables might include small reference tables or any tables intended to be read by using a full-table scan. Remember, the cache option requires a table to be:

- Defined as cached (**ALTER TABLE CUSTOMER CACHE;**)

- Smaller than the value of **cache_size_threshold**

- Accessed with a full-table scan

In summary, the table cache option is useful in cases where a small, frequently referenced table needs to remain in the buffer cache for a longer period than traditional table scans. This occurs when the table is frequently reread by many transactions. It is implemented with **ALTER TABLE** and **CREATE TABLE** commands or cache hints, and it only works when the table is small and read with a full-table scan.

Now, let's take a look at the use of clustered indexes within Oracle. Clustering can greatly reduce I/O in certain conditions, and reduction of I/O is the number one goal of Oracle performance tuning.

Clustered Indexes

Before you can take a look at the I/O path to data, you need to consider two factors: the logical I/Os (calls) and the physical I/Os required to service the request. As Oracle scans an index, you know that each node of the index tree is read before you access the data row. To illustrate, let's look at the simple example shown in Table 7.1.

> **Note:** This example has been oversimplified to illustrate the principle of clustered tables, and it does not consider other data block overhead, such as block headers and space management pages.

Now, you can run an index report from the Oracle data dictionary to see the following characteristics of **last_name_idx**:

```
SQL> @idx_list

Index            Level   Clust Ftr      # rows      reorg   dist. Keys
-----            -----   ---------      ------      -----   ----------
LAST_NAME_IDX      3     788,934      1,105,458     0.713   1,105,458
```

Table 7.1   Table and index sizes.

Object	Customer Table	last_name_idx
ROWS	1,000,000	100,000
ROW LENGTH	160	
BLOCK SIZE	16K	16K
DATA BLOCKS	10,000	4,000

This is a typical index for an Oracle database. As you can see, the index has a three-level index tree with just over 1 million rows and distinct keys. This means that Oracle would perform four logical I/Os (three through the index and one to the data block) to retrieve each row when the index is scanned. Therefore, a 1 million row table would require 4 million logical I/Os to sweep the table in index order.

As you may know, performance is impeded by physical I/Os, not logical I/Os. But how do you translate 4 million logical I/Os into a number of physical I/Os? Let's assume the index requires 4,000 data blocks and resides in contiguous data blocks, but the **CUSTOMER** table is not stored in **last_name** sequence. This means that as you read each bottom-level node of the index, you are unlikely to find that the data block is already in your buffer because the table is ordered in a different sequence than your index (see Figure 7.6).

Now, let's examine the difference when the data table is stored in the same sequence as the index. Assume you have an index that is used more frequently than your other indexes. For example, let's say you have indexed on your **customer_last_name (last_name_idx)**, and this index is used for more than 90 percent of your database queries.

If it were possible to physically order the **CUSTOMER** table in last name sequence, then you could save a considerable amount of physical I/O against the table. Using the same example, if the index data blocks are stored in the same sequence as the data table blocks, a full sweep of the table still requires 4 million logical I/Os, but a much smaller number of physical I/Os (see Figure 7.7).

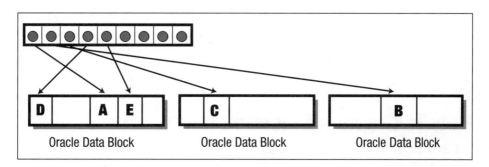

Oracle Data Block   Oracle Data Block   Oracle Data Block

Figure 7.6
Physical I/O for a non-clustered index.

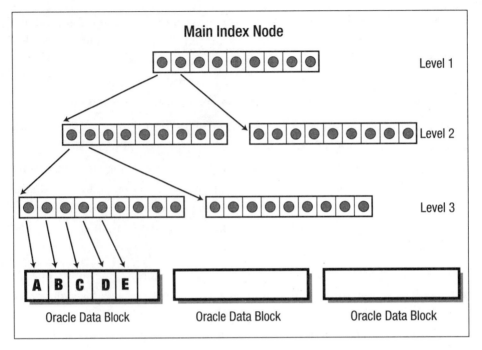

Main Index Node

Level 1

Level 2

Level 3

A B C D E

Oracle Data Block   Oracle Data Block   Oracle Data Block

Figure 7.7
Physical I/Os for a clustered table index.

Here, you can see that you still need to read all 4,000 index blocks to scan the index, but because 100 rows reside on each data block (160-byte rows in 16K blocks), you only need to read 10,000 data blocks to scan the entire table. The difference in physical I/Os is dramatic, and the reduction from 40,000 to 14,000 physical I/Os dramatically reduces the execution time for a full-index scan. Also, note that if it could guarantee that the data is in the proper physical order, Oracle could perform a full-table scan and would not need to use the index at all. Unfortunately, you cannot guarantee the physical row order—you can only approximate it.

How To Create A Clustered Index

For each table, there can only be one clustered index because only one index will be stored in the same physical order as the table. Unfortunately, Oracle does not give the DBA a simple method for ensuring the physical ordering of rows within a table. There are, however, some tricks that can be used to resequence a table to give it a different physical order. Beware, however, that the index could become out of physical sequence quickly as new rows are added to the end of the table and key values are updated to change the logical sequence in the index.

For Oracle, updates are usually done on a time-based formula, so the issue becomes one of resequencing the index and ensuring that additions to the index are managed. In most cases, the obvious key for an Oracle database is the date column. Oracle databases are updated in batch mode periodically, so the physical sequence of the data with the index could be maintained if you ensure that the new records are presorted in date order.

Here are the options for appending new rows onto the end of a physically sequenced Oracle table:

- You can copy the table with **CREATE TABLE AS SELECT** using an index hint to force the table sequence.

- Presort the extract files in index key order, and load with SQL*Loader.

- Extract the data directly from an Oracle OLTP system using date predicates, as follows:

```
INSERT INTO WAREHOUSE_TABLE
    SELECT *
    FROM
        OLTP_TABLE@remote_instance
    WHERE
        trans_date > '01-JAN-1998'
    ORDER BY
        trans_date;
```

Oracle export/import utilities have no mechanism for changing the physical sequence of tables, and they cannot be used to cluster an index.

Now, let's look at a dictionary query that will tell us the structure of our indexes (see Listing 7.7). Note that the query assumes that the Oracle database is using the cost-based optimizer and the tables have been analyzed with the **ANALYZE TABLE** command. In Listing 7.7, you can see that the indexes are grouped according to the tables they are built on. You can also see that the clustering factor for each index is computed as a percentage of the number of rows in the index.

Listing 7.7   An SQL*Plus routine to locate clustered indexes.

```
REM idx_bad1.sql, © 1997 by Donald K. Burleson
SET PAGESIZE 60;
SET LINESIZE 100;

COLUMN c0 HEADING 'Table'     FORMAT a8;
COLUMN c1 HEADING 'Index'     FORMAT a18;
COLUMN c2 HEADING 'Level'     FORMAT 999;
COLUMN c3 HEADING 'Clust Ftr' FORMAT 9,999,999;
COLUMN c4 HEADING '# rows'    FORMAT 99,999,999;
COLUMN c5 HEADING 'Clust Pct' FORMAT 999.9999;
COLUMN c6 HEADING 'Dist. Keys' FORMAT 99,999,999;
SPOOL idx_bad1.lst;

BREAK ON c0 SKIP 1;

SELECT
  DBA_INDEXES.table_name                           c0,
  index_name                                       c1,
  blevel                                           c2,
  clustering_factor                                c3,
  num_rows                                         c4,
  decode(clustering_factor,0,1,clustering_factor)/
  decode(num_rows,0,1,num_rows)                    c5,
  distinct_keys                                    c6
FROM DBA_INDEXES, DBA_TABLES
WHERE
DBA_INDEXES.owner NOT IN ('SYS','SYSTEM')
AND
DBA_TABLES.table_name = DBA_INDEXES.table_name
AND c5 < .25
ORDER BY c0, c5 desc;

SPOOL OFF;
```

Listing 7.8 shows a sample listing from idx_bad1.sql.

Listing 7.8   A sample listing from idx_bad1.sql.

```
SQL> @idx_bad1


Table   Index              Level Clust Ftr  # row   Clust Pct  Dist. Keys
-----   -----              ----- ----- ---  ------  ---------  ----------
```

```
INV_LINE  INV_LINE_ITEM_PK    2      62,107  1,910,034   .0325  1,912,644
          ILI_FK_INV          2     164,757  1,910,034   .0339  1,659,625
          ILI_FK_ACT          2     283,343  1,910,034   .0436         47
          ILI_EK_CCHS_ACCT    3   1,276,987  1,910,034   .1450     25,041
```

Now, let's inspect Listing 7.8 to see the clustering status of our indexes. The indexes are listed within each table heading in descending order of their clustering factor, with the most clustered indexes at the bottom of the list. The listing shows the **INV_LINE_ITEM_PK** index with a clustering factor of 62,107, indicating that the **INV_LINE** table has been loaded in nearly the same physical order as the index.

If the value for the clustering factor approaches the number of blocks in the base table, then the index is said to be clustered. If the clustering factor is greater than the number of blocks in the base table and approaches the number of rows in the base table, then the index is unclustered.

Determining When To Rebuild Indexes

One of the problems with many Oracle databases is their huge size. For very large databases, performing a database reorganization is impractical because of the amount of time required to export the data to tape, drop the Oracle database, and re-create the database using Oracle's import utility. Because of this time issue, a database manager must find alternative methods for ensuring that the Oracle database remains well-tuned from a physical data perspective.

In Oracle, a large index can take a long time to rebuild, and a prudent data administrator must carefully choose the right conditions that warrant an index rebuild. If very large database tables have been horizontally partitioned—where a large table is split into subtables according to date—there will be several smaller indexes to re-place a single, very large index.

In general, indexes seldom require rebuilding in Oracle unless there has been a high amount of update or delete activity against the index columns. SQL **INSERT** operations, which are common for loads of new data, do not cause structural problems within an Oracle index structure.

So, how can you tell when an index will benefit from being rebuilt? There are two Oracle views that provide index statistics: **DBA_INDEXES** and **INDEX_STATS**.

The **DBA_INDEXES** view contains statistical information that is placed into the view when the **ANALYZE INDEX xxx** command is issued. Unfortunately, the **DBA_INDEXES** view is designed to provide information to the cost-based SQL optimizer, and it does not keep statistics about the internal status of Oracle indexes.

To see the internal structure for an Oracle index, you must use the **ANALYZE IN-DEX xxx VALIDATE STRUCTURE** SQL command to validate the structure for the index. This command creates a single row in a view called **INDEX_STATS**. The **INDEX_STATS** view is a table that contains columns that describe the internals of the index. Here is a sample session:

```
SQL> ANALYZE INDEX DON.DON_FK_PLT VALIDATE STRUCTURE;

Index analyzed.

SQL> SELECT * FROM INDEX_STATS;

HEIGHT                         3
BLOCKS                      5635
NAME               DON_FK_PART
LF_ROWS
LF_BLKS                   196103
LF_ROWS_LEN                 2382
LF_BLK_LEN               3137648
BR_ROWS                     3900
BR_BLKS BR_ROWS_LEN         2381
BR_BLK_LEN                    18
DEL_LF_ROWS                41031
DEL_LF_ROWS_LEN             3956
DISTINCT_KEYS                  7
MOST_REPEATED_KEY            112
BTREE_SPACE                  125
USED_SPACE                 56220
PCT_USED                 9361008
ROWS_PER_KEY             3178679
BLKS_GETS_PER_ACCESS     787.912
```

*The Oracle **INDEX_STATS** view will never contain more than one row. There-fore, you must perform the **ANALYZE INDEX xxx VALIDATE STRUC-TURE** command and **SELECT * FROM INDEX_STATS** before issuing the next **ANALYZE INDEX** command. The script id1.sql on the accompanying CD-ROM provides a method for getting a complete report for all indexes.*

Oracle's version of b-tree indexing uses an algorithm where each index node can contain many index keys. As new key values are added to the index, Oracle must manage the configuration of each index node. As mentioned earlier in this chapter, Oracle index nodes are managed with splitting and spawning operations. Splitting occurs when a new node is created at the same index level as the existing node. As each level becomes full, the index could spawn, or create a new level to accommodate the new rows.

The **INDEX_STATS** view contains information about the internal structure of a b-tree index that can be useful when determining whether to rebuild the index. The following columns of **INDEX_STATS** are especially useful:

- **height**—Refers to the maximum number of levels encountered within the index. An index could have 90 percent of the nodes at three levels, but excessive splitting and spawning in one area of the index could cause some nodes to have more than three levels. Whenever the value of **height** is more than 3, you might benefit from dropping and re-creating the index. Oracle indexing will not spawn a fourth level on a clean rebuild until more than about 10 million nodes have been added to the index.

- **del_lf_rows**—Refers to the number of leaf rows that have been marked as deleted from the index. This occurs when heavy index update activity occurs within the index tree and indicates that the index will benefit from being dropped and re-created.

- **distinct_keys**—Indicates the number of distinct key values in an index. This is called the cardinality of the index, and values less than 20 are candidates for being re-created as bitmapped indexes.

- **most_repeated_key**—Counts the number of times the most frequent key value in a non-unique index appears in the b-tree.

Because the **INDEX_STATS** view will only hold one row at a time, it is not easy to create an SQL*Plus routine that will produce an **INDEX_STATS** report for all of the indexes on a system. The SQL presented in Listing 7.9 will perform an **ANALYZE INDEX xxx VALIDATE STRUCTURE** for each index in the schema and report the resulting values in **INDEX_STATS**.

> **Note:** Running id1.sql on the accompanying CD-ROM will invoke id2.sql through id5.sql, automatically producing the unbalanced index report. Just

*be sure that id1.sql through id5.sql are present in a common directory when
starting id1.sql.*

Despite the complexity of dealing with a one-row **INDEX_STATS** table, it is easy
to use the script presented in Listings 7.9 through 7.14 to get **INDEX_STATS** for
all indexes. In operational use, the unbalanced index report should be run whenever
a DBA suspects update activity has unbalanced the indexes.

Listing 7.9   The SQL*Plus script to generate the report for
             INDEX_STATS.

```
REM   id1.sql   The main driver routine for reporting index_stats
REM © 1997 by Donald K. Burleson
REM id1.sql
SET PAGES 9999;
SET HEADING OFF;
SET FEEDBACK OFF;
SET ECHO OFF;

SPOOL id4.sql;

SELECT '@id2.sql' FROM DUAL;

SELECT 'ANALYZE INDEX '||owner||'.'||index_name||
       'VALIDATE STRUCTURE;','@id3.sql;'
FROM DBA_INDEXES
WHERE
owner NOT IN ('SYS','SYSTEM');

SPOOL OFF;

SET HEADING ON;
SET FEEDBACK ON;
SET ECHO ON;

@id4.sql
@id5.sql
```

Listing 7.10   The SQL to create a temporary table for the
              INDEX_STATS report.

```
REM © 1997 by Donald K. Burleson
REM id2.sql
```

```
SELECT
  name                  ,
  most_repeated_key     ,
  distinct_keys         ,
  del_lf_rows           ,
  height                ,
  blks_gets_per_access
FROM INDEX_STATS;
```

Listing 7.11   The SQL to insert the data from **INDEX_STATS** into the temporary table.

```
REM © 1997 by Donald K. Burleson
REM id3.sql
INSERT INTO TEMP_STATS
(SELECT
  name                  ,
  most_repeated_key     ,
  distinct_keys         ,
  del_lf_rows           ,
  height                ,
  blks_gets_per_access
FROM INDEX_STATS
);
```

Listing 7.12   The SQL generated from running id1.sql.

```
REM © 1997 by Donald K. Burleson
REM id4.sql

ANALYZE INDEX DON.SHL_EK_TRUCK_LINK_NUM VALIDATE STRUCTURE;

@id3.sql;

ANALYZE INDEX DON.SHL_UK_FACT1_ID_SRC_CD_LOB VALIDATE STRUCTURE;

@id3.sql;

ANALYZE INDEX DON.PURCH_UNIT_PK VALIDATE STRUCTURE;

@id3.sql;
```

Listing 7.13   SQL*Plus script that generates the clustering report.

```
REM © 1997 by Donald K. Burleson
REM id5.sql - This creates the unbalanced index report
```

```
REM and the rebuild syntax
SET PAGESIZE 60;
SET LINESIZE 100;
SET ECHO OFF;
SET FEEDBACK OFF;
SET HEADING OFF;

COLUMN c1 FORMAT a18;
COLUMN c2 FORMAT 9,999,999;
COLUMN c3 FORMAT 9,999,999;
COLUMN c4 FORMAT 999,999;
COLUMN c5 FORMAT 99,999;
COLUMN c6 FORMAT 9,999;

SPOOL idx_report.lst;

PROMPT
PROMPT
PROMPT '                   # rep      dist.    # deleted              blk gets
PROMPT Index              keys       keys     leaf rows   Height     per access
PROMPT -----              -----      ----     ---------   ------     ----------

SELECT distinct
   name                 c1,
   most_repeated_key    c2,
   distinct_keys        c3,
   del_lf_rows          c4,
   height               c5,
   blks_gets_per_access c6
FROM TEMP_STATS
WHERE
   height > 3
   OR
   del_lf_rows > 10
ORDER BY name;

SPOOL OFF;

SPOOL id6.sql;

SELECT 'alter index '||owner||'.'||name||' rebuild tablespace'
       ||tablespace_name
FROM TEMP_STATS, DBA_INDEXES
```

```
WHERE
  TEMP_STATS.name = DBA_INDEXES.index_name
  AND
  (height > 3
  OR
  del_lf_rows > 10);

SELECT 'analyze index '||owner||'.'||name||' compute statistics;'
FROM TEMP_STATS, DBA_INDEXES
WHERE
  TEMP_STATS.name = DBA_INDEXES.index_name
  AND
  (height > 3
  OR
  del_lf_rows > 10);

SPOOL OFF;
```

Listing 7.14 Completed unbalanced index report.

Index	# rep keys	dist. keys	# deleted leaf rows	Height	blk gets per access
DON_EK	159,450	25,420	934	4	41
DON_FK_ACT	1,009,808	542	101	3	1,705
INV_EK_INV_NUM	4	1,586,880	122	3	4
INV_FK_CAR	546,366	1,109	315	3	725
INV_FK_SRC	1,041,696	309	31	3	2,591
LOB_FACT1_PK	1	3,778,981	66,918	4	5
RAT_FK_JEN	37	2,736,262	436,880	3	4
RAT_FK_JEN	37	2,736,262	436,880	3	4
RAT_FK_JEN	37	2,736,262	436,880	3	4
RAT_FK_JEN	37	2,736,262	436,880	3	4

JEN_FK_SHP	88	1,464,282	97,473	4	6
JEN_FK_SHP	88	1,464,282	97,473	4	6
DON_FK_LEG	342,290	1,350	301	4	933
DON_FK_LEG	342,290	1,350	301	4	933
DON_FK_LEG	342,290	1,350	301	4	933
DON_FK_LEG	342,290	1,350	301	4	933

Dropping and re-creating an index has inherent problems and is not the best way to rebuild an Oracle index. The most common problem occurs when an extended index is dropped and then fails to re-create due to a lack of space in the index tablespace. For example, if you have an index with an initial size of 100MB with 20 extents of 5MB, you can drop the index, redefine the index with an initial extent of 200MB, and re-create the index. Of course, first, you will need to ensure that there are 200MB of free space within the index before you try this operation. Also, you might need to coalesce free index extents in the tablespace to make more contiguous space.

Index Tablespace Issues

When a large database has been created, it is not uncommon to see yearly aggregate values purged and recomputed on a scheduled basis. When this happens, the table and index extending will not be a problem because the tablespace will coalesce all free extents within the tablespace.

But, what about the indexes? After a large purge, indexes can become out of balance, and additional I/O might be required to access particular records. The logical remedy to out-of-balance indexes would be to drop and rebuild all of the Oracle indexes. However, this poses another problem. To understand this process, let's examine a snapshot of an index tablespace prior to dropping all indexes in the tablespace using Oracle's Tablespace Manager (shown in Figure 7.8).

Now, let's drop the indexes, and look at the tablespace after the drop (shown in Figure 7.9).

In Figure 7.9, you can see that there are lots of empty extents in the tablespace because the empty storage has not been coalesced. Now, if you use Oracle7.2 or

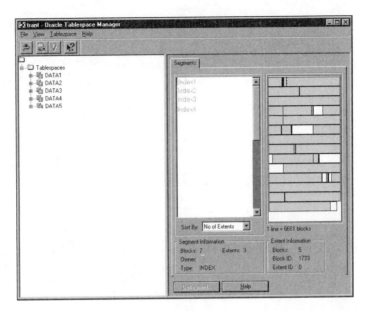

Figure 7.8

An Oracle index tablespace as seen by Oracle Tablespace Manager.

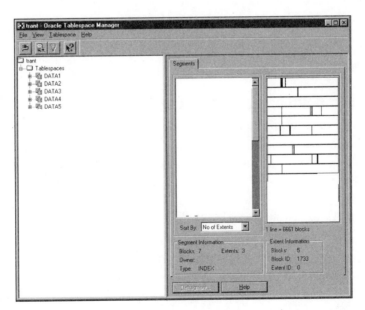

Figure 7.9

An Oracle index tablespace after dropping an index.

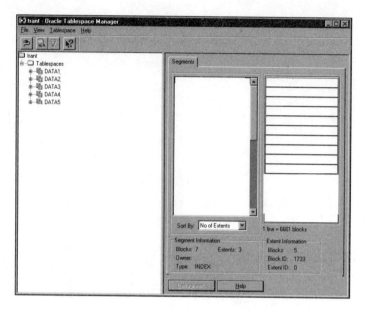

Figure 7.10
An Oracle index tablespace after coalescing the tablespace.

above, you can issue the **ALTER TABLESPACE xxx COALESCE** command (see Figure 7.10). With the tablespace clear, the index can easily be re-created to reside in a single extent.

Rebuilding Unbalanced Indexes

So, what's the solution to rebuilding an unbalanced index? Oracle (version 7.3 and above) provides a facility that rebuilds an index in place without having to drop and re-create the index. This is done by issuing an **ALTER INDEX** command, as follows:

```
ALTER INDEX xxx REBUILD TABLESPACE yyy;
```

*You must specify the tablespace name when using the **ALTER INDEX** command. If the tablespace name is not present, Oracle will attempt to rebuild the index in the default tablespace name of the connected user who is issuing the command.*

Let's take a look at what happens in an in-place rebuild of an Oracle index. An index rebuilt in place has the same number of extents as the original index. Hence, this command is not useful for reorganizing an index into a single extent. Each index node will be rebuilt in place, and the excessive levels and deleted leaf rows will be fixed. The goal of a data manager is to rebuild only those indexes that have more than three levels or lots of deleted leaf rows, so effective DBAs can use the id5.sql script to generate the rebuild commands directly from the **TEMP_STAT** table and store the output as id6.sql.

While Oracle does not publish how the rebuild command works internally, you must have extra space, equal to the index size, in each tablespace in order to issue the rebuild command. If Oracle cannot get enough scratch space in the target tablespace, the existing index will remain intact, and you will receive the message FAILED TO ALLOCATE AN EXTENT OF SIZE xxx IN TABLESPACE yyy.

Listing 7.15 shows a list of indexes to be rebuilt, specifying the tablespace names. Please note that Oracle's index **REBUILD** command is very fast when compared to dropping and re-creating an index. Using internal benchmarks of the **REBUILD** command, a 1GB index can be completely rebuilt in 20 seconds. This is because Oracle reads the existing index in order to gather the index node information for the new index. After the index has been read, Oracle replaces the old index tree in the same spot in the tablespace as the old index. For even faster execution time, the **UNRECOVERABLE** clause can be used with the **REBUILD** command.

Listing 7.15 The output from rebuilding indexes.

```
ALTER INDEX DON.DON_EK REBUILD TABLESPACE INDX_1;

index rebuilt

ALTER INDEX DON.DON_FK_ACT REBUILD TABLESPACE INDX_1;

index rebuilt

   . . .
```

Summary

While this chapter is devoted to the obvious DBA issues relating to performance and tuning, it is imperative that Oracle DBAs are intimate with the various areas of Oracle tuning. The DBA, more than any other participant in the development of the system, has the ability to influence a system's overall performance. For more information about tuning as it relates to Oracle8 data warehouses, see Chapter 10, *Tuning Oracle Data Warehouse And OLAP Applications.*

Performance And Tuning For Distributed Oracle Databases

CHAPTER

8

Performance And Tuning For Distributed Oracle Databases

Performance and tuning of Oracle systems is anything but trivial with distributed database environments because so many components within the database software contribute to the overall performance. The number of concurrent users, the availability of space within the buffer and lock pools, and the balancing of application access can all affect database performance. This chapter addresses the following topics:

- Replication of Oracle tables

- Parallelism and Oracle databases

- Planning for growth

- Designing expert systems for performance measurement

- Load sharing and Oracle

- Heterogeneity

- Tuning the Oracle WebServer

When a client/server application must access several remote databases in a single transaction, another dimension of complexity is added to the system. The database administrator (DBA) must look at more than each individual database and must consider transactions that span different servers. While accessing several servers in a distributed transaction might seem trivial, performance problems can be introduced by PC hardware, LAN and network bottlenecks, router overloads, and a plethora of other sources. Only by examining the relevant components of distributed databases can you gain a broad understanding of the issues. One of the most important tools in Oracle8 database replication is the use of Oracle snapshots. The proper use of snapshots is critical to distributed Oracle performance, and the following sections review the most important factors.

Replication Of Oracle Tables

It is interesting to note that the general attitude about data replication has shifted dramatically in the past 10 years. In the 1980s, replication was frowned upon. Database designers believed that there was no substitute for the Third Normal Form database. Today, the practical realities of distributed processing have made replication a cheap and viable alternative to expensive cross-database joins. Table replication was so successful within Oracle version 7 that Oracle introduced the concept of updatable snapshots with Oracle version 7.3. Oracle snapshots are quite stable in Oracle8 and can be used with confidence in a production environment. Oracle snapshots are very flexible and offer a huge range of options, so fully understanding Oracle's snapshot facility is a prerequisite to implementing an effective snapshot architecture.

Using Oracle Snapshots

Oracle snapshots are used to create read-only copies of tables in other Oracle databases. This is a highly effective way to avoid expensive cross-database joins of tables. As you probably know, an SQL join with a table on a remote server is far slower than a join with a local table: SQL*Net overhead increases as it retrieves and transfers data across a network. However, replication is not to be used indiscriminately, and the following guidelines exist for using replicated tables to the best advantage:

- *A replicated table should be read-only*—Obviously, a table snapshot cannot be updated because the master copy of the table is on another server.

- *A replicated table should be relatively small*—Ideally, a replicated table is small enough so that the table can be dropped and re-created each night, or the

REFRESH COMPLETE option can be used. Of course, large tables can be replicated with the REFRESH FAST option, but this involves a complicated mechanism for holding table changes and propagating them to the replicated table.

- *A replicated table should be used frequently*—It does not make sense to replicate a table if it is only referenced a few times per day, and the cost of the replication would outweigh the cost of the cross-database join.

Despite any claims by Oracle to the contrary, snapshots are not to be used indiscriminately. Only those tables that meet the preceding criteria should be placed in snapshots. In practice, snapshots are not maintenance-free, and many points of failure are possible—especially if the snapshot is created with the REFRESH FAST option. Problems can occur writing to the SNAPSHOT_LOG table, and SQL*Net errors can cause failures of updates to transfer to the replicated tables.

A snapshot is created on the destination system with the CREATE SNAPSHOT command, and the remote table is immediately defined and populated from the master table.

After creation, a snapshot can be refreshed periodically. There are two methods of refreshing: *complete* and *fast*. A complete refresh can be done in several ways, but most savvy Oracle developers drop and re-create the snapshots with a Unix **cron** job to achieve full refreshes, especially if the table is small and easily re-created. Optionally, a fast refresh can update tables with only the changes that are made to the master table. This requires additional work on the slave database to create an Oracle refresh process (in the init.ora) and the definition of a snapshot log on the master database (see Figure 8.1).

Several steps need to be completed before your Oracle system is ready to use snapshots. First, you need to run catsnap.sql, which can be found in your $ORACLE_HOME/rdbms/admin directory. This script will populate the Oracle dictionary with the necessary system tables to manage the snapshots. You'll also need to run dbmssnap.sql, which can be found in the $ORACLE_HOME/rdbms/admin directory. This script creates the stored procedures that can be used to manipulate the snapshots.

The following parameters must also be added to the init.ora file:

- **snapshot_refresh_interval=60**—This sets the interval (in minutes) for the refresh process to wake up.

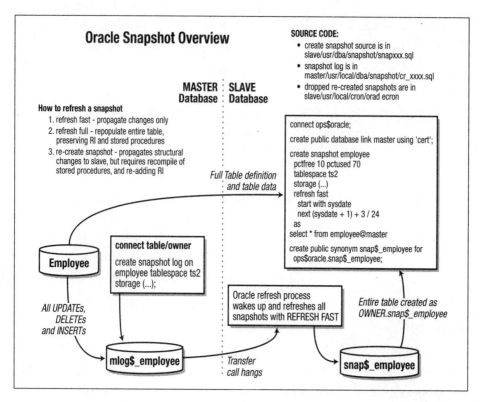

Figure 8.1
A high-level overview of Oracle snapshots.

- **snapshot_refresh_processes=1**—This is the number of refresh processes on the instance (the minimum is one).

- **snapshot_refresh_keep_connections=false**—This specifies whether the database should keep remote connections after refreshing the tables. Always use **false**.

Creating Snapshots For Small Tables

For snapshots that are small enough to be totally repopulated, the following steps are necessary. Note that it is possible to do a **REFRESH COMPLETE** or a **REFRESH FORCE** rather than a **cron** job, but using a **cron** is a simple way to guarantee that the replicated table will be fully repopulated. To avoid the **REFRESH FAST** option with a Unix **cron**, the following two steps are required:

1. Create the snapshot with the **REFRESH COMPLETE** option.

2. Alter **oracle.cron** to drop and re-create the snapshot.

Creating Snapshots For Large Tables

For snapshots of large tables, you might want to use the **REFRESH FAST** option. For **REFRESH FAST**, the following steps are required:

1. On the destination system, create the snapshot with the **REFRESH FAST** option signed on as user SYS. (Be sure to define a database link with **CONNECT TO XXX IDENTIFIED BY ZZZ,** and ensure that user XXX has select privileges against the master table.)

2. On the master system, create a snapshot log on each master table.

3. Bounce the destination system to begin the refreshes based on the interval specfied in the **CREATE SNAPSHOT.**

Listing 8.1 shows an example of a snapshot that reads a table from an instance called **london.**

Listing 8.1   The **london** snapshot.

```
CONNECT sys/xxxx;
DROP PUBLIC DATABASE LINK london;
CREATE PUBLIC DATABASE LINK london
CONNECT TO db_link IDENTIFIED BY db_pass USING 'london';
-----------------------------
DROP SNAPSHOT MY_REPLICATED_TABLE;
-----------------------------
CREATE SNAPSHOT MY_REPLICATED_TABLE
       PCTFREE 10 PCTUSED 40
       TABLESPACE ts2
       STORAGE (INITIAL 60K NEXT 10K PCTINCREASE 1)
       REFRESH FAST
               START WITH SYSDATE
               NEXT (SYSDATE+1) + 3/24
       AS SELECT * FROM ORACLE.MY_MASTER_TABLE@london;

GRANT ALL ON MY_REPLICATED_TABLE TO PUBLIC;
****************************************************
   Add the appropriate synonyms for the snapshots...
****************************************************
```

```
CONNECT /;
CREATE PUBLIC SYNONYM SNAP$_MY_REPLICATED_TABLE
FOR OPS$ORACLE.SNAP$_MY_REPLICATED_TABLE;
```

Here, you can see that the **MY_REPLICATED_TABLE** table is refreshed each morning at 3:00 AM, and the read-only name **SNAP$_MY_REPLICATED_TABLE** has been replaced with synonym **MY_REPLICATED_TABLE**. Here is an example of the snapshot log syntax that needs to be run on the master database:

```
CREATE SNAPSHOT LOG ON CUSTOMER_TABLE
TABLESPACE TS2
STORAGE (INITIAL 20K NEXT 20K);
```

The **dbms_snapshot.refresh_all** procedure can be run at any time on the destination system to refresh the snapshot tables. To force a refresh of an individual table, execute the following command:

```
EXECUTE dbms_snapshot.refresh('office','f');
```

Any refresh errors are written to the alert.log file.

The snapshot log is a table that resides in the same database as the master table, which can be seen in the **DBA_TABLES** view as a table with the name **MLOG$_TABLENAME**. In the preceding example, the snapshot log would be called **MLOG$_CUSTOMER**.

Now that we understand the basic facilities of Oracle snapshots, let's take a look at some proven, real-world techniques for implementing snapshots in a production environment.

Real-World Tips And Techniques For Oracle Snapshots

Even with Oracle's distributed features, it is still far faster to process a table on a local host than it is to process a remote table across SQL*Net's distributed communication lines. As such, table replication is a very desirable technique for improving processing speeds.

Several factors should influence a decision about replicating tables. The foremost consideration should be the size of the replicated table and the volatility of the tables.

Large, highly active tables with many updates, deletes, and inserts require a lot of system resources to replicate and keep synchronized with the master table. Smaller, less active tables are ideal candidates for replication because the creation and maintenance of the replicated table would not consume a high amount of system resources.

Oracle's snapshot facility is relatively mature and generally works as noted in the Oracle documentation. However, the flexibility of the snapshot tool gives a developer many choices in how a snapshot will be created and refreshed. You can refresh a replicated table in full, you can re-create a snapshot at will, you can choose periodic refreshes of a snapshot, and you can use database triggers to propagate changes from a master table to a snapshot table. While the implementation of particular snapshot techniques depends on an individual application, the general rules presented in this section can usually be applied.

If a replicated table is small and relatively static, it is usually easier to drop and re-create a snapshot than to use Oracle's **REFRESH COMPLETE** option. A crontab file can be set up to invoke the drop and re-creation at a predetermined time each day, completely refreshing the entire table.

Another popular alternative to the snapshot is using Oracle's distributed SQL to create a replicated table directly on the slave database. In the following example, the New York database creates a local table called **EMP_NY**, which contains New York employee information from the master employee table at corporate headquarters:

```
CREATE TABLE EMP_NY
AS
    SELECT
            emp_nbr,
            emp_name,
            emp_phone,
            emp_hire_date
    FROM EMP@hq WHERE department = 'NY';
```

Very large replicated tables consume too much time in dropping and re-creating a snapshot or using the **REFRESH COMPLETE** option. On the other hand, for static tables, a snapshot log would not contain very many changes, so you could direct Oracle to propagate the changes to the replicated table at frequent intervals. Let's take a look at the different refresh intervals that can be specified for a snapshot.

This example states that Oracle should take the snapshot log and apply it to the replicated table every seven days:

```
CREATE SNAPSHOT CUST_SNAP1
REFRESH FAST
    START WITH SYSDATE
    NEXT SYSDATE+7
AS SELECT cust_nbr, cust_name FROM CUSTOMER@hq WHERE department = 'NY';
```

The next example shows a table that is refreshed each Tuesday at 6:00 AM:

```
CREATE SNAPSHOT CUST_SNAP1
REFRESH FAST
    START WITH SYSDATE
    NEXT next_day(trunc(SYSDATE),'TUESDAY')+6/24
AS SELECT cust_nbr, cust_name FROM CUSTOMER@hq WHERE department = 'NY';
```

For very static tables, you can also specify refreshes to run quarterly. The following example refreshes a table completely on the first Tuesday of each quarter:

```
CREATE SNAPSHOT CUST_SNAP1
REFRESH COMPLETE
    START WITH SYSDATE
    NEXT next_day(add_months(trunc(SYSDATE,'Q'),3),'TUESDAY')
AS SELECT cust_nbr, cust_name FROM CUSTOMER@hq WHERE department = 'NY';
```

For dynamic tables that require refreshing daily, you can specify that the table is refreshed at 11:00 AM each day, as follows:

```
CREATE SNAPSHOT CUST_SNAP1
REFRESH FAST
    START WITH SYSDATE
    NEXT SYSDATE+11/24
AS SELECT cust_nbr, cust_name FROM CUSTOMER@hq WHERE department = 'NY';
```

In addition to using the time range specified in the **CREATE SNAPSHOT** syntax, you can also use Oracle stored procedures to achieve the same result. If you have run the dbmssnap.sql script, you can refresh a snapshot by issuing the following command:

```
EXECUTE dbms_snapshot.refresh('customer','c');  /* complete refresh */
EXECUTE dbms_snapshot.refresh('customer','f');  /* forced   refresh */
EXECUTE dbms_snapshot.refresh('customer','?');  /* fast     refresh */
```

But what about replicated tables that require faster propagation? Oracle first offered updatable snapshots with version 7.3, while users of previous releases of Oracle need to use database triggers to update snapshots.

Using Triggers To Update Snapshots

Users of previous releases of Oracle can use database triggers to simulate the realtime propagation of changes from a master table to replicated tables. In the following example, an update trigger has been placed on the **CUSTOMER** tables and relevant changes will be propagated to the New York branch:

```
CREATE TRIGGER ADD_CUSTOMER
    AFTER INSERT ON CUSTOMER
AS
IF :dept = 'NY' THEN
(INSERT INTO CUSTOMER@NY
    VALUES(:parm1, :parm2, :parm3);
);
```

But what can be done about rows that are deleted from the **CUSTOMER** table? Using the same technique, a delete trigger can be placed on the **CUSTOMER** table to remove rows from the replicated tables, as follows:

```
CREATE TRIGGER DELETE_CUSTOMER
    AFTER DELETE ON CUSTOMER
AS
IF :dept = 'NY' THEN
(DELETE FROM CUSTOMER@NY
    WHERE
    cust_nbr = :customer_parm
);
```

As you have seen, snapshot replication and triggers are very handy for taking a master and copying it to a remote location. But what if you only want to replicate a portion of a table? Oracle provides a method enabling you to accomplish this, as well.

Using Snapshots To Propagate Subsets Of Master Tables

Oracle provides a method for excluding certain rows and columns from a replicated table. For example, let's assume that you are replicating a central employee table for use by your New York branch. However, you only want to replicate employee records for those who work at the New York branch, and you want to exclude confidential columns, such as the employee's salary. Here is how a snapshot of a table subset would appear:

```
CREATE SNAPSHOT EMP_NY
REFRESH FAST
    START WITH SYSDATE
    NEXT next_day(trunc(SYSDATE),'TUESDAY')+6/24
AS
    SELECT
            emp_nbr,
            emp_name,
            emp_phone,
            emp_hire_date
    FROM EMP@hq WHERE department = 'NY';
```

The latest fad in the database marketplace is the widespread replication of data to mobile remote servers for updating purposes. This is often referred to as asynchronous updating.

Asynchronous Updating Of Oracle Tables

Replicating data for the purpose of updating mobile remote servers is fast becoming a widespread phenomenon within the sales community. The remote servers are completely disconnected from the central server, and the updates usually occur on laptop servers. Using asynchronous updating enables a laptop user to dial in to a central server and transfer updates at any time (see Figure 8.2).

This approach has been very popular with Oracle-based sales force automation (SFA) systems that strive to provide field sales personnel with current information from the centralized host without requiring them to continually dial in to the server. Here is how asynchronous updating of systems works when remote databases are disconnected from the central host.

Daily changes to the centralized host are collected and distributed to the remote laptop database whenever a member of the sales force dials in to the host and requests a refresh. As sales representatives make changes on their laptops, they are able to feed these changes to the central host whenever they dial in. While this might seem like a sound idea on the surface, some very serious questions arise, such as:

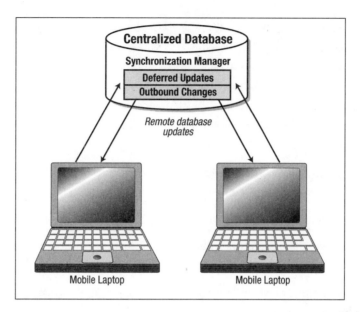

Figure 8.2
Asynchronous updating mechanisms.

- How are update anomalies handled?

- What happens when a change based on outdated information is made on a remote laptop?

- Is there a mechanism for synchronizing the remote laptops? If not, how can a working mechanism be developed?

The asynchronous approach is used almost exclusively with distributed sales systems that require salespeople in the field to have current information without having to connect to a central server via modem.

The idea is to define a subset of the database for each mobile user and then develop a mechanism to ensure that the disconnected laptop is updated each time the salesperson connects to the central database. In addition, the updates must occur quickly to minimize connect time. Most of these systems apply a date-time stamp to all relevant rows, using this date-time key to quickly retrieve the data from the master tables. Obviously, this means that every laptop is going to be out of sync with the master database to some degree.

At connect time, the system must also upload all changes that have been made to the mobile database, updating the master tables on the central server. The absence of database locks leads to some interesting update anomalies. These anomalies take two forms. The first type of anomaly occurs when a row is updated by two mobile laptops, and the upload of one row overlays the changes made by the other mobile laptop. The second type of anomaly occurs when outdated information is used as the basis for making a change while on the mobile laptop.

Most of the SFA products have developed their own rules for dealing with anomalies. The developer may choose one of the following options:

- Defer all update anomalies, writing them to a special area for manual resolution.

- The most recent update (as indicated at upload time) supersedes any prior updates.

- All end users are ranked, and the user with the highest rank supersedes all changes made by a lower-ranked employee.

Regardless of the method chosen, these tools are normally constructed using a relational database such as Oracle with a custom synchronization manager. The synchronization manager handles the downloading of information from the centralized server to the laptop and the uploading of changes to the main server.

For downloads, most of these tools prepackage the relevant information for the laptop user, keeping track of the last synchronization and writing changes to a special table. In this fashion, the laptop user does not have to wait while the server extracts the updates, and the updates can be transferred and loaded into the laptop server immediately.

For uploads, the laptop tracks all changes since the last upload—first extracting and then transferring the changes to the centralized server. The synchronization manager then inserts new information and carefully checks the date-time stamp on all rows that are marked for update. If a row has been updated since the laptop user's last time of synchronization, the data is handled according to the programmed rules in the synchronization manager. For most implementations, the safest method is to reject all potential anomalies, which triggers an exception report and requires manual resolution of the update. In practice, one of the largest problems is motivating the users of the mobile laptop to dial in frequently for their updates.

These types of systems recognize the problems that arise when trying to distribute data to mobile servers, and attempt to address the problem with custom rules and procedures. It is interesting to note that they have proven very successful in systems where up-to-the-minute information is not required for decision making and the user requires mobile access to information.

Now that we have covered Oracle snapshots, let's take a look at how Oracle's parallel features are used to improve Oracle8 performance. Parellelism is one of the most exciting features of Oracle, but remains one of the least understood areas of Oracle performance.

Parallelism And Oracle Databases

The widespread acceptance of distributed processing and multitasking operating systems has heralded a new mode of designing and implementing business systems. Instead of the traditional "linear" design of systems, tomorrow's system will incorporate massively parallel processing. The result? Many tasks could be concurrently assigned to service a database request. Indeed, the entire definition of data processing is changing. The corporate data resource has been expanded to include all sources of information, not just databases. Corporate information lies within email, Lotus Notes, and many other nontraditional sources. Many companies are collecting this information without fully exploiting its value, and multiprocessing is an ideal technique for searching these huge amounts of freeform corporate information.

Multitasking And Multithreading

Before we tackle this subject, a distinction needs to be made between *multitasking* and *multiprocessing*. Multitasking refers to the ability of a software package to manage multiple concurrent processes, thereby allowing simultaneous processing. Although OS/2 and Windows NT are good examples of this technology, multitasking can be found within all midrange and mainframe databases. Multiprocessing refers to the use of multiple CPUs within a distributed environment where a master program directs parallel operations against numerous machines. Two levels of multiprocessing are possible—the hardware level and the software level. Multiprocessing at the hardware level results when arrays of CPUs are offered. Multiprocessing at the software level occurs when a single CPU is partitioned into separate "logical" processors. The PRISM software on the IBM mainframe environment is an example of software-level multiprocessing.

In any case, multiprocessor programming techniques are quite different from linear programming techniques. Multiprocessing programming falls into two areas: data parallel programming and control parallel programming. Data parallel programming partitions data into discrete pieces, running the same program in parallel against each piece. Control parallel programming identifies independent functions that are simultaneously solved by independent CPUs (see Figure 8.3).

One of the greatest problems with implementing parallel processing systems is the identification of *parallelism*. Parallelism refers to the ability of a computer system to perform processing on many data sources at the same instant in time. Whereas many of the traditional database applications were linear in nature, today's systems have many opportunities for parallel processing.

Parallelism is especially important for scientific applications that can benefit from the opportunity to have hundreds—or even thousands—of processors working together to solve a problem. But the same concept of parallelism applies to very large databases. If a query can be split into subqueries where each subquery is assigned to

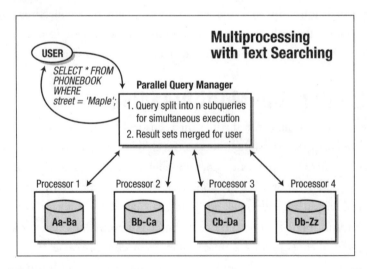

Figure 8.3
An example of a parallel query.

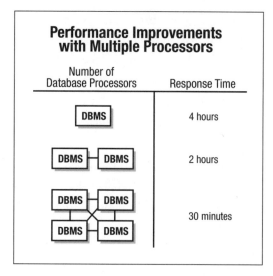

Figure 8.4
The performance benefits of adding processors.

a processor, the response time for the query can be reduced by a factor of thousands (see Figure 8.4).

Parallelism is an issue of scale. Where a linear process can solve a problem in four hours, a parallel system with 2 processors *should* be able to solve the problem in two hours, as demonstrated in Figure 8.4. While the speed improvements in Figure 8.4 are possible under certain circumstances, we must remember that parallel execution is not always possible. Speed can only be improved in situations where parallel processing is appropriate, which excludes traditional linear systems where one process can not begin until the preceding process ends.

A review of the past 30 years makes it clear that tremendous improvements have been made in the speed of processors. At the same time, processor prices have continued to decline. However, this trend cannot continue forever. The physical nature of silicon processors has been pushed to its limit and is now reaching a diminishing point of return. In order to continue to enjoy increases in performance, either silicon needs to be replaced as a medium or ways must be devised to exploit parallelism in processing.

Other facets of parallel processing can be extremely valuable. A query against a very large database can be dramatically improved if the data is partitioned. For example, if a query against a text database takes 1 minute to scan a terabyte, then partitioning the data and processing into 60 pieces will result in a retrieval time of 1 second. Another key issue is the balancing of the CPU processing with the I/O processing. In a traditional data processing environment, the systems are not computationally intensive and most of the elapsed time is spent waiting on I/O. However, this does not automatically exclude business systems from taking advantage of multiprocessing.

A continuum of processing architecture exists for parallel processing. On one end of the spectrum you find a few powerful CPUs that are loosely connected, while on the other end you can see a large amount of small processors that are tightly coupled.

Parallelism can be easily identified in a distributed database environment. For the database administrator, routine maintenance tasks such as export/import operations can be run in parallel, reducing the overall time required for system maintenance.

In an open systems environment, parallelism can be easily simulated by using a remote mount facility. With a remote mount, a data file can be directly addressed from another processor, even though the data file physically resides on another machine. This can be an especially useful technique for speeding up table replication to remote sites, as shown in Figure 8.5.

To speed up the replication of two tables, a Unix shell script directs CPU-A to begin the copy of Table A as a background task. The script then directs CPU-B to issue a

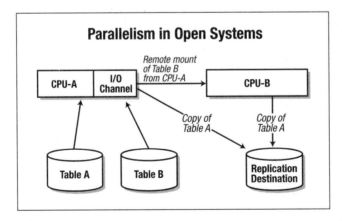

Figure 8.5
Parallelism across multiple CPUs.

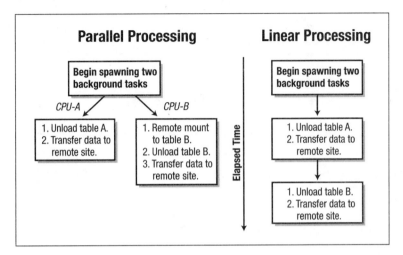

Figure 8.6
Linear versus parallel processing.

remote mount to Table B, making Table B addressable as if it were a local disk to CPU-B. The script then issues a copy of Table B, and the tables are copied simultaneously, reducing the overall processing time. (See Figure 8.6.)

Of course, the overall elapsed time will not be half of the time required for a linear process—the remote mount still requires the database on CPU-A to manage the I/O against Table B. The benefit lies in having the second processor (CPU-B) handle all the processing for the unload of Table B.

When looking at Oracle Parallel Server (OPS) and Oracle parallel query, we need to understand how the hardware architecture affects the use of these tools. The following section describes how the hardware configuration interacts with Oracle's parallel facilities.

Symmetrical Multiprocessing Vs. Massively Parallel Processing

Symmetrical multiprocessing (SMP) describes an architecture where many CPUs share a common memory area and I/O buffer. This type of architecture is not scalable because additional processors must compete for the shared memory and I/O resources. On the other hand, massively parallel processors (MPP) describes an architecture where many independent processors share nothing, operating via a common I/O bus.

An MPP system can add processors without impeding performance, and performance will actually increase as processors are added.

Using Oracle's Parallel Processes

Starting with Oracle version 7.2, some powerful new features were introduced to allow parallel processes to be used against the Oracle database. These features include:

- Parallel **CREATE TABLE**
- Parallel query
- Parallel index building
- Parallel DDL

Please note that the new parallel features are release dependent, meaning that you must be using Oracle7.3 or above to use parallel query and Oracle8 or above to use parallel Data Definition Languages (DDL). Also note that it is not necessary to have parallel processors (SMP or MPP) in order to use and benefit from parallel processing. Even on the same processor, multiple processes can be used to speed up queries. Oracle's parallel query option can be used with any SQL **SELECT** statement—the only restriction being that the query performs a full-table scan on the target table.

Parallel queries are most useful in distributed databases where a single logical table has been partitioned into smaller tables at each remote node. For example, a customer table that is ordered by customer name can be partitioned into a customer table at each remote database, such that there is a **phoenix_customer**, a **los_angeles_customer**, and so forth. This approach is very common with distributed databases where local autonomy of processing is important. However, what about the needs of those in corporate headquarters? How can they query all the remote tables as a single unit and treat the logical customer table as a single entity? The answer lies in "splitting" the table.

While splitting a table according to a key value violates normalization theory, it can dramatically improve performance for individual queries. For large queries that span many logical tables, the isolated tables can be easily reassembled using Oracle's parallel query facility, as follows:

```
CREATE VIEW ALL_CUSTOMER AS
    SELECT * FROM PHOENIX_CUSTOMER@phoenix
    UNION ALL
    SELECT * FROM LOS_ANGELES_CUSTOMER@los_angeles
    UNION ALL
    SELECT * FROM ROCHESTER_CUSTOMER@rochester;
```

> **Note:** The @ references refer to SQL*Net service names for the remote hosts.

The **ALL_CUSTOMER** view can now be queried as if it were a single database table, and Oracle parallel query will automatically recognize the **UNION ALL** parameter, firing off simultaneous queries against each of the three base tables. It is important to note that the distributed database manager will direct each query to be processed at the remote location, while the query manager waits until each remote node has returned its result set. For example, the following query will assemble the requested data from the three tables in parallel, with each query optimized separately. The result set from each subquery is then merged by the query manager:

```
SELECT customer_name
FROM ALL_CUSTOMER
WHERE
total_purchases > 5000;`
```

> **Note:** For more details on using Oracle's parallel query facility, refer to Chapter 2, Logical Performance Design.

Now that we see how parallelism can help to improve the performance of Oracle, let's take a look at how we can plan for the growth of the database system while maintaining the ability to tune the architecture.

Planning For Growth

One of the biggest problems in performance and tuning is the problem of planning for growth and ensuring that your distributed database continues to perform at an acceptable level. As you probably know, databases run within a well-defined domain of systems resources, and a shortage of system resources can lead to performance degradation. The trick is to design a database system with the ability to add resources on an as-needed basis without interrupting processing.

Growth of a database can occur in several areas. As the physical size of the database increases, so does the need for disk storage. As the volume of users increases, so does the need for increased buffer and lock pool storage. As network traffic increases, an increasing demand falls on the routers, and bandwidth might need to be increased.

Unlike the CODASYL databases of the 1980s, today's relational databases allow for tables to grow according to specified rules and procedures. In the relational model, one or more tables can reside in a tablespace. A *tablespace* is a predefined container for the tables that map to fixed files of a finite size. Tables assigned to a tablespace can grow according to the specified growth rules, but the size of the tablespace supersedes the expansion rules. In other words, a table can, according to the table definition, have more extents available, but there might not be room in the tablespace to allocate those extents.

Several allocation parameters influence table growth, including:

- **db_block_size**—The size of each physical database block.

- **INITIAL**—The initial size of each table extent.

- **NEXT**—The subsequent size of new table extents.

- **MINEXTENTS**—The minimum number of initial extents (used for striping).

- **MAXEXTENTS**—The maximum allowable number of extents (Note: the **MAXEXTENTS UNLIMITED** parameter is supported in all releases after Oracle7.3).

- **PCTINCREASE**—The percentage by which each subsequent extent grows (normally set to 1).

- **PCTFREE**—The percentage of space to be kept on each data block for future expansion.

The **PCTFREE** parameter is used to reserve space on each data block for the future expansion of row values (via the SQL **UPDATE** command). Table columns can be defined as allowing **NULL** values that do not consume any space within the row, or with **varchar** data types. A **varchar** data type specifies the maximum allowable length for the column instance, but the acceptable range of values can be anywhere from 4 bytes (the size of the length holder) to the size of the field plus 4 bytes. Hence, a **varchar(2000)** can range in size from 4 bytes to 2,004 bytes.

If an application initially stores rows with empty values and later fills in the values, the **PCTFREE** parameter can dramatically reduce I/O contention. If a block of storage is filled by the addition of a row, subsequent updates to that row to fill in column values will cause the row to fragment—usually onto the next available contiguous block. Unfortunately, it is very ironic that an Oracle developer must choose a block size when the database is initially created—a time when knowledge of system performance is extremely limited.

Block Sizing

While it is possible to use the Oracle import/export utilities to change block sizes, too little attention is given to the proper sizing of database blocks. The physical block size is set with the **db_block_size** parameter in the init.ora file. While the default for Oracle is 4K block sizes, many Oracle developers choose at least 8K block sizes for all databases, regardless of their size and usage. Some DBAs believe that 16K is the best block size, even for OLTP systems that seldom perform full-table scans. Depending on the host platform and operating system, Oracle block sizes can be set from 2K up to 32K. You should refer to the Oracle OS manual to find acceptable ranges for your operating system.

When determining the required space for your database, subtract the block header and **PCTFREE** from your calculations. Oracle block headers are a function of the **db_block_size** (in init.ora) and the value of **INITTRANS** (in tablespace definition).

The space (in bytes) required by the data block header is the result of the following formula:

```
Block Header size
  = (BLOCK_SIZE - KCBH - UB4 - KTBBH - (INITTRANS - 1)) * (KTBIT - KDBH)
  = (DB_BLOCK_SIZE - 20 - 4 - 48 - (INITTRANS - 1)) * (24 - 14)
  = (DB_BLOCK_SIZE - 72 - (INITTRANS - 1)) * 10

Where
    KCBH (block common header) = 20
    UB4 (unsigned byte 4) = 4
    KTBBH (transaction fixed header) = 48
    INITTRANS (initial number of transaction entries)
    KTBIT (transaction variable header) = 24
    KDBH (data header) = 14
```

The size (constants) of **KCBH**, **UB4**, **KTBBH**, **KTBIT**, and **KDBH** can also be found in the fixed view **V$TYPE_SIZE**.

The principle behind block sizing is simple. I/O is the single most expensive and time-consuming operation within a database. As such, the more data that can be read in a single I/O, the faster the performance of the Oracle database. This principle is especially true for databases that have many reports that read the entire contents of a table. For systems that read random single rows from the database, block size is not as important—especially with database clusters. An Oracle cluster is a mechanism whereby an owner row will reside on the same database block as its subordinate rows in other tables. For example, if the **order** rows are clustered on the same block as their **CUSTOMER** owners, Oracle will only need to perform a single I/O to retrieve the **CUSTOMER** and all of the **order** rows. Of course, in a distributed database where joins take place across different Oracle instances, clustering cannot be used. The additional I/O will be required to read the rows individually.

Bear in mind that increasing the block size of an Oracle database will also affect the number of blocks that can be cached in the buffer pool. For example, if you set the **db_block_buffers** init.ora parameter to 8MB, Oracle will be able to cache 1,000 4K blocks, but only 500 8K blocks.

Increasing the Oracle block size also increases the risk of concurrency bottlenecks, especially when the **INITTRANS** and **MAXTRANS** values are set too low. **INITTRANS** and **MAXTRANS** are Oracle tablespace creation parameters that determine the amount of space to be reserved on a block for concurrency locks. The maximum values for **INITTRANS** and **MAXTRANS** is 255, meaning that no more than 255 transactions can simultaneously access a specific database block.

If you suspect that your values are too low, a query of the **V$LOCK** table will reveal all tasks that are waiting for access to a page. Listing 8.2 shows an SQL script that can be used to check for lock contention.

Listing 8.2   locks.sql shows all locks in the database.

```
SET LINESIZE 132
SET PAGESIZE 60
COLUMN OBJECT HEADING 'Database|Object'      FORMAT a15 TRUNCATE
COLUMN lock_type HEADING 'Lock|Type'         FORMAT a4  TRUNCATE
COLUMN mode_held HEADING 'Mode|Held'         FORMAT a15 TRUNCATE
```

```
COLUMN mode_requested HEADING 'Mode|Requested' FORMAT a15 TRUNCATE
COLUMN sid HEADING 'Session|ID'
COLUMN username HEADING 'Username'                FORMAT a20 TRUNCATE
COLUMN IMAGE HEADING 'active image'              FORMAT a20 TRUNCATE
SPOOL /tmp/locks
SELECT
        C.sid,
        substr(object_name,1,20) OBJECT,
        C.username,
        substr(C.program,length(C.program)-20,length(C.program)) image,
        decode(B.type,
                'MR', 'Media Recovery',
                'RT', 'Redo Thread',
                'UN', 'User Name',
                'TX', 'Transaction',
                'TM', 'DML',
                'UL', 'PL/SQL User Lock',
                'DX', 'Distributed Xaction',
                'CF', 'Control File',
                'IS', 'Instance State',
                'FS', 'File Set',
                'IR', 'Instance Recovery',
                'ST', 'Disk Space Transaction',
                'TS', 'Temp Segment',
                'IV', 'Library Cache Invalidation',
                'LS', 'Log Start or Switch',
                'RW', 'Row Wait',
                'SQ', 'Sequence Number',
                'TE', 'Extend Table',
                'TT', 'Temp Table',
                B.type) lock_type,
        decode(B.lmode,
                0, 'None',                /* Mon Lock equivalent */
                1, 'Null',                /* NOT */
                2, 'Row-SELECT (SS)',     /* LIKE */
                3, 'Row-X (SX)',          /* R */
                4, 'Share',               /* SELECT */
                5, 'SELECT/Row-X (SSX)',  /* C */
                6, 'Exclusive',           /* X */
                to_char(B.lmode)) mode_held,
        decode(B.request,
                0, 'None',                /* Mon Lock equivalent */
                1, 'Null',                /* NOT */
                2, 'Row-SELECT (SS)',     /* LIKE */
```

```
                3, 'Row-X (SX)',            /* R */
                4, 'Share',                 /* SELECT */
                5, 'SELECT/Row-X (SSX)',    /* C */
                6, 'Exclusive',             /* X */
                to_char(B.request)) mode_requested
FROM SYS.dba_objects A, SYS.v_$lock B, SYS.v_$session C WHERE
A.object_id = B.id1 AND B.sid = C.sid AND OWNER NOT IN ('SYS','SYSTEM');
```

Listing 8.3 shows the output of locks.sql.

Listing 8.3   The results from locks.sql.

```
SQL> @locks
```

Session ID	Database Object	Username	Active Ima	Lock Type	Mode Held	Mode Requested
--	------	--------	---------	----	----	----
2	DUAL		Media	Reco	Share	None
2	SYSTEM_PRIVI		Media	Reco	Share	None
2	TABLE_PRIVIL		Media	Reco	Share	None
2	STMT_AUDIT_O		Media	Reco	Share	None
2	V$CONTROLFIL		Media	Reco	Share	None
2	V$DATAFILE		Media	Reco	Share	None
2	V$LOG		Media	Reco	Share	None
2	V$THREAD		Media	Reco	Share	None
2	V$PROCESS		Media	Reco	Share	None
2	V$BGPROCESS		Media	Reco	Share	None
2	V$SESSION		Media	Reco	Share	None
2	V$LICENSE		Media	Reco	Share	None
2	V$TRANSACTIO		Media	Reco	Share	None
2	V$LATCH		Media	Reco	Share	None
2	V$LATCHNAME		Media	Reco	Share	None
2	V$LATCHHOLDE		Media	Reco	Share	None
2	V$RESOURCE		Media	Reco	Share	None
2	V$_LOCK		Media	Reco	Share	None
2	V$LOCK		Media	Reco	Share	None
2	V$SESSTAT		Media	Reco	Share	None

```
20 rows selected.
```

Now that you know how the definition of Oracle tables can influence performance, let's move to a higher level and look at how the definition of the Oracle tablespace and the placement of objects within the tablespaces can influence Oracle8 performance.

Tablespace Considerations

Choosing how to pair tables and indexes into tablespaces has a great impact on the performance of distributed databases. As a designer, you have many choices, so it is a good idea to explore your available options. In general, the following recommendations apply to tablespaces:

- Group tables with similar characteristics in a tablespace. For example, all read-only tables could be grouped into a single, read-only tablespace. Tables with random I/O patterns could also be grouped together, all small tables could be grouped together, and so on.

- Create at least two tablespaces for use by the **TEMP** tablespaces. This approach has the advantage of allowing a designer to dedicate numerous **TEMP** tablespaces to specific classes of users. As you probably know, the **TEMP** tablespace is used for large sorting operations, and assigning appropriately sized **TEMP** tablespaces to users depending upon their sorting requirements can enhance performance. Remember, in a distributed SQL query, the rows are fetched from the remote database and sorted on the Oracle instance that initiated the request. The use of multiple **TEMP** tablespaces has the added advantage of allowing the developer to switch **TEMP** tablespaces in case of disk failure.

- Use many small, manageable tablespaces. This approach makes it easier to take a single tablespace offline for maintenance without affecting the entire system. Oracle highly recommends that no tablespace should ever become greater than 10GB, and placing all tables into a single tablespace reduces recoverability in case of media failure. However, this approach does not advocate creating a single tablespace for each table in a system. For example, Oracle recommends that the system tablespace contain only systems tables, and that a separate tablespace be created for the exclusive use of the rollback segments.

- Place the rollback segments in a separate tablespace. This isolates the activity of the rollback segments (which tend to have a high I/O rate) from the data files belonging to the application.

In addition to these general guidelines for tablespaces, the maintenance of tablespaces is also an issue with Oracle performance. The following section describes how to identify and correct tablespace fragmentation.

Tablespace Fragmentation

As rows are added to tables, the table expands into unused space within the tablespace. Conversely, when rows are deleted, a table might coalesce extents, releasing unused space back into the tablespace. As this happens, it is possible for there to be discontiguous chunks, or fragments of unused space within the tablespace. Whenever the value for a table as specified by **STORAGE (INITIAL xx)** is exceeded, Oracle will create a new extent for the table. If the **PCTINCREASE** is set to zero, a new extent of the size specified in **STORAGE (NEXT xx)** will be added to the table. If **PCTINCREASE** is non-zero, the extent size will be equal to the value of the most recent extent size multiplied by **PCTINCREASE**.

PCTINCREASE for a tablespace should not be set to zero because this will disable the automatic coalesce facility for Oracle tablespaces. In general, all tablespaces except the system tablespaces (SYSTEM, RBS) should have PCTINCREASE set to 1. The PCTINCREASE parameter for tablespaces is generally only used when a table is allocated without a STORAGE clause— although Oracle also uses it for coalescing.

This allocation of new extents will be physically contiguous to the table's initial location, as long as the next physical data blocks are empty. Unfortunately, as many tables populate a tablespace, a table might not have contiguous data blocks for its next extent, which means that it must fragment the extents onto another spot in the data file, as shown here:

```
CREATE TABLESPACE SALES
  DATAFILE '/Data/ORACLE/sales/sales.dbf'
  SIZE 500M REUSE
  DEFAULT STORAGE (INITIAL 500K  NEXT 50K  PCTINCREASE 1);
```

Here, you can see that the **SALES** tablespace has been allocated to a physical file called /Data/ORACLE/sales/sales.dbf, created at a size of 500MB. Assuming that all tables within this tablespace use default storage, they will be initially allocated at 500K and will extend in chunks of 50K.

But what happens if the tablespace gets full? Processing will cease against the tablespace, and the Oracle DBA will have to intervene to add another data file to the tablespace with the **ALTER TABLESPACE** command, as follows:

```
ALTER TABLESPACE SALES
ADD DATAFILE '/Data/ORACLE/sales/sales1.dbf'
SIZE 200M REUSE;
```

Obviously, the DBA should carefully monitor tablespace usage so that tablespaces never fill, but Oracle (version 7.2 and above) offers an alternative. The **AUTO-EXTEND** command can be used to allow a data file to grow automatically on an as-needed basis. Here are the different permutations of this command:

```
ALTER DATABASE DATAFILE '/Data/ORACLE/sales/sales.dbf' AUTOEXTEND ON;

ALTER DATABASE DATAFILE '/Data/ORACLE/sales/sales.dbf' AUTOEXTEND
    MAXSIZE UNLIMITED;

ALTER DATABASE DATAFILE '/Data/ORACLE/sales/sales.dbf' AUTOEXTEND
    MAXSIZE (500M);

ALTER DATABASE DATAFILE '/Data/ORACLE/sales/sales.dbf' RESIZE (600M);
```

When tables fragment, additional I/O is required to access the table data because the disk must access blocks on multiple noncontiguous spots on the data file. However, there are some DBAs who have conducted tests showing that extended tables are not always bad unless they are approaching the value for maximum extents. A table that has extended will spread the data across more disks, and thereby, spread the load more efficiently than a table in a single, contiguous extent. In any case, the following script will detect all tablespaces whose tables have taken more than 10 extents:

```
tblsp_fr.sql - shows all tablespaces with more than 10 extents
SET PAGES 9999;
COLUMN c1 HEADING "Tablespace Name"
COLUMN c2 HEADING "Number of Extents"
TTITLE " Tablespaces with more than 10 extents"

SELECT tablespace_name c1,
       max(extent_id) c2
FROM DBA_EXTENTS
WHERE
extent_id > 9
GROUP BY tablespace_name
;
```

Here is the output of this script:

```
SQL> @tblsp_fr

Fri Mar 15                                              page    1
                    Tablespaces with more than 10 extents

Tablespace Name                 Number of Extents
---------------                 -----------------
INDX                                   113
SALES                                   57
SYSTEM                                  56
```

Contrary to popular opinion, tables with noncontiguous extents do not necessarily cause performance problems. It is only the row fragmentation that sometimes accompanies discontiguous extents that negatively affects performance. In some studies, a table with discontiguous extents (and no row fragmentation) actually performed faster than a table that was in a single extent. Regardless, tables are dynamic, so Oracle databases will always fragment over time, and you will probably need to conduct periodic cleanups. Occasionally, you might even need to reorganize your tablespaces.

Tablespace Reorganization

In general, reorganization ensures that all tables and indexes do not have row fragmentation, and that they reside in a single extent, with all free space in a tablespace in a single, contiguous chunk. Reorganizing a tablespace can be accomplished in several ways. Rather than bring down the entire Oracle database to perform a full export/import, there are some other options.

First, let's take a look at how a tablespace can become fragmented. At initial load time, all Oracle tables within the tablespace are contiguous—that is, only one chunk of free space resides at the end of the tablespace. As tables extend and new extents are added to the tablespace, the free space becomes smaller, but it still remains contiguous.

Basically, a table can fragment in two ways:

- *A table extends (without row chaining)*—Contrary to popular belief, this is not a problem and performance will not suffer.

- *Rows fragment within the tables (due to SQL UPDATEs)*—This causes a serious performance problem, and the offending tables must be exported, dropped, and reimported.

Tablespace fragmentation occurs when "pockets" of free space exist within the tablespace. So, how do these pockets of free space appear? If tables are **DROPPED** and re-created, or if individual tables are exported and imported, space once reserved for a table's extent will become vacant.

To see the fragmentation within a tablespace, run the script shown in Listing 8.4.

Listing 8.4   tsfrag.sql shows a tablespace map.

```
REM written by Don Burleson

SET LINESIZE 132;
SET PAGES 999;

REM SET FEEDBACK OFF;
REM SET VERIFY OFF;
REM SET HEADING OFF;
REM SET TERMOUT OFF;

BREAK ON file_id SKIP PAGE;
BREAK ON FREE SKIP 1;
COMPUTE sum OF KB ON FREE;

SPOOL tsfrag;

COLUMN owner           FORMAT a10;
COLUMN segment_name    FORMAT a10;
COLUMN tablespace_name FORMAT a14;
COLUMN file_id         FORMAT 99 heading ID;
COLUMN end             FORMAT 999999;
COLUMN KB              FORMAT 9999999;
COLUMN begin           FORMAT 999999;
COLUMN blocks          FORMAT 999999;

SELECT
  tablespace_name,
  file_id,
  owner,
  segment_name,
  block_id begin,
  blocks,
```

```
    block_id+blocks-1 end,
    bytes/1024 KB,
    '' free
FROM SYS.dba_extents
WHERE tablespace_name NOT IN ('RBS','SYSTEM','TEMP','TOOLS','USER')
UNION
SELECT
    tablespace_name,
    file_id,
    '' owner,
    '' segment_name,
    block_id BEGIN,
    blocks,
    block_id+blocks+1 END,
    bytes/1023 KB,
    'F' free
FROM SYS.dba_free_space
WHERE tablespace_name NOT IN ('RBS','SYSTEM','TEMP','TOOLS','USER')
ORDER BY 1, 2, 5
;
/
SPOOL OFF;

!cat tsfrag.lst
```

Listing 8.5 shows the output of tsfrag.sql.

Listing 8.5   The results of the tsfrag.sql script.

TS_NAME	ID	OWNER	SEGMENT_NA	BEGIN	BLOCKS	END	KB	F
-------	--	-----	----------	-----	------	---	---	--
MASTER3_STAT_1	15	DON	ZIP_UPS_ZO NE_XREF	2	5	6	20	
MASTER3_STAT_1	15	DON	ACHG_TY	7	2	8	8	
MASTER3_STAT_1	15	DON	BUSN_UNIT	9	35	43	140	
MASTER3_STAT_1				44	2	45	8	F
MASTER3_STAT_1	15	DON	PLANT	46	3	48	12	
MASTER3_STAT_1				49	10	58	40	F
MASTER3_STAT_1	15	DON	DON_TABLES	59	4	62	16	
MASTER3_STAT_1	15	DON	ZONE	63	2	64	8	
							---- *	
							252	s
MASTER3_STAT_1	15			65	1216	1282	4869	F
							---- *	
							4869	s

In Listing 8.5, you can see two discontiguous chunks of free space, as indicated by the **F** column on the far right side of the report. Here, you can see that blocks 44 through 45 are free, as are blocks 49 through 58.

Oracle version 7.3 and above will automatically detect and coalesce tablespaces—provided that all affected tablespaces' default storage clauses have **PCTINCREASE** set to 1. The coalesce mechanism for tablespace coalescing is the **smon** process, which periodically wakes up to coalesce free space. Between **smon** coalesces, any transaction that requires an extent that is larger than any available free extent will trigger a coalesce on the tablespace to move all free space into a single chunk—hopefully making room for the required extent.

The dictionary view **DBA_FREE_SPACE_COALESCED** (introduced in Oracle7.3) provides details about the number of extents, bytes, and blocks that have been coalesced in each tablespace.

The following query will display coalesce information:

```
SELECT
    tablespace_name,
    bytes_coalesced,
    extents_coalesced,
    percent_extents_coalesced,
    blocks_coalesced,
    percent_blocks_coalesced
FROM
    SYS.DBA_FREE_SPACE_COALESCED
ORDER BY
    tablespace_name;
```

To change all tablespaces' **PCTINCREASE** from 0 to 1 so that tables will automatically coalesce, run the script in Listing 8.6.

Listing 8.6   coalesce.sql changes all tablespaces with
PCTINCREASE not equal to 1.

```
REM written by Don Burleson

SET LINESIZE 132;
SET PAGESIZE 999;
SET FEEDBACK OFF;
SET VERIFY OFF;
```

```
SET HEADING OFF;
SET TERMOUT OFF;

SPOOL COALESCE;

SELECT
   'alter tablespace '
   ||tablespace_name||
   ' storage ( pctincrease 1 );'
FROM DBA_TABLESPACES
WHERE
 tablespace_name NOT IN ('RBS','SYSTEM','TEMP','TOOLS','USER')
AND
 pct_increase = 0;

SPOOL OFF;

SET FEEDBACK ON;
SET VERIFY ON;
SET HEADING ON;
SET TERMOUT ON;

@coalesce.lst
```

If you detect that a single tablespace has fragmented, you can quickly coalesce it by following the steps presented here.

1. Alter session by retrieving the tablespace number from **SYS.TS$**, as follows:

    ```
    SELECT * FROM SYS.TS$:
    ```

2. In SQL*DBA, issue the command

    ```
    ALTER SESSION SET EVENTS immediate trace name coalesce level &tsnum;
    ```

    where **tsnum** is the tablespace number from Step 1.

3. Finally, to manually coalesce, issue the following command in SQL*Plus:

    ```
    ALTER TABLESPACE <xxxx> COALESCE;
    ```

While many vendor tools can aid in a database reorganization, many Oracle administrators will write a script that will export all tables within the tablespace, re-create the tablespace, and then import all of the tables and indexes to compress them into a single extent. However, be forewarned that referential integrity can make it difficult to drop a tablespace. This occurs when one tablespace contains a table that has a foreign-key constraint from a table within another tablespace.

Most often, the administrator will reorganize an entire database by performing the following steps:

1. Export the full database.
2. Generate the create database script.
3. Generate a list of data files to remove.
4. Remove the data files.
5. Create the database.
6. Import the full database.
7. Bounce the database and optionally turn on archive logging.

Now that we've covered the basic Oracle table options and their impact on performance, let's turn our attention to the situations that lead to tablespace reorganization.

Table Fragmentation

Again, it needs to be emphasized that table fragmentation does not cause performance problems. Rather, the row chaining that often accompanies table fragmentation seriously impedes performance. In fact, some Oracle DBAs have reported that extended tables (without row chaining) sometimes outperform tables that reside in a single extent. For detecting row chaining, see the next section, entitled "Row Fragmentation."

Listing 8.7 shows a simple script can be run to see the number of times that a table has extended.

Listing 8.7   tblexts.sql lists all tables with more than 10 extents.

```
SET PAUSE OFF;
SET ECHO OFF;
SET LINESIZE 150;
SET PAGESIZE 60;
COLUMN c1  HEADING "Tablespace";
COLUMN c2  HEADING "Owner";
```

```
COLUMN c3  HEADING "Table";
COLUMN c4  HEADING "Size (KB)";
COLUMN c5  HEADING "Alloc. Ext";
COLUMN c6  HEADING "Max Ext";
COLUMN c7  HEADING "Init Ext (KB)";
COLUMN c8  HEADING "Next Ext (KB)";
COLUMN c9  HEADING "Pct Inc";
COLUMN c10 HEADING "Pct Free";
COLUMN c11 HEADING "Pct Used";
BREAK ON c1 SKIP 2 ON c2 SKIP 2

TTITLE "Fragmented Tables";

SELECT   substr(SEG.tablespace_name,1,10) c1,
         substr(TAB.owner,1,10)           c2,
         substr(TAB.table_name,1,30)      c3,
         SEG.bytes/1024                   c4,
         SEG.extents                      c5,
         TAB.max_extents                  c6,
         TAB.initial_extent/1024          c7,
         TAB.next_extent/1024             c8,
         TAB.pct_increase                 c9,
         TAB.pct_free                     c10,
         TAB.pct_used                     c11
FROM     SYS.DBA_SEGMENTS SEG,
         SYS.DBA_TABLES    TAB
WHERE    SEG.tablespace_name = TAB.tablespace_name
  AND    SEG.owner = TAB.owner
  AND    SEG.segment_name = TAB.table_name
  AND    SEG.extents > 10
ORDER BY 1,2,3;
```

Listing 8.8 shows the results of the tblexts.sql script.

Listing 8.8   The results from the tblexts.sql script.

```
SQL> @tblexts

Thu Mar 14

                                                       page    1
                                               Fragmented Tables

Table              Table       Size Alloc Max Init  Next    Pct Pct Pct
space  Owner       Ext         (KB) Ext   Ext Ext(KB) Ext(KB) Inc Free Used
-----  ----        -----       ---- ---   --- -----  -----   --- ---- ----
DONT   DON         UST_CAT     5800 58    249 100    100     0   20   40
```

SYSTEM	SYS	AUD$	1724	11	249	12	840	50	10	40
		CHAINED_ROWS	684	57	249	12	12	0	10	40
		SOURCE$	1724	11	249	12	840	50	10	40

Row Fragmentation

Row fragmentation is one of the most problematic events that can occur within an Oracle system. Row fragmentation commonly takes place when an SQL **UPDATE** operation lacks sufficient room to expand the size of a row on its data block. When this happens, the row must extend onto the next available data block, causing an extra I/O when the row is accessed.

In Figure 8.7, the next four blocks are filled with rows. When an SQL update adds 1,500 bytes to row 1, the database chains to the next block. Finding no space, it chains to the next block and the next block, before finding 1,500 bytes of free space on block 4. The fragment is stored in block 4, and a chain is established from the block header of block 1 to point to the next block header, and so on, until the fragment is located.

Any subsequent retrieval of row 1 will require the database to perform four physical block I/Os in order to retrieve the entire row. I/O time is usually the largest component of overall response time, so this type of row fragmentation can greatly reduce performance.

Preventative measures can be taken to avoid row fragmentation. For example, if a row will eventually contain all of its column values, and the values are of fixed length, the table could be defined with the parameter **NOT NULL**. This reserves space in the row when it is initially stored. If a row contains variable-length columns, then the **PCTFREE** parameter can be increased to reserve space on each block for row

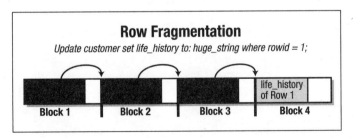

Figure 8.7
An example of Oracle row chaining.

expansion. By the way, this issue is not confined to Oracle. Most databases offer a utility that can be run periodically to check for row fragmentation. If fragments are found, the data must be exported to a flat file, the table redefined with different storage parameters, and the tables repopulated from a flat file.

Listing 8.9 contains a script called chain.sql that will detect the number of chained rows for all Oracle tables. This script is a series of queries that acquires a list of all Oracle tables and writes the **ANALYZE TABLE** syntax to an intermediate file, which is then executed to count the total number of chained rows for all tables. Remember, a chained row occurs when an SQL **UPDATE** operation has increased the size of a row, causing it to fragment onto another data block.

 Listing 8.9 creates table statistics that might force the use of the cost-based analyzer unless the database init.ora file parameter is set to RULE instead of CHOOSE.

Listing 8.9   chain.sql shows all chained rows in the database tables.

```
SET ECHO OFF;
SET HEADING OFF;
SET FEEDBACK OFF;
SET VERIFY OFF;

DROP TABLE CHAINED_ROWS;
@/opt/oracle/product/7.1.6/rdbms/admin/utlchain.sql

--define owner = &tableowner
SPOOL /opt/oracle/admin/adhoc/chainrun.sql;

SELECT 'analyze table ' || owner || '.' ||table_name ||
       ' list chained rows;'
FROM DBA_TABLES
WHERE OWNER NOT IN ('SYS','SYSTEM');
SPOOL OFF;

--!more chainrun.sql
@chainrun.sql

SELECT 'There are ' || count(*) || ' chained rows in this database.'
FROM CHAINED_ROWS;
```

```
SELECT DISTINCT owner_name, table_name, count(*)
FROM CHAINED_ROWS
GROUP BY owner_name, table_name;

PROMPT
PROMPT You may now query the chained_rows table.
PROMPT This table contains one row for each row that has chained.
PROMPT
PROMPT suggested query:  select table_name, head_rowid, timestamp
PROMPT                           from chained_rows
PROMPT

@chain

ANALYZE TABLE ORACLE.PUMPDATA LIST CHAINED ROWS;
ANALYZE TABLE ORACLE.SALESORG LIST CHAINED ROWS;
ANALYZE TABLE ORACLE.EMP LIST CHAINED ROWS;
ANALYZE TABLE ORACLE.LOB LIST CHAINED ROWS;
ANALYZE TABLE ORACLE.PRODUCT LIST CHAINED ROWS;
ANALYZE TABLE ORACLE.PAC1 LIST CHAINED ROWS;
ANALYZE TABLE ORACLE.PAC12 LIST CHAINED ROWS;
ANALYZE TABLE ORACLE.PAC23 LIST CHAINED ROWS;
ANALYZE TABLE ORACLE.MGC LIST CHAINED ROWS;
ANALYZE TABLE ORACLE.FILM_CODE LIST CHAINED ROWS;
ANALYZE TABLE ORACLE.CUST_CAT LIST CHAINED ROWS;
ANALYZE TABLE ORACLE.SALES_SUM LIST CHAINED ROWS;
ANALYZE TABLE ORACLE.DEPT LIST CHAINED ROWS;
ANALYZE TABLE ORACLE.BONUS LIST CHAINED ROWS;
ANALYZE TABLE ORACLE.SALGRADE LIST CHAINED ROWS;
ANALYZE TABLE ORACLE.DUMMY LIST CHAINED ROWS;
SQL>
SQL> SPOOL OFF;
SQL>
SQL> @chainrun.sql
SQL> SELECT 'analyze table ' || owner || '.' ||table_name ||
            ' list chained rows;'
SQL>    2   FROM DBA_TABLES
SQL>    3   WHERE OWNER NOT IN ('SYS','SYSTEM');
SQL>

SQL> ANALYZE TABLE ORACLE.LOB LIST CHAINED ROWS;
SQL> ANALYZE TABLE ORACLE.PRODUCT LIST CHAINED ROWS;
SQL> ANALYZE TABLE ORACLE.PAC1 LIST CHAINED ROWS;
SQL> ANALYZE TABLE ORACLE.PAC12 LIST CHAINED ROWS;
SQL> ANALYZE TABLE ORACLE.PAC23 LIST CHAINED ROWS;
SQL> ANALYZE TABLE ORACLE.MGC LIST CHAINED ROWS;
```

```
SQL> ANALYZE TABLE ORACLE.FILM_CODE LIST CHAINED ROWS;
SQL> ANALYZE TABLE ORACLE.CUST_CAT LIST CHAINED ROWS;
SQL> ANALYZE TABLE ORACLE.SALES_SUM LIST CHAINED ROWS;
SQL> ANALYZE TABLE ORACLE.DEPT LIST CHAINED ROWS;
SQL> ANALYZE TABLE ORACLE.BONUS LIST CHAINED ROWS;
SQL> ANALYZE TABLE ORACLE.SALGRADE LIST CHAINED ROWS;
SQL> ANALYZE TABLE ORACLE.DUMMY LIST CHAINED ROWS;
```

Listing 8.10 shows the results from the chain.sql script.

Listing 8.10   The results from the chain.sql script.

```
There are 16784 chained rows in this database.

SQL>
SQL> SELECT DISTINCT owner_name, table_name, count(*)
  2    FROM CHAINED_ROWS
  3  GROUP BY owner_name, table_name;

ORACLE                    SALESNET                  16784
ORACLE                    SALES                       432
ORACLE                    CUST                     126744
```

Now that we see how the physical definitions of Oracle objects affect system performance, it should be obvious that the process of identifying and correcting performance problems is a very well-structured task. As such, you should be able to create an environment whereby you can automatically search for unusual situations and alert the Oracle professional to the potential problem. The following section explores how such software might be created.

Designing Expert Systems For Performance Measurement

When a centralized database is split into multiple distributed systems, the overall maintenance requirements for each database increase significantly. While the overall costs for the system hardware will decline as companies abandon their mainframes, human resources will increase as redundant personnel are added to perform system and database administration tasks at each node.

Many distributed database shops are responding to this challenge by creating systems that automate the common performance tracking for each remote database, alerting the DBA staff when predefined thresholds are exceeded. This type of automation can be extended with statistical trend analysis tools such as the SAS product to give forecasts of database maintenance and performance trends.

While these systems can become very sophisticated, I recommend an evolutionary approach to the design of expert systems for performance and tuning. The work in 1981 by Robert Bonczeck into the theoretical structure of expert systems applies very well to performance and tuning applications. Bonczeck identifies a generalized framework for solving problems that consists of three components: states, operators, and goals. This approach assumes that the initial state is identified (namely, a performance degradation), and a series of operators is applied to this state until the goal state is achieved (i.e., acceptable performance). This "state-space" approach to problem solving is especially useful for systems that collect and analyze performance and tuning information.

The idea is to create a knowledge system to store relevant statistical information, periodically feeding this knowledge system into a problem-processing system, as illustrated in Figure 8.8. The problem-processing system contains the decision rules that are used to analyze trends in usage and alert the DBA if a parameter has been exceeded.

This technique also relies on the knowledge that database performance and tuning does not require human intuition. While the decision rules applied to the problem are very complex, performance analysis is nothing more than the application of well-structured rules to problem data. Therefore, an automated system can be devised to replicate the DBA's expertise in performance analysis.

The following steps can be used to create an expert system for performance and tuning:

1.   Identify the packaged utilities to be used, which can include:

   •   SQL trace facility

   •   Tablespace reports

   •   Log analysis reports

   •   Operating system-specific reports

   •   Performance monitor reports

2.   Schedule the reports to run on a periodic basis, and direct the output to a file.

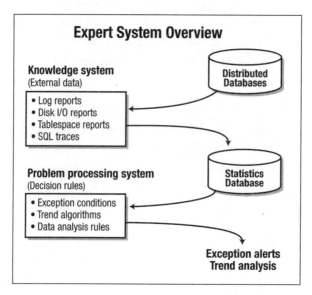

Figure 8.8
The architecture of expert systems.

3. Write a summary program to interpret the reports, and write summary statistics to a master file.

4. Create a problem processing system to read the knowledge system, generating trend reports and DBA alerts.

Many tools are available for performance analysis. Reports can be run against the database logs to produce reports containing statistics about every task in the database. The SQL trace utility can be turned on for a few minutes each day to attempt to identify inefficient SQL statements. Operating system reports can be generated containing information on disk contention and I/O bottlenecks. Performance monitors can also be used to detect information about database deadlocks and incomplete transactions.

Scheduling can be performed to fire the reports at specific time intervals. Unix utilities such as **cron** can be used for time-dependent scheduling, but it is convenient to have a gateway into the scheduler so that exception-based reporting can be conducted. For example, if a Unix monitor detects excessive hardware contention against a disk, it could trigger a user-exit to start an SQL trace to obtain detailed information.

Most database reports contain so much irrelevant information that a simple program written with C or even COBOL could be used to read the output from the reports, storing critical information into a table. This table would be used to feed the problem processing system, enabling the creation of exception reports and trend analysis reports. While this may sound complex, the data from the knowledge system can be fed directly into a canned statistical package such as SAS or SPSS to produce trend reports.

Table 8.1 shows a typical weekly exception report. All tasks for the day are analyzed and compared with a running average for their historical response time. If the response time for the task exceeds 15 percent of the historical average, the variance is noted in the right-hand column.

This type of report can provide very useful information about the overall operation of a distributed database. Note, for example, the performance degradation on Wednesday (97908). You can see that all the tasks in the system were running below their historical average on that day, so you can assume that some external influence could have caused a systemwide response problem.

Other common reports can compare the buffer utilization among distributed databases, comparing the ratio of **blocks_requested** to **blocks_in_buffer**. This can be used as a simple method of monitoring changes in buffer utilization over time. DBAs

Table 8.1 Southern Meadows' weekly task exception report for the week ending 09/12/97.

Task Name	Day of Week							Times Invoked	Historical Response Variance
	97906	97907	97908	97909	97910	97911	97912		
PC01	.55	.54	.68	.56	.54	.57	.00	21932	.55
PC02	.05	.04	.08	.06	.04	.07	.00	3444	.01
PC03	.22	.23	.40	.21	.23	.21	.22	129342	.24
PC04	.05	.08	.09	.02	.04	.01	.00	3444	.01
PC05	.35	.33	.42	.33	.32	.40	.31	3444	.31

who have implemented this type of system find that it removes the need for the tedious report analysis they once conducted by hand, providing a base for more sophisticated performance and tuning automation. For specific information about designing an Oracle system for performance monitoring, refer to Chapter 11, *Oracle Application Monitoring*.

Now that we understand the role of performance monitoring, let's take a look at how the latest hardware architectures are being used to share processing resources. Today's hardware has the ability to spread CPU consumption across many Oracle instances, and this load sharing capability can be very helpful for Oracle performance.

Load Sharing And Oracle

With the recent advances in symmetric multiprocessing (SMP), it is interesting to note that many companies are investigating tools that allow processors to be added and removed from a system on an as-needed basis. Load sharing, or the ability to dynamically add and remove processors, is the result of the shared memory cluster technology. By clustering multiple SMP processors, system administrators have the ability to easily scale-up a specific application, providing additional processing power on an as-needed basis.

System administrators can link and unlink clusters of SMP hosts as they see fit, achieving the proper balance of processing power for an application. This new technology also relieves system planners from the chore of predetermining the full amount of CPU that an application will require. With multiple SMP clusters, the system can start small and new processors can be added as demands on the system grow.

This sections looks at Platform's Computing Load Sharing Facility (LSF) as an example of load sharing technology. While not an endorsement, the discussion of this product serves as a good example of the types of software that are being used to distribute processing power in distributed environments. While each vendor offers different tools to achieve CPU load sharing, LSF provides insight into the internal functioning of these types of tools. LSF is a distributed computing system that turns a cluster of Unix computers from several vendors into a "virtual supercomputer." Platform's LSF supports fully transparent load sharing across Unix systems from different vendors, representing the enabling technology for the rapidly emerging cluster computing market.

The performance of low-cost workstations has been improving rapidly, and a cluster of workstations represents a tremendous amount of computing power. Up until now, however, such computing resources have been scattered over the network. Harnessing them to run user jobs has proven to be difficult.

Platform's LSF automates cluster computing by hiding the network and heterogeneous computers from users. Instead of running all compute jobs on the local computers like most Unix networks, LSF transparently distributes the jobs throughout the network—taking into consideration the architecture, the operating system, and the amount of resources required by the jobs, such as memory, disk space, and software licenses. LSF supports all types of applications—parallel and serial—submitted either interactively or in batch mode.

Distributed computing has been gaining importance over the last decade as a mode preferred over centralized computing. It has been widely observed that usage of computing resources in a distributed environment is usually "bursty" over time and uneven among the hosts. A user of a workstation might not use the machine all the time, but might require more than it can provide while actively working. Some hosts could be heavily loaded, whereas others remain idle. Along with the dramatic decrease in hardware costs, resource demands of applications have been increasing steadily with new, resource-intensive applications being introduced rapidly. It is now (and will remain) too expensive to dedicate a sufficient amount of computing resource to each and every user.

Load sharing is the process of redistributing the system workload among hosts to improve performance and accessibility to remote resources. Intuitively avoiding the situation of load imbalances and exploiting powerful hosts could lead to better job response times and resource utilization. Numerous studies on load sharing in the 1980s confirmed this intuition. Most of the existing research, however, is confined within the environment of a small cluster of homogeneous hosts and focuses on the sharing of the processing power (CPU). With the proliferation of distributed systems supporting medium to large organizations, system scale has grown from a few time-sharing hosts to tens of workstations supported by a few server machines—and to hundreds and thousands of hosts. For effective load sharing, computing resources beyond the processing power of memory frames, disk storage, and I/O bandwidth should also be considered.

Heterogeneity

Another important development in distributed systems is heterogeneity, which can take a number of forms. In configuration heterogeneity, hosts can have different processing power, memory space, and disk storage. In addition, hosts can execute the same code on different hosts. Operating system heterogeneity occurs when system facilities on different hosts vary and might be incompatible. Although heterogeneity imposes limitations on resource sharing, it also presents substantial opportunities. First, even if both a local workstation and a more powerful remote host are idle, the performance of a job could still be improved if executed on the remote host rather than the local workstation. Second, by providing transparent resource locating and remote execution mechanisms, any job can be initiated from any host without considering the location of the resources needed by the task. Thus, a CAD package that, at one time, could only be executed on a Sun host can now be initiated from an HP workstation.

As mentioned earlier, little research has been conducted regarding issues of large scale and heterogeneity in load sharing, yet they represent two of the most important research problems in load sharing in current and future distributed systems. As system scales for load sharing become inadequate, new research issues emerge.

Besides demonstrating the feasibility of a general purpose load-sharing system for large heterogeneous distributed systems by building a system that is usable in diverse system and application environments, the two main contributions of research to the field of resource sharing in distributed systems are:

- Algorithms designed for distributing load information in systems with thousands of hosts, as well as task placements based on tasks' resource demands and hosts' load information.

- A collection of remote execution mechanisms that are highly flexible and efficient, thus enabling interactive tasks that require a high degree of transparency (as well as relatively fine-grained tasks of parallel applications) to be executed remotely and efficiently.

Now that we see how hardware can be used to balance Oracle resources, let's turn our attention to tuning Oracle databases that are used on the Internet. Oracle's WebServer is becoming very popular with Oracle8, and the following section presents tip and techniques for tuning WebServer applications.

Tuning Oracle WebServer

There are several factors that influence the performance of a WebServer application. While most of the factors are within the control of Oracle developers, some issues, such as Internet communications, are beyond the developer's control. Consequently, you can only address performance and tuning of WebServer applications from the time a URL request is intercepted by the Web Listener until the completed request has been serviced and returned to the client. During this period, the following steps occur:

1. The request is intercepted by the Web Listener.

2. The request is forwarded to the CGI or the Web Request Broker (WRB).

3. The request is handed to Oracle.

4. Oracle services the request and passes the data back to the CGI or WRB.

5. The Web document is prepared and sent through the Web Listener to the requesting client.

Oracle WebServer achieves acceptable performance through a variety of mechanisms. The upcoming sections discuss some of the mechanisms affecting WebServer's performance.

Oracle WebServer Performance Issues

Response time with the Oracle WebServer is a function of the interaction between numerous components. The following components are listed in order of their impact on WebServer performance:

- Internet (speed of data transmission across the Internet)

- Oracle database (speed of servicing data requests)

- Web Listener (speed of spawning Oracle requests)

- Web Request Broker (speed of building HTML pages)

- PL/SQL agent (speed of loading and executing Oracle stored procedures)

You have no control over the speed of the Internet, but you do have some control over the Oracle components. Let's take a look at some of the performance and tuning issues surrounding the other components of the Oracle8 WebServer, including the Web Request Broker and PL/SQL Agent. For detailed information about tuning the Oracle WebServer, see the book *Oracle Databases on the Web*, by Robert Papaj and Donald Burleson (1997, Coriolis Group Books).

Web Request Broker

The Web Request Broker (WRB) accepts connections from the Web Listener. These requests are in the form of URLs. When the WRB first receives a request, it interrogates the URL to determine the type of object being requested. The request could be for an Oracle stored procedure, a Java routine, or any routine that has been defined with a socket. The determination of the type of object being requested is a function of the path name in the URL. The internal meaning of path names is governed by the WebServer configuration. For example, you can design your Web site so that the WebServer passes URL requests beginning with */oraproc* to the PL/SQL agent and URL requests beginning with */java* to the Java interpreter.

PL/SQL Agent

Interacting with a PL/SQL agent is generally much easier than interacting with Oracle using LiveHTML or Java. In addition, the PL/SQL agent is much faster than it was in WebServer version 1.0. This is due to a change in the architecture, whereby each instance of the PL/SQL agent stays connected to Oracle between database requests. Continuous connection does not mean that a run-unit connection is maintained with Oracle. Rather, it means that a communication connection to Oracle has been established, but no database connection has been made via SQL*Net. As you probably know, when someone establishes a connection to SQL*Plus, you can see the connection by selecting from the **V$SESSION** view within Oracle. This is not the case with WebServer because the PL/SQL agent only connects to Oracle during the servicing of the request. The servicing of a PL/SQL request consists of the following steps:

1. Retrieving the stored procedure from Oracle.

2. Executing the stored procedure.

3. Performing the specified database access.

Because each HTTP request initiates a new SQL*Net session, Oracle is technically logging off and reestablishing an SQL*Net session each time a URL request is made.

However, this process happens quickly because the Oracle server connection is maintained between URL requests.

Summary

Considering the myriad of factors that contribute to system performance, it is not surprising that there is no magic formula that can be applied to distributed databases to ensure acceptable performance. In a way, performance and tuning for distributed systems is easier than centralized systems because each remote site can be isolated and analyzed independently of the other remote sites. But, the complex nature of distributed processing ensures that performance and tuning will remain a complicated endeavor, and it is only with a complete understanding of the nature of performance that effective measurement methods can be devised.

Performance And Tuning For Oracle Database Connectivity Tools

CHAPTER
9

HIGH PERFORMANCE

Performance And Tuning For Oracle Database Connectivity Tools

Database connectivity is much more than establishing communications with another database—it is the glue that holds the entire data federation together. Connectivity is achieved with many mechanisms, including application programming interfaces (APIs), remote procedure calls (RPCs), and a variety of vendor solutions. Each mechanism imposes strict rules for establishing database connections, and this chapter reviews the most popular ways of making connectivity a reality. In this chapter, we'll cover the following areas:

- Database APIs
- The internals of ODBC
- Programming for portability
- Intersystem connectivity
- The internals of Oracle's SQL*Net and Net8
- Cross-database connectivity with IBM mainframes

Database APIs

A great deal of confusion exists about the functions of APIs and how they communicate with connectivity tools and databases. In fact, some client/server architectures impose so many layers of interfaces that it is often very difficult to track the flow of information as it passes though all the layers.

Ignoring the physical details, let's look at the logical methods for establishing connectivity. The most common type of logical connectivity is between remote databases of the same type. Oracle database software provides this type of mechanism with its SQL*Net and Net8 software, allowing Oracle databases to connect with each other in a seamless fashion (we'll talk more about SQL*Net and Net8 later in this chapter). Connectivity is established in Oracle by creating database links to the remote databases. Once defined by the DBA, these remote databases can participate in queries and updates from within any Oracle application. For example, a database in London and Paris can be defined to a system in Denver with the following SQL extension:

```
CREATE PUBLIC DATABASE LINK LONDON
    CONNECT TO system IDENTIFIED BY manager USING 'london';
CREATE PUBLIC DATABASE LINK PARIS
    CONNECT TO system IDENTIFIED BY manager USING 'paris';
```

Any tables can now be included from these remote sites by qualifying their remote site name in the SQL query. The following example joins three tables: a local **ORDER** table in Denver, a **CUSTOMER** table in Paris, and an **ORDERLINE** table in London.

```
SELECT CUSTOMER.customer_name, ORDER.order_date,
ORDERLINE.quantity_ordered
    FROM CUSTOMER@london, ORDER, ORDERLINE@paris
    WHERE
    CUSTOMER.cust_number = ORDER.customer_number
    AND
    ORDER.order_number = ORDERLINE.order_number;
```

But what about remote databases that reside in other relational systems, such as Sybase or FoxPro? And what about legacy data from a hierarchical database, like IMS, or a network database, such as CA-IDMS? Here, you enter a more complicated scenario—fortunately, you can choose from a variety of tools to accomplish this type of cross-architecture connectivity. The most popular connectivity gateway is Microsoft's Open Database Connectivity (ODBC) product (more about Microsoft's ODBC later in this chapter). However, many users have successfully implemented cross-architecture systems using custom-written RPCs and APIs.

An API is an interface that is generally embedded into an application program to interface with an external database. Database APIs come in two flavors: embedded and call-level. Embedded APIs are placed within an application program to interface with the database management system. Listing 9.1 shows a sample COBOL program that has embedded SQL commands.

Listing 9.1   A COBOL program.

```
WORKING-STORAGE SECTION.

01  CUST-RECORD.

    05  CUSTOMER_NAME        PIC X(80).
    05  CUSTOMER_ADDRESS     PIC X(100).
    05  CUSTOMER_PHONE       PIC 9(7).

EXEC-SQL     INCLUDE SQLCA     END-EXEC.

PROCEDURE DIVISION.

OPEN INPUT INPUT-FILE.
READ INPUT-FILE AT END MOVE 'Y' TO EOF-SWITCH.

EXEC-SQL

    CONNECT TO :REMOTE_SITE;

END-EXEC.

EXEC-SQL

    SELECT * FROM CUSTOMER
    WHERE
    DB_CUST_NAME = INPUT_CUSTOMER_NAME

END-EXEC.

IF SQLCODE <> 0 THEN PERFORM NOT-FOUND-ROUTINE.

NOT-FOUND-ROUTINE.

    DISPLAY "ERROR IN READING DATABASE"

CLOSE INPUT-FILE.
END RUN.
```

Here, you can see SQL has been embedded in a COBOL program for access to a relational database. Unlike a regular COBOL program, special sections are embedded into the code that are foreign to the COBOL compiler. In this sample, the SQL commands are started with **EXEC-SQL** and ended with **END-EXEC**. An SQL precompiler is invoked to preprocess these statements, commenting them out and replacing them with native calls that the COBOL compiler can recognize. In Listing 9.2, you can see that the native SQL has been replaced with calls to a routine called RDBINTC. The RDBINTC routine will place the SQL calls on behalf of the program.

Listing 9.2   The RDBINTC routine.

```
WORKING-STORAGE SECTION.

01   CUST-RECORD.

     05   CUSTOMER_NAME        PIC X(80).
     05   CUSTOMER_ADDRESS     PIC X(100).
     05   CUSTOMER_PHONE       PIC 9(7).

*  EXEC-SQL     INCLUDE SQLCA    END-EXEC.

01 SQLCA.
     05 SQL-FIELD1    PIC 99.
     05 SQL-FIELD2    PIC X(20).

PROCEDURE DIVISION.

OPEN INPUT INPUT-FILE.
READ INPUT-FILE AT END MOVE 'Y' TO EOF-SWITCH.

*    EXEC-SQL

*    CONNECT TO :REMOTE_SITE;

*    END-EXEC

CALL RDBINTC USING (SQLCA,45,:REMOTE_SITE);

*    EXEC-SQL
*    SELECT * FROM CUSTOMER
*    WHERE
*    DB_CUST_NAME = INPUT_CUSTOMER_NAME
*    END-EXEC
```

```
CALL RDBINTC USING (SQLCA,23,"CUSTOMER", DB-CUST-NAME,
    INPUT-CUSTOMER-NAME);
IF SQLCODE <> O THEN PERFORM NOT-FOUND-ROUTINE.

NOT-FOUND-ROUTINE.

    DISPLAY "ERROR IN READING DATABASE"

CLOSE INPUT-FILE.
END RUN.
```

At execution time, the COBOL program will interface with the database by making native calls to the database interface, called RDBINTC in this example. The interface will manage the I/O against the database on behalf of the COBOL program, and will pass the result set (or a cursor) back to the application program using the SQL Communications Area (SQLCA).

Notice how the COBOL program checks the value of the **SQLCODE** field. When the database is accessed from a remote program, the calling program must explicitly check the value of the **SQLCODE** to ensure successful execution of the intended statement.

As you saw in this demonstration, APIs can provide database connectivity, including a type of cross-architecture connectivity. But there are variations to this approach. In fact, the most popular cross-architecture connectivity gateway is Microsoft's Open Database Connectivity (ODBC) product. The following section will discuss the architecture of ODBC and show how it is used to establish connectivity with Oracle8 and other database engines.

The Internals Of ODBC

The Open Database Connectivity (ODBC) product was initially developed by Microsoft as a generic database driver. Its architecture has now been generalized, and many vendors offer open database connectivity products based on ODBC. ODBC is the predominant common-interface approach to database connectivity and is a part of Microsoft's Windows Open Service Architecture (WOSA). ODBC and WOSA define a set of standard data access services that can be used by a variety of other products when interfacing with an MS-Windows application.

ODBC consists of more than 50 functions that are invoked from an application using a call-level API. The ODBC API does not communicate with a database directly. Instead, it serves as a link between the application and a generic interface routine. The interface routine, in turn, communicates with the database drivers via a Service Provider Interface (SPI), as shown in Figure 9.1.

Each custom application within Windows will have call-level API calls to the ODBC database driver, and, in turn, the ODBC driver directs the request to the appropriate database driver for execution. The database driver manages the communication between the database and the program, and handles all returning data and messages, passing them back to the ODBC driver. Then, the ODBC driver passes the data back to the invoking application.

As ODBC becomes more popular, database vendors are creating new ODBC drivers that will allow ODBC to be used as a gateway into their database products. A word of caution is in order: Although most programmers can be successful with ODBC in simple applications, effective use of ODBC in multidatabase environments is very difficult. Programmers in a multidatabase environment need to be aware of all the dialects of SQL, and they must also be aware of the native API to the database engines. However, the tips presented in this chapter can help ease the effort, despite the steep learning curve.

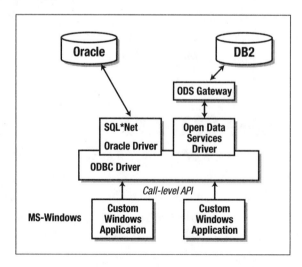

Figure 9.1
The ODBC architecture for Oracle.

Essentially, ODBC serves as the traffic cop for all data within the client/server system. When a client requests a service from a database, ODBC receives the request and manages the connection to the target database. ODBC manages the database drivers, checking the status information as it arrives from the database drivers.

It is noteworthy that the database drivers should be able to handle more than just SQL. Many databases have a native API that requires ODBC to map the request into a library of functions. An example is an SQL Server driver that maps ODBC functions to database library function calls. Databases without a native API (i.e., non-SQL databases) can also be used with ODBC, but they go through a much greater transformation than the native API calls.

When accessing multiple databases with ODBC, it is up to the API programmer to manage the multiple database connections and the multiple SQL requests that are being directed to the connections. In ODBC, *handles* are used to point to each database connection. A handle is usually a pointer into the database, and the value of the handle is a record key, a row ID, or an object ID.

Most people associate ODBC with SQL. While SQL is now the single most common access method for databases, there are many non-SQL databases that are widely used. Popular non-SQL databases include IMS, CA-IDMS, BASISplus, and almost all of the new object-oriented databases. It is a misconception that a database that does not support SQL cannot use ODBC.

Now that we have discussed the basics of interdatabase communications, we can take a look at programming for portability. When dealing with multiple relational database products, creating generic SQL is extremely important for seamless database communications.

Programming For Portability

The key to success with ODBC in a distributed relational database environment is to create the illusion of location transparency. This transparency is ideally maintained by requiring that all cross-database applications handle their queries with *vanilla* SQL. The term *vanilla* refers to the common features of SQL that are shared by all vendors. Determining which features are vanilla is often difficult because each major database vendor implements SQL with its own "enhancements" not shared by other vendors. Fortunately, most of these differences are found in the **CREATE**

TABLE and referential integrity syntax, which are not germane to SQL queries. For queries, the most common extensions relate to syntax tricks used to force SQL to use a specific index. For example, in Oracle SQL, a null string can be concatenated into the query to force the transaction to use a specific index.

As an alternative to using vanilla SQL, ODBC can also interrogate the system tables of the target database to determine which SQL features are supported. In other words, with additional programming effort, an ODBC routine can be written to interrogate the metadata in the target database and determine the SQL features that are supported by the database product. For example, a database such as Oracle can be interrogated to see if it has stored procedures associated with a database event. If so, these procedures can be accessed by ODBC and displayed as a list. System users can then choose from the list if they want ODBC to use a stored procedure. This approach can be very cumbersome, and most ODBC users recommend the generic, vanilla SQL approach.

The selection of vanilla SQL must be done very carefully because of the differences in implementation of vendors' SQL. These include support for stored procedures and built-in functions that the vendor adds to enhance programmer productivity. Several problems arise when using non-ANSI SQL:

- *The SQL is rejected as a syntax error.* This is the simplest problem to correct and can be fixed in the testing phase, long before delivery of the completed system. The introduction of a new database into the federation can cause problems if the existing SQL relies on nonstandard extensions not supported by the new SQL dialect.

- *Cross-database referential integrity is difficult to enforce.* When business rules span physical databases, the enforcement of those rules can be very hard to accomplish. Because Oracle cannot enforce RI across servers, developers must create procedural mechanisms to ensure that the rules are maintained. For example, a business rule that prohibits any rows in **tokyo.order** without parent entry in **cleveland.customer** will have to write an extended two-phase commit transaction to roll back the entire transaction if one piece of the distributed update fails.

- *The SQL performance is different on each target database.* This happens when the SQL optimizer uses different access paths for different implementations of SQL.

For example, an identical SQL request that is valid for both Oracle and DB2 will return identical result sets, but each database will use different access methods to retrieve the data. For example, DB2 SQL uses the concept of sargeable predicates to determine the optimization of an SQL query. Depending on how the SQL request is phrased, the SQL optimizer might choose to invoke sequential prefetch, use a merge scan, or utilize other access techniques that can affect performance. Whenever possible, it is recommended that a programmer ignores this issue initially, because rewriting an SQL query for performance reasons can be very time consuming. Of course, performance remains a valid issue, but SQL tuning can be left to the final stages of the project.

Anyone considering ODBC as a connectivity tool should be aware that ODBC does not support all of the SQL extensions that a database server offers. In order to accommodate these nonstandard features, ODBC offers a back door that the programmer can use to send native API commands directly to the target database. Again, this procedure is not recommended unless the feature is absolutely necessary to the application. Mixing ODBC calls with native API calls creates a confusing jumble of access methods and makes the application much more difficult to support. Another obstacle with this approach to ODBC is maintaining the portability of the application. As new releases of the database add new extensions to the SQL, the ODBC component must be changed to accommodate these enhancements.

Some people argue that the "least common denominator" approach to ODBC SQL is too limiting. They state that learning the common syntax and facilities of SQL is too time consuming, and that a generalization of SQL would remove the most powerful features, making the system far less functional. On the other hand, it is clear that interdatabase communications cannot happen if developers rely on the vendor-supplied extensions to SQL.

Now that we see the role of ODBC in interdatabase communications, let's move on to take a look at how connectivity is achieved in a distributed environment where there may be many independent instances of Oracle8 on different hosts.

Intersystem Connectivity

In homogeneous systems that allow cross-database access, a very common method of distribution uses the idea of horizontal partitioning, which can be done without

ODBC by using Oracle's distributed database capabilities. For example, customer service organizations commonly allow their remote sites to maintain customer information while maintaining a location-transparent access mode to every customer, regardless of their physical location. Horizontal partitioning is achieved by taking a subset of each remote site's customer table and populating a master lookup table that is accessible from any node in the distributed system, as shown in Figure 9.2.

In a Unix-based distributed system, the **cron** utility can be used to schedule a periodic refresh of the master table. The **cron** utility is a time-dependent task activation utility, and it starts tasks at predetermined dates and times. For example, an SQL script could automatically extract **customer_name** from the remote site and repopulate the master customer table, leaving the customer details at the remote site. The Oracle SQL might look like this:

```
/*  Delete remote rows in the master table... */

DELETE FROM CUSTOMER@master
WHERE
LOCATION = :OUR_SITE;

/*  Repopulate the master table...  */
```

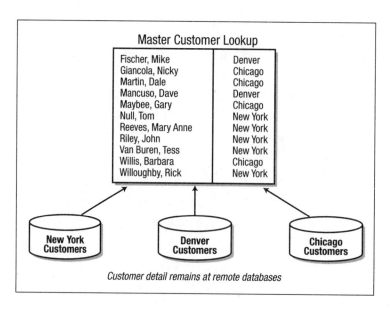

Figure 9.2
Horizontal data partitioning.

```
SELECT customer_name, ':OUR_SITE'
FROM CUSTOMER@:OUR_SITE
AS
INSERT INTO CUSTOMER@master
VALUES customer_name, site_name;
```

Once populated, the master lookup table can be accessed by any node and used to redirect the database query to the appropriate remote database for customer details, as shown in Figure 9.3.

Because of dynamic substitution in SQL, a common application can be made to access any customer in a federation (regardless of location) without making any changes to the application code. Dynamic transparency is especially useful for situations where remote locations have "ownership" of the data, while a corporate entity requires access to the data at a central location.

Now that we have a foundation for understanding distributed database communications, let's take a look at the details of establishing cross-database communications within Oracle. Oracle8 provides a very robust set of mechanisms for linking remote databases with the Net8 product.

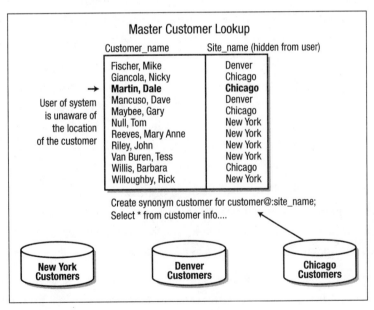

Figure 9.3
Dynamic location transparency.

The Internals Of Oracle's SQL*Net And Net8

In its most basic form, Net8 is a software tool that allows a network of Oracle clients and servers to communicate transparently on top of any underlying network topology or protocol using SQL. Originally called SQL*Net (pronounced sequel-net), this product has gone through several evolutions, from SQL*Net version 1, to version 2, a promise of version 3, the renaming to Net3 (for about a month), and finally to its current name of Net8.

The difference between SQL*Net and Net8 is very superficial—basically, Oracle changed the name to get the version numbers in sequence with the database engine. Essentially, there are no functional differences between SQL*Net 2.0 and Net8. However, Net8 has added the ability to support multiplexed users, and has also added a self-generating environment file (tnsnames.ora). Other than these features, Net8 can be thought of as being identical to SQL*Net 2.0. Throughout this chapter, I will often refer just to Net8, though the process is identical for SQL*Net 2.0.

Although Net8 is a very robust and sophisticated tool, you must appreciate the inherent complexity that goes along with the flexibility of Net8. This section provides a no-nonsense overview of the Net8 architecture. All of the examples are based on Unix.

Due to the sophisticated architecture of Net8, it is not trivial to install on the client or the server. For Unix systems, the following files are necessary to operate Net8. The tnsnames.ora and listener.ora files are found in the ORACLE_HOME/network/admin directory, and are soft linked to the /etc directory on HP-UX systems and in the /var/opt/oracle directory for Solaris and AIX:

- *tnsnames.ora*—This file is used for outgoing database requests. It contains the database names (**SID**s) running on the processor, as well as the domain name, protocol, host, and port information. When a new database is added to a box, you must update this file (changes to tnsnames.ora become effective instantly).

- *listener.ora*—This file contains a list of local databases for use by incoming connections. When you add a new destination database to a Unix host, you must also add it to this file.

- */etc/hosts*—This file lists your network addresses.

- */etc/services*—This file lists the Net8 services.

In SQL*Net version 2.0 and Net8, Oracle has added several important enhancements. Aside from the badly needed bug fixes, SQL*Net 2.0 and Net8 now allow multiple community access. A community is a group of computers that share a common protocol (such as TCP/IP to LU6.2). In addition, since version 7.1, the Oracle database engine now defines a multithreaded server (MTS) for servicing incoming data requests. In the MTS, all communication to the database is handled through a single dispatcher. In SQL*Net version 1.0, a separate process is spawned for each connection. These connections are easily viewed by using the Unix **ps** command.

When upgrading from SQL*Net 1.0 to SQL*Net 2.0 or Net8, you should be aware of subtle differences between how the two versions handle communications. (See Figure 9.4.) SQL*Net 1.0 uses an **orasrv** component on the destination database to listen for incoming requests, while SQL*Net 2.0 and Net8 use a process called **tnslsnr** (TNS listener). In addition, SQL*Net 1.0 cannot use the multithreaded server.

When a connection is made to SQL*Net or Net8, it passes the request to its underlying layer, the transparent network substrate (TNS), where the request is transmitted to the appropriate server. At the server, the software receives the request from TNS and passes the SQL to the database. *Transparent network substrate* is a fancy phrase meaning a single, common interface to all protocols that allows you to connect to databases in physically separate networks. At the lowest level, TNS communicates to other databases with message-level send/receive commands.

On the client side, the User Programmatic Interface (UPI) converts SQL to associated **PARSE**, **EXECUTE**, and **FETCH** statements. The UPI processes statements as follows:

1. Parses the SQL

2. Opens the SQL cursor

3. Binds the client application

4. Describes the contents of returned data fields

5. Executes the SQL

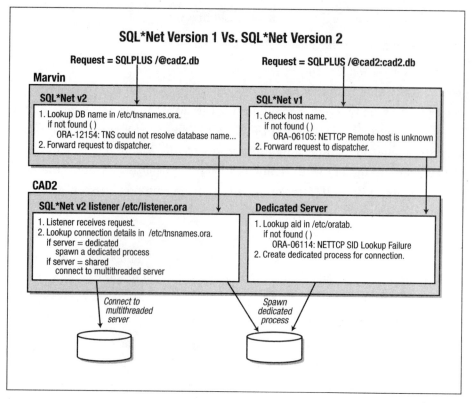

SQL*Net Version 1 Vs. SQL*Net Version 2

Request = SQLPLUS /@cad2.db   Request = SQLPLUS /@cad2:cad2.db

Marvin

SQL*Net v2
1. Lookup DB name in /etc/tnsnames.ora.
   if not found ( )
       ORA-12154: TNS could not resolve database name...
2. Forward request to dispatcher.

SQL*Net v1
1. Check host name.
   if not found ( )
       ORA-06105: NETTCP Remote host is unknown
2. Forward request to dispatcher.

CAD2

SQL*Net v2 listener /etc/listener.ora
1. Listener receives request.
2. Lookup connection details in /etc/tnsnames.ora.
   if server = dedicated
       spawn a dedicated process
   if server = shared
       connect to multithreaded server

Dedicated Server
1. Lookup aid in /etc/oratab.
   if not found ( )
       ORA-06114: NETTCP SID Lookup Failure
2. Create dedicated process for connection.

Connect to
multithreaded
server

Spawn
dedicated
process

Figure 9.4
SQL*Net 1.0 vs. SQL*Net 2.0 and Net8.

6.   Fetches the rows

7.   Closes the cursor

Oracle attempts to minimize messages to the server by combining UPI calls whenever possible. On the server side, the Oracle Programmatic Interface (OPI) responds to all possible messages from the UPI and returns requests.

No UPI exists for server-to-server communication. Instead, a Network Programmatic Interface (NPI) resides at the initiating server, and the responding server uses its OPI.

Net8 and SQL*Net support network transparency such that a network's structure can be changed without affecting the application. Location transparency is achieved with database links and synonyms.

Let's trace a sample data request through Net8. Essentially, Net8 will look for the link name in the database link table (**DBA_DB_LINKS**) and extract the service name. The service name will then be located in the tnsnames.ora file, and the host name will be extracted. As you can see, this is a three-tiered process involving the link name, service name, and host name.

In Unix environments, the host name is found in a host file (/etc/hosts), and the Internal Protocol (IP) address is gathered. For the purposes of the following example, let's say **london_unix** translates into an IP address of 143.32.142.3. The following steps illustrate how Net8 takes a remote request and translates it into the IP address of the destination database:

1. *Issue a remote request*—Check the database link called **london**:

   ```
   SELECT * FROM CUSTOMER@london
   ```

2. *Database link*—Get the service name (**london_unix_d**) using the **link_name** (**london**):

   ```
   CREATE PUBLIC DATABASE LINK london
   CONNECT TO london_unix_d;
   ```

3. *tnsnames.ora*—Get the **SID** name (**london_sid**) using the service name (**london_unix_d**):

   ```
   london_unix_d = (description=(address=(protocol=tcp) (host=seagull)
   (port=1521) (connect_data=(sid=london_sid) (server=dedicated))))
   ```

4. */etc/hosts*—Get the IP address (143.32.142.3) using the **SID** name (**london_sid**):

   ```
   143.32.142.3     london_sid        london_unix.corporate.com
   ```

As you can see, this translation occurs in a multistage process. The tnsnames.ora file specifies the name of the host containing the destination database. For Unix environments, this host name is then looked up in the /etc/hosts file to get the IP address of the destination box.

Note that the service name is looked up in tnsnames.ora—if the service exists, the IP address is found in the /etc/hosts file and a communications request is sent to the destination IP address. Also, note that both entries in this file connect to London, but **london_unix_d** directs Net8 to spawn a dedicated process, while **london_unix** uses the multithreaded server component because a shared server is specified.

Now that you have the tnsnames.ora and /etc/hosts files in place, you can include any tables from the London site by qualifying the remote site name in the SQL query. For example:

```
SELECT CUSTOMER.customer_name, ORDER.order_date
   FROM CUSTOMER@london, ORDER
   WHERE CUSTOMER.cust_number = ORDER.customer_number;
```

Note that the preceding query joins two tables at different locations: our local order table with the customer table that resides in London. Note that the database link called **london** determines how the Oracle connection will be established on the destination system. Regardless of how the connection is made to the destination, however, the user ID must have **SELECT** privileges against the customer table, or this query will fail.

The following sections discuss the internals of the SQL*Net and Net8 product for creating and maintaining database connections between remote Oracle databases.

Application Connection With SQL*Net And Net8

Connections to remote databases can be made by specifying either *service names* or *connect strings*. Connect strings use the full connection. In the following example, the **t:** means a TCP/IP connection, **host:** is the name of the remote processor, and **database** is the name of the database on that processor:

- Connect with a SQL*Net version 2 service name:

  ```
  emp@my_db
  ```

- Connect with a SQL*Net version 1 server connect string:

  ```
  sqlplus /@t:host:database
  ```

Connect strings are stored in the **DBA_DB_LINKS** table and synonyms can be created as follows:

```
CREATE SYNONYM ny_emp FOR ny_emp@t:myhost:mydatabase;
```

Now that we see how database links work, let's take a look at how SQL*Net and Net8 work in a client/server environment.

SQL*Net And Net8 For Client/Server

SQL*Net and Net8 can establish database communications in three ways: remote connection, remote request, or distributed request. A remote connection is the easiest way to make a database connection. The sending database simply makes a request by specifying a table name suffixed by @. Net8 takes it from there, seamlessly accessing the remote database and returning the data to the initiating system. Communication is established simply by making a distributed request to a remote database. Within Oracle, @ specifies the remote database name, but the functionality of the @ operator depends on where it is used. Here's an example:

```
sqlplus scott/tiger@london

SELECT count(*) FROM EMPLOYEE;

COUNT(*)
--------
162
```

In this request, **scott** is using SQL*Plus to connect to the London database, and **@london** is the service name, as defined in the tnsnames.ora file. Net8 recognizes this as a remote connection and determines the appropriate linkage to establish communications with London. Internally, Oracle will check the tnsnames.ora file to ensure that **london** is a valid destination.

Now, observe another way of connecting to London from the same database. This method is called a remote request::

```
sqlplus scott/tiger
SELECT count(*) FROM EMPLOYEE@london;

COUNT(*)
--------
162
```

Unlike a remote connection made directly from SQL*Plus, the remote request has **scott** connecting to the local copy of SQL*Plus to specify the remote table (in this case, **EMPLOYEE@london**). In order for a remote request to work, a database link must define **london**. A database link is a connection pathway to a remote database that specifies the service name of the remote database. Without the database link, the following request would fail:

```
sqlplus scott/tiger

SELECT count(*) FROM EMPLOYEE@london;
```

This request would give you an error message that reads:

```
ORA-02019: connection description for remote database not found.
```

This message appears due to the way Oracle defines the @ operator. When entering an Oracle service such as SQL*Plus, the @ operator will go directly to the tnsnames.ora file to manage the request, while the @ operator from within an Oracle program specifies the use of a database link.

To make the code functional, you must define a database link that specifies the service name used to establish the connection. Note that the database link name and the service name are the same in this example, but the database link and the connect descriptor are not related in any way:

```
CREATE DATABASE LINK london USING 'london';
SELECT Count(*) FROM EMPLOYEE@london;

count(*)
--------
162
```

Let's take a closer look at the database link. In this simple example, no mention is made of the user ID that is used to establish the connection on the remote database. Because **scott** is the user connecting to SQL*Plus, **scott** will be the user ID when the remote connection is established to the London database. Therefore, **scott** must have **SELECT** privileges against the **EMPLOYEE** table in London in order for the query to work properly. **scott**'s privileges on the initiating Oracle have no bearing on the success of the query.

*If you are using the Oracle Names facility, you must be sure that your database service names are the same as the **global_databases_names** and the **domain** init.ora parameter.*

In cases where **SELECT** security is not an issue, you can enhance the database link syntax to include a remote connect description, as follows:

```
CREATE DATABASE LINK london USING 'london'
CONNECT TO scott1 IDENTIFIED BY tiger1;
```

This way, all users who specify the **london** database link will connect as **scott1** and will have whatever privileges **scott1** has on the London system.

Once you establish a communications pathway to a remote database, it is often desirable to implement location transparency. In relational databases such as Oracle, you can obtain location transparency by creating database links to the remote database and then assigning a global synonym to the remote tables. The database link specifies a link name and a Net8 service name. You can create database links with a location suffix that is associated with a host name (in this example, **london_unix**).

You can use database links to allow applications to point to other databases without altering the application code. For data warehousing applications, where it may be necessary to copy tables to other Oracle hosts, you can replicate a table on another machine and establish links to enable the application to point transparently to the new box containing the replicated table.

To see the links for a database, query the Oracle dictionary like this:

```
SELECT DISTINCT db_link FROM DBA_DB_LINKS;
```

Keep in mind, Net8 bypasses all operating system connections when it connects to a database. All user accounts that are identified externally (that is, without an Oracle password) will not be allowed in Net8 transactions unless the init.ora parameter is changed. Oracle (version 6) used to allow the operating system to manage passwords using the **IDENTIFIED EXTERNALLY** clause (**ops$**), but because Net8 bypasses the operating system, impostor accounts could be created from other platforms. The result? Security was bypassed. Consequently, Oracle now recommends that **IDEN-TIFIED EXTERNALLY** accounts be forbidden for distributed connections.

It is interesting to note that Oracle8 still allows you to create accounts with an **ops$** prefix. Therefore, the operating system can manage its passwords, while you also have passwords within Oracle. For example, consider the following user definition:

```
CREATE USER ops$scott IDENTIFIED BY tiger;
```

Assuming that **scott** has logged onto the operating system, **scott** could enter SQL*Plus either with or without a password, as follows:

```
sqlplus /
sqlplus scott/tiger
```

This ability to connect directly to Oracle presents a confounding issue with password management. Because two sets of passwords exist—one in the operating system and another in Oracle—you might need a third-party tool to keep the passwords synchronized. (See Figure 9.5.)

Understanding The SQL*Net And Net8 Listener

To see what the Oracle listener is doing, Oracle provides a series of listener commands, including:

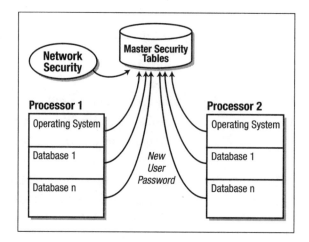

Figure 9.5
Centralized password management tool architecture.

- **LSNRCTL RELOAD**—Refreshes the listener
- **LSNRCTL START**—Starts the listener
- **LSNRCTL STOP**—Stops the listener
- **LSNRCTL STATUS**—Shows the status of the listener

Listing 9.3 shows the output of the **LSNRCTL STATUS** command.

Listing 9.3 Output of the **LSNRCTL STATUS** command.

```
[oracle]ram2: lsnrctl status

LSNRCTL for HPUX: Version 2.0.15.0.0 - Production on 16-SEP-94 15:38:00

Copyright (a)  Oracle Corporation 1993.  All rights reserved.

Connecting to (ADDRESS=(PROTOCOL=TCP)(HOST=ram2)(PORT=1521))
STATUS of the LISTENER
----------
Alias                   LISTENER
Version                 TNSLSNR for HPUX: Version 2.0.15.0.0 -
                        Production
Start Date              29-AUG-94 13:50:16
Uptime                  18 days 1 hr. 47 min. 45 sec
Trace Level             OFF
Security                OFF
Listener Parameter File /etc/listener.ora
Listener Log File       /usr/oracle/network/log/listener.log
Services Summary...
  dev7db                has 1 service handlers
  ram2db                has 1 service handlers
The command completed successfully

lsnrctl services     - lists all servers and dispatchers

[oracle]seagull: lsnrctl services

LSNRCTL for HPUX: Version 2.0.15.0.0 - Production on 16-SEP-94 15:36:47

Copyright (a)  Oracle Corporation 1993. All rights reserved.

Connecting to (ADDRESS=(PROTOCOL=TCP)(HOST=seagull)(PORT=1521))
Services Summary...
  tdb000               has 4 service handlers
    DISPATCHER established:1 refused:0 current:2 max:55 state:ready
```

```
    D001 (machine: seagull, pid: 4146)
    (ADDRESS=(PROTOCOL=tcp)(DEV=5)(HOST=141.123.224.38)(PORT=1323))
 DISPATCHER established:1 refused:0 current:2 max:55 state:ready
    D000 (machine: seagull, pid: 4145)
    (ADDRESS=(PROTOCOL=tcp)(DEV=5)(HOST=141.123.224.38)(PORT=1321))
 DISPATCHER established:0 refused:0 current:1 max:55 state:ready
    D002 (machine: seagull, pid: 4147)
    (ADDRESS=(PROTOCOL=tcp)(DEV=5)(HOST=141.123.224.38)(PORT=1325))
    DEDICATED SERVER established:0 refused:0
The command completed successfully
```

As a service request is intercepted by an Oracle server, the listener can direct the request via a dedicated server, the multithreaded server (MTS), or an existing process (prespawned shadow). The key is whether the connection contacts the listener via a service name or bypasses the listener with the **TWO_TASK** connect string. If the listener is contacted as part of the connection and the MTS params are defined to init.ora, the client will use the MTS.

There are five basic listener commands: **RELOAD**, **START**, **STOP**, **STATUS**, and **SERVICES**. Based on the request, the listener decides whether to dispatch a connection to a dedicated-server process (which it spawns) or use the MTS. The programmer has several options when deciding how Oracle will manage a process. Dedicated requests can be specified by a version 1.0 connect string or by using a service name that specifies **server=dedicated** in the tnsnames.ora file.

*Local connections will use the listener if the MTSs are defined. Even internal invocations to Oracle (for example, **sqlplus /**) will add a connection to the MTS.*

Now that we see the dynamics of SQL*Net and Net8, let's take a closer look at the Oracle tools that are used to maintain and display the interdatabase connectivity.

Managing SQL*Net And Net8 Connections

Oracle's data dictionary and **V$** structures contain some very useful information about the status of your SQL*Net or Net8 configuration, and these structures can easily be queried to gather this information. Listing 9.4 describes some of the utilities you can use to manage Net8 sessions effectively.

Listing 9.4 Commit point strength.

```
REM commit.sql - Reports the commit point strength for the database.

SET FEEDBACK OFF
COLUMN NAME  FORMAT a30 HEADING 'Name'
COLUMN TYPE  FORMAT a7  HEADING 'Type'
COLUMN VALUE FORMAT a60 HEADING 'Value'

PROMPT Commit Point-strength Report Output:
PROMPT
PROMPT
SELECT name,
       decode(TYPE,1,'boolean',
                   2,'string',
                   3,'integer',
                   4,'file') TYPE,
       replace(replace(value,'@','%{sid}'),'?','%{home}') VALUE
FROM   V$PARAMETER
WHERE  name = '\commit_point_strength';
```

This report will display a report of Oracle's **V$** structures that shows all commit point information. In the real world, it is imperative that the Oracle professional is able to view and kill all distributed connections to a database. The following section describes this process.

Showing And Killing Multithreaded SQL*Net And Net8 Sessions

On systems running SQL*Net 2.0 or Net8, you can use a session script to query the number of dedicated and shared servers on the system. For example, Listing 9.5, which appears later in this chapter, shows all connected users and their types of connections to the Oracle database. The listing shows the operating system connection and allows you to kill any runaway connections.

You can kill dedicated SQL*Net and Net8 sessions, but you cannot kill multithreaded SQL*Net and Net8 sessions directly from the Unix operating system. For example, you can identify a runaway session on a dedicated server by using the Unix **ps-ef|grep ora** command and subsequently kill it using the **kill -9 nnn** command. With the multithreaded server, operating system processes no longer exist for each separate task, so you must use the Oracle SQL **ALTER SYSTEM KILL SESSION** command to kill the task at the Oracle subsystem level.

To kill a user in a multithreaded server session, first open SQL*Plus, and enter:

```
SELECT sid, serial#, USERNAME FROM V$SESSION;

SID   SERIAL#    USERNAME
8      28        OPS$xxx
10     211       POS$yyy
13     8         dburleso
```

If **dburleso** is the session you want to kill, enter the **ALTER SYSTEM KILL SESSION '13, 8'** command.

This cumbersome method of clobbering runaway SQL*Net and Net8 connections can be very annoying in development environments where dozens of programmers are testing programs and they must call the DBA every time they want to kill a runaway task. The only alternative, however, is to grant the programmers **ALTER SYSTEM** authority on test platforms, and let the programmers kill their own tasks.

Managing The Multithreaded Server (MTS)

One of the problems with SQL*Net 1.0 was that each incoming transaction was spawned by the listener as a separate operating system task. With SQL*Net 2.0 and Net8, Oracle now has a method for allowing the listener connection to dispatch numerous subprocesses. With the MTS, all communications to a database are handled through a single dispatcher instead of separate Unix process IDs (PIDs) on each database. This translates into faster performance for most online tasks. Even local transactions will be directed through the MTS, and you will no longer see a PID for your local task when you issue **ps-ef|grep oracle**.

However, be aware that the MTS is not a panacea, especially at times when you want to invoke a dedicated process for your program. For Pro*C programs and I/O-intensive SQL*Forms applications—or any processes that have little idle time—you can derive better performance using a dedicated process.

In general, the MTS offers benefits such as reduced memory use, fewer processes per user, and automatic load balancing. However, it is often very confusing to tell whether the MTS is turned on—much less working properly.

Remember the following rules of thumb when initially starting the MTS:

- The MTS is governed by the init.ora parameters. If no MTS params are present in init.ora, the MTS is disabled.

- The MTS is used when the MTS params are in the init.ora and requests are made by service name (such as **@myplace**). In other words, you must retrieve the **ROWID** of all version 1.0 connect strings (such as **t:unix1:myplace**).

- Each user of the MTS requires 1K of storage, so plan to increase your **shared_pool_size**.

- The **V$QUEUE** and **V$DISPATCHER** system tables indicate if the number of MTS dispatchers is too low. Even though the number of dispatchers is specified in the init.ora file, you can change it online in SQL*DBA with the **ALTER SYSTEM** command, as follows:

```
SQLDBA> ALTER SYSTEM SET MTS_DISPATCHERS = 'TCPIP,4';
```

- If you encounter problems with the MTS, you can quickly regress to dedicated servers by issuing an **ALTER SYSTEM** command. The following command turns off the MTS by setting the number of MTS servers to zero:

```
SQLDBA> ALTER SYSTEM SET MTS_SERVERS=0;
```

- In order to use **ops$**, you must set two init.ora values to **TRUE** (they default to **FALSE**):

```
remote_os_authent = TRUE
remote_os_roles = TRUE
```

- When SQL*Net 1.0, 2.0, or Net8 is installed, the user can connect to the server via either a dedicated server or the MTS. However, you cannot stop and restart the listener when connecting via the MTS. You must connect to SQL*DBA with a dedicated server.

- In some cases, the instance must be bounced if the listener is stopped, or it will restart in dedicated mode. Whenever an instance is to be bounced, stop the listener, shut down the instance, restart the listener, and start up the instance.

The listener reads the MTS parameters only if it is running before startup of the instance. Therefore, bouncing the listener will disable the MTS.

Managing The Listener Process

The listener is a software program that runs on each remote node and "listens" for any incoming database requests. When a request is detected, the listener can direct the request to:

- A dedicated server

- A multithreaded server

- An existing process or prespawned shadow

Note that the configuration of an Oracle listener is a direct result of the parameters that are specified in the startup deck for the Oracle database. This parameter file is called init.ora, and it contains the following parameters to define the multithreaded server and listener:

```
# -----------
# Multithreaded Server
# -----------

MTS_DISPATCHERS = "tcp,3"

MTS_LISTENER_ADDRESS = "(ADDRESS=(PROTOCOL=tcp) (HOST=seagull)
(PORT=1521))"

MTS_MAX_DISPATCHERS = 5

MTS_MAX_SERVERS = 20

# -----------
# Distributed systems options
# -----------

DISTRIBUTED_LOCK_TIMEOUT = 60

DISTRIBUTED_RECOVERY_CONNECTION_HOLD_TIME = 200

DISTRIBUTED_TRANSACTIONS = 6
```

Miscellaneous Management Tips For SQL*Net And Net8

Just as the oratab file for SQL*Net 1.0 is interpreted at runtime, the tnsnames.ora file is also interpreted. This means that you can change it at any time without fear of bouncing anything. However, changes to listener.ora require that the listener be reloaded with **LSNRCTL RELOAD**.

When a database is accessed remotely via a database link, SQL*Net and Net8 use the temporary tablespace on the destination database, regardless of the processor invoking the task or the original database location. The moral? SQL*Net and Net8 will use the temporary tablespace on the destination database—not on the initiating database. In other words, applications on one processor that accessed another processor with a database link will use the temporary tablespaces on the terminal processor—not the processor that contains the link.

Always remember to change your $ORACLE_HOME/bin/oraenv file to unset **ORACLE_SID** and set **TWO_TASK=SID**.

Three logs appear in SQL*Net and Net8:

- **listener log**—ORACLE_HOME/network/log/listener.log

- **sqlnet log**—ORACLE_HOME/network/log/sqlnet.log

- **trace log**—destination set with the **trace_directory_listener** parameter of the listener.ora file

The following three levels of tracing are found in SQL*Net and Net8:

- **LSNRCTL TRACE ADMIN**

- **LSNRCTL TRACE USER**

- **LSNRCTL TRACE OFF**

As mentioned earlier, it is possible to run two listeners—one for version 1.0 and another for version 2.0. If a version connect string is sent, the version listener **TCPCTL** will be used. Conversely, if a TNS connect description is sent, the version listener **LSNRCTL** will be used. A connect description is the name of a database (such as **@mydata**) that maps to the tnsnames.ora on the sending side and listener.ora on the receiving side.

It is essential to note that the functions of the **ORACLE_SID** and **TWO_TASK** variables have changed. To use the MTS while you are local to the database, you should unset the **ORACLE_SID** variable and set the **TWO_TASK** to the SID name (**EXPORT TWO_TASK=mydb**). If the **ORACLE_SID** is active, you will still be able to connect—although you will not be able to take advantage of the MTS. You must change all login scripts and ORACLE_HOME/bin/oraenv files to reflect this new functionality.

You now know of three ways to establish distributed database communications with MTS. You can use a shared service name (**sqlplus /@ram2db**), a dedicated service name (**sqlplus /@d_ram2db**—prefixing the SID with **d_** will direct the listener to spawn a dedicated process for your program), or a **TWO_TASK** server connect string (**sqlplus /@t:host:sid**). The latter approach will bypass the MTS and use a dedicated process.

In a distributed Oracle environment where updates are coordinated across the databases, Oracle provides a mechanism for ensuring that a distributed update is managed as a single transaction, either committing or rolling back the transaction as a whole. This process is called a *two-phase commit*, and the following section describes how it is used in an Oracle environment.

Managing Two-Phase Commits (2PCs)

When a distributed update (or delete) has finished processing, SQL*Net and Net8 will coordinate **COMMIT** processing, which means that the entire transaction will roll back if any portion of the transaction fails. The first phase of this process is a prepare phase for each node, followed by the **COMMIT**, and then terminated by a forget phase.

If a distributed update is in the process of issuing the 2PC and a network connection breaks, Oracle will place an entry in the **DBA_2PC_PENDING** table. The recovery background process (RECO) will then roll back or commit the good node to match the state of the disconnected node to ensure consistency. You can activate the RECO background process with the **ALTER SYSTEM ENABLE DISTRIBUTED RECOVERY** command.

The **DBA_2PC_PENDING** table contains an **ADVISE** column that directs the database to either **commit** or **rollback** the pending item. You can use the **ALTER**

SESSION ADVISE syntax to direct the 2PC mechanism. For example, to force the completion of an **INSERT**, you could enter the following:

```
ALTER SESSION ADVISE COMMIT;
INSERT INTO PAYROLL@london . . . ;
```

When a 2PC transaction fails, you can query the **DBA_2PC_PENDING** table to check the **state** column. You can enter SQL*DBA and use the Recover In-Doubt Transaction dialog box to force either a rollback or a commit of the pending transaction. If you do this, the row will disappear from **DBA_2PC_PENDING** after the transaction has been resolved. If you force the transaction the wrong way (for example, rollback when other nodes committed), the RECO process will detect the problem, set the **mixed** column to **Yes**, and the row will remain in the **DBA_2PC_PENDING** table.

Internally, Oracle examines the init.ora parameters to determine the rank that the commit processing will take. The **commit_point_strength** init.ora parameter determines which of the distributed databases is to be the commit point site. In a distributed update, the database with the largest value of **commit_point_strength** will be the commit point site. The *commit point site* is the database that must successfully complete before the transaction is updated on the other databases. Conversely, if a transaction fails at the commit point site, the entire transaction will be rolled back on the other databases. In general, the commit point site should be the database that contains the most critical data.

Listing 9.5 shows a script that will identify two-phase commit transactions that have failed to complete.

Listing 9.5   pending.sql reports on any pending distributed transactions.

```
SET PAGESIZE 999;
SET FEEDBACK OFF;
SET WRAP ON;
COLUMN local_tran_id   FORMAT a22 HEADING 'Local Txn Id'
COLUMN global_tran_id  FORMAT a50 HEADING 'Global Txn Id'
COLUMN state           FORMAT a16 HEADING 'State'
COLUMN mixed           FORMAT a5  HEADING 'Mixed'
COLUMN advice          FORMAT a5  HEADING 'Advise'
```

```
SELECT local_tran_id,global_tran_id,state,mixed,advise
FROM   DBA_2PC_PENDING
ORDER  BY local_tran_id;
```

Hopefully, this section shows how distributed updates are managed within Oracle8. Now, let's move on to take a look at how SQL*Net and Net8 connections are established and maintained within an Oracle instance.

Establishing SQL*Net And Net8 Sessions

On systems running SQL*Net 2.0 or Net8, the session script can be used to query the number of dedicated and shared servers on the system. For example, Listing 9.6 shows an SQL*Plus script to view all sessions.

Listing 9.6   session.sql displays all connected sessions.

```
SET ECHO OFF;
SET TERMOUT ON;
SET LINESIZE 80;
SET PAGESIZE 60;
SET NEWPAGE 0;
TTITLE "dbname Database|UNIX/Oracle Sessions";
SPOOL /tmp/session
SET HEADING OFF;
SELECT 'Sessions on database '||substr(name,1,8) FROM V$DATABASE;
SET HEADING ON;
SELECT
        substr(B.serial#,1,5) ser#,
        substr(B.machine,1,6) box,
        substr(B.username,1,10) username,
        substr(B.osuser,1,8) os_user,
        substr(B.program,1,30) program
FROM V$SESSION B, V$PROCESS A
WHERE
B.paddr = A.addr
AND TYPE='USER'
ORDER BY spid;
TTITLE OFF;
SET HEADING OFF;
SELECT 'To kill, enter SQLPLUS>  ALTER SYSTEM KILL SESSION',
''''||'SID, SER#'||''''||';' FROM DUAL;
SPOOL OFF;
```

```
[oracle]ram2: sqlx session

Wed Sep 14
                                                        Page    1
                                                 ram2db Database
                                               Sessions for SQL*Net


ser#        box           username  os_user  program
----        ---           --------  ------   -------


DEDICATED   SYS           oracle    ram2     sqldba@ram2 (Pipe Two-Task)

DEDICATED   OPS$REDDY     reddy     ram2     runform30@ram2 (Pipe Two-Task)

DEDICATED   GLINT         lkorneke  ram2     sqlplus@ram2 (Pipe Two-Task)

DEDICATED   OPS$ORACLE    oracle    clt2     sqlplus@clt2 (TNS interface)

DEDICATED   OPS$JOKE      joke      ram2     ?  @ram2 (TCP Two-Task)

DEDICATED   OPS$WWRIGHT   wwright   ram2     runmenu50@ram2 (Pipe Two-Task)

DEDICATED   OPS$ORACLE    oracle    ensc     sqlplus@ensc (TCP Two-Task)

DEDICATED   MARYLEE       OraUser            C:\PB3\PBSYS030.DLL

DEDICATED   OPS$ORACLE    oracle    ram2     sqlplus@ram2 (Pipe Two-Task)

DEDICATED   OPS$JSTARR    jstarr    ram2     sqlforms30@ram2 (Pipe Two-Task)

DEDICATED   OPS$WWRIGHT   wwright   ram2     RUN_USEX@ram2 (Pipe Two-Task)


11 rows selected.
```

Here, you can see each of the four types of connections:

- *Pipe Two-Task*—Used for internal tasks (**sqlplus /**).

- *TNS Interface*—Used when a connection is made with a version 2.0 service name (**sqlplus /@ram2**).

- *TCP Two-Task*—Used when a connection is made with a version 1.0 connect string (**sqlplus /@t:ram2:ram2db**).

- *PC Connection Task*—Denoted by the PC DLL name (**C:\PB3\PBSYS030.DLL** = initiated via PowerBuilder DLL).

While I can only gloss over the high points here, sophisticated tools such as SQL*Net 2.0 and Net8 require a great deal of knowledge and skill to use effectively. As systems continue to evolve into complex distributed networks, interdatabase communications will become even more complex, requiring even more sophisticated tools. And, while object-orientation promises to make interdatabase communications simple, the DBA in the trenches will continue to struggle with implementing everyday distributed database communications.

Now that we understand SQL*Net and Net8, let's move to take a look at cross-architecture database communications. Even since several vendor databases were available in the 1970s, database professionals have struggled with building bridges between database products.

Cross-Database Connectivity With IBM Mainframes

A great deal of interest in database connectivity has resulted from the proliferation of companies choosing diverse database platforms. As we've discussed in this chapter, database designers are working actively to develop bridges between the divergent database systems, and many tools are becoming available to assist with multidatabase connectivity.

Currently, there are three classes of methods for database connectivity:

- Transparency products that allow applications written for a database to run on another product.

- Fourth-generation languages that access multiple databases.

- "Hook" products that allow exits to other databases.

Fortunately, we have some very simple ways to begin working with multiple databases, especially in a mainframe environment. One start at database connectivity can be achieved in the batch environment. By embedding database commands from two databases into a single COBOL program, compile procedures can be developed to

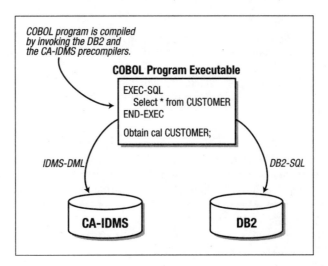

Figure 9.6
Interdatabase communications with mainframes.

separately precompile each set of database statements, creating a single program that concurrently accesses two different databases. (See Figure 9.6.)

In this example, a COBOL program was created to read DB2 tables and dynamically store them in a CA-IDMS database. The statements for DB2 and CA-IDMS remain as they would in a single database program, but a special compile procedure is set up to precompile each set of statements separately. The trick is to invoke the DB2 precompiler before the CA-IDMS precompiler. Because all DB2 commands are bracketed with **EXEC-SQL...END-EXEC**, all DB2 commands will be processed before the CA-IDMS precompiler begins its job. Listing 9.7 shows some of the mainframe Job Control Language (JCL) that works well for compiling a COBOL program to simultaneously access DB2 and CA-IDMS.

Listing 9.7   A COBOL compile job for communications between IDMS and DB2 databases.

```
//DB2IDMSC PROC  PROGRAM=,SYSTEM=PROD,DICT=LCPDICT
//***************************************************************
//*  THIS IS THE IDMS/DB2 COBOL COMPILER  (BATCH IDMS/DB2 COBOL)
//***************************************************************
//DB2 EXEC PGM=DSNHPC,PARM='HOST(COBOL),APOST,APOSTSQL,NOSOURCE,NOXREF'
//***************************************************************
```

```
//*   THIS IS THE DB2 COBOL PRECOMPILER
//DBRMLIB  DD DSN=DB2.LCP.DBRMLIB(&PROGRAM),DISP=SHR
//SYSCIN   DD DSN=&&DSNHOUT,DISP=(MOD,PASS),UNIT=SYSDA,
//            SPACE=(800,(50,50))
//SYSLIB   DD DSN=DB2.LCP.DCLGNLIB,SUBSYS=LAM
//SYSPRINT DD SYSOUT=*
//SYSTERM  DD SYSOUT=*
//SYSUDUMP DD SYSOUT=*
//SYSUT1   DD SPACE=(800,(50,50),,,ROUND),UNIT=SYSDA
//SYSUT2   DD SPACE=(800,(50,50),,,ROUND),UNIT=SYSDA
//****************************************************************
//DMLC EXEC  PGM=IDMSDMLC,REGION=1024K,PARM='DBNAME=&DICT',COND=(4,LT)
//****************************************************************
//*   THIS IS THE IDMS PRECOMPILER
//STEPLIB  DD DSN=LCP.IDMS.&SYSTEM..PRODLIB,DISP=SHR
//         DD DSN=LCP.IDMS.&SYSTEM..CDMSLIB,DISP=SHR
//SYSLST   DD DUMMY
//SYSPRINT DD SYSOUT=*
//SYSCTL   DD DSN=LCP.IDMS.&SYSTEM..SYSCTL,DISP=SHR
//SYSJRNL  DD DUMMY
//SYSPCH   DD DSN=&&WRK1WORK,UNIT=SYSDA,DISP=(NEW,PASS),
//            DCB=BLKSIZE=800,SPACE=(CYL,(5,1))
//SYSIPT   DD DSN=&&DSNHOUT,DISP=(OLD,DELETE,DELETE)
//****************************************************************
//*   THIS IS THE COBOL COMPILE STEP
//COMP     EXEC PGM=IKFCBL00,COND=(4,LT),
// PARM='&CPARM,&PAYPR,STA,LIB,DMAP,CLIST,APOST,NOSXREF,BUF=28672'
//****************************************************************
//STEPLIB  DD DSN=SYS1.VSCOLIB,DISP=SHR
//SYSPRINT DD SYSOUT=*
//SYSUDUMP DD SYSOUT=*
//SYSLIN   DD DSN=&&LOADSET,DISP=(MOD,PASS),UNIT=SYSDA,
//            SPACE=(800,(50,50),RLSE)
//SYSLIB   DD DSN=ISD.COBOL.TEST.COPYLIB,DISP=SHR
//         DD DSN=ISD.COBOL.COPYLIB,DISP=SHR
//SYSUT1   DD SPACE=(800,(50,50),RLSE),UNIT=SYSDA
//SYSUT2   DD SPACE=(800,(50,50),RLSE),UNIT=SYSDA
//SYSUT3   DD SPACE=(800,(50,50),RLSE),UNIT=SYSDA
//SYSUT4   DD SPACE=(800,(50,50),RLSE),UNIT=SYSDA
//SYSIN    DD DSN=&&WRK1WORK,DISP=(OLD,DELETE,DELETE)
//****************************************************************
//*   THIS IS THE LINK EDITOR
//LKED     EXEC PGM=IEWL,PARM='XREF,LIST,&LPARM',
//            COND=((12,LE,COMP),(4,LT,DB2))
//****************************************************************
```

```
//SYSPRINT DD  SYSOUT=*
//SYSUDUMP DD  SYSOUT=*
//SYSLIN   DD  DSN=&&LOADSET,DISP=(OLD,DELETE)
//         DD  DSN=LCP.IDMS.TEST.PROCLIB(IDMSCOB),DISP=SHR
//SYSUT1   DD  SPACE=(1024,(50,50)),UNIT=SYSDA
//SYSLIB   DD  DSN=SYS1.DB2.DSNLINK,DISP=SHR
//         DD  DSN=SYS1.VSCOLIB,DISP=SHR
//         DD  DSN=SYS1.VSCLLIB,DISP=SHR
//         DD  DSN=LCP.IDMS.&SYSTEM..CDMSLIB,DISP=SHR
//SYSLMOD  DD  DSN=LCP.IDMS.&SYSTEM..LINKLIB(&PROGRAM),DISP=SHR
//LIB      DD  DSN=LCP.IDMS.&SYSTEM..OBJLIB,DISP=SHR
//*****************************************************************
//BIND  EXEC PGM=IKJEFT01,DYNAMNBR=20,COND=((8,LT),(4,LT,DB2))
//*****************************************************************
//SYSTSIN  DD DSN=ISD.TEST.PARMCARD(PCRDB21),DISP=SHR
//DSNTRACE DD SYSOUT=*
//SYSUDUMP DD SYSOUT=*
//SYSPRINT DD SYSOUT=*
//SYSTSPRT DD SYSOUT=*
//SYSIN    DD DSN=LCP.IDMS.&SYSTEM..LINKLIB(&PROGRAM),DISP=SHR
```

The execution of the COBOL program is normally achieved by running it under the domain of the DB2 foreground processor. Listing 9.8 shows how the execution JCL for a DB2/IDMS COBOL program would appear.

Listing 9.8 The execution JCL for a cross-database COBOL program.

```
//GOFORIT  JOB (CARD)
//GOFORIT  EXEC PGM=IKJEFT01,DYNAMNBR=20
//*****************************************************************
//SYSTSIN  DD *
   DSN SYSTEM    (DB2P)
   RUN PROG      (MYCOBOL) -
   LIB           ('MY.LINK.LIB')  -
   PLAN          (MYCOBOL)
//DSNTRACE DD SYSOUT=*
//SYSUDUMP DD SYSOUT=*
//SYSPRINT DD SYSOUT=*
//SYSTSPRT DD SYSOUT=*
//STEPLIB  DD  DSN=MY.IDMS.LIBRARIES,DISP=SHR
```

With this technique, batch programs on IBM mainframes can be created to share information between architectures. While many methods to accomplish database connectivity are available, it seems certain that shops are demanding tools to allow diverse databases to communicate with each other. Rather than gravitating toward some panacea database that handles everyone's data requirements, the industry is recognizing that many different database architectures are required to meet the needs of organizations. Consequently, you are going to continue seeing the evolution of methods that allow true connectivity, regardless of the hardware platforms or database architectures that must be crossed.

Now that we see the issues involved in linking database access across platforms, let's explore the issues involved in linking between Oracle and other databases.

Linking Oracle And Non-Oracle Databases

Now is the time to take a look at the methods used to link databases from various vendors. Remember, Oracle can be made to communicate with databases of any architecture, including relational, hierarchical, network, or object-oriented databases. In general, there are three approaches to linking databases: manual consolidation, remote connection, and online applications. Following is a summary of each approach:

- *Manual consolidation*—Data is extracted from a variety of databases and loaded into a common repository. This is an approach commonly used with data warehouses. Red Brick Systems is an example of manual consolidation.

- *Remote connection*—Many databases are monitored via a common console. In this scenario, status information is shipped from a variety of databases to a common console. The common console is then used to alert operations staff to extraordinary conditions. Patrol by BMC Software is an example of this type of linking.

- *Online applications*—An online application (usually running on a PC) accesses data from a variety of databases, presenting the data to the user as if the data was coming from a single source. EDA-SQL and UNIFACE are examples of this type of linking.

As you can see, you have some options when linking multivendor databases. Let's take a look at how multivendor databases became so popular.

The History Of Multivendor Databases

There are two schools of thought when it comes to spanning applications across multiple vendor databases. One perspective maintains that a single vendor should be able to provide a global, omniscient database that is capable of supporting all types of data requirements—from online transaction processing to decision support. Many vendors foster this belief by marketing their database products as suitable for every type of application, pointing out the nightmares that result when a multivendor database application attempts to make diverse databases communicate with each other. The opposing philosophy believes the only way to successfully implement database technology is to use numerous databases, leveraging the strengths of each engine. Regardless of specific vendor philosophies, as recently as five years ago, database vendors touted their products as corporate panaceas, appropriate for all types of data and application systems.

All of this began to change around the time IBM conceded that its DB2 database was not appropriate for high-volume systems. Prior to this concession, DB2 was marketed as an all-purpose engine suitable for any application, regardless of size or performance requirements. Within time, it became apparent that DB2 was not appropriate for systems that required thousands of transactions per second. So, IBM began recommending IMS for very large, high-speed databases.

The multiple database trend kicked off as a reaction to corporate acquisitions and weak development strategies. Companies had little or no strategic direction for developing databases, and few companies probably ever purposefully decided to go heterogeneous. Heterogeneous databases means duplicating licenses and talent, and few companies have a large enough talent pool to support multiple databases. Hence, we see environments where many database products coexist and the Information Systems staff must create links between the database engines.

From this beginning, vendors began to embrace the concept of "the right database for the right application." Systems that required flexibility and ad hoc query were implemented with relational databases, while systems with complex data relationships and high performance requirements were implemented with network or hierarchical database architectures. New types of specialized database products began appearing on the scene: special word-searchable databases for textual data, databases designed especially for CAD/CAM systems, and so on. Database systems began their long march away from corporate repositories into specialized niche markets, some of which are shown in Table 9.1.

Table 9.1 Samples of specialized database products.

Type of Database	Product
Text processing	Folio, Fulcrum, Acrobat
High-speed processing	IMS, Teradata, CA-IDMS
Object support	Versant, Objectivity, ONTOS
Warehouse support	Pilot LightShip, Oracle Express, MetaCube, Fusion

Today, many products such as PowerBuilder and SAP support numerous back-end databases, and the trend has been clearly moving toward applications that are independent from the database platform.

Originally, the desire for a central repository of data was driven by the need to impose some control over data redundancy and multiple updates to the same information placed on various file systems. From this situation evolved our centralized systems, using a single-vendor database. However, end-user computing—and to some degree, slow data transmission—helped to justify a move to client/server platforms in the corporate world.

It is interesting to note that the demand for mainframe resources does not always decline after a company makes a commitment to embrace open systems. Having a single database offered definite advantages in the mainframe days, but most large IS shops are now both decentralized and distributed worldwide. To complicate matters, many of the remote locations have the authority to choose their own database—usually selecting whatever is in vogue at the time, or perhaps the cheapest database available. This approach can lead to a realtime support load problem. Interestingly, even after a large company completes its push into open systems, the largest share of costs may still be on a mainframe. Although new development is moving to open systems, companies are still seeing mainframe requirements growing at a rate of 15 to 20 percent per year—even though total dollar cost has dropped for mainframe systems. In other words, legacy systems have proven to be far more difficult to remove than planned.

As we move further away from proprietary operating systems to open systems, it seems evident that the days of single-vendor environments are numbered. We are already witnessing the shift toward a plug-and-play RDBMS environment.

Unfortunately, there has been no standard model for client/server data management. In spite of all the open systems standards (OSF, POSIX, X-Windows, IEEE, and so forth), nothing truly solid has emerged for databases. Furthermore, the standards that we have—such as SQL—are implemented in very different ways. While real-world developers wait eagerly for standards to emerge, they simply make their own decisions on the best DBMS platform. Other departments in the corporate world have followed the same thinking, choosing their idea of the best DBMS, and so on. This scattered approach has resulted in islands of information distributed among our LANs and WANs—not only distributed among different file systems on the same box, but distributed across the country and around the world. Linking these databases has become a very complicated but critical chore.

External influences have also impacted database configurations. Corporate acquisitions, mergers, and right-sizing efforts have all had the side effect of leaving a plethora of database engines within newly reformed organizations. Regardless of the wisdom (or lack thereof) of multidatabase systems, most IS departments must link more than one database, and cross-database connectivity has become commonplace. Sentry Market Research estimates that the average corporation has approximately nine different databases. End users are demanding applications that integrate legacy data from mainframes with open systems data. All the while, MIS designers are faced with the incredible challenge of making these diverse systems function as a unified whole.

While linking nonrelational databases, such as IMS and CA-IDMS, into relational databases is considered challenging, it is a common misconception that relational databases are basically the same and therefore easy to link together.

Even linking databases that share the same architecture is difficult, especially with relational databases. The idea that relational databases are "plug-and-play" is pure fantasy. For example, the popular PowerBuilder application development tool was primarily designed for use with a Sybase relational database. To accommodate PowerBuilder, Oracle had to add an init.ora parameter to cache cursors for PowerBuilder because PowerBuilder doesn't give users control over specific cursors, resulting in many SQL reparses. Locking between Oracle and Sybase is also totally different. If you use Oracle and want to build a high-performance OLTP application, you should first lock all records (an option that doesn't exist in Sybase); set a transaction boundary to roll back everything except the locks (in case of a transaction error);

then perform array operations, such as **INSERT**, **DELETE**, **UPDATE**, and **SELECT** (all of which are not supported by Sybase). Even the SQL syntax differs, and the procedural extensions to each database's SQL are never equal.

To further illustrate database stumbling blocks, consider the cost of converting an application from one relational database to another. First, do you even have the talent to make it happen when the interfaces are so diverse? Even more confounding is the lack of clarity about the "truths" of the differences. Rarely is an RDBMS chosen over another on the basis of which RDBMS is best for the type of application.

Fortunately, it is becoming clear that the differences between proprietary databases will become less of a problem as robust interfaces are developed. Very little theoretical reason can support remaining bound to the technology of a single database vendor. We are in an era where cross-platform joins are demanded. Vendors who do not provide the capability to do so will be viewed as hampering the flow of information, thereby decreasing productivity. This doesn't mean that vendors will abandon their notable differences in favor of a standardized database environment. In fact, differences are likely to intensify with the addition of new functionality because each RDBMS will need to emphasize its strengths to establish superiority over the competition.

Some vendors have seen a market opportunity for a tool that can easily access multivendor databases, both for retrieval and updates. One such product is called Passport. Passport is an object-oriented tool that makes the development of three-tiered multivendor applications unbelievably easy. Passport started out as a front-end tool when Oracle and Ingres dominated the market. It wasn't long, however, before customers wanted to mix and match databases. For example, users might want one database for the tool set and another database for the SQL. Either case requires a tool that quickly allows a developer to switch databases on an as-needed basis.

The challenge of linking multivendor databases is not one of syntax—that can be solved through standard query languages, data dictionaries, and the like. The real challenge is one of semantics: How can meaning be extracted from data contained in many different locations? I believe this challenge can only be met by building executable business models that pull related information out of multiple databases as a side effect of their ongoing operations.

Even the major DBMS vendors are recognizing that extensions into other products are necessary for their survival. The crux of the situation is becoming evident: Most shops are not capable of moving their data into a single database. In response to the realities of linking multivendor databases, just about every database vendor has created a tool that claims to allow seamless communications between its engine and other vendors' products. These tools are called *gateways*.

Gateways

Nowadays, most vendors provide tools, or gateways, within their database engines to link multivendor databases. Some large IS shops have had great success using gateway technology to link multiplatform databases. For example, consider a company that supports IMS, DB2, and Oracle. After looking at various solutions to make these databases communicate, the company might choose two different gateway products. One gateway might be Oracle's transparent gateway to handle communication from Oracle applications to DB2 and IMS, and the other gateway could be IBM's DDCS and DataJoiner to handle communication from DB2 to Oracle. Many companies use Oracle's transparent gateway because it allows them to treat calls to DB2 as if DB2 was just another Oracle database. The gateway product takes care of the translation into DB2 SQL. The company will then have the capability to join two DB2 tables, each on a separate processor, from within an Oracle application. While these gateway solutions are definitely functional, the long-term goal for most companies is to avoid gateways altogether and move into a three-tiered architecture with a protocol layer such as CORBA or DCE. But for now, gateways play an important role in multivendor database technology.

Oracle Corporation has provided a leading-edge approach to interfacing with other databases. Oracle's gateway philosophy emphasizes the need for a smooth transition path for non-Oracle databases by offering a three-phase program. Oracle recognizes that customers can't be expected to shift to Oracle overnight, so Oracle's gateway strategy allows for a smooth transition into an Oracle environment.

In phase one, Oracle applications provide gateways into non-Oracle databases, allowing Oracle applications to make calls (using Oracle SQL) to non-Oracle databases. The converter then translates the Oracle SQL into the native SQL for the foreign database. Now the developer can use the robust extensions found in Oracle

SQL with a non-Oracle database, while the Oracle open gateway relies on *SQL compensation* to perform Oracle SQL functions against the non-Oracle database. To illustrate, this technology allows an Oracle application to join a DB2 table with a Sybase table—all within the gateway product. Oracle believes in connectivity into all databases—not just relational databases. For this reason, Oracle is packaged with Information Builders Incorporated, using its EDA-SQL product to help insulate the front-end application from the foreign data source. This takes the form of an access manager that handles the communications to and from the Oracle database, allowing Oracle to access nonrelational databases. (See Figure 9.7.)

While this approach seems noble, Oracle has experienced some problems with a few of its SQL extensions that do not have equivalents in other relational databases. For example, Oracle's **decode** function cannot be implemented in Informix because the **decode** verb has no direct equivalent in Informix SQL. The multivendor SQL converter must somehow manage the translation between different dialects of SQL.

Phase two of Oracle's strategy allows a foreign application to access Oracle. For example, let's say a CICS COBOL customer requires access to Oracle data. In phase two of the Oracle gateway, the non-Oracle application on the mainframe can access Oracle as if the non-Oracle database is on a local host. However, some middleware vendors (more about middleware in a moment) do not feel that the gateway ap-

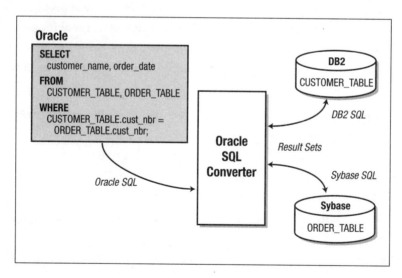

Figure 9.7
Oracle's transparent gateway—phase one.

proach is the best long-term solution for database connectivity. Unlike the gateway products that have a single interface, some products have separately tuned drivers for each target database. This movement away from general interfaces such as ODBC is primarily for performance reasons, and it is not uncommon for each product to have its own custom interface for each database that is supported.

Phase three of Oracle's strategy is heterogeneous replication. Phase three provides a solution that allows database designers to replicate data from a variety of sources and import the table data into Oracle. The Oracle gateway also provides a mechanism to constantly update the replicated non-Oracle data. The gateway approach is commonly used with data warehouse applications, but it also allows updates to non-Oracle data to be quickly transported into a replicated Oracle database, as shown in Figure 9.8.

Now that we understand the organizational issues revolving around multi-vendor database access, let's take a look at some of the techniques that are being used to create these links. The foremost approach is the creation of replication between the databases.

Data Replication

Data replication can work both ways—importing foreign tables into Oracle or taking Oracle tables and propagating them into a foreign database (where they behave as native tables within the foreign database)—as shown in Figure 9.9.

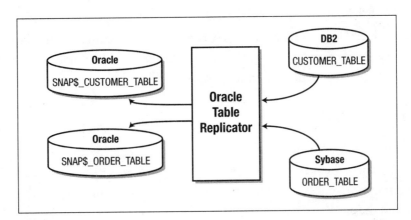

Figure 9.8
Foreign tables imported into Oracle.

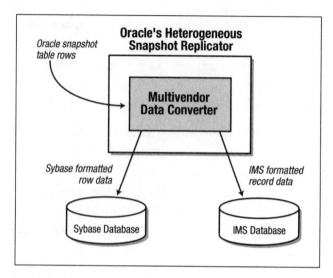

Figure 9.9
Oracle tables exported into foreign databases.

The ability to replicate in both directions gives the database design an enormous flexibility in choosing the best approach to replication, based on the needs of the client/server application. However, developers need to be aware that replication interfaces are complicated and often require manual intervention, especially when data is transferred from one hardware architecture to another. For example, populating EBCDIC data from DB2 tables into the ASCII world of Oracle involves translating characters that are unknown to ASCII, such as the cent sign.

There are several ways to create links between diverse databases, but with the growing popularity of three-tiered client/server systems, the middleware has become an increasingly popular avenue for creating these links.

Middleware

There are three components in a three-tiered client/server architecture: the application layer, where the presentation software resides; the server layer, where the data resides; and the middleware, which handles the communication between the application and the database.

Many of the new middleware packages allow applications to be developed independently of the databases, providing drivers for more than 25 database products. Some products, such as UNIFACE, accomplish this with *data choreography*, where the developer specifies the data with query by example. The developer does not have to write SQL, and UNIFACE takes care of all of the I/O and relationship management. A middleware product capable of enforcing business rules across database architectures is also needed. One important aspect of UNIFACE is the ability to enforce referential integrity across platforms. For example, a customer database could exist at corporate headquarters using Oracle, but orders are taken in the field using a C/ISAM database. The middleware tool will maintain the business rules between the tables, even though they are in different databases at different locations.

Some of the new middleware products have the capability of leveraging on their object-oriented architecture to easily access multiple databases. For example, some middleware treats each database as an object with its own attributes and behaviors. This treatment makes it trivial to swap out one database for another. These middleware products have an inherent distributed database model to manage two-phase commits across numerous midrange and PC databases, thereby enabling a single update screen to display data from many different databases. When update time comes, the tool uses synchronous communications to ensure that all databases are updated.

From a database administration perspective, another common technique for monitoring diverse databases has become increasingly popular. Remote measurement uses a special approach to link multivendor databases with a common interface layer.

Remote Measurement

Another trend in the marketplace is linking diverse databases with a common tool such that the common tools accesses the diverse databases as if they were all of the same architecture. This approach is used primarily for measuring database and system performance. For example, the Patrol product by BMC Software provides a common interface to numerous relational databases. Patrol uses a *knowledge module* on each database to collect information on each remote database, shipping exception information to the master console. This is called *fat-agent technology* because most of the processing is done on the agent. Each agent contains the protocols necessary to communicate with the master console, regardless of the agent's platform. The knowledge modules also abstract the user interface, making it possible for the knowledge module to adapt to a Unix or MVS view of the data and providing a way to cover up to 5,000 databases from a single console. A complete overview of Patrol's features can be found in Chapter 11, *Oracle Application Monitoring*.

Today, designers are seeing more heterogeneous database platforms than ever before. Data continues to reside on many platforms and within many different databases. Methods need to be created for building bridges between these islands of information. The immediate future for managing cross-database communications lies in emerging standards, such as the OMG's CORBA specification (discussed in Chapter 12) and Microsoft's OLE 2 standard. It is only within these frameworks that true, seamless distributed systems will be practical.

Summary

Now that we have addressed database connectivity issues, including Oracle client/server systems, we need to take a look at techniques for linking a client/server application with a non-Oracle data server. It's time to look at Oracle open gateway architecture as well as numerous vendors and programmatic solutions.

HIGH PERFORMANCE

Tuning Oracle Data Warehouse And OLAP Applications

HIGH PERFORMANCE

CHAPTER
10

Tuning Oracle Data Warehouse And OLAP Applications

As more companies begin to embrace the concept of creating a historical data repository for online analytical processing (OLAP) and decision support systems (DSS) applications, new client/server issues have emerged. Developers are struggling to create Oracle-based client/server applications that will perform acceptably. This chapter approaches the client/server issues from a data warehouse perspective, with a focus on creating fast Oracle applications. Topics in this chapter include:

- Data warehouses and multidimensional databases

- History of OLAP

- Oracle data warehouse features

- Table and index partitioning

- Parallel operations

- Join optimization

Data Warehousing And Multidimensional Databases

A great deal of interest has surfaced in the application of data warehousing and multidimensional databases to advanced systems. These systems, including expert systems and decision support systems, have been used to solve semistructured and even unstructured problems. Traditionally, these types of systems combine inference engines and relational databases in order to store the knowledge processing components. Unfortunately, very little work has been done with the application of warehouse databases for decision support and expert systems. The following sections cover the foundations of decision support systems and expert systems, and discusses how they are used with data warehouse technology.

Expert System

Expert system is a term that is used very loosely in the computer community regarding anything from a spreadsheet program to any program that contains an **IF** statement. In general terms, an expert system is one that models the well-structured decision process of the human mind, applying that reasoning process to a real-world situation. Any decision-making process with quantifiable rules can have the rules stored in an *inference engine*. An inference engine is used to drive the information-gathering component of the system, eventually arriving at the solution to the problem.

It has been said that an expert system makes a decision *for* a user, while a decision support system makes a decision *with* a user. This distinction is essentially true, because an expert system makes no provision for human intuition in the decision-making process. Many real-world management decisions do not require human intuition. For example, one of the crucial jobs of a retail manager is the choice of what goods to order, the quantity, and the ordering time frame. These decisions can be represented by a model called economic order quantity (EOQ). If the EOQ equation knows the velocity at which the goods are leaving the retail store, the delivery time on reorders, the average time on the shelf, and the cost of the goods, the computer can confidently produce automatic daily reports specifying which goods to order in what quantity without human input. Also, an expert system can presummarize data so that the manager can quickly take a high-level look at the relevant figures, as shown in Figure 10.1.

Decision Support Systems

Decision support systems (DSS) are generally defined as a type of system that deals with a semistructured problem. In other words, the task has a structured component as well as a component that involves human intuition. The well-structured compo-

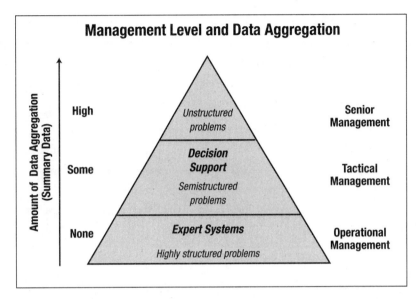

Figure 10.1
Defining different levels of aggregation.

nents are the decision rules that are stored as the problem-processing system. The intuitive or creative component is left to the user.

The following list represents some examples of semistructured problems:

- Choosing a spouse

- Building a factory

- Choosing magazine artwork

- Building a new sports car

- Designing a Graphical User Interface (GUI) for an OODBMS

Decision support technology recognizes that many tasks require human intuition. For example, the process of choosing a stock portfolio is a task that has both structured and intuitive components. Certainly, rules are associated with choosing a stock portfolio, such as diversification of the stocks and choosing an acceptable level of risk. These factors can be quantified easily and stored in a database system, allowing the user of the system to create "what-if" scenarios. However, just because a system has well-structured components does not guarantee that the entire decision process is well-structured.

One of the best ways to tell if a decision process is semistructured is to ask the question, "Do people with the same level of knowledge demonstrate different levels of skill?" For example, it is possible for many stock brokers to have the same level of knowledge about the stock market. However, brokers clearly demonstrate different levels of skill when assembling stock portfolios.

Computer simulation is one area that is used heavily within the modeling components of decision support systems. In fact, one of the first object-oriented languages was SIMULA, which was used as a driver for these what-if scenarios, and was incorporated into decision support systems so that users could model a particular situation. The user would create a scenario with objects that were subjected to a set of predefined behaviors.

The general characteristics of a decision support system include:

- *Solves a nonrecurring problem*—DSS technology is used primarily for novel and unique modeling situations that require the user to simulate the behavior of some real-world problem.

- *Requires human intuition*—DSS makes the decision *with* the user, unlike expert systems that make the decision *for* the user.

- *Requires knowledge of the problem being solved*—Unlike an expert system that provides the user with answers to well-structured questions, decision support systems require the user to thoroughly understand the problem being solved. For example, a financial decision support system, such as the DSSF product, would require the user to understand the concept of a stock Beta. Beta is the term used to measure the covariance of an individual stock against the behavior of the market as a whole. Without an understanding of the concepts, a user would be unable to effectively utilize a decision support system.

- *Allows ad hoc data query*—As users gather information for their decision, they make repeated requests to the online database, with one query answer stimulating another query. Because the purpose of ad hoc query is to allow freeform query to decision information, response time is critical.

- *Produces more than one acceptable answer*—Unlike an expert system that usually produces a single, finite answer to a problem, a decision support system deals with problems that have a domain or range of acceptable solutions. For example, a user of DSSF might discover many "acceptable" stock portfolios that match the selection criteria of the user. Another good example is a manager who needs to place production machines onto an empty warehouse floor. The goal would be to maximize the throughput of work in process from raw materials to finished goods. Clearly, the manager could choose from a number of acceptable ways of placing the machines on the warehouse floor in order to achieve this goal. This is called the *state space* approach to problem solving: First a solution domain is specified, then the user works to create models to achieve the desired goal state.

- *Uses external data sources*—For example, a DSS might require classification of customers by Standard Industry Code (SIC) or customer addresses by Standard Metropolitan Statistical Area (SMSA). Many warehouse managers load this external data into the central warehouse.

As you can see in Figure 10.2, a decision support system works with three components: the end user, the problem processing system, and the knowledge system, allowing the end user to make the decision. An expert system, on the other hand, works with the end user and an inference engine, returning a solution to the problem that is being solved.

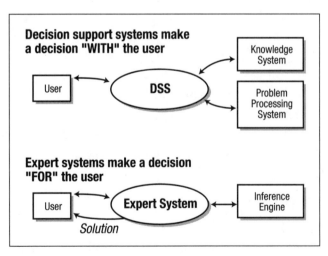

Figure 10.2
Comparing decision support and expert systems.

Decision support systems allow users to create what-if scenarios. These futuristic glimpses are essentially modeling tools that allow the user to define an environment and simulate the behavior of that environment under changing conditions. For example, the user of a DSS for finance could create a hypothetical stock portfolio and then direct the DSS to model the behavior of that stock portfolio under different market conditions. Once these behaviors are specified, the user can vary the contents of the portfolio and view the results.

The types of output from decision support systems include:

- *Management Information Systems (MIS)*—Standard reports and forecasts of sales.

- *Hypothesis testing*—Answers questions, such as: Did sales decrease in the eastern region last month because of changes in buying habits? This involves iterative questioning, with one answer leading to another question.

- *Model building*—Creating a sales model and validating its behavior against the historical data in the warehouse. Predictive modeling is often used to forecast behaviors based on historical factors.

- *Discovery of unknown trends*—Data mining tools answer questions in instances where you might not even know what specific questions to ask. For example, Why are sales up in the eastern region?

The role of human intuition in this type of problem solving has stirred great debate. Decision support systems allow the user to control the decision-making process, applying his or her own decision-making rules and intuition to the process. However, the arguments for and against using artificial intelligence to manage the intuitive component of these systems has strong proponents on both sides. Now that we see the theoretical foundation of expert systems and decision support systems, let's take a look at how these systems are used within the domain of the data warehouse.

Data Warehouses

Multidimensional databases, or data warehouses, are approaching the DSS market through two methods. The first approach is through niche servers that use a proprietary architecture to model multidimensional databases. Examples of niche servers include Arbor and IRI. The second approach is to provide multidimensional front ends that manage the mapping between the RDBMS and the dimensional representation of the data. Figure 10.3 offers an overview of the various multidimensional databases.

In general, the following definitions apply to data warehouses:

- *Subject-oriented data*—Unlike an online transaction processing application that is focused on a finite business transaction, a data warehouse attempts to collect all that is known about a subject area (e.g., sales volume, interest earned, and so forth) from all data sources within the organization.

- *Read-only during queries*—Data warehouses are loaded during off hours and are used for read-only requests during day hours.

- *Highly denormalized data structures*—Unlike an OLTP system with many "narrow" tables, data warehouses pre-join tables, creating "fat" tables with highly redundant columns.

- *Preaggregated data*—Unlike OLTP, data warehouses precalculate totals to improve runtime performance. Note that preaggregation is antirelational, meaning that the relational model advocates building aggregate objects at runtime, only allowing for the storing of atomic data components.

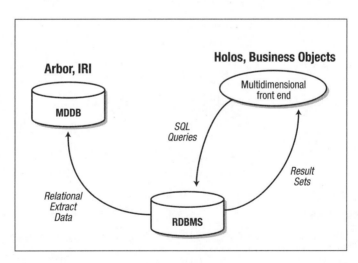

Figure 10.3
The major types of multidimensional databases.

- *Features interactive, ad hoc query*—Data warehouses must be flexible enough to handle spontaneous queries by the users. Consequently, a flexible design is imperative.

When you contrast the data warehouse with a transaction-oriented, online system, the differences become apparent. These differences are shown in Table 10.1.

Aside from the different uses for data warehouses, many developers are using relational databases to build their data warehouses and simulate multiple dimensions. Design techniques are being used for the simulations. This push toward STAR schema design has been somewhat successful, especially because designers do not have to buy a multidimensional database or invest in an expensive front-end tool. In general, using a relational database for OLAP is achieved by any combination of the following techniques:

- *Pre-joining tables together*—This is an obtuse way of saying that a denormalized table is created from the normalized online database. A large pre-join of several tables is sometimes called a fact table in a STAR schema.

- *Presummarization*—This prepares the data for any drill-down requests that come from the end user. Essentially, the different levels of aggregation are identified, and the aggregate tables are computed and populated when the data is loaded.

- *Massive denormalization*—The side effect of very inexpensive disks has been the rethinking of the merits of Third Normal Form. Today, redundancy is widely accepted, as seen by the popularity of replication tools, snapshot utilities, and

Table 10.1   Differences between OLTP and data warehouse.

	OLTP	Data Warehouse
Normalization	High (3NF)	Low (1NF)
Table sizes	Small	Large
Number of rows/table	Small	Large
Size/duration of transactions	Small	Large
Number of online users	High (1,000s)	Low (< 100)
Updates	Frequent	Nightly
Full-table scans	Rarely	Frequently
Historical data	< 90 days	Years

non-First Normal Form databases. If you can pre-create every possible result table at load time, your end user will enjoy excellent response time when making queries. The STAR schema is an example of massive denormalization.

- *Controlled periodic batch updating*—New detail data is rolled into the aggregate table on a periodic basis while the online system is down, with all summarization recalculated as the new data is introduced into the database. While data loading is important, it is only one component of the tools for loading a warehouse. There are several categories of tools that are used to populate a warehouse, including:

  - *Data extraction tools*—Tools for different hardware and databases

  - *Metadata repository*—Storage area for common definitions

  - *Data cleaning tools*—Tools for ensuring uniform data quality

  - *Data sequencing tools*—RI rules for the warehouse

  - *Warehouse loading tools*—Tools for populating the data warehouse

As you probably know, most data warehouses are loaded in batch mode after the online system has been shut down. In this sense, a data warehouse is bimodal, with a highly intensive loading window during the night, and an intensive read-only window during the day. Because many data warehouses collect data from nonrelational databases such as IMS or CA-IDMS, no standard methods for extracting data are available for loading into a warehouse. However, there are a few common techniques for extracting and loading data:

- *Log "sniffing"*—Apply the archived Oracle redo logs from the OLTP system to the data warehouse by using a "false recovery."

- *Using update, insert, and delete triggers*—Fire off a distributed update to the data warehouse.

- *Use snapshot logs to populate the data warehouse*—Update the replicated tables and change log files.

- *Run nightly extract/load programs*—Retrieve the operational data, and load it into the warehouse.

There are several methods that can be used to aggregate data within OLAP servers, depending on the processing requirements. One popular method, shown in Figure 10.4, extracts data from the relational engine, summarizing the data for display. Another popular method preaggregates the data and keeps the summarized data ready for retrieval.

Two major changes have occurred over the past several years that have driven the movement toward data warehousing:

- *Disk space is becoming inexpensive*—One gigabyte of disk carried a price tag of $100,000 in 1988. Today, one gigabyte of disk storage is less than $1,000 on Unix and less than $200 on PC platforms. To support large data warehouses, it is not uncommon to require terabytes of disk storage.

- *The movement into open systems*—The migration away from centralized processors has led to data residing on a plethora of different computer and database architectures.

Data is collected from a variety of sources, so many warehouse installations find it necessary to create a metadata repository. But, what is the role of a metadata reposi-

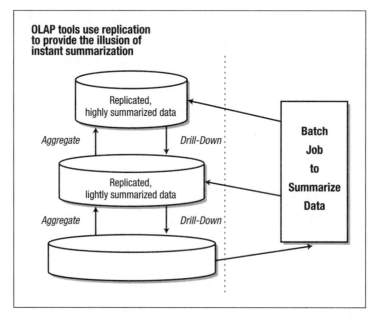

Figure 10.4
Aggregation and OLAP servers.

tory? When data is consolidated from a variety of diverse systems, many intrasystem problems can arise. These issues include:

- *Homonyms*—Different columns with the same name

- *Synonyms*—The same column with different names

- *Unit incompatibilities*—Inches versus centimeters, dollars versus yen, and so on

- *Enterprise referential integrity*—Business rules that span operational systems

- *The warehouse design rules*—Determinations concerning how tables will be built, including:

    - Horizontal denormalization (fat tables)

    - Vertical denormalization (chunking tables based on time periods)

    - Multidimensional front-end usage

There are other alternatives to using a "pure" multidimensional database (MDDB). One common approach is to insert a metadata server between the OLTP relational database and the query tool, as shown in Figure 10.5.

Examples of this approach include:

- DSS Agent, by MicroStrategy

- MetaCube, by Stanford Technology Group

- Holos by Seagate

When embarking on a data warehousing project, many pitfalls can cripple the project. Characteristics of successful data warehouse projects generally include the following:

- *Clear business justification for the project*—Measurable benefits must be defined for the warehouse project (e.g., sales will increase by 10 percent, customer retention will increase by 15 percent, and so forth). Warehouses are expensive, and the project must be able to measure the benefits.

- *Properly trained staff*—Warehousing involves many new technologies, including SMP, MPP, and MDDB. The staff must be trained and comfortable with the new tools.

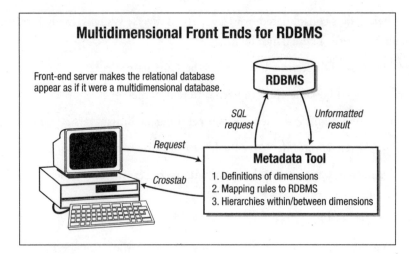

Figure 10.5
Using metadata repositories for multidimensional databases.

- *Data quality and consistency*—Warehouses deal with historical data from a variety of sources, so care must be taken to create a metadata manager that ensures common data definitions and records changes of historical data definitions.

- *Subject privacy*—Gathering data from many sources can lead to privacy violations. A good example is the hotel chain that targeted frequent hotel customers and sent a frequent-user coupon to their home addresses. Some spouses intercepted these mailings, leading to numerous divorces.

- *Starts small and evolves*—Some projects fail by defining too broad of a scope for the project. Successful projects consider their first effort a "prototype" and continue to evolve from that point.

- *Intimate end-user involvement*—Data warehouses cannot be developed in a vacuum. The system must be flexible enough to address changing end-user requirements, and the end users must understand the architecture so they are aware of the limitations of their warehouse.

- *Properly planned infrastructure*—A new infrastructure must be designed to handle communications between data sources. Parallel computers must be evaluated and installed, and staff must be appropriately educated.

- *Data modeling validated and stress tested*—The data model must be validated and stress tested so that the finished system performs at acceptable levels. A model that works great at 10GB might not function as the warehouse grows to 100GB.

- *Avoiding the wrong tools*—Many projects are led astray because of vendor hype. Unfortunately, many vendors inappropriately label their products as warehouse applications or exaggerate the functionality of their tools.

Now that we understand the basics of data warehouse projects, we can take a look at how relational data can be summarized and preaggregated for data warehouse applications.

Data Aggregation And Drill-Down In The Data Warehouse

One of the most fundamental principles of the multidimensional data warehouse is the idea of aggregation. As you know, managers at different levels require different levels of summarization to make intelligent decisions. To allow the manager to choose the level of aggregation, most warehouse offerings have a "drill-down" feature, allowing the user to adjust the level of detail, eventually reaching the original transaction data. For obvious performance reasons, the aggregations are precalculated and loaded into the warehouse during off hours.

Of the several types of aggregation, the most common is called a *roll-up aggregation*. An example of this type of aggregation would be taking daily sales totals and rolling them up into a monthly sales table—making it relatively easy to compute and run. The more difficult type of aggregation is the aggregation of boolean and comparative operators. For example, assume that a salesperson table contains a boolean column called **turkey**. A salesperson is a turkey if his or her individual sales are below the group average for the day. A salesperson can be a turkey on 15 percent of the individual days but, when the data is rolled up into a monthly summary, the salesperson could become a turkey—even with only a few (albeit very bad) sales days. Table 10.2 shows the differences between the presentation and display styles for OLAP and MDDB servers.

Table 10.2   Differences between OLAP and MDDB.

	OLAP	MDDB
Presentation display	List	Crosstab
Extraction	Select	Compare
Series variable "dimensions"	Columns	User-defined

The base rule is simple: If the data looks like it would fit well into a spreadsheet, it is probably well-suited to an MDDB—or at least an MDDB representation. Now that we have reviewed the basics of multidimensional data representation, let's take a look at how relational database vendors are reacting to the need for multidimensional data representation.

Relational Answers To MDDB

Dr. Ralph Kimball, founder of Red Brick Systems, popularized the term *STAR schema* to describe a denormalization process that simulates the structure of a multidimensional database. With a STAR schema, the designer can simulate the functions of a multidimensional database without having to purchase expensive third-party software. Kimball describes denormalization as the pre-joining of tables, such that the runtime application does not have to join tables. At the heart of the STAR schema is a *fact table*, usually comprised entirely of key values and raw data. A fact table is generally very long and can have millions of rows.

Surrounding the fact table is a series of *dimension tables* that serve to add value to the base information in the fact table. For example, consider the E/R model for a sales database shown in Figure 10.6.

Here, you can see a standard Third Normal Form (3NF) database used to represent the sales of items. No redundant information is given; therefore, salient data, such as the total for an order, would have to be computed from the atomic items that comprise the order. In this 3NF database, a list of line items would need to be created, multiplying the quantity ordered by the price for all items that belong in order 123.

Note that the state-city table hierarchy in this example is very deliberate. In order to be truly in Third Normal Form, you do not want to allow any redundant information (except, of course, foreign keys). Given that this example has been fully normalized, a query that would appear very simple to the end user would have relatively complex SQL.

For example, the SQL to calculate the sum of all orders in the western region might look very complex, involving a five-way table join, as follows:

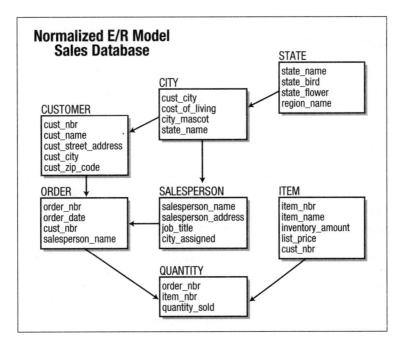

Figure 10.6
A sample fully normalized schema design.

```
CREATE TABLE TEMP AS
SELECT (QUANTITY.quantity_sold * ITEM.list_price) line_total
FROM QUANTITY, ITEM, CUSTOMER, CITY, STATE
WHERE
QUANTITY.item_nbr = ITEM.item_nbr      /* join QUANTITY and ITEM */
AND
ITEM.cust_nbr = CUSTOMER.cust_nbr      /* join ITEM and CUSTOMER */
AND
CUSTOMER.cust_nbr = CITY.cust_nbr      /* join CUSTOMER and CITY */
AND
CITY.state_name = STATE.state_name     /* join CITY and STATE */
AND
STATE.region_name = 'WEST';
```

In the real world, of course, you would introduce enough redundancy to eliminate the **CITY** and **STATE** tables. The point is clear—a manager who wants to analyze a series of complete order totals would need to do a huge amount of realtime computation. Here's the basic tradeoff: If you want true freedom from redundant data, you must pay the price at query time.

Remember, the rules of database design have changed. Ten years ago, normalization theory emphasized the need to control redundancy and touted the benefits of a structure that was free of redundant data. Today, with disk prices at an all-time low, the attitude toward redundancy has changed radically. Oracle8 is now offering a plethora of tools to allow snapshots and other methods for replicating data. With the Oracle8 object option, Oracle now allows for non-First Normal Form implementations. Today, it is perfectly acceptable to create First Normal Form implementations of normalized databases—pre-joining the tables to avoid the high performance costs of runtime SQL joins.

The basic principle behind the STAR query schema is the introduction of highly redundant data for performance reasons. Let's evolve the 3NF database into a STAR schema by creating a fact table to hold the quantity for each item sold. Essentially, a fact table is a First Normal Form representation of the database, with a very high degree of redundancy being added into the tables. This denormalized design, shown in Figure 10.7, greatly improves the simplicity of the design—but at the expense of redundant data.

At first glance, it is hard to believe that this representation contains the same data as the fully normalized database. The new fact table will contain one row for each item on each order, resulting in a tremendous amount of redundant key information. Of course, the STAR query schema is going to require far more disk space than the 3NF database from which it was created, and the STAR schema would most likely be a read-only database due to the widespread redundancy that has been introduced into the model. Also, the widespread redundancy would make updating difficult, if not downright impossible.

Also, note the dimension tables surrounding the fact table. Some of the dimension tables contain data that can be added to queries with joins, while other dimensions such as **REGION** do not contain any data and only serve as indexes to the data.

Considering the huge disk space consumption and read-only restriction, what does this STAR schema really give us? The greatest benefit is the simplicity of data retrieval. Once you have a STAR schema, you can formulate SQL queries to quickly get the information that you desire.

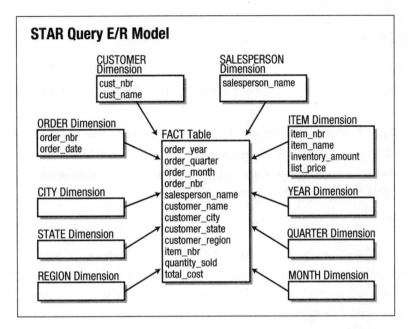

Figure 10.7
The completed STAR schema.

For example, getting the total cost for an order now becomes simple:

```
SELECT sum(total_cost) order_total
FROM FACT
WHERE
FACT.order_nbr = 123;
```

By doing some of the work up front, the realtime query becomes both faster and simpler.

Now, let's consider what would happen if the user of this schema wanted to analyze information by aggregate values. Assume your manager wants to know the breakdown of sales by region. The data is not organized by region, but you can easily query the fact table to find the answer.

At this point, retrieving the sum of all orders for the western region becomes trivial, as shown in the following snippet:

```
SELECT sum(total_cost)
FROM FACT
```

```
WHERE
region = 'WEST';
```

In addition to making the query simpler in structure, the table joining has been eliminated, so you can easily get the extracted information from the STAR schema.

> **Note:** A value such as **region** would be an ideal candidate for bitmapped indexes, which were first introduced in Oracle7.3. Columns that have less than 20 distinct values can see dramatic performance improvements by utilizing the bitmapped index technique. Bitmapped indexes are described later in this chapter.

The natural consequence of this approach is that many IS shops will keep two copies of their production databases: one in Third Normal Form for online transaction processing and another denormalized version of the database for decision support and data warehouse applications.

Populating STAR Schemas With Distributed SQL

Although it is evident at this point that having several copies of the same database can sometimes be desirable, problems arise with this dual approach when attempting to keep the STAR schema in sync with the operational database. Fortunately, Oracle provides several mechanisms to assist in this synchronization. It is safe to assume that the STAR schema will be used by executives for long-range trend analysis, so it is probably not imperative that the STAR schema be completely up-to-date with the operational database. Consequently, you can develop an asynchronous method for updating the STAR schema.

If you make this assumption, then a single SQL statement can be used to extract the data from the operational database and populate the new rows into the STAR schema. In Listing 10.1, it is assumed that the STAR schema resides at corporate headquarters in London. The table is called the **FACT_TABLE**.

Listing 10.1   Updating the STAR schema.

```
INSERT INTO FACT_TABLE@london
VALUES
(SELECT
    order_year,
    order_quarter,
    order_month,
    order_nbr,
    salerperson_name,
    customer_name,
    customer_city,
    customer_state,
    customer_region,
    item_nbr,
    quantity_sold,
    price*quantity_sold
FROM QUANTITY, ITEM, CUSTOMER, CITY, STATE
WHERE
QUANTITY.item_nbr = ITEM.item_nbr    /* join QUANTITY and ITEM */
AND
ITEM.cust_nbr = CUSTOMER.cust_nbr    /* join ITEM and CUSTOMER */
AND
CUSTOMER.city_name = CITY.city_name /* join CUSTOMER and CITY */
AND
CITY.state_name = STATE.state_name   /* join CITY and STATE */
AND
order_date = SYSDATE                 /* get only today's transactions */
);
```

This is a very simple method for achieving the extraction, normalization, and insertion of the operational data into the STAR schema. Specifying the **SYSDATE** in the **WHERE** clause ensures that only the day's transactions are extracted and loaded into the STAR schema **FACT_TABLE**. Of course, you are still undertaking a very large five-way table join, but hopefully this extraction would run during off hours, when the retrieval would not impact the production users.

Now, what about rows that have been deleted? While uncommon, you still need to account for the possibility that some orders might be canceled. You need a mechanism for updating the STAR schema to reflect deletions.

The most obvious method for removing deleted orders from the STAR schema is to create a **DELETE** trigger on the **ORDER** table of the operational system. This **DELETE** trigger will fire off a remote delete from the trigger to delete all rows from the STAR schema that are no longer valid. For example:

```
CREATE TRIGGER DELETE_ORDERS
    AFTER DELETE ON ORDER
AS
(DELETE FROM FACT_TABLE@london
    WHERE
    order_nbr = :del_ord
);
```

You now have a mechanism for keeping your data warehouse in relative synchronization with the operational database.

What are you going to do as the **FACT_TABLE** expands beyond normal table capacity? Let's assume that your organization processes 20,000 orders daily, leading to 7.3 million rows per year. With Oracle's efficient indexing, a table this large can create unique performance problems, primarily because the index must spawn many levels to properly index 7.3 million rows. Whereas a typical query might involve three index reads, a query against a 7-million-row table might involve five index reads before the target row is fetched.

To alleviate this problem, many designers partition their tables into smaller subtables, using the data as the distinguishing factor. As such, you might have a table for each month, with a name such as **FACT_TABLE_1_97**, **FACT_TABLE_2_97**, and so on.

Whenever you need to address multiple tables in a single operation, you can use the SQL **UNION ALL** verb to merge the tables together, as follows:

```
SELECT * FROM FACT_TABLE_1_97
UNION ALL
SELECT * FROM FACT_TABLE_2_97
UNION_ALL
SELECT * FROM FACT_TABLE_3_97
ORDER BY order_year, order_month;
```

In addition to having the benefit of smaller table indexes, this type of table partitioning combined with the UNION ALL statement has the added benefit of allowing Oracle's parallel query engine to simultaneously perform full-table scans on each of the subtables. In this case, a separate process would be invoked to process each of the three table scans. Oracle query manager would then gather the result data and sort according to the ORDER BY clause. In the preceding example, you could expect a 50 percent performance improvement over a query against a single FACT_TABLE. In addition, Oracle8 provides for automatic table partitioning, so Oracle8 developers can use table partitioning as described later in this chapter.

A STAR schema has now been defined and populated, and contains the **total_sales** for each order for each day. While it is easy to see the total for each order, rarely do the users of a decision support require this level of detail. Most managers would be more interested in knowing the sum of sales or units sold—aggregated by month, quarter, region, and so on.

Aggregation, Roll-Ups, And STAR Schemas

Even with a STAR schema, aggregation can be hard to compute at runtime with an acceptable response time. Essentially, you can either aggregate at runtime or preaggregate the data offline, making the totals available without realtime computation. One simple alternative to realtime aggregation is to write SQL to preaggregate the data according to the dimensions that the end user might want to see. In our example, let's assume that management wants to aggregate monthly sales by region, state, item type, and salesperson. You have four possible dimensions, so you can generate a list of the following six aggregate tables to precreate. Assume that all of the tables would have a **month_year** field as their primary key:

- *Region by state*—This table would have **region_name**, **state_name**, and **monthly_sales** as columns.

- *Region by item type*—This table would have **region_name**, **item_type**, and **monthly_sales** as columns.

- *Region by salesperson*—This table would have **region_name**, **salesperson_name**, and **monthly_sales** as columns.

- *State by item type*—This table would have **state_name**, **item_type**, and **monthly_sales** as columns.

- *State by salesperson*—This table would have **state_name**, **salesperson_name**, and **monthly_sales** as columns.

- *item type by salesperson*—This table would have **item_type**, **salesperson_name**, and **monthly_sales** as columns.

The SQL to produce these tables can be run easily as a batch task at end-of-month processing. For example, the SQL to create the **REGION_ITEM_TYPE** table might look like this:

```
INSERT INTO REGION_ITEM_TYPE
VALUES
(SELECT '3', '1997', region_name, item_type, monthly_sales)
FROM FACT_TABLE_3_97
GROUP BY region_name, item_type
);
```

The sample **REGION_ITEM_TYPE** table might look like the one in Table 10.3.

Table 10.3 A sample **REGION_ITEM_TYPE** table.

DATE	REGION	TYPE	MONTHLY_SALES
3/97	WEST	Clothes	$113,999
3/97	WEST	Hardware	$56,335
3/97	WEST	Food	$23,574
3/97	EAST	Clothes	$45,234
3/97	EAST	Hardware	$66,182
3/97	EAST	Food	$835,342
3/97	SOUTH	Clothes	$1,223
3/97	SOUTH	Hardware	$56,392
3/97	SOUTH	Food	$9,281
3/97	NORTH	Clothes	$826,463
3/97	NORTH	Hardware	$77,261
3/97	NORTH	Food	$43,383

These aggregate tables can be built in the middle of the night if need be—right after the master fact tables have been populated with the day's sales. The next morning, the prior day's sales will have been rolled up into these summaries, giving management an accurate, fast, and easy-to-use tool for decision support.

Of course, these tables are two-dimensional, but they can easily be massaged by an application to provide a tabular representation of the variables. Table 10.4 presents this tabular form.

> **Note:** This technique replicates the functionality of a multidimensional database where an end user can specify the axis of interest and the multidimensional database (MDDB) will build a tabular representation of the data.

But, what if management wants to look at quarterly summaries instead of monthly summaries? What about yearly summaries? Of course, this same technique can be used to roll up the monthly summary tables into quarterly summaries, yearly summaries, and so on, according to the demands of the end user.

Now that we see how multidimensional data representation functions within a relational database, let's explore the role of Online Analytical Processing (OLAP).

History Of OLAP

Dr. E. F. (Ted) Codd first coined the term *OLAP* in a 1993 report that was sponsored by Arbor Software. In addition to coining the term, Codd also created specific rules for OLAP, but no OLAP vendor has ever created a product that has met all of Codd's criteria for OLAP. In the 1970s, Dr. Codd also developed a set of rules for

Table 10.4   REGION versus TYPE.

	Clothes	Food	Hardware
WEST	$113,999	$23,574	$56,335
EAST	$45,234	$835,342	$66,182
NORTH	$826,463	$43,383	$77,261
SOUTH	$1,223	$9,281	$56,392

relational databases, and while interesting, no single relational database vendor has ever met all of Codd's relational rules. Despite the claim that OLAP is a new technology, some offerings such as IRI date to the early 1970s.

 The Internet offers a popular newsgroup forum that discusses OLAP issues. It is called comp.database.olap.

Now that we have a historical perspective of OLAP, we can take a look at how we can easily use a relational database to simulate cubic data representation.

Simulation Of Cubic Databases

For an illustrative example, consider the sample customer table in Table 10.5. Assume that this table is physically stored in data order. You can imagine how this data might look as a cubic table by reviewing Figure 10.8.

Of course, the cubic representation requires that the data be loaded into a multidimensional database or a spreadsheet that supports pivot tables. When considering an MDDB, two arguments emerge. The relational database vendors point out that MDDBs are proprietary—they feel that the more open relational databases should be used. The MDDB vendors point out some serious inadequacies with SQL that make it very difficult to use a relational database.

Keep in mind that dimensions can be hierarchical in nature, adding further confusion. A time dimension, for example, can be represented as a hierarchy with **year**,

Table 10.5 A sample customer table.

Customer Name	# Sales	YY-MM	City	State
Bob Papaj & Assoc.	300	91-01	NY	NY
Mark Reulbach Inc.	400	91-01	San Fran	CA
Rick Willoughby Co.	120	91-02	NY	NY
Kelvin Connor Co.	300	91-02	San Fran	CA
Jame Gaston Inc.	145	91-03	NY	NY
Linda O'Dell Assoc.	337	91-03	Fairport	NY
Rick Wahl & Assoc.	134	91-03	San Fran	CA

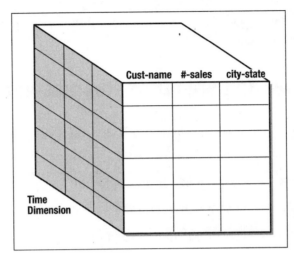

Figure 10.8

Cubic representation of relational data.

quarter, **month**, and **day**. Each of these "levels" in the dimension hierarchy can have its own values. In other words, a cubic representation with **time** as a dimension can be viewed in two ways:

- As a series of cubes, one for **year**, another for **quarter**, and another with **full_date**

- As a five-dimension table

MDDBs are most commonly used with data that is a natural fit for pivot tables, and it should come as no surprise that most MDDB sites are used with finance and marketing applications. Unfortunately, most multidimensional databases do not scale up well for warehouse applications. For example, the largest supported database for Essbase is about 20GB, whereas data warehouses with sizes measured in terabytes are not uncommon.

It is important to note that defining aggregation of a multidimensional database is no different than defining aggregate tables to a relational database. At load time, the database will still need to compute the aggregate values. MDDBs also employ the concept of sparse data. Because data is aggregated and presliced, some cells on a cube might not contain data. For example, consider a cube that tracks sales of items across a large company. The cells representing sales of thermal underwear would be null for Hawaii, while the sales of surfboards in Wyoming would also be null. Nearly all of the product offerings are able to maintain a mechanism for compressing out these types of null values.

Alternatives To Cubic Data Representation

Many traditional database designs can be used to simulate a data cube. One alternative to the cubic representation would be to leave the table in linear form, using SQL to join the table against itself to produce a result, as shown in Figure 10.9.

Let's take a look at a query that might require the self-joining of a table:

- Show all customers in Hawaii who purchased products more than 500 times.

- Show all customers in L.A. who purchase less than 10 times/month.

- Show all large customers (buying more than 100 items per month) in Alaska whose usage dropped more than 10 percent in 1996.

- Show all customers in New York whose usage in March of 1996 deviated more than 20 percent from their usage in March of 1997.

- Show all customers in California where the company name contains "Widget" and usage has dropped more than 20 percent in 1997.

In this example, you compare all user sites where usage of your product has experienced a negative usage variance of greater than 5 percent. A subset of this data can

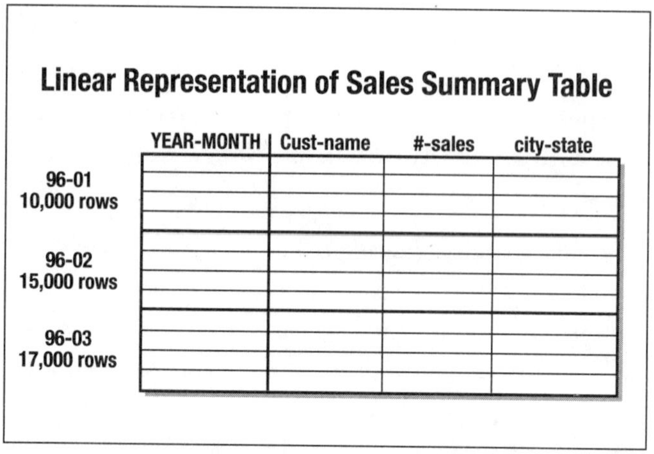

Figure 10.9
Joining a relational table against itself.

easily be extracted such that only California sites with more than 100 uses per month are displayed. For display, the user chose percentage variance, number of requests, site number, ZIP code, and city. Note the sort order of the report—it is sorted first by ZIP code, followed by city, and then by percentage variance within city:

```
SELECT integer
((((E.number_of_sales - S.number_of_sales) / S.number_of_sales) * 100) ,
E.customer_name , E.city_name , E.zip , S.number_of_sales ,
    E.number_of_sales

FROM DETAIL S , DETAIL E

WHERE
S.customer_name = E.customer_name
 AND
E.state_abbr = 'CA'
 AND
E.date_yymm = 9601
 AND
S.date_yymm = 9701
 AND
E.number_of_sales < S.number_of_sales - (.05 * S.number_of_sales)

ORDER BY E.zip asc , E.city_name asc , 1 ;
```

As you can see, the variance analysis is done directly in the SQL statement. This case displays California users whose usage has dropped by more than 5 percent (comparing January 1996 to January 1997).

But, what if a user wants to compare one full year with another year? The table is structured for simple comparison of two specific month dates, but the SQL query could be modified slightly to aggregate the data, offering comparison of two ranges of dates.

The query shown in Listing 10.2 will aggregate all sales for an entire year and compare 1996 with 1997. Here, you can meet the request "Show me all customers in California whose sales have dropped by more than 5 percent between 1996 and 1997."

Listing 10.2 Aggregating sales for an entire year.

```
SELECT integer
((((E.number_of_sales - S.number_of_sales) / S.number_of_sales) * 100) ,
```

```
E.customer_name , E.city_name , E.zip , S.number_of_sales ,
    E.number_of_sales

FROM DETAIL S , DETAIL E

WHERE
S.customer_name = E.customer_name
 AND
E.state_abbr = 'CA'
 AND
substr(E.date_yymm,1,2) = '96'
 AND
substr(S.date_yymm,1,2) = '97'
 AND
E.number_of_sales < S.number_of_sales - (.05 * S.number_of_sales)

ORDER BY E.zip asc , E.city_name asc , 1 ;
```

On the surface, it appears that SQL can be used against two-dimensional tables to handle three-dimensional time-series problems. It also appears that SQL can be used to roll up aggregations at runtime, alleviating the need to do a roll up at load time, as with a traditional database. While this implementation does not require any special multidimensional databases, two important issues need to be resolved:

- *Performance*—Joining a table against itself—especially when comparing ranges of dates—can create many levels of nesting in the SQL optimization and poor response time.

- *Ability*—Few end users would be capable of formulating this type of sophisticated SQL query.

If one strips away the marketing hype and industry jargon, you can see that a data warehouse and a multidimensional database can be easily simulated by pre-creating many redundant tables, each with precalculated roll-up information. In fact, the base issue is clear. Complex aggregation needs to be computed at runtime—or when the data is loaded.

There are many different types of OLAP and MDDB products on the market today, as shown in Table 10.6. Each has its own relative advantages and disadvantages, and they are all fighting to achieve recognition for their strengths.

Table 10.6   OLAP/MDDB product information.

Vendor	Tool	Description
Oracle	Express	Excel spreadsheet extension, true OO
Oracle	Oracle 7.3	STAR query hints, parallel query, bitmap indexes
MicroStrategy	DSS Agent	MDDB queries against RDBMS
D&B Pilot Software	Pilot LightShip	OLAP w/custom and spreadsheet GUI
IBI	FOCUS Fusion	MDDB engine
VMARK	UniVerse	NT-based MDDB engine
Kenan	Acumate ES	MDDB with PC-OLAP GUI
Arbor	OLAP Builder	Extracts data from DW for Essbase
Arbor	Essbase	MDDB engine w/Excel spreadsheet GUI
Think Systems	FYI Planner	PC-GUI with MDDB and OLAP server

The recent interest in data warehousing has created many new techniques and tools for getting useful information out of these behemoth databases. Data mining is one area that holds a great deal of promise for users of data warehouses.

Data Mining And OLAP

In traditional decision support systems, the user was charged with formulating queries against the database and deciphering any trends that were present in the data. Unfortunately, this approach is only as good as the user of the system, and many statistically valid associations between data items can be missed. This is especially true in data warehouse systems where unobtrusive trends can be present. For example, the Psychology Department at the University of Minnesota—developers of the hugely popular Minnesota Multiphasic Personality Inventory (MMPI)—have discovered some startling patterns correlating a psychological diagnosis to seemingly unrelated, ordinary questions. The results provide unobtrusive measures for human personality. For example, they found that people with low self-esteem tend to prefer baths to showers. While no "reason" for this preference is obvious, the statistically valid correlation between self-concept and cleaning preferences remains.

These types of unobtrusive trends also plague the business world, and it is the goal of data mining software to identify these trends for warehouse users. In addition to simply identifying trends, some data mining software goes one step further in an attempt to analyze other data and determine the underlying reasons for the trend.

While basic statistical tools are adequate for doing correlations between a small number of related variables, large databases with hundreds of data items are quickly bogged down in a mire of multivariate chi-square techniques that are hard to follow for even the most experienced statisticians. As such, the new data mining tools are meant to accept only general hints from the users, and then go forth into the data probing for trends.

In other cases, data mining techniques are used to prove a hypothesis based on existing data. For example, a marketing person might speculate that those with an income between $50,000 and $80,000 are likely to buy a particular product. A quick verification of this hypothesis can be run, thereby confirming or disproving the hypothesis.

Yet another class of tools uses a relatively straightforward exception detection mechanism to cruise the database looking for unexpected trends or unusual patterns. Many data mining tools use techniques borrowed from Artificial Intelligence (AI), including fuzzy logic, neural networks, fractals, and a sundry of other statistical techniques. Many of these tools perform a huge amount of internal processing, so many of them read selected information from the relational database into a proprietary, internal data representation for analysis. No widely used data mining tools are available that run directly against the relational database, although there are several promising start-up companies, as shown in Table 10.7.

While there is still a great deal of interest in data mining applications, no single vendor has stepped up to claim market leadership. It will probably be many years before all owners of a data warehouse have tools that will be able to fully exploit their data resources.

While data mining and data warehousing are very popular buzzwords, there is still a great deal that can be done to support Oracle data warehousing without buying expensive third-party products. The following sections looks at Oracle's data warehouse features.

Table 10.7 Data mining product information.

Vendor	Tool	Description
Thinking Machines	Darwin	Neural nets
MIT GmbH	DataEngine	Fuzzy logic
Reduct & Lobbe Technologies	DataLogic	Fuzzy sets
IBM	Data Mining Toolkit	Fuzzy logic
Epsilon	Epsilon	Rule-based
Cross/Z	F-DBMS	Fractals
Info. Discovery	IDIS	Rule-based
Info. Harvester	InfoHarvester	Rule-based
Angoss Software	KnowledgeSEEKER	Rule-based
Software AG	NETMAP	Neural networks
NeuralWare	NeuralWorks	Neural nets
Nestor	PRISM	Neural nets
Cognitive Systems	ReMind	Inductive logic

Oracle Data Warehouse Features

Features of Oracle introduced with version 7.2 and above will not be activated unless the following init.ora parameter has been set:

```
COMPATIBILITY=8.0.0.0.0
```

With Oracle version 7.3 and above, several new features (presented in the upcoming sections) can dramatically improve performance of Oracle data warehouse and decision support systems.

Parallel Query For Data Warehouses

It is a common misconception that parallel processors (SMP or MPP) are necessary to use and benefit from parallel processing. Even on the same processor, multiple processes can be used to speed up queries. Data warehouses generally employ parallel technology to perform warehouse loading and query functions. These include:

- *Parallel backup/recovery*—Some parallel tools are capable of rates in excess of 40GB/hour.

- *Parallel query (SMP and MPP)*—Multiple processes are used to retrieve table data.

- *Parallel loading*—Multiple processes are used to simultaneously load many tables.

- *Parallel indexing*—Multiple processes are used to create indexes.

For parallel query, the most powerful approach deals with the use of the SQL **UNION** verb in very large databases (VLDBs). In most very large Oracle data warehouses, it is common to logically partition a single table into many smaller tables in order to improve query throughput. For example, a sales table that is ordered by **date_of_sale** can be partitioned into **1997_SALES**, **1998_SALES**, and **1999_SALES** tables. This approach is often used in data warehouse applications where a single logical table might have millions of rows. While this splitting of a table according to a key value violates normalization, it can dramatically improve performance for individual queries. For large queries that can span many logical tables, the isolated tables can be reassembled easily using Oracle's parallel query facility, as shown here:

```
CREATE VIEW ALL_SALES AS
    SELECT * FROM 1997_SALES
    UNION ALL
    SELECT * FROM 1998_SALES
    UNION ALL
    SELECT * FROM 1999_SALES;
```

You can now query the **ALL_SALES** view as if it were a single database table. Oracle parallel query will automatically recognize the **UNION ALL** parameter, firing off simultaneous queries against each of the three base tables. For example, the following query will assemble the requested data from the three tables in parallel, with each query being separately optimized. The result set from each subquery is then merged by the query manager, as follows:

```
SELECT customer_name
FROM ALL_SALES
WHERE
sales_amount > 5000;
```

We'll discuss Oracle's parallel query features later in this book. In addition, for more details on using Oracle's parallel query facility, refer to Chapter 3, *Physical Performance Design.*

Now that we have seen how SQL can be used to improve performance, let's take a look at how Oracle's STAR query hints can greatly improve the speed of certain types of queries.

STAR Query Hints And STAR Joins With Oracle

The STAR schema design involves creating a main fact table that contains the primary keys in the related tables. This massive denormalization of the database structure means that just about any query against the STAR schema is going to involve the joining of many large tables—including a large fact table and many smaller reference tables. With this new optimization, data warehouse queries can run at blistering speeds, in some cases dozens of times faster than the original query.

The STAR query featured with the release of Oracle7.3 detects STAR query joins and invokes a special procedure to improve performance of the query. Prior to the release of Oracle7.3, this feature only worked with up to five tables, but this restriction has been eliminated. Also, release 7.3 (and above) no longer require the use of STAR query hints. However, hints are still allowed in the SQL syntax and are generally a good idea for documentation purposes. With the Oracle8 implementation of STAR query joins, the STAR query requires a single concatenated index to reside in the fact table for all keys. To invoke the STAR query path, the following characteristics must be present:

- There must be at least three tables being joined, with one large fact table and several smaller dimension tables.

- There must be a concatenated index on the fact table with at least three columns, one for each of the table join keys.

- You must verify with an explain plan that the **NESTED LOOPS** operation is being used to perform the join.

Oracle follows a simple procedure for processing STAR queries. Oracle will first service the queries against the smaller dimension tables, combining the result set into a Cartesian product table that is held in Oracle memory. This virtual table will contain the columns from all of the participating dimension tables. The primary key for this virtual table will be a composite of the keys for the dimension tables. If this key matches the composite index on the fact table, then the query will be able to process very quickly. Once the sum of the reference tables has been addressed, Oracle will perform a nested-loop join of the intermediate table against the fact table. This approach is far faster than the traditional method of joining the smallest reference table against the fact table and then joining each of the other reference tables against the intermediate table. The speed is a result of reducing the physical I/O. The indexes are read to gather the virtual table in memory, and the fact table will not be accessed until the virtual index has everything it requires to go directly to the requested rows via the composite index on the fact table (see Figure 10.10).

TIP *The STAR query can be very tricky to implement, and careful consideration must be given to the proper placement of indexes. Each dimension table must have an index on the join key, and the large fact table must have a composite*

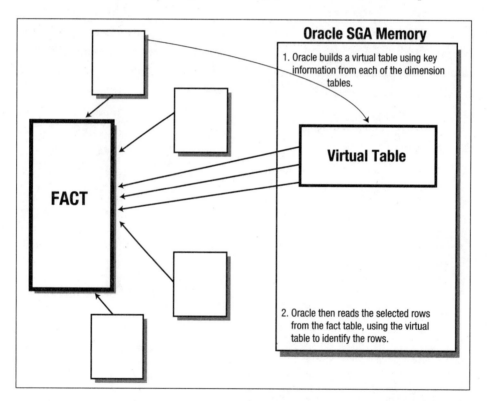

Figure 10.10
Oracle STAR query processing.

index consisting of all of the join keys from all of the dimension tables. In addi-
tion, the sequencing of the keys in the fact table composite index must be in the
correct order, or Oracle will not be able to use the index to service the query.

Now that we see how STAR query joins function within Oracle8, let's look at one of
the most exciting Oracle8 features, the bitmapped index.

Using Oracle's Bitmapped Indexes

For data warehouse applications that must elicit as much performance as possible,
some special situations can arise where Oracle bitmapped indexes can be useful. As
you know, the sheer volume of rows in very large tables can make even a trivial query
run for a long time. Oracle introduced bitmapped indexes with release 7.3 in an
attempt to improve index lookup performance for queries, especially decision support type queries that can have many conditions in the **WHERE** clause. In Oracle8,
bitmapped indexes continue to make performance improvements, and they are stable
enough to run in production applications.

The bitmap approach to indexing is very different from the traditional b-tree style of
indexes. In a traditional index, the index keys are sorted and carried in several tree
nodes. In a bitmapped index, an array is created. This array has all possible index
values as one axis, while the other axis contains all rows in the base table. For example, consider a bitmapped index on the **region** field of the **SALES** table, where
the regions are **North**, **South**, **East**, and **West**. If the **SALES** table contains 1 million
rows, the bitmapped index would create an array of 4×1 billion to store the possible
key values.

Within this array, the index data is binary. If a value is **TRUE**, it is assigned a binary
1—a **FALSE** reading is set to binary **0** (see Figure 10.11).

In Figure 10.11, you can see how this query runs faster than a traditional query. The
Oracle optimizer will notice that the items in the **WHERE** clause have bitmapped
indexes, scan for non-zero values in the proper array column, and quickly return the
row ID of the columns. A fast merge of the result set will then quickly identify the
rows that meet the query criteria.

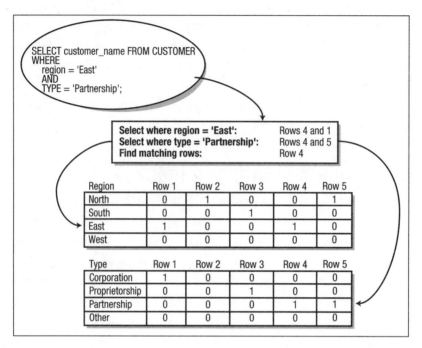

Figure 10.11
An Oracle bitmapped index.

While it might appear that the index is very large, Oracle has developed a compression method whereby all of the binary zeros are omitted from the bitmap. This makes it very compact.

While this might look reasonable at first glance, some drawbacks to bitmapped indexing have to be considered. The first and most obvious is that bitmapped indexes work best for columns that only have a small amount of possible values. For columns that have many values, such as **state_name** or **city_name**, the index overhead would probably exceed any performance gains that might accrue from using bitmapped indexes.

However, for columns such as **sex**, **color**, and **size** that have a small number of finite values, bitmapped indexes will greatly improve query retrieval speeds. Bitmapped indexes are especially useful for decision support systems where many conditions are combined to a single **WHERE** clause.

Oracle provides another method for speeding up decision support and warehouse queries. This method, also first introduced with Oracle7.3, is called the *hash-join*.

Using Oracle Hash-Joins

A hash-join is a technique where Oracle bypasses the traditional sort-merge join technique and replaces it with an algorithm that performs a full-table scan, placing the rows into memory partitions. Partition pairs that do not fit into memory are placed in the **TEMP** tablespace. Oracle will then build a hash table on the smallest partition, using the larger partition to probe the newly created hash table. This technique alleviates the need for in-memory sorting and does not require indexes to exist on the target tables.

The following init.ora parameters must be set to use hash-joins:

- **optimizer_mode=COST**

- **hash_join_enabled=TRUE**

- **hash_multiblock_io_count=TRUE**

- **hash_area_size=SIZE**

To execute a hash-join, the hash-join hint must be used. Consider this example:

```
SELECT /* USE_HASH */
FROM CUSTOMER, ORDER
WHERE
CUSTOMER.cust_no = ORDER.cust_no
AND
credit_rating = 'GOOD';
************************************************************
```

The **USE_HASH** hint directs the Oracle8 optimizer to use a hash-join to service this query. Now that we have reviewed the basics of hash-joins, let's turn our attention to the new features that were introduced with Oracle release 8.0.

Using Oracle8's New Features

The new Oracle8 architecture focuses primarily on the introduction of objects into the relational model and there are only a few new features that directly address data warehousing. The new features for data warehouses in Oracle8 fall into the following three categories:

- *Table and Index Partitioning*—Rather than manually splitting tables into horizontal partitions by date, Oracle8 provides a method for creating partitioned tables and indexes. This new feature allows a set of partitioned tables and indexes to function as a single entity, thereby providing better manageability.

- *New Parallel Operations*—Oracle8 allows for parallel DML and parallel index scans, and provides for parallelism within the new partitioned table and index structures.

- *Improved Join Optimization*—The join optimizer has been altered to allow faster joins when utilizing partitioned tables and indexes. This improvement cuts down the overhead involved when joining large partitioned tables. Of course, this is entirely transparent to the Oracle professional, and there is nothing needed to turn on this feature.

In the upcoming sections, we'll take a detailed look at table and index partitioning, as well as the new parallel operations in Oracle8.

Table And Index Partitioning

The ability to partition tables and indexes will have a very positive impact on managers of Oracle data warehouses, or any Oracle database that requires very large tables. The partitioning of tables and indexes will allow DBAs to enhance the availability of databases by making structural maintenance simpler. In addition, Oracle databases will perform faster because the Oracle engine will recognize partitions and only query the partitions required to service a query.

Increased Availability With Partitioning

Because table and index partitions exist as separate physical entities within the Oracle database, they can be maintained independently without affecting the availability of the other partitions. (See Figure 10.12.)

In any large Oracle8 database, there are many times when this partitioning feature will be extremely useful. As we discussed, most large Oracle8 databases are far too

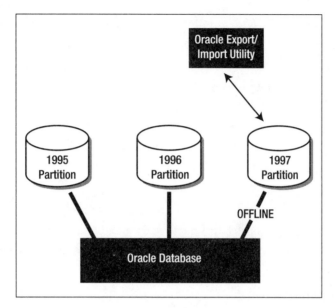

Figure 10.12
Partitions can be brought offline for maintenance.

big for a complete, periodic reorganization, and there are specific times when tables and indexes require rebuilding. These conditions include:

- *Disk failures*—When a disk crashes, the object partition can be taken offline, restored, and rolled forward without impacting the availability of the other partitions.

- *Backup of objects*—With object partitioning, portions of tables and indexes can be backed up without affecting the availability of the other partitions.

- *Tables with too many chained rows*—Sometimes a data warehouse table can be initially loaded with **NULL varchar** columns that are later updated to insert expanded values. When this occurs, the rows can fragment into other data blocks, requiring additional I/O to access the rows. To detect this condition, run the chain.sql script found on the CD-ROM.

- *Tables approaching maximum extents*—In tables with a finite number of extents, the insertion of new rows will cause a table to extend. While table extending is not a problem, if the table approaches its maximum values for extents, new rows will not be allowed into the table until it has been exported and imported into a single extent.

- *Static tables with **PCTFREE** set too high*—Because data warehouses are data sensitive, it is common to see a "rolling" effect, where the most current partition of a table gets heavy updates. As this partition becomes older, it is no longer updated, and space can be reclaimed by exporting the partition and re-creating it with smaller **PCTFREE** values, thereby packing the rows onto the data blocks and saving significant disk space. Sometimes, the data warehouse DBA might also want to migrate these partitions onto read-only tablespaces on CD-ROM while the current partition remains in an updatable tablespace.

- *Indexes that have too many deleted leaf blocks*—Oracle data warehouse indexes can become unbalanced if there are too many deleted leaf blocks within the index. When this happens the Oracle warehouse DBA will want to drop and re-create the index. For a script to detect this condition, see the id1.sql script on the CD-ROM.

- *Indexes with more than four levels*—With heavy update activity, it is not uncommon to see a data warehouse index spawn to deeper levels in certain spots within the index. When this happens, the data warehouse DBA will want to drop and re-create the index, thereby balancing the levels. For a script to detect this condition, see the index.sql script on the CD-ROM.

- *Base-table indexes are not clustered with the base table*—In Oracle, it is possible to have one index that is physically sequenced in the same order as the table. As rows are added onto the end of the table, the index will become less clustered. In these cases, the Oracle DBA will extract and sort the table, and then replace it and rebuild the clustered index.

With table partitioning, some automatic clustering of the data with the index will take place automatically because new table rows will be directed to the partition that contains similar partition values. However, clustering within the partition can get out of synchronization when too many rows are added to the end of the partition.

When any of these conditions occur, a DBA can take the offending partition offline, rebuild the object, and reintroduce it into the data warehouse with minimal service interruption.

Increased Performance With Partitioning

As mentioned, the Oracle8 architecture allows for the physical segregation of table and index partitions. The Oracle8 engine takes advantage of this in several ways:

- *Query optimization*—The Oracle8 optimizer can detect the values within each partition and access the partitions necessary to service the query. Because each partition can be defined with its own storage parameters, the Oracle8 SQL optimizer can choose a different optimization plan for each partition.

- *Load balancing*—Table and index partitioning allows the Oracle data warehouse DBA to segregate portions of very large tables and indexes onto separate disk devices, thereby improving disk I/O throughput and ensuring maximum performance.

- *Parallel Query*—The partitioning of objects also greatly improves the performance of parallel query. When Oracle8 detects that a query is going to span several partitions, such as a full-table scan, Oracle can fire off parallel processes, each of which will independently retrieve data from each partition. This feature is especially important for indexes because parallel queries will not need to share a single index.

Now that we have reviewed the compelling reasons for using partitioning with Oracle tables and indexes, let's take a more in-depth look at how table partitioning and index partitioning are implemented within the Oracle8 architecture.

Table Partitioning With Oracle8

As discussed earlier, the concept of table partitioning can greatly improve the manageability of very large data warehouse tables. Now, Oracle8 provides a method to automatically partition tables in a horizontal fashion at table creation time. (See Figure 10.13.)

While, at first glance, this might seem to be a simple method of chunking tables, Oracle has also included the ability for each partition to have its own values for **PCTFREE**, **PCTUSED**, **INITTRANS**, and **MAXTRANS**. This feature can be especially useful when a table is partitioned such that only the most recent partition is updated. In this case, the earlier partitions would have **PCTUSED** set to **100** and

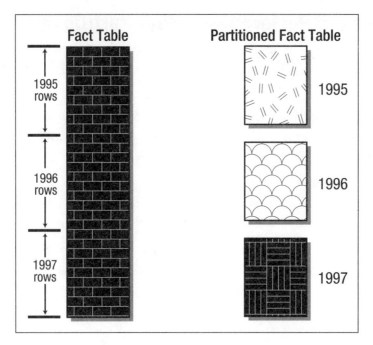

Figure 10.13
Horizontal partitioning of tables.

PCTFREE set to **0**. By allowing control over the partitions as if they are separate tables, a DBA can "pack" static data into the Oracle blocks and save space. The current partition would have **PCTFREE** set to a higher number to allow for row expansion as the rows are updated.

Partitioning Syntax

The process of creating a partitioned table with Oracle8 is very straightforward. For example, if you have a table called **ALL_FACTS**, you would first need to choose a partition key for the operation. A partition key is generally a date value and specifies the range of rows that will participate in each partition. For some data warehouse applications, the partition key could be a non-date value, such as when an employee table is partitioned according to the value of each employee's department column. Listing 10.3 shows the SQL used to create a table partition in Oracle8.

Listing 10.3 A partitioned table definition for Oracle8.

```
CREATE TABLE ALL_FACTS
(
    order_date                  date,
    order_year                  number(2),
    order_quarter               char(2),
    order_month,                number(2),
    order_nbr                   number(5),
    salerperson_name            varchar(20),
    customer_name               varchar(20),
    customer_city               varchar(20),
    customer_state              varchar(2),
    customer_region             char(1),
    item_nbr                    number(5),
    quantity_sold               number(4)
)
PARTITION BY RANGE
    (order_date)
(
PARTITION
    year_1995
    VALUES LESS THAN '01-JAN-1996'
    TABLESPACE year_1995
    STORAGE (INITIAL 500M, NEXT 5M, PCTUSED 99, PCTFREE 1),
PARTITION
    year_1996
    VALUES LESS THAN '01-JAN-1997'
    TABLESPACE year_1996
    STORAGE (INITIAL 500M, NEXT 5M, PCTUSED 99, PCTFREE 1),
PARTITION
    year_1997
    VALUES LESS THAN (MAXVALUE)
    TABLESPACE year_1997
    STORAGE (INITIAL 500M, NEXT 50M, PCTUSED 60, PCTFREE 40),
);
```

Let's review this syntax. Each table partition is defined as having the **order_date** column as the partition key, and you can see that the **VALUES LESS THAN** parameter determines which rows are partitioned into which tablespace. Note that the last partition (**year_1997**) specifies **VALUES LESS THAN (MAXVALUE)**, which means that all other rows that do not meet the selection criteria will be placed into this partition. Also, note that even though the selection parameters for the **year_1996** partition reads **VALUES LESS THAN 1996**, the 1995 rows will not be stored into the **year_1996** partition because the value check is preceded by the filter for the **year_1995** partition.

In addition, each partition has been created with different tablespace storage parameters, and it appears in this example that only the last partition will be updated, as evidenced by the value of the **PCTFREE** parameter in the **year_1997** tablespace. At SQL **INSERT** time, the DDL is consulted, and the value specified in **order_date** determines which partition the rows are stored in within the table.

This partitioning of tables also allows each partition to be referenced as a unique entity, thereby saving resources within the database. For example, you can still query the entire table as a whole, like this:

```
SELECT sum( quantity_sold)
FROM ALL_FACTS
WHERE
order_year = 97
AND
customer_city = 'Albuquerque';
```

However, it would be simpler and less resource intensive to rework this query to implicitly specify the target partition in the query, as follows:

```
SELECT sum( quantity_sold)
FROM ALL_FACTS PARTITION (year_1997)
WHERE
order_year = 97
AND
customer_city = 'Albuquerque';
```

In the same fashion, partitions can be used to limit update statements to a single partition. For example, if you have a huge employee table partitioned by department, you could give a 10 percent raise to the MIS department, as follows:

```
UPDATE ALL_EMPLOYEE PARTITION ('MIS')
SET
    salary = salary*1.1;
```

Now that we have a feel for how partitioned tables are defined within Oracle8, let's move on to take a look at how we can migrate Oracle7 tables into a partitioned structure.

Migration Into Partitioned Table Structures

Migration into partitioned tables is very simple using Oracle8. If you look at the sample table definition in Listing 10.3, you can easily migrate the data from an old Oracle7 fact table into the new partitioned structure, as follows:

```
INSERT INTO ALL_FACT PARTITION (year_1995)
(
SELECT * FROM OLD_FACT
WHERE
order_year = 95
);

INSERT INTO ALL_FACT PARTITION (year_1996)
(
SELECT * FROM OLD_FACT
WHERE
order_year = 96
);

INSERT INTO ALL_FACT PARTITION (year_1997)
(
SELECT * FROM OLD_FACT
WHERE
order_year = 97
);
```

> **Note:** In the preceding example, the **WHERE** clause is redundant. The partition definition will automatically filter out the rows that do not match the selection criteria for each partition.

Now that you understand how Oracle tables can be partitioned, let's take a look at how Oracle indexes can be partitioned. In many ways, the ability to partition Oracle indexes has more performance potential than table partitioning because indexes are a common source of contention within Oracle data warehouses.

Index Partitioning With Oracle8

In addition to a nonpartitioned index, Oracle8 allows for two methods for the partitioning of indexes. The first partitioned index method is called a local partition. A local partitioned index creates a one-for-one match between the indexes and the partitions in the table. Of course, the key value for the table partition and the value for the local index must be identical. The second method is called global and allows the index to have any number of partitions.

The partitioning of the indexes is transparent to the SQL, but the Oracle8 query engine will only scan the index partition that is required to service the query. In addition, the Oracle8 parallel query engine will sense that the index is partitioned and fire simultaneous queries to scan the indexes.

Local Partitioned Indexes

In a local partitioned index, the key values and number of index partitions will exactly match the number of partitions in the base table. Of course, it follows that there can be only one local partitioned index for each table. This is generally done to allow the DBA to take individual partitions of a table and indexes offline for maintenance without affecting the other partitions in the table:

```
CREATE INDEX year_idx
  ON ALL_FACT (order_date)
LOCAL
    (PARTITION name_idx1),
    (PARTITION name_idx2),
    (PARTITION name_idx3);
```

Oracle will automatically use equal partitioning of an index based on the number of partitions in the indexed table. For example, if in the preceding definition you created four indexes on **ALL_FACT**, the **CREATE INDEX** would fail because the partitions do not match. This equi-partition also makes index maintenance easier because a single partition can be taken offline and the index re-built without affecting the other partitions in the table.

Global Partitioned Indexes

A global partitioned index is used for all other indexes except the one used as the table partition key. A global index partitions OLTP applications such that fewer index probes are required than if the OLTP application used local partitioned indexes. In the global index partitioning scheme, the index is harder to maintain because the index can span partitions in the base table. (See Figure 10.14.) For example, when a table partition is dropped as part of a reorganization, the entire global index will be affected. When defining a global partitioned index, the DBA has the complete freedom to specify as many partitions for the index as they desire.

Now that you understand the concept of global partitions, let's examine the Oracle **CREATE INDEX** syntax for a globally partitioned index. For example:

```
CREATE INDEX item_idx
  on ALL_FACT (item_nbr)
GLOBAL
    (PARTITION city_idx1 VALUES LESS THAN (100)),
    (PARTITION city_idx1 VALUES LESS THAN (200)),
    (PARTITION city_idx1 VALUES LESS THAN (300)),
    (PARTITION city_idx1 VALUES LESS THAN (400)),
    (PARTITION city_idx1 VALUES LESS THAN (500));
```

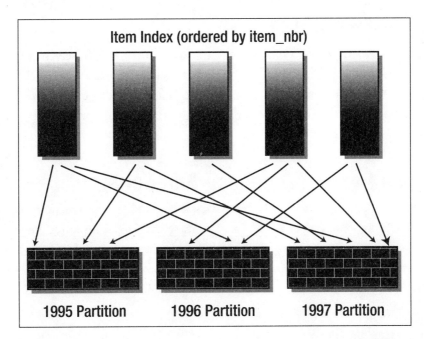

Figure 10.14
A global partitioned index.

Here, you can see that the item index has been defined with five partitions, each containing a subset of the index range values. Note that it is irrelevant that the base table is in three partitions. In fact, it is acceptable to create a global partitioned index on a table that does not have any partitioning.

These new Oracle8 data warehouse features continue to underscore Oracle Corporation's commitment to supporting very large data warehouse architectures. It will be very exciting to see how these features continue to improve in Oracle8.2, when some of the object-oriented features will be available for the data warehouse. Especially exciting will be the support for class hierarchies and inheritance because these features will greatly improve the ability of the Oracle data warehouse designer to implement ad hoc classifications of data attributes.

This concludes our discussion of Oracle8's approach to table and index partitioning. Now, let's move on to the next area of Oracle8's data warehouse advancements—parallel operations.

Parallel Operations

Oracle8's parallel operations incorporate parallel databases, parallel servers, and parallel queries. We'll begin our discussion with a review of Oracle8's Parallel Server (OPS). Then, we'll move on to take a look at Oracle's parallel query capabilities. Parallel query is very different from parallel server, and the following sections will explain the distinction.

Oracle Parallel Database And Server

In general, a *parallel database* is defined as a database that has several memory regions that share a common disk drive. Within Oracle, several Oracle instances run within RAM memory, and each independent instance shares access to the same Oracle tables. Within the Oracle parallel server, this is called the *shared-nothing parallel server configuration.* Figure 10.15 shows a shared-nothing parallel server configuration.

Oracle also supports symmetric multiprocessing (SMP) configurations where a single host contains multiple processors (see Figure 10.16). In SMP configurations, you can see that the multiple processors will provide concurrent processing, but that all

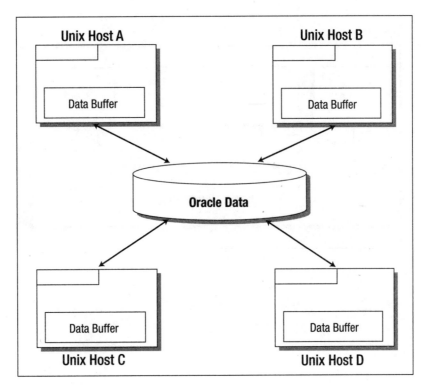

Figure 10.15
A shared-nothing parallel server configuration.

of the processors must share a common buffer pool. In short, a symmetric multiprocessor configuration is a configuration where a number of processors share common memory and disk resources.

There is a great deal of confusion about the difference between Oracle's parallel server and parallel query. While Oracle's parallel query can be used with any computer configuration (including standalone processors, SMP, or MPP), Oracle's parallel server can only be used on MPP systems. As you may know, MPPs are systems where a number of independent nodes, each with its own memory, share a common disk resource. As such, SMP is sometimes called shared memory multiprocessing and MPP is called shared-nothing multiprocessing. Examples of SMP processors include IBM SP2 and the IBM SP3, which contains eight processors. In parallel server parlance, a processor is called a *node*.

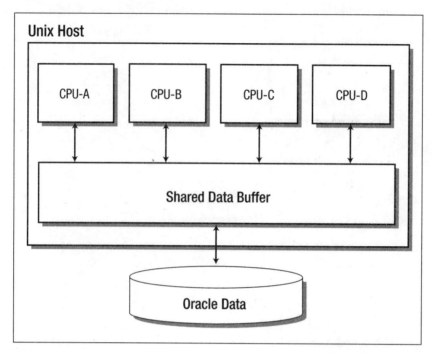

Figure 10.16
A shared memory SMP configuration.

Oracle parallel server only works with MPP because each node on the MPP box requires its own memory area for the Oracle SGA. To illustrate, consider the example shown earlier in Figure 10.15. There, you can see that a four-processor system has been configured to share a common data resource. As such, any user, on any node, will get a complete view of the entire database. For example, user **Scott** could log in to node one and create a public access table called **TIGER**. Immediately after creation, another user on node four could also access that table.

In parallel server, careful consideration must be given to the uses of parallelism because the resulting system can perform slower than a single-node system. For example, in parallel server, the DLM can force the Oracle database writer to write transactions to the database more frequently than a standalone Oracle database.

When planning for parallel server tasks, it is a good idea to segregate specific types of tasks to specific nodes (as shown in Figure 10.16). For example, common update routines against tablespace A could be segregated onto node one, while queries against tablespace B could be segregated onto node two. Because each Oracle instance has its own complete SGA, a full-table scan on one node will not flush any data out of the buffer pool of another node.

Of course, it is not always possible to segregate all data into separate buffer pools, especially with a highly denormalized data warehouse. An Oracle designer can partition the Oracle instances such that similar data queries are launched from the same instance, thereby improving the probability that the data will be waiting in the buffer.

It is possible to run Oracle parallel query on an Oracle parallel server system. In this case, the MPP system would allocate the subqueries evenly across the nodes, and the concurrency manager would coordinate the receipt of data from each subquery. Of course, this type of parallel query would run faster than a parallel query on an SMP box because the MPP box has isolated buffer pools. With SMP, the concurrent queries read their data into a common buffer pool.

Parallel processing is ideal for the Oracle data warehouse. Warehouse requests generally involve some type of aggregation (sum, average) and also require full-table scans. As such, parallelism can be used to dramatically reduce the execution time for these types of queries.

The parallel query option behaves the same regardless of whether the Oracle parallel server option has been installed. For more information, see the "Oracle Parallel Query" section later in this chapter.

Tuning The Parallel Server

To fully appreciate the facilities of the Oracle parallel server, we need to discuss the two types of parallelism: internal and external.

- *Internal parallelism*—Oracle takes an SQL query and fires off concurrently executing processes to service the SQL request.

- *External parallelism*—The operating system parallels the query.

Oracle recommends that data warehouse applications use parallel server if the hardware is clustered or arranged in an MPP environment. For SMP, parallel query can be used, but in SMP cases, the data is usually loaded into Oracle at night, and the warehouse is read-only during the day.

To understand the difference between tuning an Oracle warehouse on a single instance versus tuning a warehouse mapped to multiple servers, you need to take a look at the differences between these two approaches.

In a warehouse mapped to a single Oracle instance, DBAs tend to look for those resources that appear to be the most active. This could be a "hot" data file on a disk, excessive paging of the buffer cache (buffer hit ratio), or any number of other factors. As we have discussed, in a parallel server configuration, there are many independent Oracle instances sharing the same database.

In a sense, you can think of the shared-nothing configuration as having numerous, independent Oracle instances, and you can expect to tune each instance as if it were an independent entity. However, you must always bear in mind that each Oracle instance is competing for the same data resources. This competition is directly measured by the DLM.

Oracle parallel server only achieves a high degree of parallelism when careful planning has partitioned the tasks onto each instance in such a way that no two instances are constantly competing for data resources. If you find evidence that two Oracle instances are frequently accessing the same data blocks, the first remedy is to move common tasks into the same instance, where they can share the same buffer cache and eliminate calls to the DLM.

Indeed, tuning a parallel server is all about DLM lock contention. Your goal should be to independently tune each Oracle instance and keep a careful eye on how these instances interact with each other to manage internode locks. When DLM lock contention is identified, you have numerous options, including repartitioning the application to move tasks to other instances, adding multiple freelists to frequently accessed blocks, or using table replication techniques to alleviate I/O contention.

Here is a very simple approach to tuning a parallel server warehouse:

- *Monitor statistics independently for each Oracle instance.* The goal should be to minimize physical I/O by tuning the buffer cache and providing input into an overall load plan. For example, if you discover one instance is heavily loaded when compared to other instances, you can take a look at the partitioning of tasks and rebalance the load by moving tasks onto other instances.

- *Monitor each instance's buffer cache, looking for common data blocks.* If the same data blocks show up in multiple buffer caches, move one of the tasks into a common Oracle instance. Remember, the idea of tuning parallel server is to segregate common tasks into common instances.

- *Monitor for multiple tasks that modify rows on the same block.* When multiple tasks contend for the updating of rows on the same data block, adding freelists or freelist groups might relieve the bottleneck.

- *Monitor the DLM for lock conversions.* If the maximum lock convert rate for your DLM has been reached, you will need to repartition the application to balance "alike" transactions into common instances.

It should be apparent that the inherent complexity of parallel processing makes it very difficult to come up generic tuning techniques. Every parallel system is unique, and the Oracle professional must analyze each system carefully, considering its unique structure and behavior.

Oracle Parallel Query

One of the most exciting performance features of Oracle version 7.3 and above is the ability to partition an SQL query into subqueries and dedicate separate processors to concurrently service each subquery. At this time, parallel query is only useful for queries that perform full-table scans on long tables, but the performance improvements can be dramatic.

In order to be most effective, the table should be partitioned onto separate disk devices, such that each process can do I/O against its segment of the table without interfering with the other simultaneous query processes. However, the client/server environment of the 1990s relies on RAID or a logical volume manager (LVM), which scrambles data files across disk packs in order to balance the I/O load. Consequently, full utilization of parallel query involves *striping* a table across numerous data files, each on a separate device.

Parallel Create Table As Select

Parallel Create Table As Select (PCTAS) can be very useful in an Oracle data warehouse environment where tables are replicated across numerous servers or when preaggregating roll-up summary tables. Parallel Create Table As Select is also very useful when performing roll-up activities against your Oracle warehouse. For example, you could specify the number of parallel processes to compute the monthly summary values from your fact table. The following example assigns five processes to simultaneously read the blocks from a **CUSTOMER** table.

```
CREATE TABLE REGION_SALESPERSON_SUMMARY_03_97
PARALLEL (degree 5)
AS
SELECT region, salesperson, sum(sale_amount)
FROM FACT
WHERE
    month = 3
AND
    year = 1997;
```

Here, five query servers are dedicated to extract the data from the fact table and five query servers populate the new summary table (see Figure 10.17).

Again, you must remember that it is not necessary to have SMP or MPP hardware to benefit from parallel query techniques. Even a single-processor Unix system will experience some improvement from using parallel processes, even though all of the processes are running on the same CPU.

Now that we understand parallel server operations, let's take a look at how some common Oracle8 operations can be performed in parallel.

Parallel Index Building

Parallel index builds are often useful to the Oracle database administrator who needs to rebuild indexes that have either spawned too many levels or contain too many deleted leaf rows. Parallel index creation is also useful when importing Oracle data warehouse tables. Because data warehouses are so large, Oracle exports never capture the indexes and only export the row values. If a recovery of a table becomes necessary, the Oracle DBA can use parallel create to speed up the index re-creation. Parallel index creation takes place by allowing the degree of parallelism to be specified in the **ALTER INDEX** statement. For example:

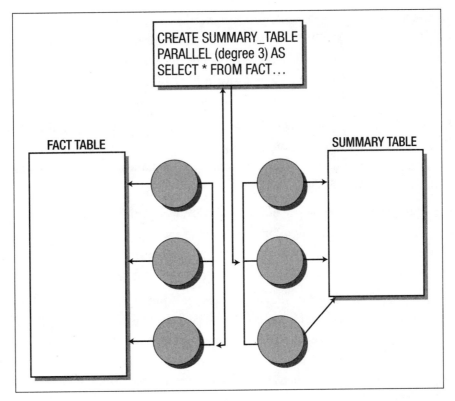

CREATE SUMMARY_TABLE
PARALLEL (degree 3) AS
SELECT * FROM FACT...

FACT TABLE

SUMMARY TABLE

Figure 10.17
Parallel Create Table As Select.

```
ALTER INDEX customer_pk
REBUILD PARALLEL 10;
```

Because this type of index creation always involves reading the old index structure and processing a large sort operation, Oracle is able to dedicate numerous, independent processes to simultaneously read the base index and collect the keys for the new index structure. Just like parallel query, each subquery task returns row ID and key values to the concurrency manager. The concurrency manager collects this information for input in the key sorting phase of the index rebuild. For very large data warehouse tables, parallel index creation can greatly reduce the amount of time required to initially create or rebuild indexes.

Some Oracle professionals mistakenly believe that it is necessary to have parallel processors (SMP or MPP) in order to use and benefit from parallel processing. Even on the same processor, multiple processes can be used to speed up queries. Oracle's parallel query option can be used with any SQL **SELECT** statement—the only restriction being that the query performs a full-table scan on the target table.

Even if your system uses RAID or LVM, some performance gains are available with parallel query. In addition to using multiple processes to retrieve a table, the query manager will also dedicate numerous processes to simultaneously sort the result sets from a large query. (See Figure 10.18.)

However, parallel query works best with SMP boxes, which have more than one internal CPU. Also, it is important to configure the system to maximize the I/O bandwidth, either through disk striping or high-speed channels. Because of the parallel sorting feature, it is also a good idea to beef up the memory on the processor.

While sorting is no substitute for using a pre-sorted index, the parallel query manager will service requests far faster than a single process. The data retrieval will not be significantly faster because the retrieval processes are competing for a channel on the same disk, but each sort process has its own sort area (as determined by the **sort_area_size** init.ora parameter), which speeds along the sorting of the result set.

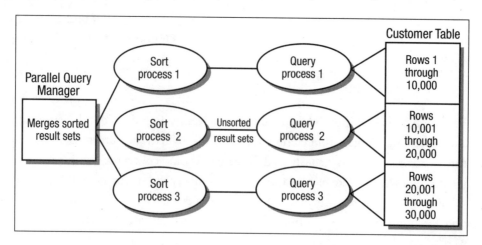

Figure 10.18
A sample parallel sort.

In addition to full-table scans and sorting, the parallel query option allows for parallel processes for merge joins and nested loops.

Invoking the parallel query option requires all indexing to be bypassed. And, most important, the execution plan for the query should specify a full-table scan. If the output of the explain plan does not indicate a full-table scan, the query can be forced to ignore the index by using query hints.

The number of processors dedicated to servicing an SQL request is ultimately determined by the Oracle query manager, but the programmer can specify the upper limit on the number of simultaneous processes. When using the cost-based optimizer, the **PARALLEL** hint can be embedded into the SQL to specify the number of processes. For example:

```
SELECT /*+ FULL(EMPLOYEE_TABLE) PARALLEL(EMPLOYEE_TABLE, 4) */
    employee_name
    FROM
    EMPLOYEE_TABLE
    WHERE
    emp_type = 'SALARIED';
```

If you are using SMP with many CPUs, you can issue a parallel request and leave it up to each Oracle instance to use its default degree of parallelism, as follows:

```
SELECT /*+ FULL(EMPLOYEE_TABLE) PARALLEL(EMPLOYEE_TABLE,
    DEFAULT, DEFAULT) */
    employee_name
    FROM
    EMPLOYEE_TABLE
    WHERE
    emp_type = 'SALARIED';
```

The following important init.ora parameters have a direct impact on parallel query:

- **sort_area_size**—The higher the value, the more memory available for individual sorts on each parallel process. Note that the **sort_area_size** parameter allocates memory for every query on the system that invokes a sort. For example, if a single query needs more memory and you increase the **sort_area_size**, all Oracle tasks will allocate the new amount of sort area, regardless of whether they will use the space.

- **parallel_min_servers**—The minimum number of query servers that will be active on the instance. System resources are involved in starting a query server, so having the query server started and waiting for requests will speed up processing. Note that if the actual number of required servers is less than the value of **parallel_min_servers**, the idle query servers will be consuming unnecessary overhead, and the value should be decreased.

- **parallel_max_servers**—The maximum number of query servers allowed on the instance. This parameter will prevent Oracle from starting so many query servers that the instance is unable to service all of them properly.

To see how many parallel query servers are busy at any given time, the following query can be issued against the **V$PQ_SYSSTAT** table:

```
SELECT * FROM V$PQ_SYSSTAT
WHERE STATISTIC = 'Servers Busy';

STATISTIC              VALUE
---------              -----
Servers Busy            30
```

In this case, you can see that 30 parallel servers are busy at this moment in time. Do not be misled by this number. Parallel query servers are constantly accepting work or returning to idle status, so it is a good idea to issue the query many times over a one-hour period. Only then will you have a realistic measure of how many parallel query servers are being used.

This wraps up our discussion of Oracle8's approach to parallel operations. Now, let's move on to the final area of Oracle8's data warehouse advancements—improved join optimization.

Summary

Now that you have seen how Oracle8 data warehouse applications function in a client/server environment, we can move on and discuss networking issues and how Oracle servers can be monitored for performance.

Oracle Application Monitoring

CHAPTER

11

Oracle Application Monitoring

Because Oracle is the world's leading relational database, many vendors offer tools that claim to monitor Oracle and alert DBAs to performance problems. Even Oracle has entered the monitoring marketplace with its Oracle Expert tool, first released in the second quarter of 1996. These tools fall into two broad categories: proactive tools, which monitor a database and search for trouble before it impacts a user, and reactive tools, which diagnose a problem after it has been reported.

Proactive Vs. Reactive Measuring Systems

When deciding how to monitor your servers, the first choice you need to make is whether to adopt a proactive or a reactive system. It is unfair to judge either method because each has a legitimate place in Oracle monitoring.

The first category of monitoring systems, proactive tools, consist of tools that constantly monitor a database and create *alerts* for unusual conditions. These tools allow a developer to set predefined thresholds. When a threshold is exceeded, the tool triggers an alert. Alerts can take a number of forms, including a report, telephone call, or pager notification. Some of the more sophisticated tools, such as BMC's Patrol, allow a developer to program corrective actions directly into the rule base and automatically take corrective action when an alert occurs. For example, if a table's next extent is 10MB but only 8MB of free space exist in the tablespace, an alert can alter the table's next extent size to 5MB and alert the DBA. This automatic action buys valuable time for a DBA and provides an opportunity for the DBA to investigate a problem before a stoppage occurs.

In comparison, an example of a reactive tool is the AdHawk tool by Eventus Software. AdHawk allows a DBA to rapidly view database locks and SQL in graphical format, quickly pinpointing the cause of a specific performance problem. This type of tool is especially useful in situations where only a few users are plagued with poor performance while other users on the database are not experiencing problems. Table 11.1 offers a compact glimpse of the various monitoring tools available in today's market, complete with vendor.

In this chapter, we'll review both monitoring methods in detail. Keep in mind that a proactive system is one that makes *forecasts* based on statistical information and determines that intervention is necessary in order to prevent a performance problem. A reactive system is used *after* performance problems have been noted. These types of systems give detailed information about the current status of an Oracle instance and allow a DBA to quickly see—and hopefully correct—a problem. While there are many reactive products in the marketplace, there are few tools that can be purchased to proactively monitor Oracle resource consumption over time. The next section explains how a simple, yet robust, proactive Oracle monitor can be created using the existing Oracle8 utilities.

Table 11.1 Representative Oracle monitoring tools.

Tool	Vendor
DBAnalyzer	Database Solutions
iVIEW Performance Logger	Independence Technologies
Patrol	BMC Software
EcoTOOLS	Compuware
DBVision	Platinum Technology
AdHawk	Eventus Software
R*SQLab	R*Tech Systems

Creating A Proactive Oracle-Based Monitor

Now, let's take a look at designing an expert system for monitoring Oracle performance over time. Before you begin, you'll need to address the following issues:

- What data will you collect, how will you collect it, and how will you display it?

- How will you create a centralized repository for the performance information?

- How will the centralized performance database be accessed?

- How will you automate the exception reporting?

As you probably know, the **V\$** tables are of limited value for performance monitoring because they keep running statistics for the total time that an Oracle instance has been running. Instead, you can alter the existing statistics report to collect information and store it in a database that you define especially for this purpose. Once you have the data on your local hosts, you can transfer the performance and tuning data into a single Oracle database. This database will be the foundation for the creation of automated exception reporting, as well as alerts. Once the requirements for your Oracle monitor have been determined, you are ready to begin gathering the performance statistics to meet your requirements.

Gathering The Oracle Performance Statistics

The fastest and simplest way to check the status of a database is to interrogate the **V\$** tables. While this provides only a crude measure of the overall health of the database, it is one of the first techniques that you should use. Remember, the **V\$** tables aren't really tables at all, but in-memory structures that hold accumulated statistics since Oracle startup. Hence, the **V\$** is used to compute long-term averages since startup, and this information can be useful if you frequently shut down and restart your Oracle database. For example, if you shut down your database each night, then the **V\$** information can provide an overall average for the day. However, if you only shut down your Oracle database once each month, the monthly running average provided by the **V\$** tables are not likely to be useful. The script in Listing 11.1 is a collection of the most useful **V\$** scripts, all packaged into a single collection.

Listing 11.1 snapshot.sql—a full snapshot of the **V$** tables.

```
REM    Remember, you must first run $ORACLE_HOME/rdbms/admin/catblock.sql
REM    before this script will work. . .
SET LINESIZE 75;
SET PAGESIZE 9999;
SET PAUSE OFF;
SET ECHO OFF;
SET TERMOUT ON;
SET SHOWMODE OFF;
SET FEEDBACK OFF;
SET NEWPAGE 1;
SET VERIFY OFF;


--spool /tmp/snap;


PROMPT ************************************************************
PROMPT  Hit Ratio Section
PROMPT ************************************************************
PROMPT
PROMPT          ==========================
PROMPT          BUFFER HIT RATIO
PROMPT          ==========================
PROMPT (SHOULD BE > 70, ELSE INCREASE db_block_buffers IN init.ora)

--SELECT trunc((1-(sum(decode(name,'physical reads',value,0)))/
--              (sum(decode(name,'db block gets',value,0)))+
--            (sum(decode(name,'consistent gets',value,0)))))
--          )* 100) "Buffer Hit Ratio"
--FROM V$SYSSTAT;


COLUMN "logical_reads" FORMAT 99,999,999,999
COLUMN "phys_reads"    FORMAT 999,999,999
COLUMN "phy_writes"    FORMAT 999,999,999
SELECT A.value + B.value  "logical_reads",
       C.value            "phys_reads",
       D.value            "phy_writes",
       round(100 * ((A.value+B.value)-C.value) / (A.value+B.value))
         "BUFFER HIT RATIO"
FROM V$SYSSTAT A, V$SYSSTAT B, V$SYSSTAT C, V$SYSSTAT D
WHERE
   A.statistic# = 37
AND
   B.statistic# = 38
AND
```

```
    C.statistic# = 39
AND
    D.statistic# = 40;

PROMPT
PROMPT
PROMPT           ==============================
PROMPT           DATA DICT HIT RATIO
PROMPT           ==============================
PROMPT (SHOULD BE HIGHER THAN 90 ELSE INCREASE shared_pool_size
PROMPT IN init.ora)
PROMPT


COLUMN "Data Dict. Gets"            FORMAT 999,999,999
COLUMN "Data Dict. cache misses"    FORMAT 999,999,999
SELECT sum(gets) "Data Dict. Gets",
       sum(getmisses) "Data Dict. cache misses",
       trunc((1-(sum(getmisses)/sum(gets)))*100)
       "DATA DICT CACHE HIT RATIO"
FROM V$ROWCACHE;


PROMPT
PROMPT           ==============================
PROMPT           LIBRARY CACHE MISS RATIO
PROMPT           ==============================
PROMPT (IF > 1 THEN INCREASE THE shared_pool_size IN init.ora)
PROMPT
COLUMN "LIBRARY CACHE MISS RATIO"       FORMAT 99.9999
COLUMN "executions"                     FORMAT 999,999,999
COLUMN "Cache misses while executing"   FORMAT 999,999,999
SELECT sum(pins) "executions", sum(reloads)
       "Cache misses while executing",
       (((sum(reloads)/sum(pins)))) "LIBRARY CACHE MISS RATIO"
FROM V$LIBRARYCACHE;


PROMPT
PROMPT           ==============================
PROMPT           LIBRARY CACHE SECTION
PROMPT           ==============================
PROMPT HIT RATIO SHOULD BE > 70, AND PIN RATIO > 70
PROMPT
COLUMN "reloads" FORMAT 999,999,999
SELECT NAMESPACE, trunc(gethitratio * 100) "Hit ratio",
       trunc(pinhitratio * 100) "pin hit ratio", reloads "reloads"
FROM V$LIBRARYCACHE;
```

```
PROMPT
PROMPT          ===================================
PROMPT          REDO LOG BUFFER
PROMPT          ===================================
PROMPT (SHOULD BE NEAR 0, ELSE INCREASE SIZE OF LOG_BUFFER IN init.ora)
PROMPT
SET HEADING OFF
COLUMN VALUE FORMAT 999,999,999
SELECT substr(name,1,30),
       value
FROM V$SYSSTAT WHERE NAME = 'redo log space requests';

SET HEADING ON
PROMPT
PROMPT
PROMPT ******************************************************************
PROMPT Free memory should be > 1,000
PROMPT ******************************************************************
PROMPT


COLUMN BYTES FORMAT 999,999,999
SELECT NAME, BYTES FROM V$SGASTAT WHERE NAME = 'free memory';


PROMPT
PROMPT ******************************************************************
PROMPT   SQL SUMMARY SECTION
PROMPT ******************************************************************
PROMPT
COLUMN "Tot SQL run since startup"     FORMAT 999,999,999
COLUMN "SQL executing now"             FORMAT 999,999,999
SELECT sum(executions) "Tot SQL run since startup",
       sum(users_executing) "SQL executing now"
FROM V$SQLAREA;


PROMPT
PROMPT
PROMPT ******************************************************************
PROMPT   Lock Section
PROMPT ******************************************************************
PROMPT
PROMPT          ===================================
PROMPT          SYSTEMWIDE LOCKS - all requests for locks or latches
PROMPT          ===================================
PROMPT
```

```
SELECT substr(username,1,12)   "User",
       substr(lock_type,1,18) "Lock Type",
       substr(mode_held,1,18) "Mode Held"
FROM SYS.dba_lock A, V$SESSION B
WHERE lock_type NOT IN ('Media Recovery','Redo Thread')
AND A.session_id = B.sid;


PROMPT
PROMPT          ============================
PROMPT          DDL LOCKS - These are usually triggers or other DDL
PROMPT          ============================
PROMPT
SELECT substr(username,1,12) "User",
       substr(owner,1,8)  "Owner",
       substr(name,1,15)  "Name",
       substr(A.type,1,20)  "Type",
       substr(mode_held,1,11) "Mode held"
FROM SYS.dba_ddl_locks A, V$SESSION B
WHERE A.session_id = B.sid;


PROMPT
PROMPT          ============================
PROMPT          DML LOCKS - These are table and row locks...
PROMPT          ============================
PROMPT
SELECT substr(username,1,12) "User",
       substr(owner,1,8)  "Owner",
       substr(name,1,20)  "Name",
       substr(mode_held,1,21) "Mode held"
FROM SYS.dba_dml_locks A, V$SESSION B
WHERE A.session_id = B.sid;


PROMPT
PROMPT
PROMPT **********************************************************
PROMPT  LATCH SECTION
PROMPT **********************************************************
PROMPT If miss_ratio or IMMEDIATE_MISS_RATIO > 1 then   latch
PROMPT Contention exists, decrease LOG_SMALL_ENTRY_MAX_SIZE IN init.ora
PROMPT
COLUMN "miss_ratio"          FORMAT .99
COLUMN "immediate_miss_ratio" FORMAT .99
SELECT substr(L.name,1,30) name,
       (misses/(gets+.001))*100 "miss_ratio",
```

```
        (immediate_misses/(immediate_gets+.001))*100
        "immediate_miss_ratio"
FROM V$LATCH L, V$LATCHNAME LN
WHERE L.latch# = LN.latch#
AND (
(misses/(gets+.001))*100 > .2
OR
(immediate_misses/(immediate_gets+.001))*100 > .2
)
ORDER BY L.name;

PROMPT
PROMPT
PROMPT ******************************************************************
PROMPT   ROLLBACK SEGMENT SECTION
PROMPT ******************************************************************
PROMPT If any count below is > 1% of the total number of requests
PROMPT for data then more rollback segments are needed
PROMPT If free list > 1% then increase freelist in init.ora

SELECT CLASS, COUNT
FROM V$WAITSTAT
WHERE CLASS IN ('free list','system undo header','system undo block',
                'undo header','undo block')
GROUP BY CLASS,COUNT;

COLUMN "Tot # of Requests for Data" FORMAT 999,999,999
SELECT sum(value) "Tot # of Requests for Data" FROM V$SYSSTAT
WHERE
NAME IN ('db block gets', 'consistent gets');

PROMPT
PROMPT              ==============================
PROMPT              ROLLBACK SEGMENT CONTENTION
PROMPT              ==============================
PROMPT
PROMPT   If any ratio is > .01 then more rollback segments are needed

COLUMN "Ratio" FORMAT 99.99999
SELECT NAME, WAITS, GETS, waits/gets "Ratio"
FROM V$ROLLSTAT A, V$ROLLNAME B
WHERE A.usn = B.usn;
COLUMN "total_waits"    FORMAT 999,999,999
COLUMN "total_timeouts"  FORMAT 999,999,999
PROMPT
```

```
PROMPT
SET FEEDBACK ON;
PROMPT *********************************************************
PROMPT  SESSION EVENT SECTION
PROMPT *********************************************************
PROMPT IF average_wait > 0 THEN CONTENTION EXISTS
PROMPT
SELECT substr(event,1,30) event,
       total_waits, total_timeouts, average_wait
FROM V$SESSION_EVENT
WHERE average_wait > 0 ;
--OR total_timeouts > 0;


PROMPT
PROMPT
PROMPT *********************************************************
PROMPT QUEUE SECTION
PROMPT *********************************************************
PROMPT Average wait for queues should be near zero ...
PROMPT
COLUMN "totalq"   FORMAT 999,999,999
COLUMN "# queued" FORMAT 999,999,999
SELECT paddr, type "Queue type", queued "# queued", wait, totalq,
       decode(totalq,0,0,wait/totalq) "AVG WAIT" FROM V$QUEUE;

SET FEEDBACK ON;
PROMPT
PROMPT
PROMPT *********************************************************
PROMPT  MULTITHREADED SERVER SECTION
PROMPT *********************************************************
PROMPT
PROMPT    If the following number is > 1
PROMPT    Then increase MTS_MAX_SERVERS parm in init.ora
PROMPT
SELECT decode( totalq, 0, 'No Requests',
               wait/totalq || ' hundredths of seconds')
               "Avg wait per request queue"
FROM V$QUEUE
WHERE TYPE = 'COMMON';

PROMPT
PROMPT If the following number increases, consider adding
PROMPT dispatcher processes
PROMPT
```

```
SELECT decode ( sum(totalq), 0, 'No Responses',
                sum(wait)/sum(totalq) || ' hundredths of seconds')
                "Avg wait per response queue"
FROM V$QUEUE Q, V$DISPATCHER D
WHERE Q.type = 'DISPATCHER'
AND Q.paddr = D.paddr;
SET FEEDBACK OFF;
PROMPT
PROMPT
PROMPT            ===============================
PROMPT            DISPATCHER USAGE
PROMPT            ===============================
PROMPT (If Time Busy > 50, then change MTS_MAX_DISPATCHERS in init.ora)
COLUMN "Time Busy" FORMAT 999,999.999
COLUMN busy        FORMAT 999,999,999
COLUMN idle        FORMAT 999,999,999
SELECT name, status, idle, busy,
       (busy/(busy+idle))*100 "Time Busy"
FROM V$DISPATCHER;

PROMPT   .
PROMPT
SELECT count(*) "Shared Server Processes"
FROM V$SHARED_SERVER
WHERE STATUS = 'QUIT';

PROMPT
PROMPT
PROMPT High-water mark for the multithreaded server
PROMPT

SELECT * FROM V$MTS;

PROMPT
PROMPT ***************************************************************
PROMPT File I/O should be evenly distributed across drives.
PROMPT

SELECT
       substr(a.file#,1,2) "#",
       substr(a.name,1,30) "Name",
       A.status,
       A.bytes,
```

```
        B.phyrds,
        B.phywrts
FROM V$DATAFILE A, V$FILESTAT B
WHERE A.file# = B.file#;

SELECT substr(name,1,55) system_statistic, VALUE
FROM V$SYSSTAT
ORDER BY name;
SPOOL OFF;
```

Listing 11.2 shows the output of the snapshot script.

Listing 11.2   The output of snapshot.sql.

```
SQL> @snapshot


*****************************************************************
Hit Ratio Section
*****************************************************************


============================
BUFFER HIT RATIO
============================
(SHOULD BE > 70, ELSE INCREASE db_block_buffers IN init.ora)

logical_reads    phys_reads      phy_writes    BUFFER HIT RATIO
-------------    ----------      ----------    ----------------
46,961,377       2,194,393       154,145             95



============================
DATA DICT HIT RATIO
============================
(SHOULD BE HIGHER THAN 90 ELSE INCREASE shared_pool_size IN init.ora)


 Data Dict. Gets  Data Dict. cache misses  DATA DICT CACHE HIT RATIO
 ---------------  -----------------------  -------------------------
 380,780          13,797                            96


============================
LIBRARY CACHE MISS RATIO
============================
(IF > 1 THEN INCREASE THE shared_pool_size IN init.ora)
```

```
executions   Cache misses while executing   LIBRARY CACHE MISS RATIO
----------   ----------------------------   ------------------------
380,971                2,437                         .0064
```

```
============================
LIBRARY CACHE SECTION
============================
```

HIT RATIO SHOULD BE > 70, AND PIN RATIO > 70 ...

NAMESPACE	Hit ratio	pin hit ratio	reloads
SQL AREA	95	97	1,253
TABLE/PROCEDURE	88	93	1,174
BODY	98	97	10
TRIGGER	50	50	0
INDEX	3	31	0
CLUSTER	44	33	0
OBJECT	100	100	0
PIPE	100	100	0

```
============================
REDO LOG BUFFER
============================
```

(SHOULD BE NEAR 0, ELSE INCREASE SIZE OF LOG_BUFFER IN init.ora)

```
redo log space requests              29
```

```
******************************************************************
Free memory should be > 1,000
******************************************************************
```

NAME	BYTES
free memory	54,820

```
******************************************************************
SQL SUMMARY SECTION
******************************************************************
```

Tot SQL run since startup	SQL executing now
60,390	2

```
**********************************************************************
Lock Section
**********************************************************************


=============================
SYSTEMWIDE LOCKS - All requests for locks or latches
=============================


User            Lock Type            Mode Held
----            ---------            ---------
OPS$G449488     DML                  Exclusive
DATAPUMP        PL/SQL User Lock     Share


=============================
DDL LOCKS - These are usually triggers or other DDL
=============================


User          Owner     Name              Type              Mode held
----          -----     ----              ----              ---------
OPS$G241107   GENESIS   VALID_DOMAIN_VA   Table/Procedure   Null
OPS$G499058   GENESIS   REB0004_PKG       Body              Null
OPS$G499058   GENESIS   REB0004_PKG       Table/Procedure   Null
OPS$G241107   SYS       DBMS_STANDARD     Body              Null
OPS$G499058   GENESIS   INSERT_REBPGMCH   Table/Procedure   Null
OPS$G499058   GENESIS   INSERT_REBPGMCH   Table/Procedure   Null


=============================
DML LOCKS - These are table and row locks...
=============================


**********************************************************************
LATCH SECTION
**********************************************************************
If miss_ratio or IMMEDIATE_MISS_RATIO> 1 then  latch
Contention exists, decrease LOG_SMALL_ENTRY_MAX_SIZE IN init.ora
NAME                          miss_ratio     immediate_miss_ratio
----                          ----------     --------------------
cache buffers lru chain          ####               .59
redo copy                        ####               .01


**********************************************************************
ROLLBACK SEGMENT SECTION
**********************************************************************
```

If any count below is > 1% of the total number of requests for data
then more rollback segments are needed
If free list > 1% then increase FREELIST in init.ora

CLASS	COUNT
free list	0
system undo block	0
system undo header	0
undo block	0
undo header	6

Tot # of Requests for Data

46,961,805

============================
ROLLBACK SEGMENT CONTENTION
============================

If any ratio is > .01 then more rollback segments are needed

NAME	WAITS	GETS	Ratio
SYSTEM	0	1431	0.00000
ROLB1	0	10808	0.00000
ROLB2	0	11225	0.00000
ROLB3	0	11832	0.00000
ROLB4	0	9976	0.00000

****
SESSION EVENT SECTION
****
If average_wait > 0 THEN CONTENTION EXISTS

 no rows selected

****
QUEUE SECTION
****

```
Average wait for queues should be near zero ...


no rows selected


*********************************************************************
MULTITHREADED SERVER SECTION
*********************************************************************


============================
DISPATCH USAGE
```

This is an excellent quick-and-dirty way to see the internal state of your Oracle database. It essentially provides a snapshot of the state of the Oracle databases. However, be aware that some of the data can be misleading. For example, the above report shows the buffer hit ratio to be 95 percent, the average since database startup. The "real" buffer hit ratio at the moment that the report was run is not available, and the **utlbstat-utlestat** report must be used to see the current hit ratios.

Now, let's take a look at how we can create a performance database by using the Oracle utilities that are provided as a part of Oracle8.

Collecting Oracle Statistics

A need has already been identified for collecting database statistics from the Oracle instances. In short, you desire a proactive performance and tuning system that will:

- Predict future resource needs (DASD, memory, CPU) based on historical consumption rates.

- Allow ad hoc query to determine where tuning resources are needed.

- Provide an empirical measure of the benefits from adding resources to a database—both human and hardware (e.g., a 20MB memory increase improved buffer hit ratio by 13 percent).

Now the question arises: How do you extract this information and place it into your Oracle database? The following section describes a simple approach that builds an Oracle database to hold performance statistics.

Creating A Performance Repository With Oracle Utilities

The basic premise of a performance repository in Oracle is to demonstrate how a DBA can automate the tedious analysis tasks within Oracle databases and be automatically alerted in extraordinary conditions. While many products exist that perform this function, a DBA can benefit from an understanding of the internal workings of the Oracle SGA as well as from insights into the complex interactions that contribute to response time.

In general terms, Oracle tuning can be divided into two areas: disk tuning and memory tuning. Many shops now use RAID or LVM to stripe data files across disks, so disk tuning has become a moot issue for most Oracle DBAs.

Memory tuning is another story. An Oracle instance resides in the real memory of the host. The allocation of memory pages and the configuration of the SGA is a primary concern for understanding performance. SGA tuning for Oracle involves two areas: parameters in the init.ora file and parameters used when an individual table is created. The init.ora file is used at startup time by Oracle to allocate the memory region for the instance, and the parameters in the init.ora control this allocation. Other parameters used at table creation time (such as **FREELIST** and **PCTUSED**) can influence performance, but we will focus on the systemwide tuning parameters here.

When tuning Oracle, two init.ora parameters become more important than all of the others combined:

- **db_block_buffers**—The number of buffers allocated for caching database blocks in memory.

- **shared_pool_size**—The amount of memory allocated for caching SQL, stored procedures, and other nondata objects.

These two parameters define the size of the in-memory region that Oracle consumes on startup and determine the amount of storage available to cache data blocks, SQL, and stored procedures.

*It is a good idea to set your **db_block_size** as large as possible for your system. For example, HP-9000 computers read 8K blocks; hence, **db_block_size** should be set to 8K.*

Keep in mind that many of these tuning issues change for future releases of Oracle8.x. Future releases of Oracle8 have promised to allow for the dynamic modification of the SGA. For example, it will not be necessary to bounce an instance to change the amount of **db_block_size**, and utilities will soon appear to detect extraordinary conditions and dynamically reconfigure the SGA.

Preparing The SGA For Packages And Stored Procedures

Oracle's shared pool is very important, especially if the system relies heavily on stored procedures and packages. This is because the code in the stored procedures is loaded into memory. The shared pool consists of the following subpools:

- Dictionary cache

- Library cache

- Shared SQL areas

- Private SQL area (exists during cursor open-cursor close; contains persistent and runtime areas)

Both the data buffer and the shared pool utilize a least-recently used algorithm to determine which objects are paged out of the shared pool. As this paging occurs, *fragments*, or discontiguous chunks, of memory are created within the memory areas.

Imagine the shared pool as being similar to a tablespace. Just as the ORA-1547 error appears when insufficient contiguous free space occurs in the tablespace, similarly, you will encounter an ORA-4031 error when contiguous free space is not available in the shared pool of the SGA. This means that a large procedure that initially fit into memory might not fit into contiguous memory when it is reloaded after being paged out. For example, consider a problem that occurs when the body of a package has been paged out of an instance's SGA because of other more recent/frequent activity. Fragmentation occurs, and the server cannot find enough contiguous memory to reload the package body, resulting in an ORA-4031 error.

To effectively measure memory, a standard method is recommended. It is a good idea to regularly run the **estat/bstat** utility (usually located in ~/rdbms/admin/ utlbstat.sql and utlestat.sql) for measuring SGA consumption over a range of time.

As we know, the hit ratios are a measure of change over time and cannot be captured with a single measurement. The following section provides guidelines for creating the "begin" and "end" ranges for determining these ratios.

Using Oracle utlbstat And utlestat Utilities

The standard utilities for creating a performance report are known as **estat/bstat**, found in $ORACLE_HOME/rdbms/admin. The names of the utilities are utlbstat.sql (begin statistics) and utlestat.sql (end statistics). You must enter the following SQL*DBA commands to run the reports:

```
$ > cd $ORACLE_HOME/rdbms/admin
$ sqldba mode=line
SQLDBA > connect internal
connected.
SQLDBA > @utlbstat
...
5 rows processed
SQLDBA > @utlestat
```

The **utlbstat** utility samples the database and stores the results in a temporary table. When **utlbstat** is run and the database is sampled again, a report is made by comparing the differences in values between the begin snapshot and the end snapshot. The output is spooled to a file called report.txt. Although the report is very ugly and hard to read, the salient data is included. Listing 11.3 presents a sample of how the statistics report might appear.

Listing 11.3   The output from the **bstat/estat** Oracle utility.

```
oracle@myhost:mtty-61>more report.txt
SQLDBA>
SQLDBA> SET CHARWIDTH 12
SQLDBA> SET NUMWIDTH 10
SQLDBA> REM Select Library cache statistics...The pin hit rate should
SQLDBA> REM be HIGH.
SQLDBA> SELECT NAMESPACE LIBRARY,
     2>         gets,
     3>         round(decode(gethits,0,1,gethits)/decode(gets,0,1,gets),3)
     4>            gethitratio,
     5>         pins,
     6>         round(decode(pinhits,0,1,pinhits)/decode(pins,0,1,pins),3)
     7>            pinhitratio,
     8>         reloads, invalidations
     9> FROM STATS$LIB;
```

```
LIBRARY       GETS    GETHITRATI  PINS   PINHITRATI  RELOADS  INVALIDATI
-------       ----    ----------  ----   ----------  -------  ----------
BODY             9         1         9        1          0          0
CLUSTER          0         1         0        1          0          0
INDEX            8      .125        12     .333          0          0
OBJECT           0         1         0        1          0          0
PIPE             0         1         0        1          0          0
SQL AREA       490      .935      1675     .937         21         20
TABLE/PROCED   111      .865       281     .911          8          0
TRIGGER          0         1         0        1          0          0

8 rows selected.


SQLDBA>
SQLDBA> SET CHARWIDTH 27;
SQLDBA> SET NUMWIDTH 12;
SQLDBA> REM The total is the total value of the statistic between the
SQLDBA> REM time bstat was run and the time estat was run...Note that
SQLDBA> REM the estat script logs on as "internal" so the per_logon
SQLDBA> REM statistics will always be based on at least one logon.
SQLDBA> SELECT N1.name "Statistic",
    2>          N1.change "Total",
    3>          round(N1.change/trans.change,2) "Per Transaction",
    4>          round(N1.change/logs.change,2)  "Per Logon"
    5> FROM STATS$STATS N1, STATS$STATS TRANS, STATS$STATS LOGS
    6> WHERE TRANS.name='user commits'
    7> AND   LOGS.name='logons cumulative'
    8> AND   N1.change != 0
    9> ORDER BY N1.name;
Statistic                   Total    Per Transact   Per Logon
---------                   -----    ------------   ---------
CR blocks created              45            15            9
DBWR buffers scanned        49630      16543.33         9926
DBWR checkpoints               13          4.33          2.6
DBWR free buffers found     49389         16463       9877.8
DBWR lru scans               1515           505          303
DBWR make free requests      1513        504.33        302.6
DBWR summed scan depth      49634      16544.67       9926.8
DBWR timeouts                  38         12.67          7.6
background timeouts           114            38         22.8
calls to kcmgas               136         45.33         27.2
calls to kcmgcs                16          5.33          3.2
calls to kcmgrs              1134           378        226.8
```

```
cleanouts and rollbacks - c        4            1.33            .8
cleanouts only - consistent       90              30            18
cluster key scan block gets      266           88.67          53.2
cluster key scans                114              38          22.8
consistent changes                48              16           9.6
consistent gets               111477           37159       22295.4
cursor authentications            90              30            18
data blocks consistent read       48              16           9.6
db block changes                1292          430.67         258.4
db block gets                   1286          428.67         257.2
deferred (CURRENT) block cl      112           37.33          22.4
enqueue releases                2277             759         455.4
enqueue requests                2282          760.67         456.4
enqueue timeouts                   4            1.33            .8
execute count                    605          201.67           121
free buffer inspected            146           48.67          29.2
free buffer requested          28628         9542.67        5725.6
immediate (CR) block cleano       94           31.33          18.8
immediate (CURRENT) block c       13            4.33           2.6
logons cumulative                  5            1.67             1
messages received               1610          536.67           322
messages sent                   1610          536.67           322
no work - consistent read g   109953           36651       21990.6
opened cursors cumulative        387             129          77.4
parse count                      502          167.33         100.4
physical reads                 28505         9501.67          5701
physical writes                  213              71          42.6
recursive calls                 6838         2279.33        1367.6
redo blocks written              607          202.33         121.4
redo entries                     769          256.33         153.8
redo size                     282490        94163.33         56498
redo small copies                723             241         144.6
redo synch writes                 33              11           6.6
redo wastage                    2306         7686.67          4612
redo writes                       94           31.33          18.8
rollbacks only - consistent       44           14.67           8.8
session logical reads         112714        37571.33       22542.8
session pga memory            629940          209980        125988
session pga memory max        629940          209980        125988
session uga memory             14248         4749.33        2849.6
session uga memory max        228624           76208       45724.8
sorts (memory)                    23            7.67           4.6
sorts (rows)                    5957         1985.67        1191.4
table fetch by rowid           36144           12048        7228.8
table fetch continued row      31679        10559.67        6335.8
table scan blocks gotten        5884         1961.33        1176.8
```

```
table scan rows gotten          123829        41276.33       24765.8
table scans (long tables)           11            3.67           2.2
table scans (short tables)          19            6.33           3.8
user calls                         188           62.67          37.6
user commits                         3               1            .6
write requests                     100           33.33            20
64 rows selected.
SQLDBA>
SQLDBA> SET CHARWIDTH 27;
SQLDBA> SET NUMWIDTH 12;
SQLDBA> REM Systemwide wait events.
SQLDBA> SELECT  N1.event "Event Name",
     2>         N1.event_count "Count",
     3>         N1.time_waited "Total Time",
     4>         (N1.time_waited/N1.event_count) "Average Time"
     5> FROM STATS$EVENT N1
     6> WHERE N1.event_count > 0
     7> ORDER BY N1.time_waited desc;


Event Name                      Count    Total Time    Average Time
----------                      -----    ----------    ------------
smon timer                          2             0               0
buffer busy waits                   3             0               0
control file sequential rea         8             0               0
rdbms ipc reply                    12             0               0
log file sync                      39             0               0
pmon timer                         57             0               0
latch free                         73             0               0
Event Name                      Count    Total Time    Average Time
----------                      -----    ----------    ------------
log file parallel write            93             0               0
db file parallel write             96             0               0
client message                    190             0               0
db file scattered read            635             0               0
rdbms ipc message                1600             0               0
db file sequential read         25071             0               0
13 rows selected.
SQLDBA>
```

The output of **utlbstat** and **utlestat** can offer some very valuable performance information. Listing 11.3 shows the basic statistics for the database during the period between your **bstat** (begin statistics) and the **estat** (end statistics). While all the information can be important, you can view several critical performance statistics here, including:

- **BUFFER BUSY WAITS**—A high value indicates that either more buffer blocks or rollback segments are needed.

- **DBWR CHECKPOINTS**—A high value indicates a need to increase the init.ora **log_checkpoint_interval**.

- **DBWR FREE LOW**—A high value indicates a need to increase the init.ora parameter **free_buffer_requested**.

- **REDO LOG SPACE REQUESTS**—This should be zero. If not, increase the size of your redo logs.

- **SORTS (DISK)**—Sorts to disk are time consuming, so consider increasing your init.ora parm **sort_area_size**.

  *The **sort_area_size** parameter takes effect for each user who accesses Oracle, regardless of the sorting requirements of each transaction. Check your "high water mark" in your alert.log to ensure that your host has enough memory to support your choice. The formula is:*

  ```
  total_memory = oracle_high_water_mark * sort_area_size
  ```

- **TABLE SCANS (LONG TABLES)**—This should only happen in cases where reading most of the table rows would be required to answer the query.

The benefit of running **bstat/estat** is the ability to measure changes over a period of time. It is relatively simple to write a script that invokes **bstat** at a specified time and runs the **estat** utility at a later time. Some sites compute **bstat/estat** statistics each hour so that hourly variations can be easily detected.

Running the utilities is very simple. Within a script, go to $ORACLE_HOME/ rdbms/admin, enter SQL*DBA, and invoke the utlbstat.sql script. The report will be generated when utlestat.sql is invoked. The standard **estat** utility creates a report called report.txt that is dumped into the $ORACLE_HOME directory.

Once the report.txt file is created, there are two ways to extract the information. A command script in Perl, awk, or Korn shell can be written to interrogate the report, extract the information, and write it into Oracle tables. The **estat** utility can also be altered to dump data into Oracle tables while it creates the report.txt file.

Listing 11.4 shows a sample Unix script that can be invoked from a **cron** process. In this case, the script called perf would be addressed as **perf bstat** and **perf estat**.

Listing 11.4   A Unix script to gather performance information.

```
if [ $# != 1 ]
then
    echo "usage: $0 { bstat | estat }"
    exit 1
fi


if [ "${1}" != bstat -a "${1}" != estat ]
then
    echo "usage: $0 { bstat | estat }"
    exit 1
fi


SQLPATH=/usr/perfmon

if [ "${1}" = bstat ]
then
    #  Begin collection
    sqldba << !
       connect internal
       @${ORACLE_HOME}/rdbms/admin/utlbstat
       exit
!

else
    #  End data collection
    sqldba << !
       connect internal
       @${SQLPATH}/specialestat
       exit
!
    sqlplus / @${SQLPATH}/tracker ${ORACLE_SID}
fi

exit 0
```

Note that the regular **estat** utility has been replaced by a customized version called **specialestat**, and this customized **estat** utility is run in lieu of the one in $ORACLE_HOME/rdbms/admin. The **specialestat** is identical to the **utlestat** except that it does not delete the temporary tables that are used to create report.txt. In this way, the temporary tables can be interrogated and loaded into special performance tracking tables. Following **specialestat**, the tracker utility is then invoked to capture the **estat** information into permanent tables, dropping the temporary tables.

After the data has been transferred into permanent tables, the statistical information can be analyzed and graphed to show performance trends. Predictions can be extrapolated from the data using linear forecasting methods, and problems such as full tablespaces can be predicted with relative accuracy. Listing 11.5 presents a script that will load the performance tables.

Listing 11.5   tracker.ddl—an SQL script to gather performance statistics.

```
INSERT INTO track_stats
(   oracle_sid,   collection_started)
SELECT  '&1',min(stats_gather_times)
FROM    SYS.STATS$DATES;

UPDATE track_stats
SET    collection_ended =
         (SELECT  max(stats_gather_times)
          FROM    SYS.STATS$DATES),
       run_date = to_date(substr(collection_started,1,12),
                  'DD-MON-YY HH24'),
       consistent_gets =
         (SELECT  change
          FROM    SYS.STATS$STATS
          WHERE   name = 'consistent gets'),
       block_gets =
         (SELECT  change
          FROM    SYS.STATS$STATS
          WHERE   name = 'db block gets'),
       physical_reads =
         (SELECT  change
          FROM    SYS.STATS$STATS
          WHERE   name = 'physical reads'),
       buffer_busy_waits =
         (SELECT  change
          FROM    SYS.STATS$STATS
          WHERE   name = 'buffer busy waits'),
       buffer_free_needed =
         (SELECT  change
          FROM    SYS.STATS$STATS
          WHERE   name = 'free buffer requested'),
       free_buffer_waits =
         (SELECT  change
```

```
               FROM    SYS.STATS$STATS
               WHERE   name = 'free buffer waits'),
           free_buffer_scans =
             (SELECT   change
              FROM     SYS.STATS$STATS
              WHERE    name = 'free buffer scans'),
           enqueue_timeouts =
             (SELECT   change
              FROM     SYS.STATS$STATS
              WHERE    name = 'enqueue timeouts'),
           redo_space_wait =
             (SELECT   change
              FROM     SYS.STATS$STATS
              WHERE    name = 'redo log space wait time'),
           write_wait_time =
             (SELECT   change
              FROM     SYS.STATS$STATS
              WHERE    name = 'write wait time'),
           write_complete_waits =
             (SELECT   change
              FROM     SYS.STATS$STATS
              WHERE    name = 'write complete waits'),
           rollback_header_gets =
             (SELECT   sum(trans_tbl_gets)
              FROM     SYS.STATS$ROLL),
           rollback_header_waits =
             (SELECT   sum(trans_tbl_waits)
              FROM     SYS.STATS$ROLL)
WHERE  collection_ended IS NULL;


INSERT INTO LATCHES
(ls_latch_name, ls_latch_gets, ls_latch_misses,
 ls_latch_sleeps, ls_latch_immed_gets, ls_latch_immed_misses)
SELECT  name, gets, misses, sleeps, immed_gets, immed_miss
FROM    SYS.STATS$LATCHES;

UPDATE LATCHES SET
    ls_collection_started =
         (SELECT   min(stats_gather_times)
          FROM     SYS.STATS$DATES)
WHERE ls_oracle_sid IS NULL;
```

```
UPDATE LATCHES SET
    run_date = to_date(substr(ls_collection_started,1,12),
    'DD-MON-YY HH24')
WHERE ls_oracle_sid IS NULL;

UPDATE LATCHES
SET ls_oracle_sid =
        (SELECT  '&1'
          FROM    SYS.DUAL),
    ls_collection_ended =
        (SELECT  max(stats_gather_times)
          FROM    SYS.STATS$DATES)
WHERE ls_oracle_sid IS NULL;
```

Generally speaking, a "sum of the least squares" technique will suffice for forecasting, but single or double exponential smoothing techniques might yield more accurate predictions under certain circumstances. Now that we see how Oracle statistics can be collected and stored in special tables, we'll look at how to collect systemwide statistics in Oracle.

Building The Oracle Performance Database

You begin building your Oracle performance database by determining which data items you want to track, and then designing a table structure that fills your requirements (see Figure 11.1).

The philosophy for the performance and tuning repository is to collect virtually all of the information from the **bstat/estat** reports and the **V$** and **DBA** tables. The original information is collected on each remote agent and stored in local tables. For example, on Saturday at 8:00 AM, a **crontab** job could start a task to invoke the export and compress utilities that will extract the information into a flat file. Following extraction, the data would be transferred to a central host via anonymous FTP, where the extracted files would be loaded into the master Oracle tables on the central host. Each remote host would then have its performance and tuning tables re-created. At a predetermined time on Saturday, a **crontab** would verify that all remote agents have delivered their daily extract files and notify the DBA of any agents who have failed.

The next step is to translate the model into some physical Oracle tables. Now that the empty database has been created, you will need to alter the utlestat.sql program

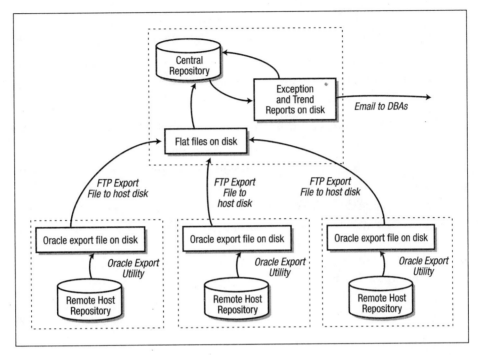

Figure 11.1

A sample schema for storing Oracle performance information.

to insert the information into your new table whenever it is invoked. Here is an example of how the hit ratios can be captured:

```
INSERT INTO ORACLE.pt_instance (buffer_hit_ratio)
(
SELECT
round(decode(gets-misses,0,1,gets-misses)/decode(gets,0,1,gets),3)
     hit_ratio,
    sleeps,
    round(sleeps/decode(misses,0,1,misses),3) "SLEEPS/MISS"
    FROM STATS$LATCHES
    WHERE gets != 0
    AND name = 'buffer cache lru'
);
```

Once the modifications have been completed, this new version of utlestat.sql will replace the older version. Whenever it is invoked, it will add rows to your performance and tuning database.

To make the utility run, it is suggested that a **cron** job be set to start utlbstat.sql at a predetermined time, followed by utlestat.sql several hours later. This way, you will receive a daily, consistent record of the status of your Oracle database at the same time each day. Of course, if you want to measure trends during the processing day, you can run this every hour, with 15 minutes between **bstat** and **estat**.

In a distributed environment, it is necessary to transfer the local Oracle statistics table data into a large, centralized Oracle database that will hold performance and tuning information for all of the Oracle instances in the enterprise. This can be easily accomplished by running a **cron** job from the main repository. This **cron** will execute the necessary SQL to select all rows from the remote table, inserting them into the main table. Finally, it will either truncate the tables or delete all rows from the remote table:

```
INSERT INTO MAIN.pt_instance
(
SELECT * FROM ORACLE.pt_instance@bankok
);
DELETE FROM ORACLE.pt_instance@bankok;
```

You can now run reports and alert scripts against the centralized repository to predict when problems will be encountered. Listing 11.6 presents an example of a query that will list any tables that have extended more than three times on the previous day.

Listing 11.6   A sample table report.

```
COLUMN c0   HEADING "SID";
COLUMN c1   HEADING "Owner";
COLUMN c2   HEADING "ts";
COLUMN c3   HEADING "Table";
COLUMN c4   HEADING "Size (KB)" FORMAT 999,999;
COLUMN c5   HEADING "Next (K)"  FORMAT 99,999;
COLUMN c6   HEADING "Old Ext"   FORMAT 999;
COLUMN c7   HEADING "New Ext"   FORMAT 999;

SET LINESIZE 150;
SET PAGESIZE 60;
BREAK ON c0 SKIP 2 ON c1 SKIP 1
TTITLE " Table Report| > 50 Extents or new extents";
SPOOL /tmp/rpt10
SELECT
DISTINCT
```

```
            B.sid                          c0,
            substr(B.owner,1,6)            c1,
            substr(B.tablespace_name,1,10) c2,
            substr(B.table_name,1,20)      c3,
            (B.blocks_alloc*2048)/1024     c4,
            C.next_extent/1024             c5,
            A.extents                      c6,
            B.extents                      c7
FROM        PERF A,
            PERF B,
            DBA_TABLES C
WHERE
            rtrim(C.table_name) = rtrim(B.table_name)
AND
            A.sid = B.sid
AND
            rtrim(A.tablespace_name) <> 'SYSTEM'
AND
            A.tablespace_name = B.tablespace_name
AND
            A.table_name = B.table_name
AND
            to_char(B.run_date) = to_char(round(SYSDATE,'DAY')-7)
            -- start with closest SUNDAY minus one week
AND
            to_char(A.run_date) = to_char(B.run_date-7)
            -- compare to one week prior
AND
(
            A.extents < B.extents
            -- where extents has increased
OR
            B.extents > 50
)
--AND
--          B.extents - A.extents > 1
ORDER BY B.sid;
SPOOL OFF;
```

Notice that this query joins the **PERF** table with itself, comparing the table data for one week against the table data for the prior week. Reports like these are the basis for automated exception reporting because they can be used to detect out-of-the-ordinary conditions and alert the developer before performance becomes a problem.

Now that we have defined the general architecture of our performance collection system, let's look at the scheduled tasks that are required to make the system function automatically. There will be scheduled tasks on each of the Oracle instances, as well as on the centralized performance and tuning database.

Daily And Weekly System Processing

The system architecture shown in Figure 11.2 has been designed to have "agents" on each remote Oracle host to perform the daily data collection, which is accomplished with two **cron** tasks (**bstat-estat**). Each remote host will have a small copy of the performance and tuning database to hold one week's worth of data. Each Saturday, the hosts will execute two **cron** jobs to accomplish the following tasks:

- **Export_p_and_t_tables** (C shell script)—This will export and compress the Oracle performance and tuning, and FTP the file to central:/$DBA/$SID/ p_and_t.

- **Create_p_add_t_tables** (C shell)—This will drop and re-create the local database tables.

After all remote sites FTP their export files, a **cron** will fire on the central database to perform the following actions:

- **Import_p_and_t_tables** (C shell) *(For example, runs each Saturday at 1:00 PM)*— It will loop through all entries in $DBA/$SID/p_and_t/hostfile (the list of SIDs) and then load the export file into the main performance and tuning database.

- Run the script $DBA/DBAX/p_and_t/reports/extract_reports.csh *(For example, runs each Saturday at 2:00 PM)*—It will loop through all entries in $DBA/$SID/ p_and_t/hostfile (the list of SIDs), and then, for each entry, execute p_and_t_rpt**.sql (where ** = 01–11), spooling the reports to SERVER.- SID.p_and_t_rpt** in directory $DBA/$SID/p_and_t/reports.

- Run the script $DBA/$SID/p_and_t/reports/mail_reports.csh *(For example, runs each Saturday at 3:00 PM)*—Loops through all entries in $DBA/p_and_t/hostfile (the list of SIDs). For each entry, it will get the email address of the primary DBA for the host (in $DBA/p_and_t/hostfile) and then email reports SERVER.SID_rpt** to the address specified in hostfile. For reference purposes,

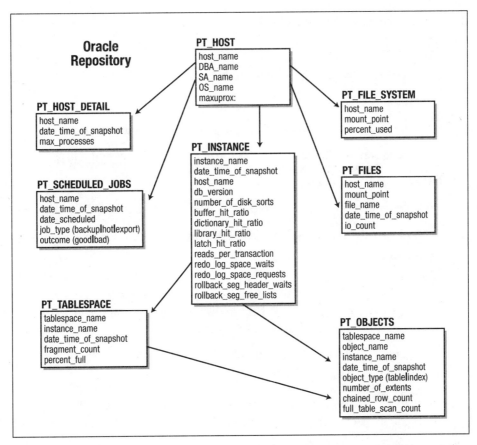

Figure 11.2

A sample performance and tuning architecture.

the reports will remain on Central as well, as explained in the next section. Now that we have reviewed the code that is used at the centralized database, let's take a look at the code that would exist on each Oracle host to initially collect the statistics.

Local Oracle Processing

On each remote host, a directory will exist to hold the code required to collect data. The central database will exist on Central repository, but each remote host will have a small, local copy of the master database to temporarily hold the performance and tuning data until the weekly upload.

Each remote host will have the following:

- Scripts (**chmod** +x)

  - **bstat**—A C shell script to start the **bstat** utility.

  - **estat**—A C shell script to run the **estat** utility.

  - **export_p_and_t_tables**—A C shell script to export and FTP the file.

  - **create_stat**—A C shell script to drop and re-create the local tables.

- **PARM** Files (**chmod 440**)

  - **pass_system**—A protected file containing the Oracle **SYSTEM** password.

  - **pass_oracle_central**—A protected file with the Unix Oracle password for Central.

- SQL Files

  - **p_and_t_collect_b_e_stats.sql**—A file that retrieves performance and tuning data from the **BSTAT-ESTAT** tables.

  - **p_and_t_collect_object_stats.sql**—A file that retrieves performance and tuning table data from DBA tables.

  - **p_and_t_collect_ts_stats.sql**—A file that retrieves performance and tuning tablespace data from DBA tables.

  - **create_p_and_t_tables.sql**—A file that contains SQL to drop and re-create the local p_and_t tables with **SYSTEM** owner.

  - **add_server_name.sql**—A file that contains SQL to add the server name to the local p_and_t tables.

  - **p_and_t_utlbstat.sql**—A customized version of **bstat**.

  - **p_and_t_utlestat.sql**—A customized version of **estat** to retain the **TEMP** tables.

- Other Files

  - **create_failed**—An error message file for **create_stat**.

  - **export_failed**—An error message file from **export_p_and_t_tables**.

- **export_p_and_t_tables.par**—A parfile for the export job.

- **Any other files in $DBA/$SID/p_and_t**—Output (i.e., log files) from running the jobs.

Now that you've seen the components for remote hosts, let's look at how you can use the Unix **cron** utility to schedule these tasks in their proper sequence.

cron Run Schedules

The **bstat** script is run each weekday at 8:00 AM, followed by the **estat** at 4:00 PM. Here is the **crontab** listing:

```
#
# Below are the cron entries for the performance & tuning database
#
00 08 * * 1-5 /u03/home/oracle/admin/p_and_t/bstat 2>&1
00 16 * * 1-5 /u03/home/oracle/admin/p_and_t/estat 2>&1
#
00 08 * * 6   /u03/home/oracle/p_and_t/export_p_and_t_tables 2>&1
30 08 * * 6   /u03/home/oracle/p_and_t/create_p_and_t_tables 2>&1
```

On the central server, weekly processes are executed to perform the following tasks:

- Uncompress and load the incoming data

- Extract the weekly performance and tuning reports

- Mail the reports to the DBAs

Here is the **crontab** listing:

```
#
#
00 13 * * 1 /u01/dba/oracle/admin/DBAX/p_and_t/import_p_and_t_tables 2>&1
#
00 14 * * 1 /u01/oracle/p_and_t/reports/extract_reports.csh 2>&1
00 15 * * 1 /u01/oracle/p_and_t/reports/mail_reports.csh 2>&1
```

Now that all of the scheduled **cron** tasks are in place, let's take a detailed look at the performance and tuning reports that can be easily generated from our new database.

Performance Reports

This system consists of 10 reports that provide detailed performance information about each Oracle component. Tables 11.2 through 11.12 show samples of each report.

Table 11.2 **MY_SID** instance hit and enqueue report data for the last seven days (07/08/96 10:06).

B/Estat Execution	Logical Reads	Physical Reads	Enqueue Waits	Hit Ratio
96/07/01 MON 08:00-09:30	127,460,970	29,344,200	192	.77
96/07/02 TUE 09:18-09:30	1,571,052	1,187,076	0	.24
96/07/03 WED 08:00-09:30	18,588	366	0	.98
96/07/04 THU 08:00-09:30	12,548	320	0	.97
96/07/05 FRI 08:00-09:30	12,372	244	0	.98
Average	25,815,106	6,106,441	38	.79
Minimum	12,372	244	0	.244
Maximum	127,460,970	29,344,200	192	.98

Table 11.3 Excerpts from **MY_SID** sort stats report for the last 21 days (07/08/96 10:06).

B/Estat Execution	Sorts (Memory)	Sorts (Disk)	Sorts (Rows)
96/06/28 FRI 09:23-09:24	42	0	636
96/06/28 FRI 09:28-16:00	600	0	13,302
96/07/01 MON 08:00-09:30	3,630	282	11,025,378
96/07/02 TUE 09:18-09:30	42	0	660
96/07/03 WED 08:00-09:30	42	0	660
96/07/04 THU 08:00-09:30	44	0	440
96/07/05 FRI 08:00-09:30	28	0	440
Average	633	40	1,577,359
Minimum	28	0	440
Maximum	3,630	282	11,025,378

Table 11.4   Excerpts from **MY_SID** user call stats report for the last 21 days (07/08/96 10:06).

B/Estat Execution	User Calls	User Commits	User Rollbacks	Recursive Calls	Call Ratio
96/06/28 FRI 09:23-09:24	270	12	0	156	.58
96/06/28 FRI 09:28-16:00	14,934	54	0	211,998	14.20
96/07/01 MON 08:00-09:30	24,468	2,970	0	2,956,938	120.85
96/07/02 TUE 09:18-09:30	270	30	0	14,868	55.07
96/07/03 WED 08:00-09:30	270	12	0	12,738	47.18
96/07/04 THU 08:00-09:30	180	8	0	8,528	47.38
96/07/05 FRI 08:00-09:30	180	8	0	8,372	46.51
Average	5,796	442	0	459,085	47.39
Minimum	180	8	0	156	.58
Maximum	24,468	2,970	0	2,956,938	120.85

Table 11.5   Excerpts from **MY_SID** fetch and scan stats report for the last 21 days (07/08/96 10:06).

B/Estat Execution	Fetch By ROWID	Fetch CtRow	Scans Long	Scans Short	Scans Rows	Scan Ratio
96/07/01 11:03-11:06	720	0	0	18	18	.00
96/07/01 11:28-16:00	3,222,765	207	144	947,241	120,345,201	.00
96/07/02 08:00-16:00	109,052,170	55	240	570,605	355,301,755	.00
96/07/03 08:00-16:00	2,456,540	164	764	25,000	310,878,908	.03
96/07/04 08:00-16:00	160	0	0	472	18,312	.00
96/07/05 08:00-16:00	19,796	0	0	532	92,844	.00
Average	22,458,692	71	191	257,311	131,106,173	.01
Minimum	160	0	0	18	18	.00
Maximum	109,052,170	207	764	947,241	355,301,755	.03

Table 11.6 Excerpts from **MY_SID** average write queue and redo wait report for the last 21 days (07/08/96 10:06).

B/Estat Execution	Summed Dirty Queue Length	Write Requests	Avg Write Queue Length	Redo Special Requests
96/06/26 WED 16:19-16:20	0	128	.00	0
96/06/27 THU 08:05-12:05	5,572	16,856	.33	28
96/06/28 FRI 09:28-16:00	18	378	.05	0
96/07/01 MON 08:00-09:30	35,784	122,334	.29	138
96/07/01 MON 08:00-12:00	41,909	38,976	1.08	126
96/07/02 TUE 08:00-12:00	2,016	22,950	.09	126
96/07/02 TUE 08:00-16:00	116,455	28,080	4.15	40
96/07/03 WED 08:00-12:00	437	2,207	.20	39
6/07/03 WED 08:00-16:00	87,396	74,064	1.18	80
96/07/04 THU 08:00-09:30	0	32	.00	0
96/07/05 FRI 08:00-16:00	0	184	.00	0
Average	30,612	18,540	.96	32
Minimum	0	32	.00	0
Maximum	116,455	122,334	4.15	138

Table 11.7 Excerpts from **MY_SID** instance B/E file stats totals by data file for last 31 days (07/08/96 10:06).

Data File	Total Reads	Total Read Time	Total Writes	Total Write Time
/Datadisks/d01/ORACLE/my_sid/mptv.dbf	6,870,264	0	100,596	0
/Datadisks/d02/ORACLE/my_sid/index.dbf	282,408	0	66,876	0
Average	806,251	0	54,535	0

(continued)

Table 11.7   Excerpts from **MY_SID** instance B/E file stats totals by data file for last 31 days (07/08/96 10:06) *(continued)*.

Data File	Total Reads	Total Read Time	Total Write	Total Write Time
Minimum	0	0	0	0
Maximum	6,870,264	0	255,474	0
Sum	7,256,258	0	490,816	0

Table 11.8   Excerpts from **MY_SID** instance B/E file totals by file system for last 7 days stats (07/09/96 09:22).

File System	Total Reads	Total Writes
/Datadisks/d01/ORACLE	373,144	45,823
/Datadisks/d02/ORACLE	22,120	67,729
/Datadisks/d03/ORACLE	449,608	9,107
/Datadisks/d04/ORACLE	1,119,456	11,920
/Datadisks/d05/ORACLE	272,716	9,703
/Datadisks/d06/ORACLE	1,051,170	37,835
/Datadisks/d09/ORACLE	746	1,186
Average	644,920	158,627
Minimum	0	0
Maximum	2,876,425	1,444,968
Sum	9,673,799	2,379,401

Table 11.9   Excerpts from **MY_SID** instance B-E rollback stats last 21 days (07/08/96). Transaction table wait ratio > .05—Add rollbacks.

B/Estat Execution	Gets	Waits	Ratio	Undo Bytes
96/06/28 FRI 09:23-09:24	28	0	.00	9,576
96/06/28 FRI 09:28-16:00	2,975	0	.00	99,988

(continued)

Table 11.9 Excerpts from **MY_SID** instance B-E rollback stats last 21 days (07/08/96). Transaction table wait ratio > .05—Add rollbacks *(continued)*.

B/Estat Execution	Gets	Waits	Ratio	Und Bytes
96/07/01 MON 08:00-07:36	94,101	0	.00	124,102,104
96/07/02 TUE 09:18-09:30	266	0	.00	501,942
96/07/03 WED 08:00-09:30	658	0	.00	9,632
96/07/04 THU 08:00-09:30	470	0	.00	6,880
96/07/05 FRI 08:00-09:30	470	0	.00	6,880

Table 11.10 Excerpts from **MY_SID** instance B-E lib stats last 40 days (07/08/96). Reparse ratio > .01—Increase **shared_pool_size**.

B/Estat Execution	Pins	Reloads	Reparse Ratio
96/06/28 FRI 09:23-09:24	728	21	.0288
96/06/28 FRI 09:28-16:00	36,330	742	.0204
96/07/01 MON 08:00-07:36	1,123,808	315	.0003
96/07/02 TUE 09:18-09:30	7,315	70	.0096
96/07/03 WED 08:00-09:30	994	0	.0000
96/07/04 THU 08:00-09:30	700	0	.0000
96/07/05 FRI 08:00-09:30	660	0	.0000
Average	167,219	164	.0084

Table 11.11 Excerpts from Table/Index extents (07/08/96 13:40). **TRANP** table report > 80—Extents or new extents data for the last 7 days.

SID	Owner	TS	Table	Size (KB)	Next (K)	Old Ext	New Ext
TRANP	HOCK	USERS_01	LOBHOCK11	7,606	352	67	69
RPT	USERS_01	USER_TABLES_RPT		660	0	12	15

Table 11.12 Excerpts from Tablespace report (07/12/96). **MY_SID** instance data file storage in Oracle megabytes (1,048,576 bytes).

Date	Tablespace	Tablesp Pieces	Tablesp Mbytes	Free Mbytes	Free Mbytes	Percent Free
03-JUL-96	INDEXG	5	600	20	17	3
03-JUL-96	GSA_DATA	4	600	61	57	10
03-JUL-96	INDEXH	1	200	21	21	10
03-JUL-96	INDEXE	3	400	42	38	10
03-JUL-96	PROSPECTING01	1	900	99	99	11
03-JUL-96	PERSON	1	200	30	30	15
03-JUL-96	PROSPECTING02	7	750	165	82	22
03-JUL-96	ADDRESS	1	200	49	49	24
03-JUL-96	INDEXB	2	400	114	62	29
03-JUL-96	RESPONSIBILITY	1	150	45	45	30
03-JUL-96	TOOLS	2	10	3	3	32
03-JUL-96	ORGANIZATION	1	300	121	121	40

Tablespace And Table Data Gathering

While the estat/bstat utilities are great for measuring memory usage, a DBA might still want to capture information about Oracle tables and tablespaces. For example, an alert report can easily be generated that shows all tables and indexes that have extended more than twice in the past 24 hours. A tablespace alert report could be written to display all tablespaces that have free space less than 10 percent of the tablespace size.

A routine can easily be written to interrogate all tablespaces and dump the information into a statistical table, as shown in Listing 11.7, and this tablespace information can be tracked to predict the rate of growth and the time when it will become necessary to add a data file to the tablespace.

Listing 11.7 A tablespace data gathering script.

```
INSERT INTO TABLESPACE_STAT VALUES (
SELECT   DFS.tablespace_name,
         round(sum(DFS.bytes)/1048576,2),
```

```
        round(max(DFS.bytes)/1048576,2)
FROM     SYS.dba_free_space DFS
GROUP BY DFS.tablespace_name
ORDER BY DFS.tablespace_name);
```

Tables are usually tracked to provide information on unexpected growth. A high growth rate can indicate that the table was undersized on the **NEXT** parameter, or it can indicate an upturn in end-user processing. In either case, the DBA wants to be informed whenever any table extends more than twice within any 24-hour period.

Gathering the table extent information is a simple matter, as shown in Listing 11.8. This script can be attached to a **cron** process to gather the extent information at a specified time interval.

Listing 11.8   A table data gathering script.

```
INSERT INTO TAB_STAT VALUES(
SELECT   DS.tablespace_name,
         DT.owner,
         DT.table_name,
         DS.bytes/1024,
         DS.extents,
         DT.max_extents,
         DT.initial_extent/1024,
         DT.next_extent/1024,
         DT.pct_increase,
         DT.pct_free,
         DT.pct_used
FROM     SYS.dba_segments DS,
         SYS.dba_tables DT
WHERE    DS.tablespace_name = DT.tablespace_name
AND    DS.owner = DT.owner
AND    DS.segment_name = DT.table_name
ORDER BY 1,2,3);
```

Once these tables have been populated, it is a relatively simple matter to write some SQL to generate alert reports for the DBA.

A tablespace alert report can be defined by the DBA, but it would usually contain a list of tablespaces where the largest fragment is less than 10 percent of the size of the tablespace. Regardless, data created from table analysis routines can be used to generate variance reports that alert the DBA to possible problems in the databases. (See Listing 11.9.) Note the clever method of joining the extents table against itself to show all tables that have extended in the past week.

Listing 11.9 A table extents report.

```
BREAK ON c0 SKIP 2 ON c1 SKIP 1
TTITLE " Table Report| > 50 Extents or new extents";
SPOOL /tmp/rpt10
SELECT
DISTINCT
        B.sid                             c0,
        substr(B.owner,1,6)               c1,
        substr(B.tablespace_name,1,10)    c2,
        substr(B.table_name,1,20)         c3,
        (B.blocks_alloc*2048)/1024        c4,
        C.next_extent/1024                c5,
        A.extents                         c6,
        B.extents                         c7
FROM    TAB_STAT         A,
        TAB_STAT         B,
        DBA_TABLES       C
WHERE
        rtrim(C.table_name) = rtrim(B.table_name)
AND
        A.sid = B.sid
AND
        rtrim(A.tablespace_name) <> 'SYSTEM'
AND
        A.tablespace_name = B.tablespace_name
AND
        A.table_name = B.table_name
AND
        to_char(A.run_date) = to_char(B.run_date-7)
        -- compare to one week prior
AND
(
        A.extents < B.extents
        -- where extents has increased
OR
        B.extents > 50
)
ORDER BY B.sid;
```

While the marketplace is full of fancy tools for measuring Oracle performance, an Oracle DBA can benefit from extending the basic Oracle performance tools to create a proactive, customized framework for Oracle tuning. Today, Oracle DBAs must automate as many functions as possible in order to maximize productivity. One way a developer can maximize productivity is to create a menu-based interface to assist in running the Oracle performance reports. With a friendly front end, Oracle professionals can easily run reports at will without knowing any of the interface language.

Online Menu For The Performance System

Once a mechanism has been put in place to deliver statistics to a centralized Oracle database, a menu-based system can be created to allow reports to be generated against the data. Here is a sample menu for such a system:

Performance Reports for Oracle

MAIN MENU

1. SGA waits and Buffer hit ratio report

2. Cache hit ratio report

3. Data Dictionary report

4. File report

5. Tablespace report

6. Table report

7. Index report

8. SGA—hit ratio/wait count alert

9. Tablespace—fragment/free space alert

10. Table—Increased extents alert

11. Index—Increased extents alert

12. Audit

14. Exit

Enter choice ==>

This menu is driven by a Korn shell script, as shown in Listing 11.10.

Listing 11.10   A Korn shell script to extract Oracle performance data.

```
trap "exit 0" 1 2 3 4 5 6 7 8 10 15


USER_NAME='id -un'
#if [ "$USER_NAME" != "root" -a "$USER_NAME" != "oracle" ]
if [ "$USER_NAME" != "root" ]
then
  echo
  echo "You must be ROOT to execute this script."
  echo
  return 0
fi

# Set PATH
        PATH=/bin:/u01/bin:/etc:/u01/contrib/bin:/u01/oracle/bin:/
          u01/oracle/etc:/u01/lib:/u01/lib/acct:/u01/backup/bin
        export PATH

# Set up Oracle environment
        ORACLE_HOME=/u01/oracle
        ORAKITPATH=/u01/oracle/resource
        FORMS30PATH=/u01/oracle/resource
        MENU5PATH=/u01/oracle/resource
        export ORACLE_HOME ORACLE_SID ORAKITPATH FORMS30PATH MENU5PATH
        PATH=$PATH:${ORACLE_HOME}/bin:
        export PATH
        ORAENV_ASK=NO

TWO_TASK=perfdb
export TWO_TASK
unset ORACLE_SID

get_sid()
{
echo
echo "Enter the database name: \c"
read DBNAME1
END1=${DBNAME1}
export END1
}
```

```
get_parms()
{

#*********************************************************************
# Prompt for database name
#*********************************************************************
echo
echo "Enter the database name: \c"
read DBNAME1


case $DBNAME1 in

   ""            ) END1="\" \""
       ;;

   *             )  END1="\" and upper(rtrim(brndb.sid))
                    =upper('"${DBNAME1}"')\""
       ;;
esac

export END1
} #  End of get_parms()

get_date()
{
#*********************************************************************
# Prompt for start date
#*********************************************************************
echo
echo "Enter a start date:(mm/dd/yy) (or press enter for none) \c"
read DATE1

if [ $DATE1 ]
then
   END2="\" and run_date >=to_date('$DATE1','MM/DD/YY')\""
else
   END2="\" and run_date >=to_date('01/01/01','MM/DD/YY')\""
fi

export END2

#*********************************************************************
# Prompt for end date
#*********************************************************************
```

```
echo
echo "Enter an end date:(mm/dd/yy) (or press enter for none) \c"
read DATE2

if [ $DATE2 ]
then
    END3="\" and run_date <=to_date('$DATE2','MM/DD/YY')\""
else
    END3="\" and run_date <=to_date('12/31/99','MM/DD/YY')\""
fi

export END3

} # end of get_date...

get_extents()
{
#*********************************************************************
# Prompt for number of extents
#*********************************************************************
echo
echo "Where number of extents is greater than (default 0):\c"
read EXT1

if [ $EXT1 ]
then
    END4="\" and extents > $EXT1\""
else
    END4="\" and extents > 0\""
fi

export END4
} # end of get_extents...


three_mess()
{
echo " "
echo "Data for this report is collected directly from the remote host."
echo " "
echo "Therefore, you may not want to run this against a database"
echo "unless you are prepared to wait awhile."
echo " "
}
```

```
#*******************************************************************
#  Main routine loop
#*******************************************************************
while true ; do
  clear

  echo "                    PER Reports for Oracle"
  echo
  echo "     1. SGA waits & Buffer hit ratio report"
  echo "     2. Cache hit ratio report"
  echo "     3. Data Dictionary report"
  echo "     4. File report"
  echo "     5. Tablespace report"
  echo "     6. Table report"
  echo "     7. Index report"
  echo
  echo "     8. SGA        - hit ratio/wait count alert "
  echo "     9. Tablespace - fragment/free space alert"
  echo "    10. Table      - Increased extents alert"
  echo "    11. Index      - Increased extents alert"
  echo
  echo "    12. Audit      - Check a database for security violations"
  echo
  echo "    14. EXIT"
  echo
  echo $MESS1
  echo

  echo "Enter choice ==> \c:"
  read PICK


  case $PICK in

    "1") PREFIX=ps
         one_mess;
         get_parms;
         get_date;
         /u01/oracle/per/perf/rpt1.sh
         MESS1="Report has been spooled to  /tmp/rpt1.lst"
         ;;
    "2") PREFIX=ds
         one_mess;
         get_parms;
         get_date;
```

```
          /u01/oracle/per/perf/rpt2.sh
          MESS1="Report has been spooled to  /tmp/rpt2.lst"
          ;;
    "3") PREFIX=ls
          one_mess;
          get_parms;
          get_date;
          /u01/oracle/per/perf/rpt3.sh
          MESS1="Report has been spooled to  /tmp/rpt3.lst"
          ;;
    "4") PREFIX=fs
          one_mess;
          get_parms;
          get_date;
          /u01/oracle/per/perf/rpt4.sh
          MESS1="Report has been spooled to  /tmp/rpt4.lst"
          ;;
    "5") get_parms;
          get_date;
          /u01/oracle/per/perf/rpt5.sh
          MESS1="Report has been spooled to  /tmp/rpt5.lst"
          ;;
    "6") get_parms;
          get_date;
          get_extents;
          /u01/oracle/per/perf/rpt6.sh
          MESS1="Report has been spooled to  /tmp/rpt6.lst"
          ;;
    "7") get_parms;
          get_date;
          get_extents;
          /u01/oracle/per/perf/rpt7.sh
          MESS1="Report has been spooled to  /tmp/rpt7.lst"
          ;;
    "8") nohup /u01/oracle/per/perf/rpt8.sh > /tmp/rpt8.lst 2>&1 &
          MESS1="Report will be spooled to  /tmp/rpt8.lst"
          ;;
    "9") nohup /u01/oracle/per/perf/rpt9.sh > /tmp/rpt9.lst 2>&1 &
          MESS1="Report will be spooled to  /tmp/rpt9.lst"
          ;;
   "10") nohup /u01/oracle/per/perf/rpt10.sh > /tmp/rpt10.lst 2>&1 &
          MESS1="Report will be spooled to  /tmp/rpt10.lst"
          ;;
   "11") nohup /u01/oracle/per/perf/rpt11.sh > /tmp/rpt11.lst 2>&1 &
          MESS1="Report will be spooled to  /tmp/rpt11.lst"
          ;;
```

```
"12") three_mess;
      get_sid;
      /u01/oracle/per/perf/rpt12.sh
      MESS1="Report has been spooled to  /tmp/rpt12.lst"
      ;;
"14") echo bye
      break
      ;;
esac
```

This Korn shell script provides complete access to the reports in the database. Note that reports one through seven can be parameterized, and the system will ask you to specify the database name and the date ranges.

Running The Oracle Reports And Alerts

The following parameters are required to run the script from Listing 11.10. The script will prompt the user for the following values:

1.   Database name (default is *all* databases)

2.   Start date (default is 2000 BC)

3.   End date (default is today)

Reports 6 and 7 (table and index reports) prompt you to enter the number of extents that are used in the table or index query. The user will receive the following prompts:

```
Enter the database name: (or press enter for all databases) cusdb
Enter a start date:(mm/dd/yy) (or press enter for none) 06/01/95
Enter an end date:(mm/dd/yy) (or press enter for none)
Where number of extents is greater than (default 0):30
```

Also note that reports 8 through 11 are the alert reports. Alert reports do not prompt for additional information.

While this approach is excellent for creating a proactive (i.e., long-term) infrastructure for monitoring Oracle, there are many vendor offerings that can be used for reactive monitoring. As I mentioned earlier, reactive Oracle monitoring is done by continuously polling for exceptions and sending alerts when some Oracle threshold has been exceeded. Oracle offers crude alert monitor tools within the Oracle Enterprise Manager Console, but robust tools for Oracle alert monitoring have been around for years. One of the most popular is Patrol, by BMC Software. The following section takes a closer look at Patrol and how it is used to continuously monitor Oracle performance.

A Closer Look—BMC's Patrol

In the fiercely competitive marketplace of system monitoring tools, vendors are striving to create products that take care of the routine and mundane administrative tasks, freeing DBAs and system administrators to do more high-level work. With the advent of open systems and geographically diverse networks of distributed databases, a centralized tool for monitoring system performance has become indispensable. Patrol is a product that fulfills this need.

> **Note:** A fully-functional demonstration copy of BMC's Patrol can be found on the CD-ROM accompanying this book.

Marketed as an alert monitor, Patrol positions itself against products such as DBVision, by Platinum Software, and a host of other SNMP-compliant monitors. The goal of this type of tool is to provide an intelligent agent that will constantly monitor the database and operating environment, detecting extraordinary conditions (called events). Once detected, an event can trigger an intelligent script to automatically correct a problem while calling the DBA's beeper number (or triggering another alert). While this might sound like a lofty goal, Patrol has been very successful in creating a framework that removes much of the tedious monitoring from DBAs' and SAs' jobs. Patrol is friendly enough that a naive operator can monitor dozens of hosts, drilling down quickly to identify the nature of many problems.

Patrol offers the ability to manage a variety of relational databases from a single console, and it currently supports a host of relational databases, including Oracle, Sybase, Informix, DB2 version 2, OpenVMS, and CA-Ingres. In addition, Patrol offers special submodules for monitoring vendor application packages, such as Oracle Financials. The ability to provide a common monitor for many diverse databases is one of the features of Patrol that appeals to large, multivendor database sites.

For such a sophisticated product, the installation of Patrol is relatively straightforward and consists of two steps: the installation of the "console" (the host that monitors the databases) and the installation of agent software on each agent that will be monitored. The installation guide is compact and well-written, and describes the procedures for loading the Patrol installer that is run to install the specific product components.

The front end for the console is Motif-based, offering an excellent GUI environment with a very intuitive drill-down capability. In fact, Patrol is so intuitive that an experienced DBA can instantly use the console to view a problem without any prior training. The main screen consists of one icon for each host, and the host turns red to indicate that an event has been triggered within the knowledge module (see Figure 11.3).

Clicking on a host icon will drill down into a set of database icons—one for each database on the host—and will also show icons for other components on the host, including file systems and disk devices. A drill-down from the database icon will show numerous database statistics. Despite these superior display capabilities, Patrol's real value comes from its management of the user-defined rules that tell Patrol when something is amiss. Figure 11.4 displays Patrol's drill-down screen.

Anyone who has ever used an alert monitor in a production environment knows that the effective use of a tool depends on its ability to identify salient problems while avoiding false alerts (precision). At the same time, no real problems can be missed (recall). This balancing act between precision and recall requires a very flexible set of customizable rule bases—an area in which Patrol is very effective.

Patrol's Knowledge Module

Patrol supports a dynamic knowledge base that allows DBAs to continually customize specific events within their systems. For example, a DBA might be interested in knowing when a file system is nearly full. However, file systems dedicated to database files will always be full—falsely alerting the DBA about a condition that does not require any intervention. Patrol collects these decision rules and calls them *knowledge modules* (KMs). To Patrol, a knowledge module consists of a set of parameters with meaningful names, such as **BufferBusyRate** and **CacheHitRatio**. (See Figure 11.5.) A knowledge module can be versioned, customized, and stored on the main console (the global KM) or on each remote agent (the local KM).

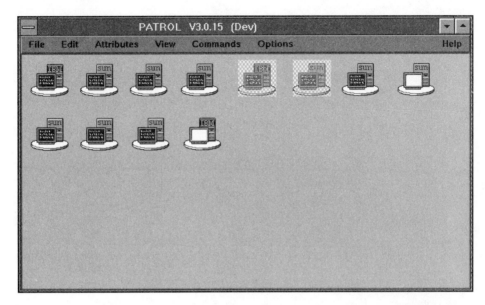

Figure 11.3
The main Patrol console screen.

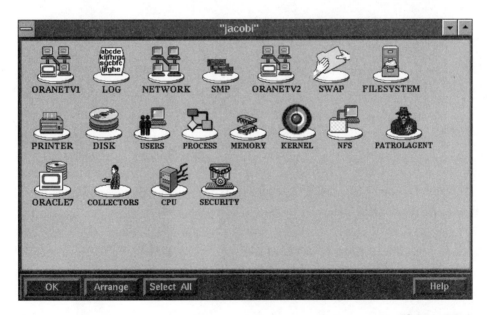

Figure 11.4
The drill-down Patrol screen.

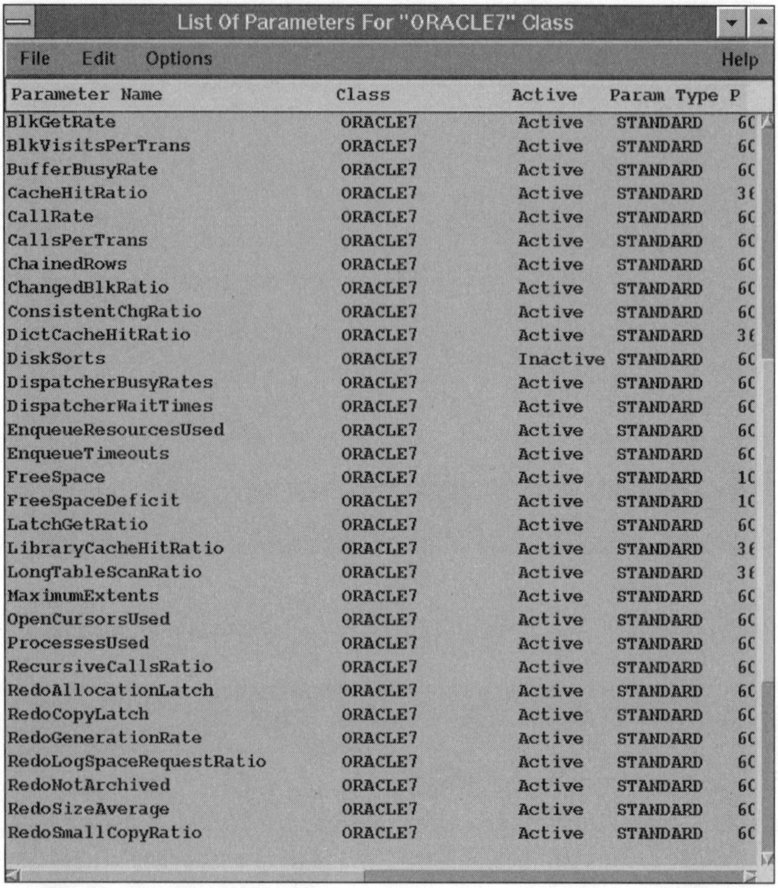

Figure 11.5
The Patrol Oracle parameter list.

The Patrol architecture provides a mechanism whereby the global knowledge module is referenced first, followed by any additional rules specific to an agent. This feature is especially useful for databases that have unique characteristics. For example, the value of **LongTableScanRatio** should stay below 80 percent for online transaction processing systems, but a **LongTableScanRatio** of 60 percent is perfectly acceptable for a batch-oriented reporting database that relies on full-table scans.

These parameters contain the following attributes:

• *Poll Time*—A parameter that can be scheduled to "fire" on a schedule.

- *Automated Recovery*—Specific actions that can be programmed to notify the DBA and trigger actions to automatically correct the problem.

- *Output Range*—Values that trigger an alert condition. For example, by default, the value of **MaximumExtents** will trigger a warning when a table reaches 90 percent of available extents, and an alarm when reaching 95 percent of available extents.

- *Manual Recovery*—This is a knowledge base that advises the DBA as to an appropriate corrective action. For example, the value of **LibraryCacheHitRatio** for Oracle correctly advises the DBA that increasing the value of **shared_pool_size** could relieve the problem. This feature of Patrol is especially nice for the newbie DBA who is not intimately familiar with corrective actions for database problems (see Figure 11.6).

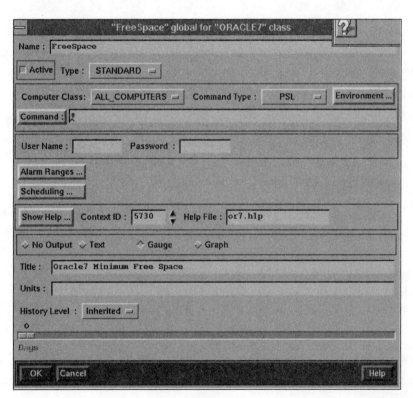

Figure 11.6
The Patrol Oracle parameter maintenance screen.

Each parameter can be manually adjusted to reflect specific conditions that exist at specific sites. This customization is achieved by changing the Output Range Values and the polling times. For example, a transaction-oriented system could be customized to stop polling in the evenings when batch reporting occurs.

It is important to note that Patrol measures systemwide statistics and not just the behaviors of each database on the host. Patrol currently supports Unix-level measurement on Bull, DC-OSX, DG, HP, SCO, Sequent, SGI, Solaris, Sun4, and SVR4. With the Unix knowledge module, a system administrator would be able to use Patrol to measure "swap" memory usage, paging within the Unix buffer cache, and just about every possible kernel component. Unfortunately, Patrol does not offer a "recovery" section for the Unix component. (Possibly the developers at BMC assumed that system administrators would be offended by a tool that suggests possible remedies for problems.)

Customized events can also be incorporated into Patrol's knowledge modules. A customized event might be a backup process that is run every Tuesday morning at 1:00 AM. Patrol can be customized to check for the successful completion of the backup, and trigger an alert if a problem is encountered.

Patrol also comes with a set of menu options that allows a manager to create reports and view salient information about the system.

Patrol Reports

Patrol's report facility is very robust and comprehensive, replacing the need to have additional database reports for all but the most specific queries. A couple of interesting menu option are Patrol's CPU Hog Percentage and All Problem Users, which can be programmed to detect runaway processes on the host and alert DBAs about the event. For example, any process that consumes more than 30 percent of the overall CPU might be a runaway process, and Patrol can be programmed to detect these conditions (see Figure 11.7).

As a natural extension of its reporting feature, Patrol provides a means of handling exceptions, whereby the Oracle professional can set thresholds. When these thresh-

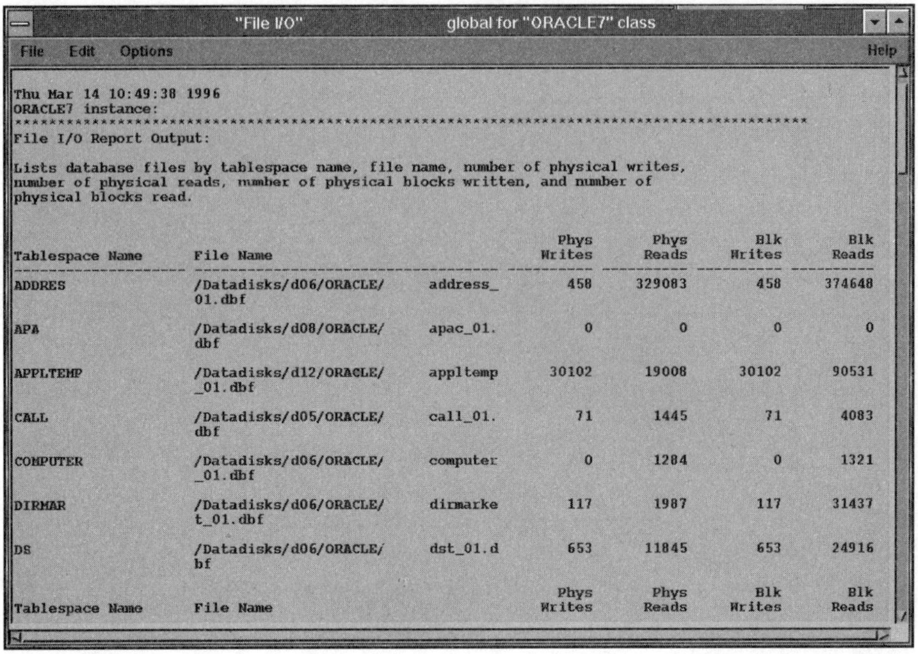

```
                     "File I/O"                 global for "ORACLE7" class

File   Edit   Options                                                        Help

Thu Mar 14 10:49:38 1996
ORACLE7 instance:
********************************************************************************
File I/O Report Output:

Lists database files by tablespace name, file name, number of physical writes,
number of physical reads, number of physical blocks written, and number of
physical blocks read.

                                                      Phys      Phys      Blk       Blk
Tablespace Name     File Name                        Writes     Reads    Writes     Reads

ADDRES              /Datadisks/d06/ORACLE/  address_    458    329083      458    374648
                    01.dbf

APA                 /Datadisks/d08/ORACLE/  apac_01.      0         0        0         0
                    dbf

APPLTEMP            /Datadisks/d12/ORACLE/  appltemp  30102     19008    30102     90531
                    _01.dbf

CALL                /Datadisks/d05/ORACLE/  call_01.     71      1445       71      4083
                    dbf

COMPUTER            /Datadisks/d06/ORACLE/  computer      0      1284        0      1321
                    _01.dbf

DIRMAR              /Datadisks/d06/ORACLE/  dirmarke    117      1987      117     31437
                    t_01.dbf

DS                  /Datadisks/d06/ORACLE/  dst_01.d    653     11845      653     24916
                    bf

                                                      Phys      Phys      Blk       Blk
Tablespace Name     File Name                        Writes     Reads    Writes     Reads
```

Figure 11.7
A Patrol Oracle report.

olds are exceeded, alerts are sent to those individuals who are responsible for fixing the performance problem.

Patrol Exception Handling

Patrol provides preset automated recovery actions. For example, the Oracle component allows Patrol to automatically resize a table's **NEXT EXTENT** size, thereby averting possible downtime. To illustrate this feature, assume a customer table has been defined to grow in chunks of 5MB (for example, **NEXT=5MB**). If the tablespace that contains the table only has 4MB available, Patrol will automatically downsize the table to **NEXT=3MB**, allowing the table to extend one more time and buying time for the DBA to be notified and add a data file to the tablespace before the table becomes locked. In this way, the DBA can add a data file to the tablespace without disruption of the system (see Figure 11.8).

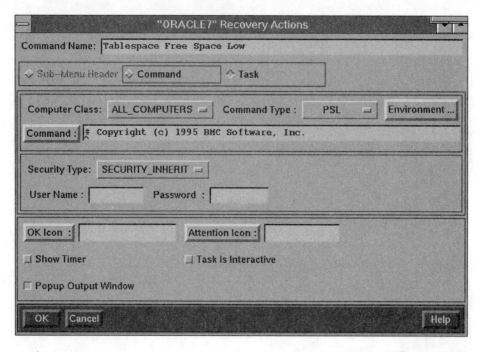

Figure 11.8
A Patrol recovery action.

Patrol offers extensions into its base system using a proprietary language called Patrol Script Language (PSL). PSL is used to extend the base functionality of the software and automatically handle sophisticated recovery, where numerous conditions must be checked. Internally, PSL is a large library of more than 100 prewritten functions. These functions, in turn, are called from within a small framework of 10 commands. The functions also include calls to SNMP modules for interfacing with other SNMP-compliant tools.

In short, Patrol is a very robust and comprehensive system and database monitoring tool. Like any powerful monitor, Patrol is not plug-and-play—it requires a significant investment in up-front customization. However, once the framework is in place, Patrol delivers as promised by continually monitoring your system, alerting you when necessary, and correcting problems. The result? The elimination of many tedious and time-consuming chores for systems and DBA staffs.

Another exciting system tool for Oracle developers is Oracle's Performance Pack. Let's take a look at this product, as well.

Oracle Tools For Performance Monitoring

Oracle's Performance Pack is a fairly new tool that assists in the complex task of tuning Oracle databases. The Performance Pack is sold as an addition to Oracle's Enterprise Manager. Let's take a high-level, overview look of the basic components of the Performance Pack and see how it can help DBAs monitor their Oracle databases.

Top Sessions

The Top Sessions monitor begins by allowing a developer to choose from a list of sorting criteria for the top sessions. This is an extremely useful tool because the top tasks can be sorted by just about every conceivable measurement criteria. These criteria include the number of clean outs and rollbacks, the number of consistent gets, the amount of CPU used by a session, I/O performed by a session, calls to SQL*Net, and many other options. Figure 11.9 shows the starting screen to Top Sessions, where sorting criteria are chosen. In the real world, a developer can iterate through the sort criteria selection screen in order to sort the top Oracle tasks by several different criteria. This is done to help understand whether a task is CPU bound or I/O bound.

The Top Sessions screen then displays the top sessions (accompanied by useful top session information) according to the sort criteria. Note that the Oracle background processes are also listed on this screen. While statistics for all tasks can be gathered, details about an SQL explain plan can only be viewed for those tasks marked *ACTIVE*.

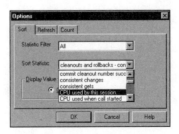

Figure 11.9
Selecting the Top Sessions sorting criteria.

To view details about any task on this list, simply double-click on the task, and a screen similar to the one shown in Figure 11.10 will appear. This screen has four tabs: General, Statistics, Cursors, and Locks. Figure 11.10 shows the general infor mation reported about an Oracle task.mation reported about an Oracle task.mation reported about an Oracle task.mation reported about an Oracle task.

To display even more details about an Oracle task, the Statistics tab can be chosen. This screen provides some very useful information about a data warehouse query, including SQL*Net activity from client to server, CPU usage, and consistent gets.

In my opinion, the real value of the Session Details screen is gained by pressing the Cursors tab. For all SQL marked *ACTIVE* on the main screen, you can see the actual SQL as it exists in the library cache. Note that the Explain Plan button can be pressed to review the explain plan for the SQL.

In Figure 11.11, you can see the Explain Plan for SQL that is currently executing. This is one of the most powerful features of OPP because Explain Plan information can be captured and printed easily for further reference. In many cases, database

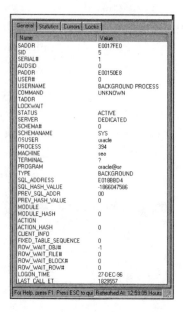

Figure 11.10
The general data for an individual Oracle task.

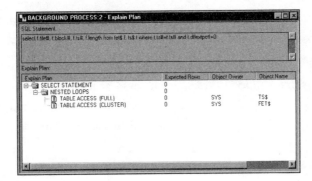

Figure 11.11
The Explain Plan for an SQL query.

queries can be shown to be performing full-table scans, even though the developers thought the queries were using indexes. This is especially important for systems where a lot of ad hoc queries are executed.

Now that you understand how individual tasks are investigated using OPP's Top Sessions tool, let's take a quick look at some of the systemwide tuning tools, starting with the Oracle Expert.

Oracle Expert

The Oracle Expert aids DBAs in the performance and tuning of Oracle databases. Based on decision rules, Oracle Expert interrogates a database instance and schema definition, and recommends changes. In addition, Oracle Expert contains a facility for implementing suggested changes. Oracle Expert makes tuning recommendations for three areas: instance tuning, application tuning, and structure tuning.

- *Instance Tuning*—Involves changes to the parameters that affect the configuration of an Oracle instance, including the following:

  - *Initialization Parameters*—SGA parameters, such as **shared_pool_size** and **db_block_buffers**.

  - *I/O Parameters*—Parameters such as **checkpoint_processes** and **db_multiblock_read_count**.

  - *Parallel Query Parameters*—Parameters such as suggested settings for **parallel_min_servers** and **parallel_max_servers**.

- • *Sort Parameters*—Parameters such as suggestions for **sort_area_size**, **sort_area_retained_size**, and **sort_direct_writes**.

- *Application Tuning*—Involves tuning SQL statements, but only includes SQL statements that happen to reside in the SGA at the time Oracle Expert is running. Oracle Expert examines the applications, transactions, and SQL statements that are running at the moment. Application tuning categories include the following:

  - • *SQL Similarity Identification*—Oracle Expert identifies similar SQL statements that are treated as different SQL statements due to differences in capitalization and spacing. These duplicate SQL statements must be parsed as new SQL statements, causing unnecessary overhead for Oracle.

  - • *Index Placement*—Oracle Expert examines existing SQL and determines if any queries might benefit from new indexes. Oracle Expert can also make recommendations to remove indexes that are not used or change existing indexes (such as suggesting to add columns).

- *Structure Tuning*—Involves database structure tuning. Oracle Expert can create recommendations about the size and placement of database tables and indexes. The categories of structure tuning are as follows:

  - • *Segment Size*—Oracle Expert makes recommendations for default storage parameters of a tablespace. These parameters provide default initial allocation and growth rate of segments created within a tablespace.

  - • *Segment Placement*—Oracle Expert makes recommendations to isolate tables and indexes in separate tablespaces.

  - • *User Analysis*—Oracle Expert makes recommendations on the proper assignment of default and temporary tablespaces.

It needs to be noted that Oracle Expert is still rather primitive and sometimes makes naive recommendations. For example, while Oracle recommends that **PCTINCREASE** be set to **1** for a tablespace in order for the tablespace coalesce feature to work, Oracle Expert will detect the non-zero value and recommend that **PCTINCREASE** be reset to **0**. However, Oracle has made a resource commitment to improving the intelligence of Oracle Expert, so future releases of this product will undoubtedly show greater intelligence.

Also, the runtime for Oracle Expert can be frustrating, especially when Oracle Expert is asked to examine a database. Oracle Expert dutifully walks through indexes and tables, looking to make recommendations, but it does not report back to an end user about where the Expert is during the process. Even a relatively small database could take hours to examine, and the user often runs the risk that the SQL*Net connection might get dropped during these long-running examinations of the data.

Oracle Expert has tremendous potential to be a successful tool that automates the task of routine performance and tuning audits. Clearly, Oracle has made a commitment to this type of tool, and it will be exciting to see the Oracle Expert evolve into a robust and intelligent tool for tuning the database. With that said, let's take a look at one of the most popular tools in the OPP tool set, Oracle's Performance Manager.

Oracle Performance Manager

The Oracle Performance Manager component of OPP is a very simple package that graphically displays salient system measures using pie charts and histograms. While this is not a new concept, Oracle has created numerous shortcuts to allow the quick, visual display of a database's performance. The most commonly used display is achieved by opening the Display menu and choosing the Overall option. This command provides a high-level graphical view of your system, as shown in Figure 11.12.

The Oracle Performance Manager tool is generally used to get a fast, high-level overview of the health of an instance. With just a few mouse clicks, the Oracle DBA can generate a report that displays the hit ratios, number of users logged on, number of active users, users waiting for locks, memory used, file I/O, system I/O, and system throughput.

The Oracle Performance Manager is an excellent tool for identifying high-level characteristics of an Oracle warehouse. In addition to the Oracle Expert and Performance Manager tools, Oracle provides two other especially noteworthy components in the Performance Pack arsenal, namely the Trace tool and the Tablespace Manager.

Oracle Trace

The Oracle Trace tool is generally used to enable a developer to directly view data that is accessed while an SQL statement is executing. As a general rule, the Oracle Trace facility is only used when a very critical SQL statement is giving strange results

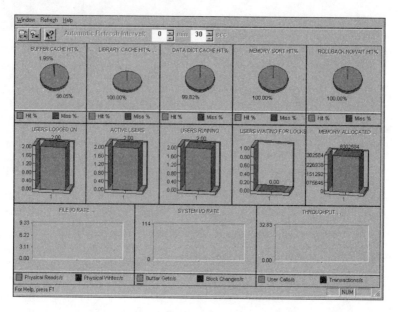

Figure 11.12
The overall statistics in the Performance Manager.

and is seldom used by Oracle database administrators. Oracle Trace is a graphical representation of the Oracle TKPROF utility that has been available since Oracle7.

Oracle Trace produces huge volumes of output, since it displays the contents of all the Oracle rows as they are retrieved from the database, and then sorted, aggregated, and displayed. Because of this huge volume of output, Oracle Trace is generally used when an SQL statement returns unexpected results and it is important to understand the interaction between the Oracle data and the SQL statement execution.

Oracle Tablespace Manager

Another exciting addition to Oracle's performance pack is the Tablespace Manager tool. This tool is indispensable for the identification of data warehouse file placement within the data warehouse. At last, the Oracle DBA has a tool that can display where tables reside within a tablespace. The Oracle Tablespace Manager can drill into schema owners and investigate any tablespace.

Figure 11.13 shows the details of a tablespace. On the left side, you can see the data files that comprise the tablespace. On the right side, you can see a list of segment

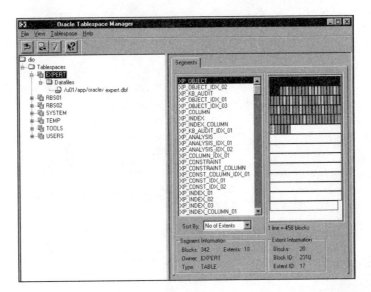

Figure 11.13

The tablespace detail display screen for the Oracle Tablespace Manager.

names (tables or indexes) sorted by any number of selection criteria. In this example, the tablespaces are sorted in descending order by the number of extents. From this

Overall, the Oracle Performance Pack is a direct competitor to numerous other third-party products used to monitor the Oracle database. In time, OPP will become increasingly popular by virtue of its tight integration with Oracle and because Oracle is committed to enhancing the tool set.

Summary

Now that we have investigated database performance monitoring techniques, we can wrap up this text by looking at the future of relational database tuning, with a focus on object-orientation, and entertain a discussion about how objects will change the way databases are implemented and tuned.

The Future Of Oracle8 Technology

CHAPTER
12

HIGH PERFORMANCE

The Future Of Oracle8 Technology

While Oracle has made tremendous strides in database object orientation with Oracle8, there are many exciting new Oracle features looming on the horizon. This chapter will take a look at some of the emerging technologies and how Oracle may choose to implement these new features. This chapter will begin with an overview of the Object Management Group and their evolving standards, take a look the possible new extensions to Oracle8 objects, explore the new 64-bit option of Oracle, and look at preparing Oracle8 for the year 2000. All of these topics are leading-edge, and we can certainly expect to see exciting new developments in these areas over the next few years.

The Future Of Database Object Standards

Many organizations recognize the importance of standards in the emerging area of object-oriented systems development, and Oracle is no exception. In the spring of 1992, the Object Management Group (OMG), a nonprofit corporation dedicated to developing object standards, published the *Common Object Request Broker Architecture* (CORBA) standard for object-oriented development. CORBA was developed jointly by Sun, Hewlett-Packard, Digital Equipment Corporation, NCR, and HyperDesk Corporation. CORBA creates a standard protocol for an object to place requests and receive responses from other objects. It is interesting to note that these competing vendors—all with vested interests in proprietary software—have agreed to adhere to the CORBA standard in the development of new object-oriented systems.

Object Management

Most of the major distributed operating systems state that they adhere to CORBA. Consequently, an understanding of the foundation architecture for distributed systems is critical. This section is from the *Object Management Architecture Guide* and is reproduced with the permission of the Object Management Group.

Chris Stone, President and CEO of the Object Management Group, states:

The OMG's goal is to get everybody to agree on a messaging format and how objects talk to each other; get them to agree to the language and a model of how to structure the data; get them to agree to some common interfaces; get them to agree on how to do security and containment.... The real significance of the CORBA specification is for application developers who want to build new client/server applications that will work across disparate platforms.

Twin business pressures of decentralization and globalization prompted technology to come to the rescue in the form of the personal computer and desktop computing. All information of a business, however, was distributed throughout the many computing resources of the business. In addition, software often creates additional hurdles, including the time to develop the software, maintenance and enhancement of software, limitations on program complexity for profitable software sales, and time required to learn and use the software. These hurdles herald the major issues facing corporate information systems today—the quality, cost, and lack of interoperability of software. Hardware costs are plummeting, but software costs are rising.

The Object Management Group formed to help reduce complexity, lower costs, and hasten the introduction of new software applications. OMG has plans to accomplish this through the introduction of an architectural framework with supporting detailed interface specifications. These specifications drive the industry towards interoperable, reusable, portable software components based on standard object-oriented interfaces.

The mission of OMG is as follows:

- OMG is dedicated to maximizing the portability, reusability, and interoperability of software. OMG is the leading worldwide organization dedicated to producing the framework and specifications for commercially available object-oriented environments.

- OMG provides a reference architecture with terms and definitions upon which all specifications are based. OMG will create industry standards for commercially available object-oriented systems by focusing on Distributed Applications, Distributed Services, and Common Facilities.

- OMG provides an open forum for industry discussion, education, and promotion of OMG-endorsed object technology. OMG coordinates its activities with related organizations and acts as a technology/marketing center for object-oriented software.

- OMG defines the object management paradigm as the ability to encapsulate data and methods for software development. This models the "real world" through representation of program components called objects. This representation results in faster application development, easier maintenance, reduced program complexity, and reusable components. A central benefit of an object-oriented system is its ability to grow in functionality through the extension of existing components and the addition of new objects to the system.

OMG envisions a day when software users start up applications as they start up their cars, with no more concern about the underlying structure of the objects they manipulate than the driver has about the molecular composition of gasoline.

The members of OMG share the goal of developing and using integrated software systems. These systems are built using a methodology that supports modular production of software; encourages reuse of code; allows useful integration across lines of developers, operating systems, and hardware; and enhances long-range maintenance of code. Members of OMG believe that the object-oriented approach to software construction best supports their goals.

Object orientation, both at the programming language and applications environment levels, provides a terrific boost in programmer productivity, and it greatly lends itself to the production of integrated software systems. Not necessarily promoting faster programming, object technology allows constructing more with less code. This is partly due to the naturalness of the approach and to its rigorous requirement for interface specification. Only a set of standard interfaces for interoperable software components is missing.

The Benefits Of Object Orientation

As mentioned, the technological approach of object technology (or object-orientated technology) was chosen by OMG member companies—not for their own sake, but to attain a set of end-user goals.

End users benefit in a number of ways from the object-oriented approach to application construction, and this section points out many of the benefits. To start, an object-oriented user interface offers many advantages over more traditional user interfaces. In an object-oriented interface, *applications objects* (computer-simulated representations of real-world objects) are presented to end users as objects that can be manipulated in a manner similar to real-world objects. Examples of such object-oriented interfaces can be seen in systems such as Xerox Star, Apple Macintosh, Apple's OPENSTEP, OSF Motif, HP NewWave, and, to a limited degree, Microsoft Windows. CAD systems represent another good example of design components that can be manipulated in a way similar to that of real components. The end result is a reduced learning curve with a common look and feel to multiple applications. After all, "seeing and pointing" is much easier than "remembering and typing."

A more indirect end-user benefit of object-oriented applications, provided that the users cooperate according to some standard, is that independently developed general-purpose applications can be combined in a user-specific way. OMG's central purpose is to create a standard that allows interoperability among independently developed applications across heterogeneous networks of computers. This means that multiple software programs will appear as one to the user of information, regardless of where the programs reside.

Common functionality in different applications—storage, retrieval, mailing, printing, creation and deletion of objects, help, and computer-based training—is realized by common shared objects leading to a uniform and consistent user interface. Sharing information drastically reduces documentation redundancy. Consistent access across multiple applications allows increased focus on application creation, as opposed to application education.

The transition to object-oriented application technology does not make existing applications obsolete. Existing applications can be embedded (with different levels of integration) in an object-oriented environment.

Pragmatic migration of existing applications gives a user control over computing resources, as well as how quickly these resources change. Likewise, application developers benefit from object technology and object-oriented standards. These benefits fall into two general categories: modular architecture (encapsulation) and reuse of existing components.

- Encapsulation of object data applications are built in a truly modular fashion, preventing unintended interference. In addition, it is possible to build applications in an incremental way, preserving correctness during the development process.

- Reusing existing components, specifically when the OMG standard is in effect, standardizes interaction among independently developed applications (and application components). Cost and lead time can be saved by using existing object class implementations.

In developing standards, OMG keeps these benefits of object orientation in mind, together with the following set of overall goals:

- *Heterogeneity*—Integration of applications and facilities are available across heterogeneous networks of systems, independent of networking transports and operating systems.

- *Customization Options*—Common facilities are customizable to meet specific end-user or organizational requirements and preferences.

- *Management and Control*—Examines issues such as security, recovery, interruptability, auditing, and performance.

- *Internationalization*—OMG is an international group, and its standards reflect built-in support for internationalization of software.

- *Technical Standards*—Standards that meet user goals are the central focus of the OMG.

In addition to developing object-orientation standards and goals, the OMG has created an object model for developers. We'll look at the OMG object model in a moment, but first, let's view the big picture by looking at the components used in object management architecture.

The Object Management Components

The components of the object management architecture provide a complete set of tools for the interoperation of objects in a distributed environment. These components include:

- Object Request Broker

- Object Services

- Common Facilities

- Application Objects

Let's take a quick look at each component.

The Object Request Broker (ORB) component of the Object Management Architecture (OMA) is the communications heart of CORBA. The ORB provides an infrastructure that allows objects to communicate independently of specific implementation platforms and techniques for addressed objects. The Object Request Broker component guarantees portability and interoperability of objects over a network of heterogeneous systems.

The Object Services component standardizes the life cycle management of objects. Functions create objects (the Object Factory), control access to objects, keep track of relocated objects, and control relationships among species of objects (class management). The Object Services component provides the generic environment in which single objects perform their tasks. Standardization of Object Services leads to consistency over different applications and improved productivity for the developer.

The Common Facilities component provides a set of generic application functions configured to the individual requirements of a specific configuration. Examples are printing, database, and email facilities. Standardization leads to uniformity in generic operations and allows end users to manipulate their configurations as opposed to configuring individual applications.

The Application Objects part of the architecture represents the application objects performing specific tasks for users. One application is typically built from a large number of basic object classes—partly specific for the application, partly from the set of Common Facilities. New classes of application objects are built by modification of existing classes through generalization or specialization of existing classes (inheritance), as provided by Object Services. This multiobject class approach to application development leads to improved productivity for developers and enhances the ability of end users to combine and configure their applications.

This short summary should give you a general idea of the main components in the object management architecture. Now, let's take a closer look at the OMG object model and see how it is structured. Remember, the OMG object model is the foundation for the Common Object Request Broker Architecture (CORBA), which is the architecture chosen by Oracle8 for implementation of their plug-in cartridges.

The OMG Object Model

The OMG model defines a common object's semantics, specifying the externally visible characteristics of objects in a standard and implementation-independent way. The common semantics characterize objects existing in an OMG-compliant system, which performs operations and maintains states for objects. The following discussion presents the building blocks of the OMG object model, namely the interface, objects, types, and implementation details.

- *Interface*—An interface describes the externally visible characteristics of objects, consisting of operation signatures. The external view of both object behavior and object state (information needed to alter the outcome of a subsequent operation) are modeled in terms of operation signatures.

- *Objects*—Objects are grouped into types, and individual objects are instances of their respective types.

- *Types*—A type determines which operations are applied to its instances. Types participate in subtype/supertype relationships that affect the set of operations applicable to their instances. Types also have implementations. An implementation of an object type is typically a set of data structures constituting a stored representation and a set of methods or procedures that provide the code to implement each of the operations' defined type.

- *Implementation Details*—Implementation details are encapsulated by operations and are never directly exposed in the external interface. For example, the stored representation is only observable or changeable through an operation request. Formally, the OMG Object Model states nothing regarding implementations of a type. It only claims their existence and the possibility that a given type can have multiple implementations (note that systems are not required to support multiple implementations).

The OMG Object Model defines a core set of requirements that must be supported in any system that complies with the Object Model standard. This set of required capabilities is termed the *Core Object Model.* The core serves as the basis for portability and interoperability of object systems across all technologies, as well as across implementations within technology domains.

While the Core Object Model serves as the common ground, the OMG Object Model also allows for extensions to the core to enable even greater commonality within different technology domains. The Object Model defines the concept of components that are compatible extensions to the core Object Model, but are not required to be supported by all systems. For example, relationships are defined as components. The OMG Object Model Components guide contains descriptions of components that are accepted as a standard.

The Object Model also defines a mechanism, referred to as *profiles,* for technology domains to group pertinent components. Profiles are groups of components combining as a useful set of extensions for particular domains.

The Object Management Architecture (OMA)

An OMA-compliant application consists of a set of interworking classes and instances interacting via the Object Request Broker (the ORB is discussed in more detail later in this chapter). Compliance, therefore, means conformance to the OMA and the protocol definitions. Using ORB, objects make and receive requests and responses. To recap, the Object Management Architecture mainly consists of the following components:

- *Object Request Broker (ORB)*—A utility that provides mechanisms by which objects transparently make and receive requests and responses.

- *Object Services (OS)*—A collection of services with object interfaces providing basic functions to realize and maintain objects.

- *Common Facilities (CF)*—A collection of classes and object interfaces providing general purpose capabilities, useful in many applications.

- *Application Objects (AO)*—Objects that are specific to particular end user applications.

In general terms, the Application Objects and Common Facilities have an application orientation, while the ORB and Object Services are oriented to the system or infrastructure aspects of distributed object management. However, there is some overlap. For example, Common Facilities provides higher-level services, such as transactions and versioning, that use primitives provided within Object Services.

The categories reflect a partitioning in terms of functions—from basic functions common to most applications or classes of standardized applications, to those that are too application-specific or special-purpose to be standardized. Therefore, the ORB, Object Services, and Common Facilities are focal to OMG standardization efforts.

Object Services, Common Facilities, and Application Objects intercommunicate using the Object Request Broker. Objects can also use non-object interfaces to external services, but these are outside the scope of the OMA. Although not explicitly stated in the reference model, objects can communicate with the Object Services via object interfaces. For example, the addition of a new class is a request to an object providing this service. If this were done manually, it would be performed by editing a class definition script or a C++ include file.

Application Objects and Common Facilities use and provide functions and services via object interfaces. In general, objects issue as well as process requests for services, and Application Objects provide services for other applications or facilities. For example, an application-specific service, such as printer rendering, is cast as an application object invoked by a Common Facility, like print queue. Common Facilities objects use services provided elsewhere.

Note that applications need only provide or use OMA-compliant interfaces to participate in the Object Management Architecture. Applications do not have to be constructed using the object-oriented paradigm, which also applies to the provision of Object Services. For example, existing relational or object-oriented database management systems provide some or all of the Object Services. Existing applications, external tools, and system support software are embedded as objects participating in the Object Management Architecture, using class interface front ends, also known as *adapters* or *wrappers*.

The reference model does not impose any restrictions on how applications and common facilities are structured and implemented. Objects of a given application class deal with the presentation of information, interaction with the user, semantics, functionality, the persistent storage of data, or any combination of the preceding functions.

The OMA assumes that underlying services provided by a platform's operating system and lower-level basic services (such as network computing facilities) are available and usable by OMA implementations. Specifically, the Object Management Architecture does not address user interface support. The interfaces between applications and windowing systems or other display support are the subjects of standardization efforts outside the OMG. Eventually, however, Common Facilities might provide standard user interface classes. In addition, the reference model does not deal explicitly with the choice of possible binding mechanisms, such as compile time, load time, and runtime.

Now that we have reviewed the basic object architecture, let's explore the details behind the OMG Object Request Broker.

Object Request Broker

The ORB provides mechanisms by which objects transparently make and receive requests and responses. In so doing, the ORB provides interoperability between applications on different machines in heterogeneous distributed environments and seamlessly interconnects multiple object systems.

The OMG Object Model defines an object request and its associated result (response) as the fundamental interaction mechanism. A request names an operation and includes zero or more parameter values, any of which can be object names identifying specific objects. The ORB arranges processing of the request. This entails identifying and calling some method to perform the operation using the parameters. After the operation terminates, the ORB conveys results to the requester.

The ORB itself can not maintain all the information needed to carry out its functions. The ORB can generate requests of its own to Object Services or use them in the process of conveying a request. In other words, to find the specific method executed for a given request, the ORB uses a class dictionary service or searches runtime method libraries.

In order to satisfy the OMG Technical Objectives, the ORB is expected to address—at least to some degree—the following areas:

- *Name Services*—The Object name-mapping services map the object names in the naming domain of the requester into equivalent names in the domain of the method to be executed. The OMG Object Model does not require object names to be unique or universal. Object location services, involving simple attribute lookups on objects, use the object names in the request to locate the method to perform the requested operation. In practice, different object systems or domains have locally preferred object naming schemes.

- *Request Dispatch*—This function determines the invocation method. The OMG Object Model does not require a request to be delivered to any particular object. As far as the requester is concerned, it does not matter whether the request first goes to a method that operates on the variables of objects passed as parameters or whether it goes to any particular object in the parameter list.

- *Parameter Encoding*—These facilities convey the local representation of parameter values in the requester's environment to equivalent representations in the recipient's environment. To accomplish this, parameter encodings can employ standards or de facto standards, such as OSF/DCE, ONC/NFS/XDR, NCA/SCS/NDR, and ANSI.

- *Delivery*—Requests and results are delivered to the proper location characterized by a particular node, address, space, thread, or entry point. These facilities use standard transport protocols, such as TCP/UDP/IP and ISO/TPN.

- *Synchronization*—Synchronization primarily deals with handling the parallelism of the objects making and processing a request, and the rendezvousing of the requester with the response to the request. Possible synchronization models include asynchronous (request with no response), synchronous (request and await reply), and deferred synchronous (proceed after sending request and claim reply later).

- *Activation*—Activation is the housekeeping process that is necessary before invoking a method. Activation and deactivation (passivation) of persistent objects obtains the object state for use when the object is accessed and saves the state when it no longer needs to be accessed. For objects holding persistent information in non-object storage facilities, such as files and databases, explicit requests must be made to objects for activation and deactivation.

- *Exception Handling*—Object location failures and attempted request delivery failures will report to either the requester or recipient in ways that distinguish them from other types of errors. Needed actions recover session resources and resynchronize the requester and the recipient. The ORB coordinates recovery housekeeping activities.

- *Security Mechanisms*—The ORB provides security enforcement mechanisms supporting higher-level security control and policies. These mechanisms ensure secure conveyance of requests among objects. Authentication mechanisms ensure identities of requesting and receiving objects, threads, address spaces, nodes, and communication routes. Protection mechanisms ensure integrity of conveyed data and ensure that the data is accessible only to authorized parties. Access enforcement mechanisms control access and licensing policies.

OMG is very active in establishing standard interfaces for object-oriented distributed systems. OMG's CORBA is widely accepted. Vendors are developing distributed object technology tools that promise to revolutionize the software market in the 1990s and beyond. IBM, Hewlett-Packard, DEC, and many others recognize the huge market potential for object-oriented distributed systems.

Now that we understand the basics of CORBA, we can see why Oracle has chosen to model their cartridges on this standard approach. Now, let's change topics and take a look at how the immediate future will see additional features being incorporated into Oracle8.x releases. The most exciting promise from Oracle is to provide support for object inheritance.

Oracle Objects And Inheritance

As we have briefly mentioned in earlier chapters, *inheritance* is defined as the ability of a lower-level object to inherit or access the data items and behaviors associated with all classes that are above it in the class hierarchy. As we have noted, Oracle8 does not yet support inheritance, but there have been promises that it will be supported in future releases. While inheritance is very well-defined within procedural languages such as C++ and Smalltalk, there is still some controversy about how inheritance will be implemented within the Oracle8 database. Let's gaze into our crystal ball and take a look at how the existing Oracle8 object model may be extended to provide support for inheritance.

The Future Of Oracle—An Inheritance Example

To illustrate how inheritance might someday work within Oracle, consider the following example. In a university database, there are several types of students. The main question when designing classes is to ask whether the different types of students will have different data or different behaviors. Let's assume that our analysis of the data has derived the following data definitions for students:

```
CREATE CLASS student (
    student_ID     number (5);
    student_name
        first_name          varchar(20),
        MI                  char(1),
        last_name           varchar(20)
  );


CREATE CLASS graduate_student
        WITHIN CLASS student
(
    undergraduate_degree       char(3)
       CONSTRAINT undergraduate_degree IN ('BA','BS'),
    undergraduate_major        varchar(20),
    undergraduate_school_name varchar(30),
    undergraduate_school_address
      street_address           varchar(20),
      city_name                varchar(20),
      zip_code                 number(9),
    mentor_name                varchar(20),
    thesis_review_date         date);

CREATE CLASS non_resident_student WITHIN CLASS student (
    state_of_origin            char(2),
    region_of_origin           char(5)
      CONSTRAINT region_of_origin IN ('NORTH', 'SOUTH','EAST','WEST'));

CREATE CLASS foreign_student WITHIN CLASS non_resident_student (
    country_of_origin          varchar(20),
    visa_expiration_date       date);
```

> *Note:* The university example does not allow foreign or nonresident students into the graduate school, which is why you can see that the **graduate_school** is only a subclass of the **student** class.

In the previous example, you can see that the **WITHIN** clause is used to indicate that a class type participates within the domain of an existing superclass definition. Now, let's examine how these data structures will be used by the Oracle8.x database at object-creation time. When a **foreign_student** object is created, a data structure will be created that contains all of the data structures from each higher-level object. For example, this is what the data structure would look like for a **foreign_student**:

```
foreign_student (
    student_ID            number (5);
    student_name
        first_name        varchar(20),
        MI                char(1),
        last_name         varchar(20),
    state_of_origin       char(2),
    region_of_origin      char(5);
        CONSTRAINT region_of_origin IN ('NORTH', 'SOUTH','EAST','WEST');
    country_of_origin     varchar(20),
    visa_expiration_date  date
);
```

Here, you can see that a **foreign_student** would inherit the data structures contained in both the **student** and **non_resident_student** classes in addition to its own class data structures. When a **foreign_student** is created, it is treated as a **student** object, but the database is aware that it is a **foreign_student** and will always check the **foreign_student** object first before looking inside other student class definitions.

Also, note that the constraint for valid values is also inherited into the data definition. Whenever a **foreign_student** object is created, the **region_of_origin** column must have one of the specified values.

While inheritance will soon revolutionize the ways in which Oracle databases are accessed, the immediate future presents some interesting challenges. While Oracle8 calls itself year 2000 compliant, this does not mean that Oracle8 applications will automatically identify and correct millennium issues. The following section explores how to prepare for the year 2000 within Oracle8.

Oracle And The Year 2000

Oracle databases are time-based; therefore, it is critical that DBAs are properly prepared for the transition into the next century. Oracle, with all of its robust features, has a very complex strategy for managing **date** data types. As such, Oracle developers must recognize pitfalls when altering date parameters, and developers must fully understand the ramifications of any date changes they implement. Even as of this writing, Oracle has a date format (**YY**) that is programmed to automatically change behavior when the year ticks to 2000.

Oracle Date Overview

The **date** data type within Oracle can be changed by setting a parameter called **nls_date_format**. Oracle's default, **DD-MON-YY**, places a **19** in front of all two-digit year values and is programmed to place a **20** in front of all two-digit years after the year 2000. **nls_date_format** accepts the following three values:

- **DD-MON-YYYY**—Four-digit years are required for query and date storage when using this value setting.

- **DD-MON-YY**—Two-digit years are used for query and date storage, and the current century is added to the date at insert time.

- **DD-MON-RR**—Two-digit years are used for queries and date storage. Where the year ranges from 00 through 49, a **20** is added for the century. For values 50 through 99, a **19** is added for the century.

The **nls_date_format** can be changed at the session level by using the **ALTER SESSION** command, or it can be permanently changed by setting the **nls_date_format** parameter in the init.ora file.

Oracle provides the following two views to assist developers in displaying current date defaults:

- **V$NLS_PARAMETERS**—This view shows the current systemwide default settings for the date parameters:

```
SVRMGR> SELECT * FROM V$NLS_PARAMETERS;

PARAMETER                                    VALUE
- - - - - - - - -                            - - - - - - - -
NLS_DATE_FORMAT                              DD-MON-YY
```

- **nls_session_parameters**—This Oracle view displays the National Language Support parameters, including the **nls_date_formate**:

```
SVRMGR> SELECT * FROM nls_session_parameters;

PARAMETER              VALUE
--------              -------
NLS_DATE_FORMAT        DD-MON-YYYY
```

Date Display

There are many ways to change the date display within Oracle. Several of the popular built-in functions (BIFs), such as **to_char** and **to_date**, are commonly used to manipulate the display of Oracle dates. Of course, BIFs can never alter the internal representation of an Oracle date, but the **nls_date_format** can change the way the century portion of a date is stored within an Oracle table.

The default **nls_date_format** for Oracle is **DD-MON-YY**. Problems might arise early in the year 2000 when SQL queries are changed to accommodate four-digit years. In the following example, a query to count all shipments after January 15, 1997 will fail to retrieve the rows because the year is interpreted as 2097:

```
SELECT count(*) FROM SHPMT
WHERE shpmt_date > '15-JAN-97';

no rows selected
```

The natural response to this failure would be to change the SQL to specify a four-digit year. Unfortunately, Oracle does not like the change, and the SQL query will fail with an error message, as follows:

```
SQL> SELECT count(*) FROM SHPMT WHERE shpmt_date > '25-OCT-1996';
ERROR:
ORA-01830: date format picture ends before converting entire
           input string

no rows selected
```

Now, it appears that you can simply change the Oracle parameter called **nls_date_format** to accommodate a four-digit year in an SQL query. Unfortunately, this change will return misleading results. When a four-digit year is used in the SQL, the query is correct, but when a two-digit year is used, an inaccurate result is returned from the SQL query. Consider the following:

```
SQL> ALTER SESSION SET nls_date_format = "DD-MON-YYYY";

Session altered.

SQL> SELECT count(*) FROM SHPMT WHERE shpmt_date > '25-OCT-1996';

COUNT(*)
------
      40

1 row selected.

SQL> SELECT count(*) FROM SHPMT WHERE shpmt_date > '25-OCT-96';

COUNT(*)
------
  176858

1 row selected.
```

It appears from these tests that two events must occur in order to achieve the goal: A four-digit date must be specified and the **nls_date_format** must be changed. In order to get SQL comparisons to work across the century boundary, developers can specify four-digit years in all SQL queries, as follows:

```
SELECT count(*) FROM SHPMT
WHERE shpmt_date
BETWEEN '15-JAN-2000' AND '15-DEC-1999';

COUNT(*)
------
  163632

1 row selected.
```

However, a developer cannot easily change the **nls_date_format** in the init.ora file until all SQL accessing the database is converted to use four-digit years in the queries. The scariest part of this issue is that two-digit year queries do not fail, they produce misleading results. Apparently, the only solution when changing to a **YYYY** format is to carefully coordinate the change to **nls_date_format** with changes to all SQL queries that reference dates.

Date Insertion

Date insertion with the Oracle default **nls_date_format** will always prefix a year with a century of **19**, and Oracle will not allow the SQL to specify a century value. Consider the following:

```
SQL> ALTER SESSION SET nls_date_format = "DD-MON-YY";

Session altered.

SQL>
SQL> INSERT INTO DT VALUES ('01-JAN-01');

1 row created.

SQL> INSERT INTO DT VALUES ('01-JAN-99');

1 row created.

SQL> INSERT INTO DT VALUES ('01-JAN-2001');
insert into dt values ('01-JAN-2001')
                            *
ERROR at line 1:
ORA-01830: date format picture ends before converting entire
           input string

SQL> INSERT INTO DT VALUES ('01-JAN-1999');
insert into dt values ('01-JAN-1999')
ERROR at line 1:
ORA-01830: date format picture ends before converting entire
           input string

SQL> SELECT * FROM DT;

DY
----
01-JAN-99
01-JAN-01
```

Let's see what happens if the **nls_date_format** is reset to **YYYY**. With the **nls_date_format** set to **YYYY**, developers can specify the century in the SQL **INSERT** statements. However, note that inserting the date 01-JAN-91 no longer stores the year as 1991. Instead, the year is stored as 91 AD, the same year the Romans began throwing Christians to the lions! Consider the following:

```
SQL> ALTER SESSION SET nls_date_format = "DD-MON-YYYY";

Session altered.

SQL> INSERT INTO DT VALUES ('01-JAN-91');

1 row created.

SQL> INSERT INTO DT VALUES ('01-JAN-1901');

1 row created.

SQL> INSERT INTO DT VALUES ('01-JAN-1999');

1 row created.

SQL> INSERT INTO DT VALUES ('01-JAN-2001');

1 row created.

SQL> INSERT INTO DT VALUES ('01-JAN-2099');

1 row created.

SQL> SELECT * FROM DT;

DY
-----
01-JAN-0091
01-JAN-1901
01-JAN-1999
01-JAN-2001
01-JAN-2099
```

One solution can be found by using the **RR** date format in **nls_date_format**. If the **nls_date_format** is set to **DD-MON-RR**, Oracle makes some assumptions about the century. If the year is in the range 00 through 49, Oracle assumes the century is

20, while years in the range 50 through 99 are prefixed with a **19**. This rule also remains true after the year 2000. Consider the following:

```
SQL> ALTER SESSION SET nls_date_format = "DD-MON-RR";

Session altered.

SQL> INSERT INTO DT VALUES ('01-JAN-49');

1 row created.

SQL> INSERT INTO DT VALUES ('01-JAN-50');

1 row created.

SQL> ALTER SESSION SET nls_date_format = "DD-MON-YYYY";

Session altered.

SQL> SELECT * FROM DT;

DY
-----
01-JAN-2049
01-JAN-1950
```

Of course, there are some drawbacks to using the **RR** date format. For applications that need to store birth dates for anyone born before 1950, developers might have date-conversion problems because 01-JAN-49 is stored as 01-JAN-2049.

Also, like the **YY** date format, the **RR** date format will not allow the century to be explicitly specified. Consider the following:

```
SQL> ALTER SESSION SET nls_date_format = "DD-MON-RR";

Session altered.

SQL>
SQL> INSERT INTO DT VALUES ('01-JAN-49');
1 row created.

SQL> INSERT INTO DT VALUES ('01-JAN-1950');
INSERT INTO DT VALUES ('01-JAN-1950')
                  *
```

```
ERROR at line 1:
ORA-01830: date format picture ends before converting entire
           input string
```

Checking Existing Century Values

The first step in year 2000 compatibility is to audit your existing databases to ensure your year values are properly stored within Oracle tables. The following code will perform this operation, selecting the distinct year values for all columns of all tables that contain date values. This query will cause full-table scans and can run for a long time, especially on data warehouses, so you might want to schedule this code to run during off hours.

```
REM  Written by Don Burleson (c) 1995

SET PAGES 9999;
SET HEADING OFF;
SET FEEDBACK OFF;

PROMPT All Distinct Year Values within all tables
PROMPT ================================================

SPOOL checkdate.sql;

SELECT 'spool date_list.lst' FROM DUAL;

SELECT 'select distinct to_char('||
       column_name||
       ',''YYYY'') from '||owner||'.'||table_name||';'
FROM dba_tab_columns
WHERE data_type = 'DATE'
AND OWNER NOT IN ('SYS','SYSTEM');

SELECT 'spool off' FROM DUAL;

SPOOL OFF;

@checkdate
```

A Suggested Implementation Plan

It is not enough to assume that your Oracle application is year 2000 compliant and assume that a wizard will instantly be able to solve your year 2000 problems. Your database could be in trouble sooner than you think, especially if your system stores dates into the next century. For example, a system that schedules projects 24 months in advance will run into problems in January of 1998 when the 00 dates are stored as 1900 instead of 2000. To achieve year 2000 compliance, you will need to choose one of the following three options.

Option One: Do Nothing

Doing nothing when the year changes to 2000 is an acceptable alternative for applications that will never issue date queries or store dates for the years 1990 through 1999. As you know, the existing default of **YY** means that all dates must be specified with two digits, and that a **20** will be assumed for the century in all queries after 1-JAN-2000. This will immediately block all SQL access to dates where the century is **19**.

Option Two: Change The nls_date_format To DD-MON-RR

This option will not change the way existing queries function. However, if the application requires the storage of dates before 1950 or after 2050, then this option cannot be used because the **RR** format will not allow these dates to be stored in Oracle tables. The overriding problem is interpretive. Some SQL queries appear backward due to the years 00 through 49 being higher than the years 50 through 99. For example, the following query will test for all rows with a date between 1998 and 2048. At first glance, it appears that this query is for rows between 1948 through 1998.

```
REM    Assume that today is 1-JAN-2001;
SELECT * FROM SHPMT WHERE DATE BETWEEN '1-JAN-48' AND '1-JAN-98';
```

In short, the **RR** option allows for an easily implemented change because no SQL changes are required and a DBA only needs to reset the **nls_date_format** parameter in the Oracle init.ora file. The downside to this approach is that some of the cross-century queries might be misinterpreted by end users and programmers.

Option Three: Change The nls_date_format To DD-MON-YYYY

This option requires existing SQL to be changed to specify four-digit years and coordinating the SQL change with the change to the **nls_date_format**. In other words, if you decide to use this option, you need to develop a plan to coordinate the changing of the **nls_date_format** parameter with the changing of all SQL that accesses your database. This process requires the following procedure:

- Direct the developers to specify four-digit years in all SQL queries. This can be done before changing the **nls_date_format** parameter.

- Change the init.ora parameter **nls_date_format** to **DD-MON-YYYY**.

- Ensure that all SQL has been changed to specify four-digit years. (Remember, specifying two-digit years after making this change will result in zeros being used as century values.)

- Scan all areas where SQL might be stored, including:

  - Stored procedures and triggers.

  - Unix code libraries that contain SQL queries.

  - External program source code, such as Pro*C source libraries.

A routine to check stored procedures for two-digit dates is relatively simple to write. The following SQL can be used to interrogate all Oracle stored procedures and display the names of all stored procedures that might reference date values:

```
SET PAGES 999;
SET HEADING OFF;

PROMPT Possible stored procedures with date manipulation
PROMPT ================================================
SELECT DISTINCT NAME FROM DBA_SOURCE
WHERE
    TEXT LIKE '%date%'
OR TEXT LIKE '%DATE%'
OR TEXT LIKE '%dt%'
OR TEXT LIKE '%DT%'
AND OWNER NOT IN ('SYS','SYSTEM');
```

Regardless of Oracle's statement that the database is year 2000 compliant, it is still the responsibility of Oracle DBAs to ensure date format changes. By following these simple steps and carefully coordinating the changes to the SQL with the change to the **nls_date_format**, you can ensure that your Oracle database will continue to function properly. It is not necessary to wait until the last minute to make changes for the year 2000. The impact and ramifications could be dramatic for those who do not carefully plan in advance.

While year 2000 issues will plague the industry for the next few years, there are exciting new advances on the horizon. The general availability of 64-bit processors will soon become a reality, and Oracle is stepping up to the challenge with their 64-bit option. The following section describes some of the huge performance gains that will come from exploiting these new hardware resources.

Oracle's 64-Bit Option—A Look Into The Future

For very large data warehouses where sub-second response time is critical, few database engines can beat the performance of Oracle with the 64-bit option. Designed for use with Digital Equipment Corporation Alpha series (DEC-Alpha), Oracle's 64-bit architecture performs more than 1,000 times faster than standard Oracle software. It is interesting to note that the DEC-Alpha family of 64-bit processors has been around since 1991, and the database vendors are only now beginning to realize their potential for data warehousing. Because most major hardware vendors have caught on and are creating 64-bit systems, let's take a look into the future by examining the existing state of Oracle's 64-bit option for data warehousing.

SQL Complexity And Response Time

As you probably know, when Oracle performs n-way joins of a very large fact table against dimension tables, Oracle denigrates in performance as the number of joined tables increases (see Figure 12.1). However, Oracle claims that using Oracle's STAR query hints with bit databases actually improves response times as the complexity of SQL queries increases. In an Oracle study, a DEC-Alpha with Oracle's 64-bit option showed response times improving as the number of joined tables increased.

An Oracle STAR query maps the selection criteria conditions from a query and creates a cross-product of the dimension tables. This cross-product is then compared to the fact table by using a multikey index in the fact table.

Using a large SGA configuration with Oracle 64 on a DEC-Alpha, Oracle corporation demonstrated that a query that took more than one hour on a Unix Oracle

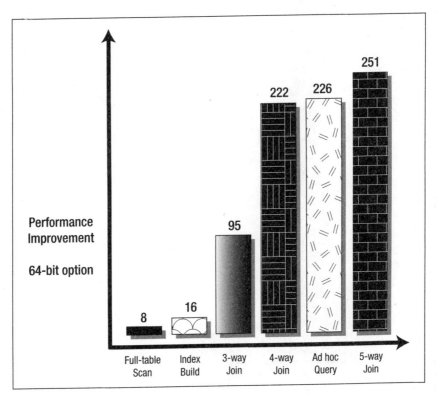

Figure 12.1
An Oracle benchmark.

database ran in less than three seconds on a 64-bit processor with a STAR schema and 6 gigabytes of data buffer (see Figure 12.2).

In addition, the Oracle 64-bit option has two enhanced features: Big Oracle Blocks (BOB) and Large SGA (LSGA).

What About BOB?

BOB is probably one of the most important features of Oracle on 64-bit machines. Because block sizes can reach 32K, an entire track of data can be read with a single I/O, and system performance can be improved dramatically. This is especially important in data warehouses that scan large ranges of tables. When used with the init.ora parameter **db_multiblock_read_count**, physical I/O for table scan operations can be greatly reduced. BOB is also very useful if you are storing non-tabular data in your Oracle database, as is the case with Oracle's spatial data option.

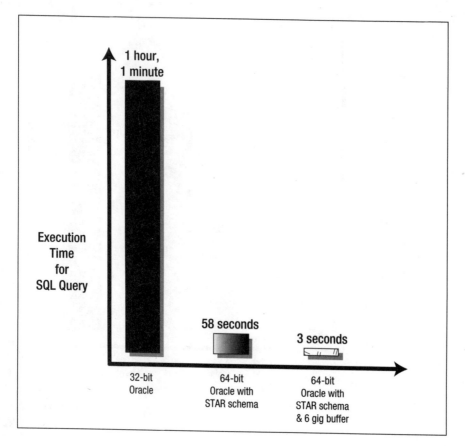

Figure 12.2
Query speed comparison—32-bit versus 64-bit processors.

In these cases, binary large objects (BLOBs), such as images, can be accessed with a single physical disk I/O.

LSGA

LSGA is extremely important in the future of Oracle data warehouse systems. As the cost of RAM memory falls, you will see huge Oracle SGAs, some of which will be able to cache an entire database. In some 64-bit Oracle warehouses, large tables are read into an Oracle data buffer using the table cache option. For example, assume you have a 10GB data warehouse with 32K blocks and **db_block_buffers** parameter set to 10,000, for a total buffer size of 320MB. In addition, you have an SGA large enough to hold the entire database, which can be read at startup where it will remain for the entire processing day without any disk I/O (assuming, of course, that you are in query mode). Because accessing RAM takes 50 nanoseconds, compared to the 50 milliseconds required to access disk I/O, you can see that I/O will proceed one million times faster in a system that does not perform disk I/O.

Sixty-four-bit architectures also remove many of the traditional barriers of Unix systems. File sizes can now exceed 2GB, SGA regions can reach up to 14GB, and database block sizes can now be made 32K, the same as Oracle's mainframe cousins.

Summary

This chapter has taken a look at the immediate future and direction of Oracle and gives us some insight into the exciting new features that we can expect to see within the next few years. As time passes, Oracle will continue to reinvent itself, and offer new features and options to the database community.

This book has hopefully provided a simple and straightforward approach to the design and implementation of Oracle8 high-speed information systems. While many of the techniques are specific to Oracle7 and Oracle8, the performance and tuning principles apply to all areas of database management and all commercial database offerings. Congratulations. You are now armed with the knowledge and resources to pragmatically tune your Oracle8 databases and to maximize all of the power that is offered within the Oracle8 engine.

Index

S